Minnesota's Best Breweries and Brewpubs

Minnesota's Best Breweries and Brewpubs

Searching for the Perfect Pint

Robin Shepard

The University of Wisconsin Press

The University of Wisconsin Press
1930 Monroe Street, 3rd Floor
Madison, Wisconsin 53711-2059

uwpress.wisc.edu

3 Henrietta Street
London WCE 8LU, England
eurospanbookstore.com

Printed in the United States of America

Library of Congress Cataloging-in-Publication Data
Shepard, Robin.
    Minnesota's best breweries and brewpubs :
    searching for the perfect pint / Robin Shepard.
    p. cm.
    Includes bibliographical references and index.
    ISBN 978-0-299-28244-8 (pbk. : alk. paper) — ISBN 978-0-299-28243-1
    (e-book)
    1. Bars (Drinking establishments)—Minnesota—Guidebooks. 2. Micro-
breweries—Minnesota—Guidebooks. 3. Breweries—Minnesota—Guidebooks.
4. Beer. I. Title.
TX950.57.M6S54 2011
663'.4209776—dc22
2010041470

Contents

Introduction   vii

The Best of Minnesota's Best   x

Tips for Finding Your Own Perfect Pint   xiii

Taster Chart   xxi

Beer and Food   xxii

The Craft Brewing Business   xxvii

The Brewing Process   xxviii

Breweries and Brewpubs Map   xxx

Central Region   1

Metro Region   21

Northeast Region   145

Northwest Region   193

Southern Region   203

Minnesota's Contract Breweries   257

Breweries to Watch   283

Minneapolis–St. Paul Airport Brews   287

Beer Tastings and Festivals   292

Books for the Beer Traveler   296

Websites for the Beer Traveler   299

Directory of Minnesota Breweries and Brewpubs   301

Directory of Just Over the Border Breweries
and Brewpubs   317

Minnesota's Brewing Past   323

Beer Styles   328

Terms Commonly Heard on Brewery Tours   347

Index   353

Introduction

The pursuit of the perfect pint is about the journey in finding the best beer Minnesota has to offer. It's a lifelong quest based on the quality of the experience, not the quantity!

Minnesota's Best Breweries and Brewpubs describes more than 45 of the state's beer makers and more than 350 Minnesota beers. If you've picked up this book, you probably like to visit local breweries and brewpubs when you travel. As a travel guide it offers insights into these businesses, with notes about their beer and food, along with a few ideas for other things to do nearby. More than just a guide to which beer to drink, it offers reflections on a quest that for the true beer lover never ends. Along the way it shares stories beyond the brewery walls, kettles, fermenters, kegs, and pint glasses that make the experience so perfect!

In my critiques, beer rankings, and pub descriptions, I have tried to offer my assessment of things as I have experienced them. I visited every brewery or brewpub listed here, and in many instances several times. I also sampled many of the beers of companies or businesses that own a beer label but not a working brewery. I even made the trip to an office or warehouse to keep my assessment honest in finding all current Minnesota beer makers.

A book like this inevitably contains dated material, and I consider that a positive statement on the nature of beer business. It's a dynamic business best described as always changing, never static, and always worth another look— or sip—to truly experience what's new. It's a good thing that there is really no way to definitively describe Minnesota's brewing industry on any given day. If that were possible, the journey would be over and the quest for that "one" perfect pint achieved! Perhaps that is why I, like so many other beer nomads, enjoy the pursuit.

This book is merely a snapshot. The observation of "no visit is the same" applies very well to Minnesota's brewpubs and breweries. Beer menus often change with the seasons, or the recipes themselves might be tweaked to improve the product. New beers might be created between visits, so there's always a reason to consider going back. And when food is added, as with brewpubs, there is yet another dynamic aspect of the total experience and reason to keep searching.

Breweries and brewpubs in this book are arranged within five Minnesota regions, the ones used by a number of state agencies, including the Minnesota Department of Tourism. By thinking about your beer exploration within these regions it's easier to locate and plan a brewery-finding adventure that allows an exploration of communities, culture, and tourism. After all, that's all part of finding the perfect pint!

Many great beer purveyors lie just beyond the Minnesota state line. While the focus of this book remains Minnesota, some very good beer makers will reward those who choose to expand their search for that perfect pint or two. At the end of each geographical section are a few abbreviated descriptions of breweries and brewpubs within a short distance past the Minnesota border. They are included for several reasons. Some make well-known products often found in Minnesota. Some make beer under contract for a Minnesota beer company and might therefore go unnoticed. Others may offer something of historical interest. Those that are included represent a sampling of nearby beer venues that are worthy of exploration when your quest for beer takes you beyond the state's borders!

Wisconsin to the east has more than sixty breweries and brewpubs, several within a short distance from the Minnesota state line. Superior, Wisconsin, is virtually inseparable from Duluth, Minnesota, a fact recognized by their Twin Ports label. In the fall the Gitchee Gummee Brewfest breaks down the border between those cities and states. Likewise, the Thirsty Pagan Brewpub of Superior is located less than a mile south of the famous Blatnick Bridge that spans the actual Twin Ports (St. Louis Bay) and connects the two cities. Just east of the Metro Region are the Rush River Brewing Company in River Falls and the eco-friendly Dave's BrewFarm in Wilson. To the southeast lies the historic beer town of La Crosse, Wisconsin. It's more than just a neighbor on the other side of the Mississippi River. La Crosse's Pearl Street Brewery is well worth the drive for its tasting room, especially for fans of the its hoppy Pearl Street Pale Ale. That Wisconsin river town was also home to the G. Heileman Brewing Company (now City Brewing Company), which was the nation's fourth largest brewery in its heyday. Any self-proclaimed beer lover in pursuit of great beer and history must visit the National Brewery Museum in Potosi, Wisconsin. While not a short drive, it would be a very worthwhile and scenic weekend trip along the Great River Road.

Beyond Minnesota's southern border, about a half-hour south of Albert Lea in the small town of Northwood, Iowa, the Worth Brewing Company is making its own mark. Worth Brewing is so small it's been called a nano-brewery.

The eastern Dakotas have a handful of brewpubs that shouldn't be skipped. Granite City Food and Brewery has locations in Sioux Falls, South Dakota, and Fargo, North Dakota. In between lies the Scottish themed Dempsey's Brewery, Restaurant, and Pub in Watertown, South Dakota, where owner Bill Dempsey is likely to be seen wearing a kilt and playing the bagpipes.

Next to every beer listed in this guide is a place for you to record your own score. I've also included my approach to evaluating beer that includes a tasting chart. It was developed in my travels to help display the finer nuances associated with beer styles, flavors, and colors. In the back of this book is a condensed directory of addresses and phone numbers as well as a list of common characteristics you can use to chart your pursuit. I am obviously enthusiastic about craft brewers in Minnesota—that is my bias. Therefore, take my observations and ratings for what they are: my personal opinions. I hope they inspire you to think about such experiences in your own terms. Try not to take all this too seriously, and enjoy the never ending pursuit of defining what a good beer is to you.

I have tried to be accurate, but if I've missed something or gotten a brewery's story a little askew, I'll correct it in a future edition. As with finding the perfect pint, this book will never be finished! This book also offers many opinions on a large number of individual Minnesota beers. However, it's up to you to define, and find, your own perfect pint. Take this book along as you search for your own meaning of "perfect pint." It just may lead you to the best of Minnesota beer as you explore the state and its beer makers on a journey created by a pursuit and passion for good beer.

In my travels I have met many beer enthusiasts along the way and have made new friendships over a pint or two while sharing tales of travel. I also very much appreciate the willingness of so many of the brewers and brewery owners who have allowed me to tell some part of their personal story in these pages.

The quest to visit all of Minnesota's breweries has been a wonderful way to experience the many things the state has to offer. And while putting together a book like this is thoroughly enjoyable, the time needed for writing far exceeded the traveling and sampling. All that would not have been possible without support from my wife, Kristi. And especially for that I'm very grateful.

Lastly, as you pursue your own perfect pint, remember the search is about appreciating the artisanal craft of making beer. Know your limits, understand moderation, and be responsible for your own actions.

The book is about appreciating the local flavors of beer with the distinctive backdrop of Minnesota's people, places, and natural beauty. I've thoroughly enjoyed my travels, and may you too, in a search for the perfect pint that lasts a lifetime.

Cheers.

The Best of Minnesota's Best

With so many great breweries and brewpubs it's almost unfair to pick favorites. However, the comparison seems appropriate given that in writing this book every Minnesota brewery was visited at least once (and most received at least three visits). While no means definitive, consider this a dynamic snapshot of favorites that I hope you will use to define your own perfect pint.

BY THE NUMBERS (2010 ANNUAL PRODUCTION)

Largest Brewery
August Schell Brewing Company, New Ulm—115,766 barrels

Largest Brewpub
Fitger's Brewhouse, Duluth—2,500 barrels

Smallest Breweries
Mantorville Brewing Company, Mantorville—30 barrels
Vine Park Brewing Company, St. Paul—90 barrels

Smallest Brewpub
Backwater Brewing Company, Winona—125 barrels

Oldest Brewery
August Schell Brewing Company, New Ulm—operated continuously by the same family since 1860 (also the second oldest in the U.S.)

BEER AND FOOD COMBOS

Barley John's Brew Pub, New Brighton—the real deal with distinctive beer and a menu that reflects house-made specialties, some from home-grown ingredients.
Great Waters Brewing Company, St. Paul—A diverse food menu that highlights, if not respects, cask-conditioned brews.

BEER GARDENS

Barley John's Brew Pub, New Brighton—There's always something interesting on the beer list to enjoy among the hop vines, trellis, and fire pit.

Minneapolis Town Hall Brewery, Minneapolis—Numerous house brews, including cask ales, combined with a couple dozen outside tables that look out over the bustling Seven Corners intersection.

A BREW AND A VIEW

Castle Danger Brewery, Two Harbors—A small 3-barrel brewhouse that's tucked in a maintenance building on a thirteen cabin resort on Lake Superior.

BREWERY EVENTS AND FESTIVALS

Autumn Brew Review, Minneapolis—Features nearly 100 breweries and 250-plus beers in September.

Summer Beer Festival, St. Paul—A summertime extravaganza at the State Fairgrounds in June.

Surly Darkness Day, Surly Brewing, Brooklyn Center—Marks the limited release of the brewery's Russian Imperial Stout called "Darkness" in October.

TOURS WITH BEER IN HAND

Flat Earth Brewing Company, St. Paul—Locals turn out for the occasional tastings that happen in late afternoons on Tuesdays and Thursdays, and full tours are held on every other Saturday.

Lake Superior Brewing Company, Duluth—It's a special treat when the tour is led by owner and head brewer Dale Kleinschmidt in a brewery that shares a building with the Department of Revenue.

Summit Brewing Company, St. Paul—Tours begin in a large reception hall that overlooks the copper-clad brew kettles before visitors move into the fermentation, bottling, and packaging areas.

HISTORICAL TOURS AND DISPLAYS

August Schell Brewing Company, New Ulm—Visitors get a sense of more than 150 years of the Schell business and family life.

Fitger's Brewhouse, Duluth—A small museum operates within the history-laden walls that date back to the early 1880s.

Potosi Brewing Company & National Brewery Museum, Potosi, Wisconsin—A destination on its own, with a museum that contains rotating breweriana exhibits from private collections.

BEER VACATIONS

Northern Tour—Duluth (Carmody Irish Pub and Brewery, Dubh Linn Irish Brewpub, Dubrue, Fitger's Brewhouse, Lake Superior Brewing Company); Ely (BoatHouse Brewpub and Restaurant); and Two Harbors (Castle Danger Brewing).

Southern and Western Tour—Mankato (Mankato Brewery); New Ulm (August Schell Brewing Company); and Lucan (Brau Brothers Brewing Company).

OVER THE BORDER

Worth Brewing Company, Northwood, Iowa—South of the Minnesota border, this "nano-brewery" makes only about seventy-five barrels per year.

Dave's BrewFarm, Wilson, Wisconsin—Owner David Anderson had to request a federal exemption to allow this brewery to be constructed in the basement of his rural Wisconsin farmhouse. It's also solar powered!

2011 EXCEPTIONAL BEERS (ALPHABETICAL ORDER)

Bender—Surly Brewing Company, Brooklyn Center
Gale Force Wheat—Castle Danger Brewery, Two Harbors
Great Northern Porter—Summit Brewing Company, St. Paul
Lake Superior Special Ale—Lake Superior Brewing Company, Duluth
Mango Mama—Minneapolis Town Hall Brewery, Minneapolis
Park Point Pilsner—Fitger's Brewhouse, Duluth
Rubus—Brau Brothers Brewing Company, Lucan
Scotch Ale—Brau Brothers Brewing Company, Lucan
Snowstorm—August Schell Brewing Company, New Ulm
West Side—Harriet Brewing, Minneapolis

Tips for Finding Your Own Perfect Pint

A travel tip not to dismiss is to always plan ahead and especially call ahead for hours and confirm tour times for that first visit. While there can be something very special about an impromptu stop at a brewery that you've never been to before or just discovered on vacation, save some hassle and call ahead. More than a few times I've invested a great amount of travel time to get to a beer venue only find that the hours were limited or the place was closed when I finally arrived. Calling ahead respects the nature of the business and allows one to inquire about current beer offerings, food menus, and the business hours of operation, all of which can greatly vary at any point during the year (for that reason, business hours have not been included in this book). You'll find this especially sound advice in areas of seasonal tourism.

Searching for beers adds a special dimension to making the most out of travel and touring. The search is as much about the journey itself as the individual pint. Anyone who plans an evening, weekend, or vacation around finding the best beer probably has some method for finding their own perfect pint. You may have your own list that helps you decide how to find the best beer when traveling, but here are a few of my tips for traveling.

Plan, but not so much that you're inflexible or unwilling to stay a little longer when you find something you like or when you receive advice from a trustworthy beer enthusiast along the way.

Scan various websites to learn about events, festival, special keg tappings, beer and food menus, and unique aspects to the cities you'll be traveling to.

Scan the local phone book for breweries, brewpubs, homebrew shops, and other beer venues.

Call a local homebrew store to ask for advice, directions, insights, and/or where the local homebrew club hangs out.

Pick up a beer newspaper and/or beer magazine and scan it for locations, addresses, special events, and special release beers.

Look for posted events while visiting a brewery or brewpub; it can be especially rewarding when you unexpectedly stumble across a brewmaster's dinner, special beer tasting, keg tapping, or even a festival.

Inquire about beer samples and taster trays, which make for a great way to learn about different beers on the menu.

Spot the bartender or waitstaff who really knows beer and one who, besides talking up their own place, isn't shy about dropping hints about other places that serve great local beer.

Understand the options for local transportation; *always* carry a local taxi cab number and never be shy about asking the bartender or waitstaff to call you a cab. Checking local bus schedules is also a good idea. It's best to avoid the hassles and extra time that come with driving and parking your own vehicle. Public transportation is an essential backup for when you enjoy the establishment just a little too much.

Always call ahead for hours and to find out what beers are on tap as well as any specials on the food menu.

BEER STYLES

Beer generally falls into two broad categories, ales and lagers. Ales are created by strains of yeast that do their work in warmer temperatures, usually at the top of the fermentation vessel. Lagers are made with strains of yeast that enjoy colder and longer fermentation periods, usually at the bottom of the vessel. The yeast, fermentation temperatures, the amount of fermentable sugars, and varieties of hops all make for many different flavors, which are described in the Beer Styles section of this book.

Broadly characterized, lagers have evolved, or at least have been perfected, more recently than ales. Lagers require more strict control of temperature and time to ferment—hence the terms "lagering" or "storing" to describe fermenting and aging beer. Ales are considered older in their invention, and they can represent an incredible range of flavors, colors, and other beer characteristics. Ale styles date back hundreds or even thousands of years.

In analyzing a beer menu or evaluating the beer at your favorite store, one of the first things to observe is the style. One can't always depend on creative and catchy names to reveal such distinctions, but if you truly want to find a type of beer that merits a place in your home refrigerator, this is a good first step. Keep in mind, however, that some brewers don't really like to be held to strict definitions, and they relish terms such as "freestyle brewing" that allow them to be creative beyond accepted beer norms. While that certainly expands the array of flavor and characteristics, it makes it rather difficult for those who enjoy finding certain styles or comparing beers. In those instances, just ask the waitstaff or brewery which of their offerings most closely matches your preferred style—then sip to see if you too find similar characteristics.

As your tasting skills improve, rank the styles next to each other. For example, pilsners, bocks, Oktoberfests, nut browns, porters, and stouts are all different and need to be appreciated for what they are. That is, evaluate porters against porters rather than against pilsners or wheats. Over the years I've found that my own preferences for porters, nut browns, and Oktoberfests cause me to be more discriminating with these beers.

If you need some help with beer styles, see the Beer Styles section in the back of the book for more specific descriptions. Comparing different beer styles is a wonderful way to find what you like in beer. A few suggestions for your approach to tasting follow.

GLASSWARE

Tasting beer requires transferring it from its packaging to some type of glassware. Granted, drinking from the bottle or can is acceptable, but it can be rather limiting in determining the beer's color and aroma. Furthermore, different styles of glassware accent the qualities of certain beers. Bottles and cans are designed for storing and selling beer, not really for accentuating the characteristics of its flavor at the time it is served.

Glassware is also a great way to distinguish brewpubs and taverns. Those that are serious about creating a beer experience will have appropriate glassware for specific beer styles. Among the most basic and commonly available are the pilsner glasses for serving pilsners. Tall and tapering to a short stem, these glasses are designed to direct the floral hop aroma to the nose. Shaker and British pint glasses, which are the most common pub glasses, are excellent for beers with abundant aromas and bouquets, but they often don't do much to enhance the beer. By contrast, weizen glasses are tall with an inward flared lip to help retain the beer's head and focus aromas. Chalices, snifters, and thistles help concentrate more subtle aromas and allow the beer to develop a head without giving you a face of foam. A mug with a wide opening allows the aroma to explode under a thick, heavy head of foam. Mugs usually have heavy glass handles that are well suited for sipping beers or for beers that you won't want to warm by handling the vessel.

THE ELEMENTS OF TASTING BEER

There are five basic elements to consistently tasting beer. Those elements have to do with sensory perceptions: smell with your nose, see with your eyes, feel with your tongue, taste with your mouth or your tongue, and perceive how the beer finishes—its aftertaste.

Before these sensory steps, however, are the presentation and the art of pouring the beer. Despite what you may have learned in college about a frothy head meaning less beer in the glass, beer with a head is what you want. As you pour the beer, start in the center of the glass—the beer needs an opportunity to explode into rich, heavy foam. Note the thickness, texture, and how long the beer's head lasts. Once you've mastered the art of the perfect pour, then you're ready to taste.

Aroma or Nose

It is usually best to make your observations about aroma before you actually taste the beer. The aroma is usually greatest at the time of pouring the beer, so it makes sense to gather your impressions as the beer initially breathes and the head begins to dissipate. Determining aroma, or the beer's nose, takes practice. It is one of the most subjective judgments you'll make. Immediately after you pour, raise the glass to your nose. Many complex flavor notes were created by malts, hops, and yeast during the brewing, fermenting, and aging processes. It may help to swirl the beer gently in the glass to release some of the carbonation and heighten the aroma. A sweet, caramel, chocolate, or coffee-like aroma comes from the malt varieties. A floral, tea-like, citrus aroma comes from hops. Fruity aromas, such as apples, bananas, or pears, are the esters. It's fun to be creative when describing the beer's nose.

While the more common terms for aroma are malty, hoppy, sour, or fruity, the more specifically you can identify the smells the more distinctive the description. If the nose is fruity, is it banana or citrus?

Chalice (left), Thistle (middle), and Snifter (right)

The wide mouth allows for the aromas to explode, while providing greater space for a thick head. The shape and the stem allow the drinker to control the warming of the beer. Chalices are often used with Belgian ales, while thistles are associated with fine Scottish ales, and snifters are often used with barley wines.

Growler

A growler is a container for beer bought by the measure, usually a half-gallon. Many brewpubs sell beer-to-go poured directly from the tap into the growler. There are several stories about how the term "growler" came to be. One story says it originated in the nineteenth century when factory workers (some say the porters of London) regularly drank beer on break or with a meal. The local taverns would sell beer in open metal pails, which children fetched for the growling stomachs of the waiting factory workers. According to another common tale, sliding the metal pails down the bar to customers produced a growling sound—and allegedly coined another term, "rushing the growler," which could also be attributed to the children rushing back to the factory with a full growler. You decide which story you like best!

Mugs

The wide open mouth allows for total exposure to the beer aroma, often recommended for strong malty beers. The obvious emphasis of the mug is on its handling ease! Mugs are often used for full-bodied beers.

Pilsner

Designed to direct the floral hop aroma to the nose. The clear glass will highlight the clear golden color and effervescence of the beer. Some versions of the pilsner glass have a small foot or stem and look similar to a large wine flute. The pilsner glass is designed for the pilsner.

Stange (pole) or Stick
A simple cylinder glass resembling the shape of a test tube. Glass sizes often vary, but traditionally its capacity is small at 0.2 liter (about 7 ounces). It is typically used for German Kölsch and Alt beers.

American Pint (left) and British Pint (right)
The most common pub glassware. Suited as general all-purpose beer glassware. The V-shaped American Pint, sometimes called a Shaker Pint, is most often used in American bars and taverns. The bulged side of the British Pint, sometimes called a Nonic Pint, makes for better handling. Both have wide openings to allow the aroma to explode.

Tulip Pint
The glass is commonly used in Ireland and England to serve ales and is especially associated with Guinness Stout. The glass expands toward the top, then flares or bows inward, which focuses the aroma and supports the beer's head. It is sometimes referred to as an Imperial Pint Glass.

Weizen
Clear, tall, and slightly bowed sides allow the aroma to concentrate and then escape while supporting a delicate head. This glass is well suited for the light fruit esters of the Weizenbier.

Willi Becher or Willy Becher
A tall V-shaped glass with an inward taper in the upper third of the glass. This is one of the best overall beer glasses because it will focus the aroma, support thick to thin heads of foam, and provide lots of glass to display clear and colorful beers. This glass is especially well suited for appreciating rich colorful lagers like Bock, Oktoberfest, Schwarzbier, and Rauch beers.

Some common aroma descriptors and their associations:

acetaldehyde—green apple

diacetyl—butter, butterscotch, toffee

estery—various fruits

hoppy—hop flowers, floral, piney, resiny

malty—sweetness of caramel or chocolate

musty—stale, earthy, moldy

phenolic—medicinal, plastic

solvent—acetone or lacquer thinners

sulfur—rotten eggs

vegetal—cooked, canned, or rotten vegetables

Appearance

The appearance of beer has two distinct elements: body color and head or foam. The color is most commonly associated with the amount and type of barley or wheat used in brewing. Colors range from light yellow, straw, gold, and amber to copper, bronze, brown, and black, with shades in between. Some styles, such as porter and stout, can even have reddish hues. Cloudiness or clarity is also an important characteristic. Unfiltered wheat beers are often cloudy yellow or golden, while pilsners take a clear and bubbly appearance. The head of a beer can be as distinctive as the body. Notice its color and especially the texture of the head. Is it thick and creamy like a stout, or is it thin and bubbly like a pilsner?

Filtering beer is a common brewing technique, especially for those making certain styles. Filtering removes yeast and any suspended particles, leaving the beer bright and clear; so for some styles, pilsners especially, this helps accentuate effervescence and overall appearance. In contrast, some beer styles are traditionally not filtered. A true German Hefeweizen is distinguished by special yeast that remains in suspension and contributes to a hazy and cloudy, golden body.

Texture or Mouth Feel

Swirl or roll the beer around in your mouth. Does the texture feel thick and creamy or thin and watery? Does it feel bubbly or even sharp? These adjectives can be helpful: crisp, silky, round, coarse. Texture can also refer to dryness that commonly goes with bitterness, or even a warming sensation that can be associated with alcohol content.

Taste

Appreciate the beer's varied flavor notes and its balance. Your tongue is stimulated in different ways: on the tip you should detect the sweetness of malt; toward the back on either side you sense bitterness from the hops. Is the taste balanced between the malt and hops, or does one dominate, such as the hoppiness of an India pale ale? You may even want to comment on the intensity of the taste.

Serious tasters, such as those who judge beer competitions, say there are more than a hundred separately identifiable flavor elements. About forty of these are common and present in most beers.

Some common taste descriptors and their associations:

bitter—bitterness derived from hops

dry—astringent, grainy, worty, sulfitic

fruity—apples, oranges, citrus

grainy—cereal-like

hoppy—flowery and aromatic hop qualities

malty—sweetness of caramel or chocolate

medicinal—chemical or phenolic, solvent

musty—earthy, moldy

sour—a sharpness or fruity tone, vinegar-like, acidic

sulfur—skunky, burnt matches, rotten eggs, onion

sweet—sugar

yeasty—yeast, bouillon

Finish

A good beer with character offers several different taste impressions, from the initial taste to the midtaste to the aftertaste or finish. A common finish for a pale ale tends to feature a dry bitterness. Beers with higher alcohol contents, such as Doppelbocks, can leave a warming sensation in the mouth. Crisp, clean-tasting beers, such as some pilsners, may not have a detectable finish.

NOTE TAKING

If you are a serious note taker, it can be fun to make written observations to help you remember what you liked about a beer. However, from one beer enthusiast to another, such obsessive note taking eventually leads to a problem with what to do with the scribbled notations on beer coasters and menus or the volumes of beer journals that one accumulates.

When you write notes, focus on the most impressive or memorable part of the beer's flavor and overall character. An easy place to begin is by describing the balance between the bitterness (hops) and the sweetness (malt). Certain styles accentuate bitterness or sweetness, and one often finds that one of those basic flavor components tends to dominate over another.

Beers also have distinctive taste segments in their overall flavor profile that stand out. The foretaste can sometimes be much different from the aftertaste or finish of a beer. Some brewers consider as many as three distinctive segments of the taste profile: foretaste or the beginning flavors, midtaste or main flavor, and finish or aftertaste.

Sometimes tastes can evoke images. If your bock has the flavor of chicken soup, a little note taking might help you steer clear the next time! The more descriptive the better.

SCORING

There are many different methods of scoring beer. It seems that nearly every beer book has its own approach. However, those used by the Beverage Testing Institute (BTI) or at sanctioned competitions of the American Homebrewers Association (AHA) are numerical and standardized, although the determination of final critical numerical score is still quite subjective. The BTI and AHA approach to evaluating beer is quite detailed because the results are used in competitions. Those processes for rating beer can be somewhat challenging for the average beer aficionado because they require in-depth knowledge of style and need to be practiced for the scores to be consistent.

For most of us at our favorite brewpub or brewery, a straightforward and simple method of comparison is sufficient. I've always been rather reluctant to get into scoring games over beer. However, I do feel general methods help me decide what I like. Therefore, I've settled on an overall rating method that attempts to describe how positive I feel about a given beer—as opposed to numerical rating schemes that seem to result in a harsh judgment by the beer style police!

The tasting card shown here, for example, uses a four-point (or mug) scale. After you've gone through a beer's taste qualities, rank your overall impression. Don't be indecisive. Make a judgment of how much you enjoy this beer. An even number of choices, such as four, requires you to take a stand. There is no middle category of undecided.

🍺🍺🍺🍺	A great beer; distinctive; you'll have this beer over others.
🍺🍺🍺	A beer you enjoy; reliable; close to its described style and/or what the brewer says the beer is supposed to be.
🍺🍺	An okay beer, but its flavor seems to lack distinction; yet, probably worth trying again (just to be sure).
🍺	You probably wouldn't recommend it to a friend; it doesn't match how the brewer describes it; or if it was described as an accepted common style it's nothing like the characteristics of that style.

It bears pointing out that not all brewers like strict style distinctions, and therefore the beer may be a combination of so-called accepted styles. In those instances, you may want to base your judgment on how close the beer came to the brewer's description.

SIGNING OFF ON YOUR VISIT

At the suggestion of readers of the previous companion books, *Wisconsin's Best Breweries and Brewpubs* and *The Best Breweries and Brewpubs of Illinois*, this book includes an autograph block near the logo of each brewpub or brewery. As you hopscotch across the Gopher State visiting beer makers, take this book along and ask the brewmaster, brewery owner, or waitperson to sign his or her name and date your visit. Don't be shy—you just might find that asking for an autograph is a great way to strike up a conversation. And who knows where that might lead the discussion?

Taster Chart

BEER RATING SHEET: Date: _____

Beer Name: _____

Brewery: _____

☐ Microbrewery   (or)   ☐ Brew Pub

City: _____

State/Province: _____

Country: _____

GPS Coordinates
N ____ ____ ____
W ____ ____ ____

Style (lager/ale) _____

Nose/Aroma: _____

Appearance: _____

Mouth Feel/Body: _____

Taste: _____

Finish: _____

Comments: _____

_____

_____

_____

_____

_____

Beer Diagram:

Hoppy   *Malty*

A L E S

L A G E R S

3   1   Dark

2

6   Light
    Color
    Light

4

5   Dark

General Character Beers

Hoppy   *Malty*

Reference Beers
1. Barley John's, Dark Knight
2. Finnegans, Irish Ale
3. Guinness, Stout
4. Miller, Budweiser
5. Spaten Oktoberfest
6. Summit, Extra Pale Ale

Overall Score For This Beer:

☐   4- 🍺🍺🍺🍺   = A great beer; distinctive; you'll have this beer over others.

☐   3- 🍺🍺🍺   = A beer you enjoy; reliable; close to its described style.

☐   2- 🍺🍺   = Problematic; lacks distinction; but probably worth trying again.

☐   1- 🍺   = A beer that isn't true to its style; you wouldn't recommend it to a friend.

Who Drank: _____

Beer and Food

Beer has qualities that make it a great food beverage. While it doesn't always receive the same attention as wine at the dinner table, its gastro combinations deserve respect. Beer offers many variations—malty sweetness, hoppy bitterness, spiciness, yeasty-earthiness, carbonation, and alcohol strength—to create endless pairing opportunities for the meal. Here are a few ideas for matching a favorite style of beer with just the right dish.

APPETIZERS AND SALADS

Finding the right combination to begin a meal can be especially challenging because appetizer choices at most restaurants can be numerous and very diverse in flavor. One of the best general approaches is to find combinations that stimulate the appetite rather than fill you up or, worse, stain the taste buds so much that the meal that follows is tainted.

The best pre-meal beers are light and complement rather than stand on their own. For example, consider matching a cool spring roll with a crisp Hefeweizen, where the sharp cleanness of cucumber, cabbage, and vermicelli rice go well with the crisp and bubbly wheat beer. A heartier example might be a spicy appetizer like jalapeño peppers or onion rings that cry out for the firm bitterness of a pale ale to cut the heat.

Salads are a bit easier, but the dressing you choose will make a big difference in selecting just the right beer. Sweet dressings tend to go better with a mildly malty amber ale or nut brown, while those with a sharper vinegar base are better suited to the crisp, firm hoppiness of a Czech pilsner. But here again, there really isn't a standard approach because appetizer and salad varieties are so vast.

CHEESE

Cheese can bring out some of the most pleasurable yet subjective pairings with beer. A light bubbly saison tends to go well with creamy brie and rind cheese, while more assertive, hoppy India pale ales accentuate the sharpness in aged cheddar. The so-called stinky cheeses may go best with some equally aggressive flavors from bold, malty sweet beers.

MAIN MEAL

A general approach to matching entrées and beers can be to think of an ale as red wine and lager as white wine. Ales generally go with meats and assertive sauces, while the lighter and crisper lagers go with seafood. However, the nature of an entrée and how it is prepared will create unique twists of flavor, so those rules don't always apply.

Consider the beer's ability to complement, contrast, cut, or cleanse flavors on the palate. The only set rule is to avoid combinations that are so competitive that one stamps out the other.

Crisp and firmly hopped beers like German pilsners (lagers) are excellent with most fish because they have just enough bitterness to cleanse oily or grilled tones. Dark and malty brews, like Scottish ales and porters (ales), go well with steaks. Golden and blonde ales are smooth and slightly malty, yet have a hoppy balance that goes well with fried foods, like chicken. Spicy foods are best left for pale ales with bitter and resiny profiles that compete with, and even cut, the pepper heat of the dish.

DESSERT AND AFTER THE MAIN MEAL

Rich caramel and chocolate flavors found in big robust malty brews will blend incredibly well with sweet desserts like chocolate cake and crème brûlée. A favorite pairing is the strong, sweet caramel flavor of a Doppelbock with apple pie.

Equally as flavorful are the Belgian lambics, such as a kriek (cherry) or framboise (raspberry), next to something from your favorite chocolatier.

THE PERFECT PAIRING

When pairing beer and food it can be fun to experiment and determine what works for you personally. The most serious beer person will likely start with a beer or style of beer first, because if you don't like the beer you're having, you probably won't like the pairing. With either beer in hand or food first, there are great ways to go about making the experience perfect. Here are a few examples.

FOOD-TO-BEER PAIRINGS

Asian

chicken or pork	Amber Lager, English Mild, Weizenbock
steak	Dortmunder, Hellesbock
vegetarian	Premium Lager
barbecue	
ribs	Bock, Doppelbock, Oktoberfest
brisket, smoked	Dry-Hopped American Pale Ale
vegetables	Brown Ale

Burgers

cheeseburger	American Pale Ale, American Pilsner
hamburger	Amber Ale

grilled chicken	Amber Lager
summer sausage & cheese	Hoppy Red Ale
veggie burger	English Porter, Schwarzbier

Cheeses

Benedictine	Belgian Abbey
blue	Doppelbock, Imperial Stout
brie	Belgian Dubbel
cheddar (mild)	Brown Ale
cheddar (sharp, well aged)	American Pale Ale, American IPA
Cocoa Cardona	Porter, Irish Stout
Emmentahaler	Barley Wine
feta/goat	Hefeweizen, American Wheat
Gruyere	Doppelbock
Gouda	Vienna Lager
Gouda (well aged)	Bock, Robust Reds
Harvarti	Belgian Dubbel, English/Sweet Stout
Limburger	Cask Ale with Hops, American Pale Ale
Mascarpone	Cherry Ale, Belgian Lambic (Kriek)
Monastery	Belgian Abbey, Belgian Trappist
Mobay	Bourbon Barrel Brown Ale, Porter
Sarvecchio/parmesan	Oktoberfest
Stilton	Belgian Dubbel
Swiss	Oktoberfest

Desserts

apple strudel	Robust Porter, Doppelbock
carrot cake	Imperial/Double India Pale Ale
chocolate	Belgian Framboise, Kriek
Crème Brûlée	Doppelbock
fruit tarts	Sweet Porter, Cream or Milk Stout
fudge brownies	Barrel Aged Stout, Coffee or Mint Stout

Fish

fried	Extra Special Bitter (ESB), Pale Ale
broiled	Belgian Pale Ale
boiled	Belgian Wit
baked	Bock, Oktoberfest
mussels/oysters	Irish/Dry Stout

Indian

chicken or pork	American Pilsner
steak	Strong Belgian Ale
vegetarian	American Wheat, Kolsch

Italian

pasta with rich sauces	Alt, English Pale Ale
lasagna, risotto	Bock, Amber Ale
pizza (varies greatly with toppings)	Pale ale, Porter

Mediterranean

chicken or pork	American Pilsner
steak	English Mild, Trappist Ale
vegetarian	Weizen, Belgian Pale Ale

Mexican

burritos, enchiladas	Amber Ale, English Mild, Red Lager
fajitas	Oktoberfest, Porter, Stout

Pork

sausages	Oktoberfest
loin, roasted	Cherry Ale, Belgian Lambic (Kriek)
ham, roasted	Saison, Apricot Ale

Poultry

chicken, fried	American Amber Lager
chicken, barbecued	American Brown Ale, Schwarzbier
duck	Belgian Dubbel, Doppelbock
turkey	Scottish Ale, Amber Lager, Red Lager

Salads

house or cobb	Hefeweizen
with fruits and nuts	Saison
with vinaigrette dressings	Bock
Caesar	American Pale Ale, India Pale Ale

Spicy

gumbo, jambalaya	English IPA
buffalo wings	American IPA
jalapeno pizza	Imperial IPA
hot chili	American IPA, American Pale Ale, Black India Ale

Steaks

grilled	Schwarzbier, Porter, Stout
broiled	ESB, English Pale Ale

Stews

beef, steak	Scottish Ale, Alt
vegetable	Amber Ale, English Pale Ale

BEER-TO-FOOD PAIRINGS

Lagers

Amber	Asian chicken or pork
American Pilsner	hamburgers and grilled sandwiches
German-style Pilsner	modestly spiced dishes, especially Indian
Bohemian-style Pilsner	modestly spiced dishes, especially sushi
Dortmunder	Asian steak
Oktoberfest/Marzen	German sausages and hams

Vienna/red	Mexican, burritos to fajitas
European-style Dark	hamburgers to bratwurst
Schwarzbier	BBQ chicken, grilled vegetables
Bock	ribs, sweet BBQ, well-aged Gouda cheese
Maibock	all kinds of rich German dishes
Doppelbock	ribs, blue cheese, Crème Brûlée
Eisbock	stews and sweet BBQ

Ales

Amber Ale	a versatile style that goes with many foods
American, Brown Ale	grilled vegetables, mild cheddars, light soups
American, Imperial/ Double (IPA)	Thai, spicy dishes
American, India Pale Ale (IPA)	spicy Asian and Indian dishes, well-aged cheddar
American, Pale Ale	burgers, modestly spiced dishes, sharp cheddar
Barley Wine	often difficult to pair, wonderful on its own
Belgian, Abbey	heavy stews,
Belgian, Dubbel	sweet stews with meat, brie and havarti cheeses
Belgian, Lambic, Framboise (raspberry)	a dessert beer, very good with dark chocolate
Belgian, Lambic, Kriek (cherry)	fruit salads, especially good with chocolate
Belgian, Pale Ale	salads with fruits and nuts, citrus-based Thai dishes
Belgian, Trappist	poultry, breads, Monastery cheese
Belgian, Tripel	chicken, shellfish, rich butter-based sauces
Belgian, White (Wit)	garden salads, boiled fish
English, Brown Ale	grilled steaks
English, India Pale Ale	chili, spicy seafood, gumbo
English, Pale Ale	fried chicken
English (sweet) Stout	beef and lamb, fruit tart desserts
ESB (Extra Special Bitter)	fried fish, crab cakes, broiled steaks
Hefeweizen	cold summer salads, young feta/goat cheeses
Imperial Stout	chocolate desserts
Irish (dry) Stout	shellfish, Cocoa Cardona cheese
Porter	steaks from grilled to BBQ
Robust Porter	heavier beef dishes, apple desserts
Saison	crisp cold lettuce salads with fruits and nuts
Scottish Ale	lamb, duck, turkey
Scotch Ale	wild game, especially venison
Weizenbock	chicken or pork with wild rice

The Craft Brewing Business

Some craft brewers actually prefer the term "artisan beer maker" in reference to their free spirit, innovation, and creativity of recipes. The industry applies the term "craft brewer" to those breweries making fewer than two million barrels of beer annually. The national Brewers Association further describes these beer makers as independent—with less than 25 percent of the brewery being owned or controlled by someone who is not a craft brewer—and traditional in what it produces—for example, an all-malt flagship beer or at least 50 percent of its volume in either all-malt beers or beers that use adjuncts to enhance rather than lighten flavor.

Another way to further describe the craft brewing industry is in the market segments and business models described by the Brewers Association:

microbrewery—A brewery that produces fewer than 15,000 barrels of beer a year. It sells at least 75 percent of its beer to the public through off-site distribution.

brewpub—A restaurant and brewery that makes and sells beer on-site. The beer is brewed primarily for sale in the restaurant. Some brewpubs, where laws allow, also distribute off-site, such as in half-gallon growlers. If more than 75 percent of sales are off-site, groups such as the Brewers Association consider it a microbrewery.

contract brewing company—A company or brewery that hires another brewery to make all or some of its beer. The entity that contracts usually handles the marketing and distributor relationships. The brewery under contract commonly takes care of brewing and packaging.

regional brewery—A brewery with annual production of more than 15,000 barrels but fewer than two million barrels.

large brewery—A brewery with annual production of more than two million barrels.

The Brewing Process

A tour of a few brewpubs or breweries will offer other insights into the brewing process. Most brewmasters and owners enjoy giving tours. They display a passion for what they create just as artists do for their paintings. Many breweries have regularly scheduled tours, usually on weekends. Brewpubs are more likely to offer tours whenever they have time and interest from patrons. Just remember, it's always a good idea to call ahead if you would like a tour.

Brewing begins with the basic ingredients of water, barley, hops, and yeast. The amounts of those ingredients and the way they are mixed, heated, cooled, and stored all contribute to creating different styles of beer. Traditionally, many small brewers take pride in stating they follow the Reinheitsgebot, or Germany Purity Law of 1516, which mandated that only barley, hops, and water be used in producing beer.

The equipment brewers use can, and often does, differ from brewery to brewery. The percentage of beer sold by craft breweries is small when compared with overall beer consumption in the United States. Approximately 1,600 craft breweries (defined by the Brewers Association as those making less than six million barrels annually) make up less than 5 percent of the beer produced and only about 7.5 percent of sales dollars. Most of Minnesota's craft breweries have annual production figures that fall between 300 and 1,000 barrels. Beyond those are breweries like August Schell (New Ulm), Summit (St. Paul), and Cold Spring (Cold Spring) with much larger production figures, in the tens-of-thousands of barrels per year. Big or small, Minnesota's beer makers have some basic elements described in the accompanying diagram.

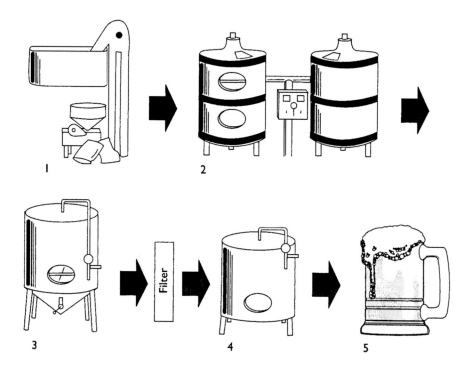

1. Milling
Malted barley is weighed, milled, and transported in a grain augering system or grain elevator.

2. Mash and Boil
The cracked malt is mixed with hot water and cooked in the mash tun, converting starches to fermentable sugars. The malt is then rinsed, or sparged, with hot water, creating the wort. The wort is boiled, and hops are added.

3. Fermentation and Lagering
The boiled wort is cooled down, yeast is added to the fermenter, and fermentation begins. Ales will take at least ten days to age and are kept at temperatures of 60 to 70 degrees Fahrenheit. Lagers take at least thirty days and ferment at temperatures of 35 to 50 degrees Fahrenheit.

4. Storage
Beer may be filtered to remove traces of yeast as it is transferred to the cold storage vessels.

5. Tapping
Brewpubs can draw beer directly from the cold storage vessels or tanks, which are usually near the bar. At breweries, beer goes into kegs, bottles, or cans.

Breweries and Brewpubs Map

1. August Schell Brewing Company (New Ulm)
2. Backwater Brewing Company (Winona)
3. Bank Beer Company (Hendricks)
4. Bard's Tale Beer Company (Minneapolis)
5. Barley John's Brew Pub (New Brighton)
6. Blue Diamond Brewing Company (St. Paul)
7. BoatHouse Brewpub and Restaurant (Ely)
8. Boom Island Brewing Company (Minneapolis)
9. Brainerd Lakes Brewery (Brainerd)
10. Brau Brothers Brewing Company (Lucan)
11. Carmody Irish Pub and Brewing (Duluth)
12. Castle Danger Brewery (Two Harbors)
13. Cold Spring Brewing Company (Cold Spring)
14. Dubh Linn Irish Brewpub (Duluth)
15. Dubrue (Duluth)
16. Finnegans Inc. (Minneapolis)
17. Fitger's Brewhouse (Duluth)
18. Flat Earth Brewing Company (St. Paul)
19. Fulton Brewery (Minneapolis)
20. Granite City Food and Brewery (Eagan)
21. Granite City Food and Brewery (Maple Grove)
22. Granite City Food and Brewery (Roseville)
23. Granite City Food and Brewery (St. Cloud)
24. Granite City Food and Brewery (St. Louis Park)
25. Great Waters Brewing Company (St. Paul)
26. Harriet Brewing (Minneapolis)
27. Hauenstein Beer (Sleepy Eye)
28. Herkimer Pub and Brewery (Minneapolis)
29. Lakemaid Beer Company (Minneapolis)
30. Lake Superior Brewing Company (Duluth)
31. Leech Lake Brewing Company (Walker)
32. Lift Bridge Brewery (Stillwater)
33. Lucid Brewing Company (Minnetonka)
34. Mankato Brewery (Mankato)
35. Mantorville Brewing Company (Mantorville)
36. McCann's Food and Brew (St. Cloud)
37. Minneapolis Town Hall Brewery (Minneapolis)
38. Olvalde Farm and Brewing Company (Rollingstone)
39. Pig's Eye Brewing Company (Woodbury)
40. Pour Decisions Brewing Company (Roseville)
41. Rock Bottom Restaurant and Brewery (Minneapolis)
42. Steel Toe Brewing (St. Louis Park)
43. Stillwater Brewing Company (Stillwater)
44. Summit Brewing Company (St. Paul)
45. Surly Brewing Company (Brooklyn Center)
46. Theodore Fyten Brewing Company and St. Croix Brewing Company (St. Paul)
47. Vine Park Brewing Company (St. Paul)

a. Brady's Brewhouse (New Richmond, Wisconsin)
b. City Brewing Company (La Crosse, Wisconsin)
c. Das Bierhaus (Menomonie, Wisconsin)
d. Dave's BrewFarm (Wilson, Wisconsin)
e. Dempsey's Brewery, Restaurant, and Pub (Watertown, South Dakota)
f. Granite City Food and Brewery (Fargo, North Dakota)
g. Granite City Food and Brewery (Sioux Falls, South Dakota)
h. Lucette Brewing Company (Menomonie, Wisconsin)
i. Pearl Street Brewery (La Crosse, Wisconsin)
j. Potosi Brewing Company (Potosi, Wisconsin)
k. Rush River Brewing Company (River Falls, Wisconsin)
l. Sand Creek Brewing Company (Black River Falls, Wisconsin)
m. South Shore Brewery (Ashland, Wisconsin)
n. Thirsty Pagan Brewing (Superior, Wisconsin)
o. Toppling Goliath Brewing Company (Decorah, Iowa)
p. Worth Brewing Company (Northwood, Iowa)

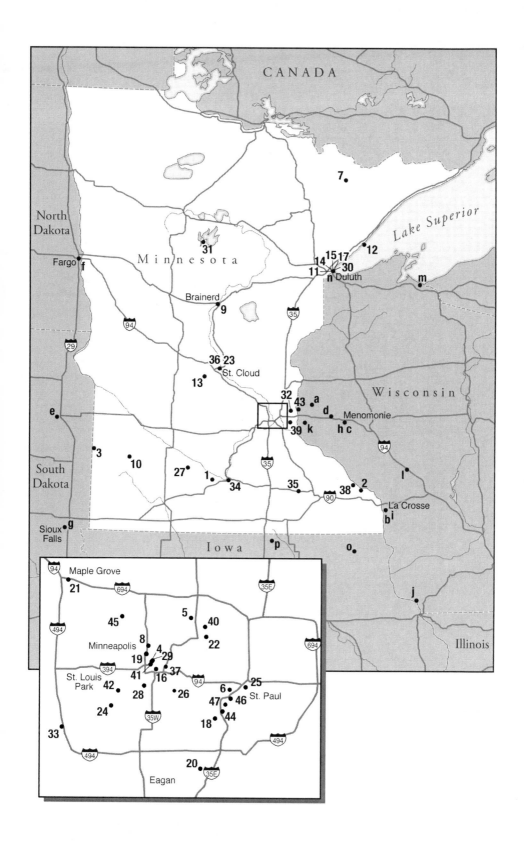

Central Region

COLD SPRING BREWING COMPANY (COLD SPRING)

GRANITE CITY FOOD AND BREWERY (ST. CLOUD)

MCCANN'S FOOD AND BREW (ST. CLOUD)

Geographically the heart of Minnesota, this region has beautiful lakes, wooded hills, and majestic farmland. Some of the best colors of the year (obviously, after the seasonal colors of beer, that is) are found in its hardwood forests each fall. The Central Region is northwest of the Twin Cities and is often described as an appealing blend of town and country life alongside many lake communities. It's also known for its scenic golf opportunities, with more than seventy courses. Before or after a round or two, there are a great many other activities that include bike and hiking trails, beautiful byways, antiquing, art galleries, theaters, lake resorts, and many romantic bed and breakfast and hotel accommodations.

Cold Spring Brewing Company
Cold Spring

Visit Date   Signed

ABOUT THE BREWERY

If you are into Minnesota brewing history, Cold Spring Brewing Company should be on your list of breweries to visit. Just don't expect a lot of signs pointing you to the brewery. It has been part of the community for nearly 140 years, so the locals know exactly where it stands. If you do get lost on your way, ask anyone who lives in Cold Spring and they'll get you there. The community is about fifteen miles south of Interstate 94 and the St. Cloud turnoffs.

The brewery's footprint is actually quite large, easily occupying over a city block in most comparable urban settings. The series of buildings that make up the sprawling complex are mostly tan and metal sided. However, older parts of the brewery are brick and wood, and they remain at the core of the brewhouse. Just take a tour and you'll walk through older parts of buildings where you will see the old copper mash tun and brick walls that are two- to four-feet thick.

Cold Spring Brewing has seen its share of ownership changes, acquisitions, and then some — even more so in recent times. In 1995 it was sold to a group of investors from Colorado known as Beverage International but within a year the ownership group had disappeared, leaving behind unpaid bills. The brewery fell back into the hands of the local bank, which put it up for sale in 1997. In 1998 a group of local investors, led by then brewery manager Maurice Bryan and former Coors executives Dan and Mabel Coborun, acquired the brewery in a sheriff's auction. In the early 2000s the brewery focused on its own Gluek brands, while turning more and more attention to contract brewing for others. In doing so it saw its portfolio of beers grow to more than thirty

3

different labels. It also was shipping about a third of its products to China, Mexico, and Puerto Rico. Beers like Aspen, Barkley Sound, Lawson Creek, Hackstein, and Hoffbrau were a few of the labels brewed under contract and marketed in the United States. Another well-known beer from the 1940s, called Stite, or what the locals refer to as "green lightning" because of its green and white can, made a comeback in 2001 when it was reintroduced in distinctive 8.3-ounce cans. Cold Spring adopted the standard 12-ounce can in 2004.

In 2008 the brewery changed its name back to Cold Spring Brewing. By 2008 it had phased out the Gluek brands. In more recent times the brewery has become a leader in the energy drink market. It makes more than eighty different "malternative" products, such as the popular Monster drink, and claims to be the nation's number one producer of energy specialty drinks. Nonbeer beverages in the Cold Spring portfolio include Guadalupe health drinks and Cold Spring Mineral Water.

The Cold Spring Brewing Company is the largest beer maker in Minnesota, with an annual production that exceeds 100,000 barrels, much of which is through contract accounts. Some of those include Blue Diamond (St. Paul), Rooster Lager and Walleye Chop for Bank Beer (Hendricks), and packaged products for the Lift Bridge Brewery (Stillwater). Among Cold Spring's own current products are John Henry Three Lick Spiker Ale, Olde Johnnie Ale, Moonlight Ale, and Cold Spring Hard Lemonade. The brewery's oldest brand, Gluek, was discontinued in 2010, ending a label that dates back to the 1850s. However, the brewery continues to keep the trademark.

HISTORY

Cold Spring Brewing was founded in 1874 by Michael Sargl, a German immigrant and brewer, near the natural springs along the Sauk River. It still operates in its original location. During its first quarter of a century, as the brewery changed hands several times, many of the owners put their own imprint on its size, equipment, and buildings. John Oster became a partner in the 1880s because he owned a steam engine that could no longer be used as a threshing machine. But because it was on wheels it could be moved around the brewery and was a big asset in grinding barley. The original malt house was built in 1880 and the brewhouse was expanded in 1899. The Cold Spring newspaper in October 1899 described it as an "immense enterprise on Red River Street . . . supplied with all the most modern machinery which skill and ingenuity could devise or money could buy . . . equipped with all the latest and best fixtures and machinery to be found only in a first class brewery . . . employing ten men all the year round and it is one of the best and most popular and thriving institutions of its kind in the northwest [with] a yearly capacity of 10,000 barrels."

In 1899 John Oster, his partner Ferdinand Peters, and brewmaster Eugene Hermanutz incorporated the business and changed its name to Cold Spring Brewing Company. All three built homes near the brewery, which remain today. Through the years of Prohibition it bottled and sold local spring and mineral waters along with tonics. It reopened in 1933 as Cold Spring Brewing Company and was able to survive industry consolidation by focusing on local markets and expanding distribution of a handful of its popular beers within the region. In the 1960s and 1970s the company was selling nearly 90 percent of its products in Minnesota. In 1969 the brewery undertook a major modernization that included buying equipment from more than twenty breweries that had gone under from the pressures of industry consolidation. In the 1970s Cold Spring embarked on a number of novelty brews. It's "Minnesota 13" was a beer named after Prohibition era spirits made in Sterns County from a University of Minnesota hybrid corn called Minnesota 13. In the late 1970s the brewery drew national attention with its Billy Beer, Elvira Beer, Goat's Breath, and Bad Frog. In the 1980s Cold Spring introduced Killebrew Root Beer, named after baseball great Harmon Killebrew who played for the Minnesota Twins from 1961 to 1974.

The Gluek connection occurred in the 1980s when Cold Spring acquired the Gluek brands from G. Heileman. However, Gluek as a brewery is more than a mere historical footnote in the business records of Cold Spring. Gluek was founded by Gottlieb Gluek in 1857 as the Mississippi Brewing Company of Minneapolis. It became Gluek Brewing when Gottlieb died and his sons took over the brewery in 1880. It continued until Prohibition, and then reopened in 1933. In the 1940s it was Gluek that originally developed the malt liquor Stite. But industry competition, insufficient marketing, and a failure to keep on top of new brewing technologies were just too much for Gluek. In 1964 the family sold the company to G. Heileman of La Crosse.

DON'T MISS THIS

Old newspaper clippings in the receiving and hospitality area describe more than a century of brewing on this site. Tours take visitors through some of the older areas of the brewery, including a walk through the brewhouse with its two-foot-thick walls.

COLD SPRING BREWS

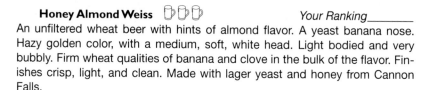

Honey Almond Weiss　🍺🍺🍺　　　　　*Your Ranking*_____

An unfiltered wheat beer with hints of almond flavor. A yeast banana nose. Hazy golden color, with a medium, soft, white head. Light bodied and very bubbly. Firm wheat qualities of banana and clove in the bulk of the flavor. Finishes crisp, light, and clean. Made with lager yeast and honey from Cannon Falls.

John Henry Three Lick Spiker Ale　🍺🍺🍺🍺　*Your Ranking*_____

An imperial stout conditioned with oak chips from barrels used to make bourbon. Its recipe includes three different dark-roasted malts that give it color and roasted flavor. Oats are added for additional body, and hops include Cascade, Willamette, and Alsace. This beer has a strong malty and bourbon nose and a deep, rich bronze color with a medium bubbly head. Full bodied with lots of chocolate, caramel, and bourbon flavor. Finishes with a firm bitterness. Some alcoholic warmth from all that malt. This is one beer from Cold Spring to not overlook. Its name recalls the mythical John Henry, who could drive a railroad spike into a tie with just three swings—thus, Three Lick Spiker Ale.

Moonlight Ale 🍺🍺🍺   *Your Ranking*_____

A combination of bock and porter styles that gets three additions of hops. A malty aroma with deep bronze color and a thin, tan head. Medium bodied. Rich caramel tones throughout main flavor profile and finish. An interesting beer with lots of different flavors.

Northern Reserve Golden Reserve 🍺🍺🍺   *Your Ranking*_____

This is what it is, a "value priced" brand for Cold Spring. A straw to golden color, with a bubbly and crisp texture. It is crisp and light, with nonoffensive balance between hops and malty graininess. Northern beer was once made by the Northern Brewing Company of Superior, Wisconsin, that closed in 1967; soon thereafter the Northern label was acquired by the Cold Spring Brewing Company. The Northern Brewing Company was a well-known regional brewery that was begun in 1890 by Louis Rueping and John Klinkert as the Klinkert Brewing Company.

OTHER COLD SPRING BREWS YOU MAY WANT TO TRY

Old Johnnie Ale   *Your Ranking*_____

Cold Spring Brewing worked with alumni of St. John's University in nearby Collegeville to resurrect an old Benedictine beer recipe from the nineteenth century that was at the heart, if not immortal soul, of this beer. It's release in 2006 coincided with the 150th anniversary of St. John's. Upon its tapping at Brother Willie's Pub in Collegeville, Abbot John Klassen "blessed the ale in perpetuity and consumed the first glass," according to a news release from St John's. Old Johnnie has a strong malty body. It is a copper-colored ale made with caramelized barley and flaked wheat. This beer is sometimes found in large 32-ounce (one quart) cans!

Stite   *Your Ranking*_____

This American pilsner was reintroduced in 2001. No nose. Clear, light golden color and a medium bubbly, marbled, white head. Light, crisp body. A sharp malty flavor with a citrus finish. Great fresh crispness that is accented by the citrus notes. Packaging changed in 2004 to larger 12-ounce cans.

MENU

None. Cold Spring Brewing Company does not serve food.

OTHER THINGS TO SEE OR DO IN THE AREA

Once a resting point on the Red River Trail, Cold Spring was founded in 1856. It was the main road for trains of ox carts bearing supplies and ammunition to the pioneer forts of the Red River valley. Today a number of private residences are listed on the National Register of Historic Places.

One of the best known businesses in town is the Cold Spring Bakery (308 Main Street). It has made donuts, buns, breads, and cookies for local citizens since 1946, and in 2004 was named Modern Baking's Bakery of the Year. Another local landmark is the headquarters of Cold Spring Granite (202 South

Third Avenue), the world's largest supplier of industrial granites with plants in Texas, California, New York, Wisconsin, and Canada.

Within ten miles of Cold Spring are twelve lakes and over thirty resorts. Year-round activities that attract many visitors include snowmobiling, cross-county and downhill skiing, golfing, boating, and fishing. The Cold Spring Area Broomball League heats up the winter with games on the ice rinks at Pioneer Park (Tenth Avenue South). A tournament is held there every February. You might catch a youth hockey game on the ice rinks at Pioneer Park. Cold Spring hosts the Springers amateur baseball team (Cold Spring Baseball Park, First Street South and Seventh Avenue South). The Springers have made more state tournament appearances (forty-eight as of 2009) than any other team. In July, Cold Spring holds its annual three-day Hometown Pride Festival with family karaoke, turtle races, arts and crafts, music, and beer garden, among many other events. In August, north and west of Cold Spring near Richmond, the Minnesota Bluegrass and Old-Time Music Festival is held at the El Rancho Manana (www.minnesotabluegrass.org). The event features entertainers, workshops, demonstrations, and dancing.

Cold Spring is home to one of the largest great blue heron rookeries in the United States. The large birds are commonly seen along the Sauk River that flows through Cold Spring. The Cold Spring Heron Colony and State Natural Area is a couple of miles east of town along Highway 23 and the river. Although you'll likely see many herons, no nesting birds have been recorded since 1989. Further west of Cold Spring, the Bruce Hitman Heron Rookery and State Natural Area is known as a nesting site. Ideal habitat for the herons, great egrets, double-crested cormorants, and black-crowned night herons is found on a small island within Lake Johanna, near Brooten, about forty miles west of Cold Spring

For interesting interaction with nature, visit Hoopers' Christmas Tree Ranch and Tibetan Yak farm (15813 Christmas Tree Road, Cold Spring). With more than forty head of yak, it boasts one of the largest herds in North America.

In the summers of 1876 and 1877 grasshoppers were destroying local farms. On April 26, 1877, the residents of Cold Spring vowed that if the Blessed Virgin would rid them of grasshoppers they would build a chapel and offer prayers to her for the next fifteen years. The next day, the grasshoppers were gone, and the people of Cold Spring kept their promise and built Assumption Chapel (one mile east of Cold Spring on Minnesota 23, then one block east on Chapel Hill Road). The chapel was made of wood and was destroyed by a tornado in 1894, seventeen years after it was constructed. In 1952 the chapel was rebuilt from local granite with the help of community members.

The area surrounding Cold Spring is the "real" Lake Wobegon, made famous by Minnesota Public Radio's Garrison Keillor. The Lake Wobegon Regional Trail provides opportunities for bicyclers, hikers, walkers, runners, skaters, and snowmobilers. It connects a number of area cities, including Avon, Albany, Freeport, Holdingford, Melrose, Sauk Centre, and St. Joseph. The trail was officially opened in 1998, and Keillor himself was on hand to ride the trail from Avon to Albany.

BREWERY RATING

	Your Rating	Shepard's Rating	General Description
Location		🍺🍺🍺🍺	Located on the north edge of Cold Spring. If you can't find it, just ask around.
Ease of Finding Location		🍺🍺🍺	Not difficult, but requires a commitment to traveling to Cold Spring.
Brewery Atmosphere		🍺🍺🍺🍺	Tours actually walk through the brewery, up close and personal, from the bottling line to the historic cellar walls that are several feet thick.
Dining Experience		n/a	Not applicable.
The Pints		🍺🍺🍺	An okay experience, especially for its tour with insights into Cold Spring history and the original brewery. Cold Spring beers are well made, yet its overall portfolio of styles and the number of its own brands is smaller than many other breweries (not counting what it contract brews for others).

DIRECTIONS

Cold Spring is about ten miles southwest of St. Cloud, following Minnesota 23. The brewery is about a half-dozen blocks north of the intersection of Minnesota 23 and County Road 2. The large tan buildings are minimally identified, but the facility with its numerous buildings really stands out on the north edge of Cold Spring, making it difficult to miss.

Granite City Food and Brewery

St. Cloud

Granite City
FOOD & BREWERY®

Visit Date	Signed

ABOUT THE BREWERY

You need not wonder too much about the name Granite City when you walk through the doors of one of the fastest growing brewpub chains. Stone accents that include large flagstone pillars and a red granite bar top reinforce the name that's a reference to St. Cloud's nickname — Granite City, a moniker that the local granite quarries inspired more than a century ago.

Granite City Food and Brewery opened in St. Cloud in 1999, the first in a chain of more than two dozen brewpubs in a dozen states, mostly in the Midwest. The company was founded in 1997 as Founders Food & Firkins by restaurant veterans Steve Wagenheim and Bill Burdick. It took them about a year and a half to develop their plans and raise the funding that opened the doors of the St. Cloud location, which began a successful business model poised for rapid expansion. The original concept that Wagenheim and Burdick worked from was to combine craft beer and food and to focus on medium-size cities, of which the Midwest has many. The final building sites often are close to major highways, regional shopping opportunities, entertainment venues, and hotels.

Wagenheim and Burdick are longtime friends with many years of experience in the hospitality industry. Wagenheim was the chief operating officer and president of Champps Americana, a sports restaurant-bar chain that eventually gave rise to the Fuddruckers chain of restaurants. Burdick owned the popular brewpub Sherlock's Home from 1989 to 2002 in Minnetonka.

The St. Cloud Granite City has a working brewery, unlike the other Granite City restaurants. The St. Cloud location does periodically brew special beers, but it also takes advantage of a Granite City trademarked process called Fermentus Interruptus that was developed by Burdick. The process involves a central wort-making facility—the worthouse—in Ellsworth, Iowa, that prepares and then ships wort to each store where yeast is added so that the fermentation begins at that specific restaurant. Ellsworth is located along Interstate 35 north of Ames, so it's ideally positioned to serve the company's chain of midwestern restaurants. Once the wort is ready it's pumped into custom-made tanker trucks that deliver the wort to one of twenty-six restaurants spread across eleven states. The facility also propagates the necessary yeast strains, which are also carried in the trucks in plastic containers much like the "water cubs" used by campers and hikers. Granite City has strong intentions to grow by doubling the number of restaurants in its family by 2015.

In 2011 Granite City began contracting with the Minhas Craft Brewery of Monroe, Wisconsin, to bottle several of its most popular beers. Its Northern Light Lager, Brother Benedict's Bock, and Duke of Wellington Pale Ale can be found in 12-ounce bottles throughout Minnesota.

HISTORY

St. Cloud has a rich history of brewing that goes back to the late 1850s. The Kramer and Seberger brewery is believed to have been one of the earliest, operating near Lake George, which is only about a mile east of Granite City Food and Brewery.

Steve Wagenheim serves as the president and CEO of Granite City Food and Brewery. His experience at Champps and prior to that as a restaurant consultant with the Minneapolis accounting firm of Laventhol and Horwath gives him long-standing credentials in the field. In 1992, when he was in charge of the Champps Franchise Development Group, he undoubtedly developed skills and concepts that now serve him and the company very well. This is especially so as Granite City expands beyond the Midwest into the Northeast and South. Wagenheim considers himself somewhat of an elder statesman in the industry, with nearly forty years in the business. He also enjoys being a familiar face, with periodic visits to each Granite City. Wagenheim goes out of his way to meet patrons, asking them about their experience and looking for creative ways to improve the business. His mantra: "Give the customer a twenty-five-dollar experience for thirteen dollars."

Bill Burdick is a modern legend in Minnesota's brewing scene, widely known by the most serious beer aficionados for the brewpub that no longer exists—Sherlock's Home. The Minnetonka pub was often visited by renowned beer writer Michael Jackson, whom Burdick enlisted in regular beer and whiskey tastings. Jackson once wrote in his column, "Sherlock's Home is too clever by half, but the beers are terrific. . . . I have a visceral dislike for fake British pubs, but Burdick's [Sherlock's] has its own character. Whatever it is—and I am not sure—it is itself." To which, in the story, Burdick commented, "We have a British allusion, but this is America, and we are not pretending otherwise."

Burdick earned an undergraduate degree in microbiology from Brown University and later a master's degree in brewing science form Heriot-Watt University in Edinburgh, Scotland. His résumé includes working for the William Younger Brewing Company in Edinburgh. In 1976 he went to Minnesota to work for the Multifood Corporation and design restaurants. By 1989 he decided to go out on his own and that's when he opened Sherlock's. In 2002 Burdick decided to close Sherlock's so he could focus more on Granite City and developing the trademarked Fermentus Interruptus process. He guided the design and construction of Granite City's worthouse in Ellsworth. Burdick handled brewing operations for Granite City until he retired in 2005.

From 1999 until spring 2011 Bob McKenzie served as head brewer at Granite City in St. Cloud and also oversaw the brewing operations at the brewpub's Twin Cities locations. In April 2011 he became brewmaster at Rock Bottom Restaurant and Brewery in downtown Minneapolis.

Cory O'Neel, Granite City's director of brewery operations, is based in Ellsworth at the worthouse and oversees quality assurance for the entire company. O'Neel grew up in Des Moines and after earning a bachelor's degree in microbiology from the University of Missouri in 1993 he headed west to Colorado. There he ended up rooming with a group of local homebrewers, and with his microbiology background it must have seemed like fate. He soon found work at the Oasis Brewery in Boulder (closed 2011). In 1996 O'Neel traveled to Hong Kong where he worked at the South China Brewing Company. When he returned in 1999 he purchased the Wolf Tongue Brewery in Nederland, Colorado, and ran it for a couple of years. He also worked for Coors in Golden, Colorado, and later the Boulder Beer Company. In 2006 he was offered a position by Granite City to help in the Ellsworth worthouse. It was very much like coming home for O'Neel, who has family in central Iowa.

O'Neel and fellow Granite City brewer R.J. Nab of Kansas City share responsibility for making site visits and training local restaurant staff in brewing techniques. O'Neel also travels to Monroe, Wisconsin, on brew days when the Minhas Brewery is making the bottled beer for Granite City.

As for the working brewhouse at St. Cloud's Grant City? Well, O'Neel might even be seen there from time to time brewing with his fellow Granite City brewers. The St. Cloud restaurant relies almost entirely on the Fermentus Interruptus process, but O'Neel says that since the restaurant has a complete brewing system it does get used occasionally. He refers to St. Cloud as "a playground for his brewers" and sees the equipment there as a great place to try things, like pilot batches and special brews. He admits that may not happen often, but he looks forward to it whenever there's time in the busy production schedule.

DON'T MISS THIS

There are a couple of unique features to Granite City's original location in St. Cloud. The first is an enclosed solarium-like room with lots of windows that makes for a separate dining area just off the bar area. The second feature is the vivid red-granite rectangular bar that seats patrons on three of four sides. Nearly all of the chain's locations display a photo of a smiling bartender hoisting two mugs. In the St. Cloud location it hangs just inside the entryway.

GRANITE CITY BREWS

Broad Axe Stout 🍺🍺🍺🍺   *Your Ranking_____*
Medium to full bodied with creamy texture from flaked oats in its recipe and served on a nitrogen tap. There is lots of rich roasted chocolate and caramel flavor.

Brother Benedict's Bock 🍺🍺   *Your Ranking_____*

A German-style lager with medium body, deep brown color, and a caramel malty flavor. Its recipe includes Munich and chocolate malts with Apollo and Tettnang hops.

Duke of Wellington 🍺🍺🍺   *Your Ranking_____*

A medium- to full-bodied, copper-colored India pale ale that has a solid malty character with a hoppy nose and finish with hints of apricot. Made with Apollo, Cascade, and Willamette hops.

Northern Light Lager 🍺🍺   *Your Ranking_____*

An American light lager, bubbly with a golden color. Features Apollo hops.

Scottish Ale 🍺🍺🍺🍺   *Your Ranking_____*

A Scottish-style export ale with a mahogany brown color, a thick, soft, tan head, and overall medium-round body. Solid and rich caramel flavor and finish. Its brown malt and Simpson's Golden Naked Oats combine for a light malty background. This beer has also gone by the name McK's Scottish Ale, a reference to its creator and former Granite City brewer Bob McKenzie.

Wag's Wheat 🍺🍺   *Your Ranking_____*

A slightly cloudy American wheat that has vivid yellow color and a thick, white head. The lightest of the Granite City beers. Made with Apollo and Glacier hops. Named after Granite City founder Steve Wagenheim.

OTHER GRANITE CITY BREWS YOU MAY WANT TO TRY

Since it has a complete brewery, the Granite City in St. Cloud has the capability to offer beers not found at the other locations. For example, you may see a couple of hand pulls on the north side of the bar that offer an inviting image, but unfortunately in recent years they have not been utilized much. Beyond cask-conditioned brew, a few of the special beers that have appeared at the St. Cloud Granite City include:

The Admiral (Two Pulls)   *Your Ranking_____*

The Admiral combines Northern Light and Duke of Wellington IPA.

Double IPA 🍺🍺🍺   *Your Ranking_____*

When released in late 2009, this beer was called the 1,000th Batch. It has a bright orange copper color and floral hoppy nose with a firm, dry, bitter finish.

Pride of Pilsen 🍺🍺🍺🍺   *Your Ranking_____*

Another special beer designed by former Granite City brewmaster Bob McKenzie, who liked to call it his baby. It was actually first made at the St. Cloud location, where the local water quality makes brewing very difficult. McKenzie took almost two years to get this recipe how he wanted it to taste. This beer doesn't return very often now that McKenzie has moved to the Rock Bottom Brewpub in Minneapolis. When it—or a similar version from the hands of O'Neel—does return, it will most likely be a summer seasonal for Granite City St. Cloud.

Two Pull *Your Ranking*_____

The Granite City Two Pull is a blended beer created by mixing Northern Light and Brother Benedict's Bock.

MENU

Granite City offers a broad menu of items that are modestly priced. While the menus across the various locations look similar, there are rotating weekly specials that add variety. Some of those choices include Sriracha Tilapia, Cajun Pasta, Sticky Fingers (honey-glazed chicken strips), and the Quarry Burger.

Granite City features many made-from-scratch menu items. Even still, if you visit more than one location you'll find quite a few similarities. No matter which Granite City restaurant you are in, the meatloaf is a favorite. Just as tasty is the London broil.

Granite City always offers extensive salad selections, ranging from a basic dinner salad to grilled Asian chicken. Expect about ten different sandwiches and a half-dozen burger choices. One of the signature items is the Bleu Peppercorn burger, a half pound of Angus beef seasoned with black peppercorns and topped with creamy bleu cheese. There are also steaks, seafood, pastas, soups, and a kids' menu. Several of the house beers are integrated into menu items, such as the ale and cheddar soup. Granite City also is well known for its Sunday brunch.

OTHER THINGS TO SEE OR DO IN THE AREA

St. Cloud was founded in 1856 when the three communities of Lower, Upper, and Middle Town merged—a fact not lost on some locals today who like to correct visitors when referring to uptown versus downtown. The first commercial brewers started making beer around 1857. Many of the early beer drinkers were loggers and quarry workers. The first of the granite quarries opened in 1863. For a better understanding of the industry that the brewpub name references, visit Quarry Park (a short drive southwest along County Road 137 in Waite Park). There you'll find hiking and biking trails and get a firsthand look at some of the early abandoned rock pits where stones were harvested. There are even swimming and scuba diving opportunities for those who are certified. The park has a fifty-five-foot-high observation deck that offers panoramic views of the area. Actually, if you have the opportunity to just walk around the "up" town, you'll want to take notice of the Stearns County courthouse, one of the many public structures that were built with local granite. The Stearns History Museum (235 South Thirty-third Avenue) has a model of a 1930s working quarry, along with exhibits of the area's natural environment and displays of early Ojibwe and Dakota settlements.

The Munsinger and Clemens Gardens (101 Riverside Drive) is another great walk that will take you past more than a thousand rose bushes that share the park with giant oaks, hemlocks, and very old pines. Continue northward, along Riverside Drive, and you'll end up in Riverside Park, which lies on the east bank of the Mississippi River and has great views of its own.

Sports fans may want to allow time for the Minnesota Amateur Baseball Hall of Fame (10 Fourth Avenue South, on the second floor of the St. Cloud Civic Center). It has rotating exhibits on hometown teams, baseball artifacts, and photographs dating back to 1857, when amateur baseball began in Minnesota. It you want to take in a ball game, the St. Cloud River Bats play in the Northwoods League at Dick Putz Field (5001 Eighth Street North). The National Hockey Center (720 Fourth Avenue South, on the St. Cloud State University campus) is home to the St. Cloud State Huskies, a Division I men's hockey team. The facility, built in 1989, has two Olympic-size hockey rinks that are also used for instruction and community recreation.

But perhaps the most famous region is the area northwest of St. Cloud that gave rise to Lake Wobegon, the fictional community portrayed by public radio's Garrison Keillor. In his weekly news and personal observations he calls this the geographic center of Minnesota. Roughly between Holdingford and Freeport, it's a place "where all the women are strong, all the men are good-looking, and the children are above average." And what is the beer of choice in Lake Wobegon? Keillor claims to be partial to Wendy's Beer, brewed in St. Wendel. (In case you go looking for it, there is no actual record in any brewery archives of Wendy's Beer.)

BREWERY RATING

	Your Rating	Shepard's Rating	General Description
Location		🍺🍺🍺	Close to shopping, entertainment, and major roads.
Ease of Finding Location		🍺🍺🍺🍺	Easy to find, off I-94 from exit 167B.
Brewery Atmosphere		🍺🍺	High ceilings, lots of stone accents, a show kitchen, and prominent beer fermenters provide a vibrant brewery feel. But those looking for unique character might be somewhat disappointed in that all Granite Citys have similar décor.
Dining Experience		🍺🍺🍺	Pub fare to family-style offerings. Food is well prepared and reasonably priced.
The Pints		🍺🍺🍺🍺	One reason to visit Granite City St. Cloud is that it's the first restaurant brewpub in the Granite City family. This Granite City has its own brewery capabilities and produces a few special beers throughout the year. For that reason it's always worth a stop while in the neighborhood.

DIRECTIONS

St. Cloud is located about an hour north and west of Minneapolis, or three hours south and east of Moorhead. From I-94, take exit 167B and head north on Minnesota 15 for about four miles to the intersection with Second Street. Granite City Food and Brewery sits on the northwest corner of this intersection.

McCann's Food and Brew
St. Cloud

Visit Date	Signed

ABOUT THE BREWERY

McCann's Food and Brew opened in 2007 under the ownership of Nick Mc-Cann and Wendel Clark. The two partners and good friends actually flipped a coin to determine which of their names the business would use. Clark handles much of the day-to-day management of the brewpub. McCann is very much involved, but also runs a local flooring business. The brewmaster, Chris Laumb, grew up in St. Cloud and learned much of his brewing skills on the job, backed up by several years of homebrewing.

Remodeled in 2007, the building has two levels. The upstairs has a small bar, the main dining room, and a small room off the main bar that houses the 10-barrel brewing system that makes up the brewhouse. Sitting at the bar, you may even catch a glimpse of Laumb through the windows that look into the brewery. The lower level of the restaurant has a banquet room, two bars, and an enclosed room containing four fermenters and five serving tanks. Much of the downstairs is also set up as a large game room with more than ten pool tables and twenty dart boards for pickup games and tournaments.

St. Cloud has a strong German heritage. In 2009 it hosted a delegation from its sister city of Spalt, which is also known as the Bavarian city of hops. Not surprisingly, it's in a region of Germany where Spalt hops are grown. The delegation was led by Spalt mayor Udo Weingart, who also manages the municipal brewery that makes Spalter Bier. During that 2009 visit Weingart spent time with Laumb, Clark, and McCann talking about beer and even sampling a few.

HISTORY

The brewpub actually began in 1996, as an expansion to the well-known O'Hara's Restaurant. Tim O'Hara had operated a restaurant in this location since 1978, the same corner where the O'Hara family had operated different businesses since 1945.

O'Hara got the inspiration for adding a brewery to his restaurant from a former employee who had moved to Colorado, discovered Coopersmith's Brewpub in Fort Collins, and sent O'Hara a brochure from Coopersmith's. After traveling around the country looking at other brewpubs, Tim called the JV Northwest brewery equipment company to help him design his brewhouse.

Brewmaster Chris Laumb had worked for O'Hara's and helped install the original equipment. So, when Clark and McCann decided to buy the business in 2007, they hired Laumb to keep making their beer. Laumb knew homebrewing and had worked at the nearby Cold Spring brewery, but humbly says he's mostly self-taught.

DON'T MISS THIS

Near the hostess stand, take notice of the Monster Burger Wall of Fame. To get your photo on the board you must polish off the two-pound Monster Burger, including its fries and onion rings, all served in the scoop of a snow shovel. To be recognized you must eat it all, and in less than one hour!

MCCANN'S BREWS

American Brown Ale 🍺🍺🍺   *Your Ranking*_____
A light malty nose. Deep hazy amber color, with a rocky tan head. Medium bodied. Mild, but firm malty body. Clean finish.

Blacked Out Oatmeal Stout 🍺🍺🍺   *Your Ranking*_____
Begins with an assertive, malty nose. Deep dark color with bronze highlights. The head is thick, soft, and tan. Full bodied, slick texture. The flavor is robust like its appearance with firm, sweet chocolate maltiness. Sweet malty and lightly roasted finish. This stout is part of the "dark seasonal" line of beers at McCann's and is offered in the winter.

Deep Seven IPA 🍺🍺🍺   *Your Ranking*_____
A combination of two English hops and two varieties of American hops plus three types of malt give "seven" special meaning. Deep Seven starts with lots of hoppy aroma. It color is rich golden to copper with a marbled, tan head. Medium bodied. There is an assertive piney hoppiness in flavor profile and finish. Chris Laumb says its name is a reference to a local quarry pit that he and friends swam in as kids and called Deep Seven.

Golden Ale 🍺🍺🍺   *Your Ranking*_____
This American golden ale is McCann's flagship beer. Begins with a light malty nose. Clear, light golden color and a thick, soft, off-white head. Light bodied with soft texture. The flavor is sharp, yet overall very clean and light. Finishes

with just a little roastedness, but remains clean and crisp. Made with Belgian pilsner malt, Munich malt, and crystal hops.

High Bank Amber Ale   Your Ranking_____
No nose. Clear copper color with a medium soft, tan head. Medium bodied and round texture. A firm caramel malt flavor that is slightly sweet. The finish is light malty with a hint of roastedness. This beer is made with Belgian pale malt and English hops.

Maple Moon   Your Ranking_____
A malty nose. Clear copper color and a thin, soft, tan head. Medium bodied and bubbly. Sweet caramel maltiness and a light roasted background that includes an assertive maple flavor from Minnesota maple syrup.

Pale Ale   Your Ranking_____
A light floral nose. Solid, clear, copper color and a thin, tan, marbled head. Medium bodied and round texture. A resiny hoppiness throughout flavor and finish. There is a light dryness that remains in the aftertaste.

Prairie Porter   Your Ranking_____
This dark and roasted porter is made with four types of malt: dark, crystal, black, and chocolate. It begins with a firm, roasted, malty nose. Very dark black color and a thin, soft, tan head. Full bodied. Strong chocolate malt flavors dominate with a sweet malty finish that has strong hints of roastedness.

Rye Pale Ale   Your Ranking_____
A seasonal brew for McCann's. This pale ale shows off spicy and dry character from rye malt added to the mash, alongside the citrus-like bitterness of Simcoe hops. Its nose is light but maltiness is firm. The color is a deep clear golden with a thin, soft, off-white head. Medium body helps bring out the spicy qualities of the main flavor profile. Finishes with a long-lasting, dry bitterness.

Trippel Trouble   Your Ranking_____
A yeasty and sweet nose. Clear golden-copper color and a medium, soft, off-white head. There is solid yeasty sweetness that is almost honey-like. That sweetness continues throughout the finish. This is a wonderful, full-bodied, big Belgian beer. Part of McCann's seasonal lineup of beers, it is offered in winter.

OTHER MCCANN'S BREWS YOU MAY WANT TO TRY

Apricot Coriander Ale   Your Ranking_____
Made with a combination of apricot, Belgian malt, and French hops. A light beer with orange citrus notes.

Raspberry   Your Ranking_____
Strong berry nose. A clear golden color with a medium, soft, white head. Light to medium bodied. An assertive raspberry flavor and finish. A lot of fruit flavoring that continues to linger long into the finish. For some who like raspberry, this is a great beer. For me, it was a little too much.

An unfiltered wheat. This bright yellow golden beer is light bodied and bubbly.

MENU

McCann's menu features many pub, tavern, and family restaurant items. Appetizer choices include cheesy garlic bread, nachos, wings, quesadillas, and a combination platter of nearly all starters. McCann's menu has a large number of burgers, sandwiches, wraps, and pastas. The menu itself highlights a few of the signature options, like the Bacon and Cheese Chicken Sandwich that is topped with smoked bacon and your choice of cheese. The McCann's Pasta is made with mushrooms, onion, peppers, and steak on penne pasta with Cajun alfredo sauce. The wraps are hearty, and choices range from Chicken Caesar to steak. Several salad options are available. The dinner side of the menu has walleye prepared either beer battered or pan seared. The Steak Tips are sirloin and served with mixed vegetables on a bed of rice. McCann's also makes pizza with about a half-dozen choices, including build-your-own.

OTHER THINGS TO SEE OR DO IN THE AREA

St. Cloud was named after Saint-Cloud—a suburb of Paris, France. In the early days it was a trading post and connection to the Red River Trail that stretched to Canada. The Mississippi River provided additional transportation, and St. Cloud was a place where steamboats would dock when water levels allowed—but with no great consistency. If you want to catch a glimpse of the Mississippi, travel north on Minnesota 15 and you'll cross the river by way of the Bridge of Hope. Students named the bridge in a contest held throughout the local school system.

St. Cloud is also known for its granite quarries, the first of which opened up 1863. The city is often referred to by its nickname—Granite City. For a better understanding, visit Quarry Park (a short drive along County Road 137 in Waite Park) where hiking and biking trails will provide an up-close look at the abandoned rock pits where stones were harvested.

Sports fans may want to allow time for the Minnesota Amateur Baseball Hall of Fame (10 Fourth Avenue South, on the second floor of the St. Cloud Civic Center). If you enjoy art, the Paramount Theatre and Visual Arts Center (913 West Germain Street) is home to professional theater performances, exhibits, and classes for aspiring artists. There are events and festivals throughout the year, but among the highlights are Granite City Days in June and the Mississippi River Fest in April.

Those traveling in this part of Minnesota might watch for the signs pointing to St. Augusta, a town about seven miles south of St. Cloud. In May 2000, the unincorporated community decided to change its name to Ventura, in honor of the governor at the time, Jesse Ventura. But the move, designed to attract positive attention, did anything but that. The following November the locals voted to change the name back to St. Augusta—by a wide margin.

Within a few miles of McCann's is another brewpub, Granite City Food and Brewery (3945 Second Street South). This was the first Granite City in a fast-growing chain of restaurants in the Midwest.

BREWERY RATING

	Your Rating	Shepard's Rating	General Description
Location		🍺🍺🍺	Located in a small shopping mall on the north edge of town.
Ease of Finding Location		🍺🍺🍺	Close to major roads and intersections, but a little advance planning will help.
Brewery Atmosphere		🍺🍺🍺	Higher marks are given for the upstairs décor, which is in the spirit of a local tavern and family restaurant. The downstairs has a sports bar theme, and a third area is a banquet hall.
Dining Experience		🍺🍺🍺	Wide selection of pub and family-oriented entrées.
The Pints		🍺🍺🍺	Good beer and a great way to experience some of the local flare when traveling through the community.

DIRECTIONS

St. Cloud is located about an hour north and west of Minneapolis, or three hours south and east of Moorhead, via I-94. McCann's Food and Brew is in an area known as the West End neighborhood of St. Cloud, but most locals just call it by its location, the intersection of "Thirty-third and Third."

From exit 167B of I-94, go north on Minnesota 15 for four miles to the intersection with Second Street (Minnesota 23 west) but keep traveling north. You might note, however, that just to the northwest of this intersection is the well-known Granite City brewpub of St. Cloud.

Continue north on Minnesota 15 for another one and a half miles, passing Crossroads Center on the west. At the intersection and stoplights marking Third Street North, turn right (east) onto Third Street and continue for about half of a mile. McCann's is located on the south side of Third Street in the Premier Plaza (intersection of Third Street North and Thirty-third Avenue North).

Metro Region

BARLEY JOHN'S BREW PUB (NEW BRIGHTON)

BOOM ISLAND BREWING COMPANY (MINNEAPOLIS)

FLAT EARTH BREWING COMPANY (ST. PAUL)

FULTON BREWERY (MINNEAPOLIS)

GRANITE CITY FOOD AND BREWERY (EAGAN)

GRANITE CITY FOOD AND BREWERY (MAPLE GROVE)

GRANITE CITY FOOD AND BREWERY (ROSEVILLE)

GRANITE CITY FOOD AND BREWERY (ST. LOUIS PARK)

GREAT WATERS BREWING COMPANY (ST. PAUL)

HARRIET BREWING (MINNEAPOLIS)

HERKIMER PUB AND BREWERY (MINNEAPOLIS)

LIFT BRIDGE BREWERY (STILLWATER)

LUCID BREWING COMPANY (MINNETONKA)

MINNEAPOLIS TOWN HALL BREWERY (MINNEAPOLIS)

POUR DECISIONS BREWING COMPANY (ROSEVILLE)

ROCK BOTTOM RESTAURANT AND BREWERY (MINNEAPOLIS)

STEEL TOE BREWING (ST. LOUIS PARK)

STILLWATER BREWING COMPANY (STILLWATER)

SUMMIT BREWING COMPANY (ST. PAUL)

SURLY BREWING COMPANY (BROOKLYN CENTER)

THEODORE FYTEN BREWING COMPANY AND ST. CROIX BREWING COMPANY (ST. PAUL)

VINE PARK BREWING COMPANY (ST. PAUL)

BRADY'S BREWHOUSE (NEW RICHMOND, WISCONSIN)

DAS BIERHAUS (MENOMONIE, WISCONSIN)

DAVE'S BREWFARM (WILSON, WISCONSIN)

LUCETTE BREWING COMPANY (MENOMONIE, WISCONSIN)

RUSH RIVER BREWING COMPANY (RIVER FALLS, WISCONSIN)

This region includes Minneapolis, St. Paul, and their neighboring communities. The Twin Cities area enjoys the largest number of breweries and brewpubs. There are endless opportunities beyond beer that include arts, architecture, terrific restaurants, museums, and professional sports. There are also greenways and lakes, and the Mississippi, Minnesota, and St. Croix rivers, which wind through and around the metro area. This region offers an incredible list of things to see and do, while supporting the state's largest concentration of local beer makers.

Barley John's Brew Pub
New Brighton

651 • 636 - 4670
781 Old Highway Eight • New Brighton MN 55112

Visit Date	Signed

ABOUT THE BREWERY

Barley John's is a beer enthusiasts' hangout. It is a must-stop for those seeking the essence of artisan brewed beer and food as a total experience. It's a small place, on the north side of the Twin Cities. While not the easiest beer venue to find, it is well worth the trek no matter where you're coming from or headed to.

Barley John's is small by anyone's assessment. It has only a half-dozen seats at the bar, and a cozy main dining room. In warm weather, or when the heaters or outside fire can keep up with the weather, there is a beer garden that nearly triples the capacity of the place. It has a roadhouse atmosphere, accented by the nearby busy intersection of County Road D and Old Highway 8. Given its compact square footage and popularity, it can become very crowded, especially when a local musician is appearing or members of the local home-brew clubs turn up.

Inside, Barley John's says handcraft in more ways than just its beer list. There are stained-glass accents and wall stencils by local artists. The bar itself was made from a split tree trunk. Once you walk through the door you have to wonder how a brewpub of such large reputation among local aficionados fits in a place this small — just a bar and dining room combined with a kitchen. If you're looking for the brewery, you'll find most of it in a glass-enclosed porch that houses the 3.5-barrel system. Beers are stored and aged below the bar in the building's basement.

Barley John's commitment to craft brewing makes this a very special stop

23

on any Minnesota beer trip. It caters to the neighborhood and is well known among the Twin Cities beer crowd. The menu ranges from a few common brewpub items to more eclectic and health-friendly dishes developed by owners John Moore and Laura Subak, who have worked in the healthcare field.

Barley John's has figured out a special niche for itself among local brewpubs. In 2010 Barley John's was picked "Best Brewpub" in the Twin Cities Guide from *City Pages*. The standard beers include Little Barley Bitter, Stockyards IPA, Wild Brunette, and Old 8 Porter. On most visits you'll come across at least a dozen being served that include familiar brands as guest beers. Moore gets a lot of attention for his big and bold "Batman Series" of brews. His Maibock and Oktoberfest are just as worthy of a pint or two.

HISTORY

Owner and brewer John Moore first tried homebrewing in the late 1980s with friends while studying microbiology at the University of Minnesota. Moore went on to receive a degree in nutrition and dietetics, and later landed a job as a nutritionist for a local hospital and subsequently the Pillsbury Company in Minneapolis. After his wife, Laura Subak, bought him a homebrew kit in 1991 his hobby really took off. So when a position to help out at the James Page Brewery opened up in 1994, John left his job at Pillsbury to manage the brewery's yeast cultures. While at James Page, John's influence was felt in a number of the early Page brews, such as the Burley Brown and the Wild Rice, both of which have won medals at the Great American Beer Festival.

After working at James Page for a couple of years, John decided to expand his brewing credentials and attended the Siebel Institute of Technology and World Brewing Academy in Chicago, graduating in 1995. A downturn in the local brewery business, the closing of Stroh's, and cutbacks at James Page prompted John and Laura to go into business for themselves. They opened Barley John's in 2000 on a corner that, over the years, had been the site of a Vienna sausage stand, an A&W Root Beer drive-in, and later a Chinese restaurant. Moore is helped out in the brewery by Colin Mullen.

DON'T MISS THIS

The bar was made from a sugar maple tree that once stood in the front yard of the home of John Moore's grandmother Hellen Cruaser. Also, take a close look at the tap handles behind the bar. John's friend Tom Rine, who works at the nearby Island Glass Company, made them. Tom had offered to make custom tap handles in the event that John should ever open his own place.

BARLEY JOHN'S BREWS

Belgian Dubbel 🍺🍺🍺   *Your Ranking_____*
A yeasty and light fruity nose. Deep copper to bronze color and a thin, off-white head. Medium bodied and bubbly. Its taste is sweet, yeasty, and spicy. Belgian influences in the type of malts, yeast, and candi sugar are part of the recipe. It also gets additions of dried cherries, which you find in the aroma and finish.

Cream Ale 🍺🍺🍺🍺   *Your Ranking_____*

This is one of Barley John's lightest beers. It's made with pilsner malt and corn, then hopped with Hallertau hops. Offers a light malty and grainy nose. Clear golden color and a medium soft, off-white head. Light bodied with a soft texture. Malty body with a crisp background and clean finish. A very nice, light, clean ale.

Dark Mild 🍺🍺🍺   *Your Ranking_____*

A malty nose. Hazy bronze color with a thin, soft, tan head. Medium bodied and bubbly. A firm caramel maltiness to the main flavor. Finishes with a malty and mildly roasted ending. The roasted tones build over a pint or two.

German Ale 🍺🍺🍺   *Your Ranking_____*

Light malty nose with a hint of smoky roastedness. Clear copper color, very effervescent and bubbly with a medium, soft, off-white head. Light to medium bodied, overall crisp mouth feel. Begins with a subtle hoppiness from German Hallertau hops. A gentle malty sweetness that lingers into the finish. Just a nice, smooth, and firm malty character.

Little Barley Bitter 🍺🍺🍺   *Your Ranking_____*

A light, faint floral nose. Hazy, light golden color with a thin, bubbly, off-white head. Medium bodied and round texture. This English-style bitter has a firm, mild, malty start with a dry, bitter background. A light bitter hoppiness grows in the finish. Overall, dry and smooth. The hoppiness will grow on you. Little Barley Bitter was named after John and Laura's son Nick. When Laura was expecting in 2000 those working on the building's renovation liked to jokingly ask, "How's little barley doing?" It was a name that stuck and soon became Nick's nickname as well as the name for one of their very first beers.

Maibock 🍺🍺🍺🍺   *Your Ranking_____*

Begins with an inviting malty, sweet nose. Light amber color and a tan, thin, and soft head. Medium bodied and round. Smooth caramel maltiness dominates but doesn't overtake a light bitter background and finish. A very nice seasonal choice.

Oktoberfest 🍺🍺🍺   *Your Ranking_____*

This seasonal has an inviting caramel nose, clear deep-bronze color, and thick, bubbly, tan head. Medium bodied and soft texture. A smooth malty start with a dry, mildly bitter finish. A smooth Oktoberfest and just a great beer to celebrate the arrival of fall.

Old 8 Porter 🍺🍺🍺🍺   *Your Ranking_____*

Lots of chocolate malt in the nose. Dark black with bronze highlights. Full bodied with rich chocolate and roasted coffee tones. Firm malty flavor. It's also a beer to respect for its 8 percent ABV. Moore's original version of this beer was fashioned to be around 7.2 percent, but when he decided to call it "Old 8" he pumped up the recipe just enough to achieve an alcohol content equal to the name. It's also a reference to Old Highway 8, which passes by the brewpub and was once the main road from Minneapolis to the New Brighton stockyards.

Stockyard IPA 🍺🍺🍺🍺

Your Ranking_____

For those who like bitter, hoppy beers, just head for the Stockyard! Aggressive flavors, including bitterness, yet a soft texture. Strong floral nose. Hazy amber color with a soft, bubbly, tan head. Light malty start adds to the softness, then the hops overtake the flavor and finish with a warm firm bitterness. Made with Northern Brewer and East Kent Goldings hops. New Brighton was once known for its stockyards.

Triple Oat Stout 🍺🍺🍺

Your Ranking_____

Light but firm roasted nose. Dark with a medium marbled tan head. Medium bodied and silky. Soft chocolate maltiness with a light bitter finish. Made with three kinds of oats and English noble hops.

Wild Brunette 🍺🍺🍺🍺

Your Ranking_____

This wild rice brown ale is the signature beer for Barley John's. Minnesota wild rice gives this ale an earthy background with notes of vanilla and almond. A sweet, slightly fruity nose. Deep, vivid, ruby-bronze color. A beautiful beer! Sweet caramel flavor with hints of toasted almond in the background. A warm, complex finish with a mild dryness. John Moore developed this recipe in the early 1990s when other brewers were making popular blondes and reds. Moore decided he would pay tribute to his wife, Laura, who is a brunette!

OTHER BARLEY JOHN'S BREWS YOU MAY WANT TO TRY

Alfred

Your Ranking_____

If you see a beer on the menu called Alfred, it's likely to lead you to a Dark Knight in days ahead. Alfred is the portion of the Dark Knight that doesn't make it into the bourbon barrel. Moore makes just enough Dark Knight to fill an oak barrel, and what doesn't fit in the barrel is called Alfred and is often released just before the Dark Knight arrives. It carries the name Alfred because that was the name of Batman's butler, and you always had to go through Alfred to get to Batman!

Dark Knight 🍺🍺🍺🍺

Your Ranking_____

A big, dark, full-bodied porter. More robust than the brewpub's Old 8. Moore hesitates to call it an imperial porter himself, but most who frequent the brewpub like to put that label on it. The beer is aged in a bourbon barrel and is double fermented with a Belgian yeast strain. This beer came from John Moore's sense of adventure with a bit of humor. After buying a used bourbon barrel to experiment with several years ago, John decided that the porter beer style might offer some unique flavors with the oak and bourbon. An intense malty recipe with added Belgian candi sugar to restart secondary fermentation makes for a strong, warm beer, with some of the qualities of a robust porter, an imperial stout, and a Belgian tripel. The beer ages in the barrel for four to five months. Annual releases of this beer fall between 13 and 14 percent ABV. The name Dark Knight is a reference to Batman. It was first released on a Halloween night not long after Barley John's first opened its doors.

Dark Knight Returns   *Your Ranking*_____

This is the same porter from which the Dark Knight comes, except it is the second batch in the same used bourbon barrel. Moore says when he first made the Dark Knight he couldn't stand to throw out the barrel after he had used it just once, so he tried filling the barrel again with Dark Knight. He liked the result and he needed a catchy name, so "Dark Knight Returns" just seemed to fit. Expect the beer to have the rich chocolate maltiness and warmth of the Dark Knight, but just a little less bourbon flavor.

Rosie's Old Ale   🍺🍺🍺🍺   *Your Ranking*_____

A triple-fermented version of an old stock ale aged in oak barrels that were once used to make bourbon. The beer is the third one to make its way through the oak casks that are used for Dark Knight and Dark Knight Returns. As the third brew through the same barrel, there is a bit more tannin and oak tones with less bourbon flavor. Rosie's has a malty nose with a hint of that oakiness. Its color is a hazy reddish-amber with a thin, bubbly, off-white head. Full bodied and warm from the start. Up-front maltiness balances nicely with the light oak. Rosie is the name of John and Laura's daughter.

MENU

The restaurant is a cozy place with about a dozen tables. Among the favorites is the grilled pizza. Simply labeled Pizza J, Pizza O, Pizza H, and Pizza N, they spell out the owner's first name. The "J" features Canadian bacon, "O" is made with portobello mushrooms, "H" offers sun-dried tomatoes and roasted garlic, and "N" is billed as not-your-average-pizza, with sausage, peppers, and kalamata olives. There's also a Pizza Laura, a vegetarian special. Other entrées include beer tenderloin, smoked pork chops, and beer-battered catfish and chips. Daily and seasonal specialties are something to watch for. In the summer you may find salads made with heirloom tomatoes, fresh strawberries, or even blueberries that are all grown in the brewpub's garden that is just a few steps from the beer garden. Appetizer selections feature hot artichoke dip, chicken quesadillas, barbecued chicken, and shrimp kabobs. The pub's signature hamburger is the build-your-own Barley Burger, a half-pound of chopped sirloin that, when topped with cheddar cheese and jalapeños, will match well with a Stockyard IPA.

OTHER THINGS TO SEE OR DO IN THE AREA

New Brighton was once surrounded by the Minneapolis Stockyard and Packing Company. Today, the annual Stockyard Days in August offers a parade, live entertainment, street dancing, 5K and 10K runs, an antique car show, bed races, and fireworks at Long Lake Regional Park. New Brighton has more than a dozen parks, and among the most popular is Long Lake, located just north of Barley John's on Old Highway 8. Another popular destination is Gibbs Farm Museum of Pioneer and Dakota Life (2097 Larpenteur Avenue West, St. Paul) with exhibits of traditional pioneer life—a farmstead, one-room schoolhouse, and the Dakotah Medicine Teaching Garden. And, if you are interested in shopping, Barley John's Brewpub isn't far from Rosedale Center, located about two miles southeast in Roseville.

BREWERY RATING

	Your Rating	Shepard's Rating	General Description
Location		🍺🍺🍺	A combination of neighborhood restaurant and light entertainment district. The major intersection of County Road D and Old Highway 8 is a great landmark, yet somewhat distracts from the beer garden atmosphere.
Ease of Finding Location		🍺🍺🍺	Easy, but requires some planning. The intersection of County Road D and Old Highway 8 can make for a navigational challenge to entering the brewpub.
Brewery Atmosphere		🍺🍺🍺🍺	A very small restaurant with an even smaller bar and yet even smaller brewhouse. Will appeal to beer enthusiasts and/or family gatherings.
Dining Experience		🍺🍺🍺🍺	Health-conscious entrées to basic pub fare and family-style offerings
The Pints		🍺🍺🍺🍺	A perfect experience that is accentuated by the quality of Barley John's small batch brews.

DIRECTIONS

Located north of Minneapolis, just west of Interstate 35W. From I-35W, exit at County Road D (exit 25A when traveling north and exit 25B when traveling south) and turn west. Within three stoplights County D will meet Old Highway 8; Barley John's is at the northeast corner on a slightly elevated lot that overlooks this intersection.

Boom Island Brewing Company

Minneapolis

ABOUT THE BREWERY

Most beer enthusiasts consider brewing an art form, similar to making music. When all the components in an orchestra come together to play a symphony, it's like when all the ingredients come together for that perfect pint. Boom Island Brewing is certainly an example of that. Brewery owner and brewmaster Kevin Welch is a classical musician who routinely plays for such groups as the Minnesota Orchestra and the Minnesota Opera. Welch's artisanship comes through not only in the brass he commands by playing the French horn, but he also has mastered other metals like copper and stainless steel that he welded and fitted together to build his own brewery nearly from scratch. Welch self-fabricated a 10-barrel brewing system, including a stainless steel mash/lauter tun and four fermenters. Welch actually applied for a patent on the process and equipment he developed to shape the stainless steel that went into the fermenters. His hand-crafted approach was inspired by travels across Belgium where he talked with brewers and even volunteered to help in exchange for learning about their systems and how they made their beer. He became so committed that when he returned from one of his trips he signed up for classes at a local technical college in order to become certified in tungsten inert gas welding. He also got the help of friends with special talents in assembling the brewery. He "tapped into" the skills of fellow musicians who enjoyed working for beer. In particular, he was assisted by two friends who are well known nationally for their repair and construction of brass musical instruments. A third friend, who is an electrical engineer and plays trombone in the orchestra with

Welsh, also regularly turned up as Boom Island took shape in a north Minneapolis warehouse. Besides helping Welch with the metal work, his talented collaborators helped him devise the mechanical system needed for a bottler filler and corker and figure out a unique design for a stir plate that he uses to culture yeast. He even got design help with his labels from a local jazz drummer.

Welch's growing up along the Mississippi River near Memphis drew him to this north side location. Boom Island is a place in the river in downtown Minneapolis — the same river he grew up around as a youth only hundreds of miles south. As a freelance musician Welch spent several years traveling and when he settled in Minneapolis the river offered a sense of coming home. When he discovered the beauty of Boom Island Park it was a natural connection to his dream of creating his brewery. The actual Boom Island is only about two blocks from Welch's brewery. It's also just a few blocks from the old Grain Belt Brewery that operated until 1975 at 1215 Marshall Street Northeast, on the east bank of the Mississippi River (Boom Island Brewing is on the west bank). The Grain Belt Brewery is listed on the National Register of Historic Places.

Kevin Welch has achieved considerable success as a musician, and that dedication helped him get off to a great start in brewing. In the years leading up to opening his brewery he claimed several awards in the Upper Mississippi Mashout homebrew competition. And some of those beers were the starting brews for his company. His Belgian blonde ale received a gold medal with a nomination for Best in Show in the 2010 Mashout. Then in 2011 his Belgian pale ale was given gold while his tripel captured silver. You'll find Boom Island beers in 750mL bottles and on select draft accounts.

HISTORY

Boom Island Brewing was established in 2011. Founder Kevin Welch grew up near Memphis along the Mississippi River. He came from a family with two sisters and a brother who made a pact with their parents that no matter what they wanted to do in the classroom or in after-school activities they had to give their best effort. While also active in sports, Kevin took up the French horn in the high school band. By tenth grade he was achieving high marks in all-state band activities and had become one of the best horn players in the state. Following high school he chose to attend the Cleveland Institute of Music and from there played for the Tulsa Philharmonic Orchestra for a year before attending Western Michigan University where he taught music theory while working on his master's degree. His freelancing as a musician brought him to the Twin Cities, where he met his wife to be, Qiuxia, who is also a French horn player. By 2000 both were living and working as freelance musicians in Minneapolis.

One evening backstage after a Duluth Superior Symphony Orchestra concert a fellow French horn player offered Welch a sample of homebrewed beer. Welch admits he was already pretty familiar with craft beer thanks to his days at Western Michigan in Kalamazoo (the home of Bell's Brewery); however, at that time he didn't know much about homebrewing. The taste was enough to spark his curiosity. His orchestra colleague loaned him Charlie Papazian's book, *The Joy of Home Brewing*, and Welch was soon learning a different tune, so to speak. By the time the next concert occurred Welch had his own homebrew to share.

In 2005 Kevin and Qiuxia traveled to China to visit her parents. During their nearly year-long stay there Kevin even taught his father-in-law about home-brewing, and he says he got pretty good at making Belgian-style Wit beers with Tibetan un-malted barley.

By 2006 Kevin and Qiuxia had returned to Minneapolis to resume their careers as classical musicians. However, Kevin couldn't get the homebrew-song out of his head and started working on a business plan for a brewery. Since then his dream has taken him on several summer trips to Belgium where he's spent weeks talking to brewmasters and volunteering to help out. On more than one of those trips Welch collected yeast samples from his favorite beers that he propagated in his own homebrewing. One trip in particular allowed Welch to spend quite a bit of time at the Brewery Boelens in the village of Belsele. There he met brewery owner Kris Boelens, who is also an accomplished copper smith and had built nearly his entire brewery himself. That was inspiring to Kevin Welch, enough so that he dared to construct his own brewery. Welch likes to laugh, "Working with copper and stainless steel has given me some real practical skills, so if this brewery flops I can at least be a technician and repairman someplace."

DON'T MISS THIS

One cannot overlook the hand-crafted and hand-assembled brewery. Kevin Welch's artisanship is evident in so much more than just his beer recipes, which makes this a must visit.

BOOM ISLAND BREWS

Brimstone 🍺🍺🍺🍺   *Your Ranking*_____
This is a very nice Belgian Tripel. A light yeasty nose and light-golden color. Medium to full bodied, round mouth feel, and bubbly. Rich yeastiness and sweetness in the early taste that seems to melt away with some dry accents and alcohol warmth in the finish. Based on a homebrew recipe that captured a silver medal at the 2011 Upper Mississippi Mashout. This beer is made with a Flanders yeast that is commonly used in beers of the Flemish region of Belgium. Kevin Welch points out that his discovery of Westmalle Tripel (Brouwerij der Trappisten van Westmalle) on a trip to Belgium was his introduction to the world of Belgian beers, which eventually led him to make those styles the central element of his own brewery.

Hoodoo 🍺🍺🍺🍺   *Your Ranking*_____
This Belgian Dubbel has a very inviting caramel and malty nose with a light hint of a sweet, plumb-like aroma. Deep amber to bronze-mahogany color and a medium, soft, tan head. Full bodied. The yeasty flavors in the beginning eventually give way to the mild and sweet fruity tones. The beer finishes sweet and warm. This beer was Best of Show at the 2011 Upper Mississippi Mashout. Its name is similar to "voodoo" folk magic and perhaps a subtle connection to the alcohol strength and warmth found in this wonderful brew.

Silvius 🍺🍺🍺🍺   *Your Ranking*_____
This Belgian pale ale is based on the beers Welch enjoyed while touring Antwerp. It has a dark golden to copper color with a soft, off-white head.

Yeasty aroma and sweetness with a dry finish. Named after a mythical Roman soldier who killed a giant that stole money from the local townspeople. The beer received a gold medal at the 2011 Upper Mississippi Mashout. This beer launched the brewery in fall of 2011.

OTHER BOOM ISLAND BREWS YOU MAY WANT TO TRY

Boom Island Quadruple   *Your Ranking*_____
A boldly flavored dark brown beer. Early recipe formulations called for additions of Minnesota wild rice.

thoprock   *Your Ranking*_____
A Belgian inspired IPA. Deep amber color. Rich depth to the sweetness and the spicy character of hops. Made following a Belgian brewing technique in which fermentable sugars are added at several points during the brewing process. This was the second beer released by Boom Island when it opened in 2011. Named after the Thoprock music festival in Bruges, Belgium.

MENU

None. Boom Island Brewing Company does not serve food.

OTHER THINGS TO SEE OR DO IN THE AREA

Boom Island, from which the brewery gets its name, is a place in the Mississippi River in downtown Minneapolis near B.F. Nelson and Nicollet Island Parks. During the heyday of logging in Minnesota, Boom Island was a place where long beams extended from derricks to help sort floating logs. Today's Boom Island Park is approximately 25 acres and it includes a playground, picnic areas, a boat launch and dock, and walking and biking paths. Boom Island Park is also the landing for the paddleboat *Minneapolis Queen*. Trips are an excellent way to see the Minneapolis skyline and views of St. Anthony Falls and the Stone Arch Bridge.

Boom Island Brewing is located just north of Minneapolis's Warehouse District and the central city itself. The character of the Warehouse District is derived from being the city's shipping hub in years past, and for those reasons it is listed on the National Register of Historic Places. While there are still many industrial buildings, many of the old factories and warehouses have been converted to commercial space. There's also a thriving arts scene, small retail stores, coffee shops, restaurants, and many bars. Also close by is Target Field, the home of the Minnesota Twins. Other breweries in the area include the Fulton Brewery (414 6th Avenue, North), Rock Bottom Restaurant and Brewery (800 LaSalle Plaza), and little further east is the Minneapolis Town Hall Brewery (1430 Washington Avenue, South).

BREWERY RATING

	Your Rating	Shepard's Rating	General Description
Location		🍺🍺🍺	Named after Boom Island, the location in the Mississippi where booms were used to gather and sort logs during Minnesota's logging days. Brewery itself is located in a rather plain industrial warehouse.
Ease of Finding Location		🍺🍺	Located north of downtown Minneapolis. Requires some careful planning to find.
Brewery Atmosphere		🍺🍺🍺🍺	You really understand hand-crafted beer when you see the hand-hammered copper mash/lauter tun that was made by owner and brewmaster Kevin Welch. One appreciates this brewery for its small nature and the artisanship of Welch.
Dining Experience		n/a	Not applicable.
The Pints		🍺🍺🍺🍺	Only a handful of brews from Boom Island and the hand-crafted system of Kevin Welch. Initial brews were all very well done. Belgian beer fans will find something to marvel about.

DIRECTIONS

From Interstate 94, take exit 229 (Washington Avenue N/West Broadway Avenue). If approaching from the south this exit will provide an immediate left-hand turn (northward) onto North Washington Avenue. You'll want to travel on North Washington Avenue northward for about four blocks to North 22nd Avenue, where you should turn right (east). Boom Island Brewing will be in approximately one bock on the northwest corner of the intersection with North 22nd Avenue and North 2nd Street. If approaching from the north at Exit 229, turn east on Broadway Street Northeast. Once you have crossed over the interstate, immediately turn left (northward) onto North Washington Avenue. After about two blocks on North Washington Avenue you should turn right (east) onto North 22nd. Boom Island Brewing will be in approximately one bock on the northwest corner of the intersection with North 22nd Avenue and North 2nd Street.

Flat Earth Brewing Company
St. Paul

ABOUT THE BREWERY

Flat Earth Brewing is tucked away in a neighborhood southwest of downtown St. Paul. It occupies a warehouse-industrial-type building with minimal evidence to identify it as a brewery. A few beer kegs, some stainless steel equipment, and wooden pallets in the parking lot provide clues if you look close enough. But on the occasional warm summer afternoon the crowds gather and the large bay doors are opened, with sampling patrons filtering in and out as they choose their next growler fill. Inside the 6,000-square-foot building is a row of shiny fermenters and the large copper brew kettle. Parts of the 15-barrel brewing system were once used to make beer for the former Steelhead Brewery in San Francisco. Flat Earth Brewing owner Jeff Williamson purchased it and had it trucked to Minnesota in two semitrailers.

Flat Earth Brewing didn't take long to establish itself with local craft brew enthusiasts. After introducing its first beer in 2007, production grew steadily. Early on, Flat Earth helped out other breweries like Lift Bridge (Stillwater) by making beer for them, but by 2010 Flat Earth was experiencing such tremendous popularity of its own brands that it cut back on contract work to focus on its own growth.

Flat Earth Brewing has an expansive list of brews. In its first three years it offered more than thirty different beers. Among the most popular are the Belgian Pale Ale, Angry Planet Pale Ale, and Northwest Passage IPA. Seasonals that have a big following include a Belgian tripel called Bermuda Triangle and the barley wine Winter Warlock. For those venturing to the brewery on growler fill days it's difficult to predict what special version of Flat Earth's porter might be available. Small batches of this dark beer get infused with a range of flavors to create limited and sometimes "one-only" offerings. The Xanadu is made with orange, but the most unique is called Grand Design and it features the flavor of S'mores.

HISTORY

Jeff and Cathie Williamson are the husband-and-wife team that started Flat Earth Brewing. Jeff grew up in Forest Lake, Minnesota; Cathie is originally from Massachusetts. On trips to the East Coast to see Cathie's family, they started enjoying visits to brewpubs and microbreweries. Then Cathie bought Jeff a homebrew kit as a birthday gift, and the hobby grew to a point where the Williamsons began thinking about starting either a brewery or a brewpub. Jeff eventually left a job as a special needs teacher for a position with Minneapolis Town Hall Brewery, where he worked as an assistant brewer. At Town Hall Jeff was involved in recipe formulations and brewing. He learned firsthand about what it takes to make beer for a brewpub. After a couple of years he and Cathie decided the time was right, only the brewery business model seemed to offer them more flexibility for their growing family. In 2007 they founded Flat Earth Brewing. In fall 2010 a local retired businessman, John Warner, purchased a major interest in Flat Earth Brewing. He and Jeff Williamson are among five co-owners of the brewery. Warner's family is well known in the Twin Cities for their Warners' Stellian appliance stores.

The name Flat Earth reflects, to some extent, the Williamsons' love of travel and finding good beer, along with their approach to making bold brews that may seem to be on the edge of mainstream beer flavors. But Flat Earth leaves lots of room for interpretation when you first hear it or see it on a label. Williamson says it was actually inspired by conversations at a local bar over beers with a friend who happens to be a former NASA rocket scientist. He introduced them to the concepts and beliefs of the Flat Earth Society, which led to suggestions of conspiracy theories in such beer names as Black Helicopter Coffee Stout, Element 115 Lager, and Ovni Ale.

DON'T MISS THIS

One of the best ways to enjoy this brewery is by joining the local fans on weekday evenings when the brewery offers tastings and growler sales. It's also an opportunity to talk about Flat Earth beer names with fellow customers, maybe even share a conspiracy theory or two. The brewery does offer tours on select Saturdays so it's best to consult the brewery's website or call ahead.

FLAT EARTH BREWS

Angry Planet Pale Ale 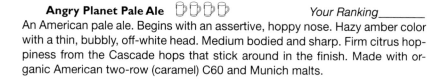   *Your Ranking_____*
An American pale ale. Begins with an assertive, hoppy nose. Hazy amber color with a thin, bubbly, off-white head. Medium bodied and sharp. Firm citrus hoppiness from the Cascade hops that stick around in the finish. Made with organic American two-row (caramel) C60 and Munich malts.

Belgian-Style Pale Ale 🍺🍺🍺🍺

*Your Ranking*_____

This was the first commercial beer made by Flat Earth and it's considered the brewery's flagship product. A light but firm, hoppy aroma. Light golden to copper color and a medium bubbly, off-white head. Medium bodied and round. A strong yeasty, sweet beginning with hints of spice, raisin, and cherry. Ends with a firm hoppy finish and light dryness.

Bermuda Triangle Tripel 🍺🍺🍺🍺

*Your Ranking*_____

This tripel is made with Belgian candi sugar and orange blossom honey. A sweet yeasty-floral aroma. Rich, clear, golden color and a soft, white head. Its medium body and bubbly texture makes it seem light, but watch out for its 9 percent ABV. Lots of sweetness with hints of a spice in the background and finish. Often seen toward the end of summer, but it's so popular it doesn't last long.

Black Helicopter Coffee Stout 🍺🍺🍺

*Your Ranking*_____

This is a traditional English oatmeal stout. However, with the name Black Helicopter one might expect some clandestine ingredients. Each batch is made with fifteen gallons of fresh cold-pressed Dunn Bros. coffee that gets added to the beer during packaging. The beer has a roasted coffee nose, deep black color and a thick, marbled brown head. Medium bodied and round mouth feel. It begins with smooth chocolate maltiness, but has firm coffee and roasted tones throughout taste and finish.

Curley Tail 🍺🍺🍺

*Your Ranking*_____

This is an English pale ale, originally made for Midway Stadium, home of the St. Paul Saints of the American Baseball Association. A light hoppy nose. Clear orange-copper color and a bubbly, tan head. Medium bodied and bubbly. A sharp hoppiness dominates with a light, crisp, bitter finish.

Cygnus X-1 Porter 🍺🍺🍺🍺

*Your Ranking*_____

An English porter with rye malt from Canada. One might easily connect the Cygnus X-1 with a black hole in space. However, there's a double meaning behind the name of this beer. It's also associated with a song from the band Rush. Initially it was called Canadian Porter, a reference to the band's origins, but federal officials who review labels felt that name implied the beer was made in Canada. The beer begins with a malty nose. Its body is deep black with a thick, soft, tan head. Medium bodied and soft texture. Smooth chocolate and caramel tones throughout the bulk of the flavor and finish.

Element 115 Lager 🍺🍺🍺

*Your Ranking*_____

A California common or steam beer. Clean nose. Deep amber color with lots of maltiness in the flavor, yet still nice balance from the hops. Its name is a reference to an undiscovered element in the periodic table that is said to allow UFOs to fly.

Extra Medium 🍺🍺🍺

*Your Ranking*_____

Flat Earth calls this an American wild ale because it's brewed with a blended strain of yeast that leaves it crisp and sour. Its nose has the aroma of tart cherries and lemon. Hazy copper color and a medium soft, tan head. Medium bodied and bubbly. It offers strong fruity sourness in beginning. There is a dryness in the finish, along with a continued sour presence. Extra Medium is brewed in the summer.

Hep Cat 🍺🍺🍺🍺   *Your Ranking*_____
An American blonde ale. Light malty nose. Clear golden color with a medium-soft, off-white head. Light to medium bodied and crisp. There's a malty middle to this beer, yet a crisp background and firm hoppiness to the finish.

Northwest Passage 🍺🍺🍺   *Your Ranking*_____
An American IPA. Strong resin-like nose. Clear copper color and a thick, soft, off-white head. Medium to full bodied with a sharpness that accentuates the crisp bitter taste. Finishes with a piney bitterness and lingers into a dryness. At 115 IBUs (international bittering units) this is one of the hoppiest beers made in Minnesota. While it does have assertive bitterness, its malty side is a nice complement so the hops don't overtake the entire flavor.

Sunburst 🍺🍺🍺   *Your Ranking*_____
This is an apricot-infused IPA. Assertive notes of apricot in the nose. Clear golden color and a medium-soft, tan head. Medium bodied. Apricots linger throughout, but this beer still has a strong hoppiness in the background and especially in the finish.

Winter Warlock 🍺🍺🍺🍺   *Your Ranking*_____
English barley wine. This is a winter seasonal usually appearing in late November and early December. If you make it to the brewery for the early release you might be fortunate enough to have the option of the current batch or an older version from a previous winter. But this beer sells quickly, so those who enjoy comparing the differences in vintages will want to inquire early. It's brewed with the same malt that is used to make Macallan's Scotch. A malty nose. Deep copper to bronze color with a thick, off-white head. Solid malty flavor with lots of caramel tones and a warmth throughout main flavor profile and finish. This beer has some mythical powers of smooth taste and alcohol around 10 percent ABV.

Xanadu (Cygnus X-1) 🍺🍺🍺   *Your Ranking*_____
An American porter infused with orange flavor. Starts with a complex orange and malty nose. Dark color and a thick, soft, brown head. There's lots of smooth chocolate malt flavor but also lots of orange in the body and finish.

OTHER FLAT EARTH BREWS YOU MAY WANT TO TRY

Mummy Train Pumpkin Ale   *Your Ranking*_____
Made with English malt, hops, and fresh pumpkin. Amber-orange color with a thin tan head. Strong pumpkin spices of nutmeg and cinnamon.

Ovni Ale   *Your Ranking*_____
A bière de garde. This is a rare treat as a Minnesota beer. Its name is French for unidentified flying object.

Rode Haring Your Ranking_____

A Flanders red ale with lots of characteristic sourness and tartness.

Flat Earth has a very diverse lineup of beers. Among its more popular are the flavor-infused porters, or versions of Cygnus X-1. Because they are often made in small batches and are offered only in growlers at the brewery, the may or may not appear again. A few favorites that have created a buzz among Flat Earth enthusiasts are listed below.

Big Money Oak Porter *Your Ranking_____*

An oak-infused porter. Oak chips soaked in Jack Daniel's are added to Flat Earth's Cygnus X-1. Growlers get a few extra chips!

Grand Design *Your Ranking_____*

A S'more-infused porter.

Monkey Business *Your Ranking_____*

A coconut-infused porter

MENU

None. Flat Earth Brewing does not serve food.

OTHER THINGS TO SEE OR DO IN THE AREA

All along West Seventh Street you can find places to eat. Downtown St. Paul is about two miles north and east (up) Seventh Street. Famous Dave's (1930 Seventh Street West), an icon in the world of Minnesota BBQ restaurants, is a short walk from Flat Earth. It's actually a good landmark; the brewery is roughly behind Famous Dave's, one block south on Benson Avenue.

Along the Mississippi River channel, just a few blocks south of Flat Earth, are a number of parks and hiking and biking opportunities. The bluff-lined river is quite beautiful. The water attracts boating and fishing, while the trails along the river will connect all the way to Minneapolis

Along the river and southwest of Flat Earth is historic Fort Snelling (junction of Minnesota highways 5 and 55, just east of the Minneapolis–St. Paul International Airport). In 1805 Lieutenant (later General) Zebulon M. Pike made a treaty with the Dakota to purchase the tract on which the fort was built in 1820–24. The Minnesota Historical Society runs a living-history museum there.

Fort Snelling is at the confluence of the Minnesota and Mississippi rivers—an area known as Mendota ("meeting of the waters") in the Siouan language. The fortress itself is only a small part of Fort Snelling State Park, which covers nearly 3,000 acres along the river.

Not far from Fort Snelling is the historic village of Mendota. One of Minnesota's oldest towns, Mendota emerged from an early nineteenth-century fur-trading center. Its attractions include the Henry H. Sibley House (1357 Sibley Memorial Highway), built in 1838 for the one-time Minnesota governor who also managed the American Fur Company (1825–53), and, next door, the Jean Baptiste Faribault House, built in 1839. Both offer tours.

Following the Mississippi River toward Minneapolis, you come to Minne-

38 *Flat Earth Brewing Company*

haha Park. Well worth a stop, it's one of the Twin Cities' most popular parks and contains the fifty-three-foot waterfall made famous by Henry Wadsworth Longfellow's epic poem *The Song of the Hiawatha*.

Flat Earth is actually one of four breweries within just a few miles of each other. Summit Brewing (910 Montreal Circle) is only a few blocks east of Flat Earth. So is Vine Park (1254 West Seventh Street). Further into downtown St. Paul, but only a couple miles north and east, is Great Waters Brewing (426 St. Peter Street) in the historic Hamm's building.

BREWERY RATING

	Your Rating	Shepard's Rating	General Description
Location		🍺🍺🍺	Located just a block off busy Seventh Street West, among commercial and residential neighbors, in a nondescript industrial building.
Ease of Finding Location		🍺🍺🍺	Not too difficult to find. Planning is important because the building sits off main roads and offers minimal exterior evidence that it is a working brewery.
Brewery Atmosphere		🍺🍺🍺🍺	This is a working brewery. This is especially fun on tasting days, enjoying beers with the crowd of Flat Earth fans!
Dining Experience		n/a	Not applicable.
The Pints		🍺🍺🍺🍺	The beers of Flat Earth are distinctive and truly on the edge!

DIRECTIONS

Flat Earth is located about three-quarters of a mile west of Interstate 35E on West Seventh Street (exit 103B). When approaching from I-35E, watch for the Famous Dave's restaurant and then turn left on South Homer Street. Within one intersection turn left, again, onto Benson, and Flat Earth will be immediately on your left.

Fulton Brewery
Minneapolis

_____   _____
Visit Date   *Signed*

ABOUT THE BREWERY

The Fulton Brewery is an example of what can happen when a homebrewing hobby outgrows the neighborhood garage where it all began. As the passion for beer grew and the demands from fellow beer drinkers got louder, the four friends who started Fulton found themselves constructing a brewery that looked like a mad scientist's creation. Beginning with some large-scale homebrew equipment and a bed frame they found abandoned in an alley, they cut, welded, drilled, and cobbled things together to create a beer-making monster — a true Frankenstein system. Their creativity helped them modify, tinker, and tweak things. They even searched Craigslist for what could be retrofitted to their needs. Homebrewers would envy the 10-gallon system and admire the planning and problem solving (including duct tape) that put it all together, while others might just see what appears to be a few turkey roasters welded together to heat a bunch of half-barrel kegs. Actually Fulton's first brewery expansion involved moving from one friend's one-car garage to another's larger two-car garage. These humble beginnings are reflected in the company's mantra, "Ordinary Guys Brewing Extraordinary Beer."

In 2009 the four homebrewers determined they were supplying friends, families, parties, holiday gatherings, and weddings with more of their beer than they were getting to enjoy themselves. That revelation led them to look for other beer-making options and a commercial brewer who would follow their recipes. They wanted help in providing enough beer that they could build a good beer reputation, establish some loyal tap accounts, and build up the financial resources that just might lead them to owning their own brewery. That year they founded the Fulton Beer Company and entered into contract with Sand Creek Brewing in Black River Falls, Wisconsin, to make and bottle their beer.

That contract route proved successful for Fulton. By summer 2010 interest in their beers, especially the IPA Sweet Child of Vine, gave the four homebrewers turned beer company owners enough courage and perhaps enough cash to buy a building in downtown Minneapolis. The building that is home to Fulton Brewery was constructed in the 1950s and for many years was used by a sheet metal manufacturing company. In the 1990s it contained a sewing business called Home Beautiful. Fulton's owners started looking for a place in 2010 but after several months were getting frustrated with their choices, until this building actually found them. The building's owner discovered Fulton's website and sent them an e-mail saying he was a fan of their beer and asking if they would like to rent his building. After a meeting, a tour, and some negotiations Fulton had found a home.

The brewhouse is composed of a 20-barrel Diversified Metal Engineering (DME) system with four 40-barrel stainless steel fermenters and one 40-barrel bright tank. Even though the downtown Minneapolis brewery produces beer for kegs, growlers, and limited release bottles, Fulton continues to contract with Sand Creek Brewing Company for packaged beer. The Fulton Brewery also has a gift shop and a sizable taproom for serving up to sixty guests at a time.

Fulton began with just one beer, Sweet Child of Vine, at a launch party in October 2009 at the Happy Gnome bar in St. Paul. Soon after it added Lonely Blonde as its second brew. Worthy Adversary and Libertine became more regular after Fulton got its brewing equipment up and running in 2011. By the way, the original 10-gallon garage-made brewing system is still used occasionally for recipe development and small specialty brews. It's also a fixture on the tours at the downtown brewery.

HISTORY

The Fulton Brewery was established in 2009 by Jim Diley, Brian Hoffman, Peter Grande, and Ryan Petz. (Before it built its own brewery in Minneapolis its name was Fulton Beer Company. Once the brewery became operational it started using Fulton Brewery.) Three of the company founders have other jobs. Diley is a local attorney, Hoffman a clinical researcher for Boston Scientific in St. Paul, and Petz has a marketing position for General Mills in the food service division in Golden Valley. Prior to opening the brewery in downtown Minneapolis, Grande was a residential construction contractor. Peter became Fulton's first full-time brewmaster in 2011.

Each of the Fulton owners contributed in his own way to getting the company started. In particular, brewery president Ryan Petz's graduate work at the University of Minnesota's Carlson School of Management provided many early ideas and approaches that formed the basis for Fulton's business plan. Brian Hoffman is the facility manager and he handles events and promotions. Jim Diley has his own law practice, which proved invaluable as the owners navigated the many rules and regulations associated with company formation. Peter Grande's expertise in residential carpentry, wiring, and plumbing was critical as they built their elaborate homebrewing and commercial test-batch brewery. The others joke that if they break anything, Peter will fix it — skills very important to being a brewmaster.

Petz, Diley, and Hoffman met while students at St. John's University and were roommates after they graduated. Grande got involved with the group after his sister gave her husband, Diley, a Mr. Beer kit. At first, they admit, their beer wasn't the best, but over time batches improved and their friends started asking for more. According to Petz, "The first time one of our batches turned out good, after that initial sip, we thought, 'Oh, wow, what would it be like to do it as a job?'"

DON'T MISS THIS

By making a commitment to more than just beer, the Fulton Brewery clearly wants to be a fixture in this Minneapolis neighborhood for years to come. Part of the company's business model created the Ful 10 Program where other small businesses and local entrepreneurs can "tap" into the success of Fulton. The brewery targets 10 percent of its own profits to the Ful 10 Program as a loan pool for others with ideas. As loans are made and paid back, the Ful 10 fund grows, and, it's hoped, so too do self-sustaining small businesses in their area.

FULTON BREWS

Lonely Blonde 🍺🍺🍺   *Your Ranking_____*
A light hoppy nose. Clear golden color with a thick, creamy, tan head. Light to medium bodied and bubbly. A malty start with a light fruitiness in the background. Fruity finish. Made with Czech Saaz hops. Its malts include German pilsner, crystal, and white wheat.

Sweet Child of Vine 🍺🍺🍺   *Your Ranking_____*
This is the beer that started it all, the first beer introduced by Fulton in 2009 and the only beer the company made commercially until summer 2010. It's aroma is assertively hoppy. Hazy copper color and a thick, bubbly, off-white head. Medium to full bodied and bubbly texture. Light resiny start with a malty-biscuity background. Dry hoppy finish. Sweet Child of Vine is an IPA that gets its bitterness from Simcoe and Glacier hops. The Simcoe hops provide core bitterness, while the Glacier are part of the dry hopping process for aroma. This beer gets its strong malty backbone from two-row American pale malt, caramel malt, and a fair amount of white wheat. Its name plays on the Guns and Roses tune "Sweet Child o' Mine."

OTHER FULTON BREWS YOU MAY WANT TO TRY

Libertine   *Your Ranking_____*
An imperial red ale. Loaded with lots of malt, including Maris Otter and Caramel 60, with some additional rye malt. It has a reddish hue and some dryness. The name signifies that Fulton doesn't play by the rules and liberates itself from beer styles and preconceived notions of strict brewing definitions.

Wagging Tail Pale Ale   *Your Ranking_____*

This beer was originally planned as Fulton's first beer but came in second to their IPA. A complex flavor profile with firm hoppiness from Cascade and Perle hops, yet well balanced from American barley and caramel malt. Named in honor of Libby, Jim Diley's yellow lab and Fulton's unofficial mascot. Libby's tail wagging is considered Fulton's seal of approval!

Worthy Adversary   *Your Ranking_____*

This imperial stout is very dark and full bodied. Firm coffee and chocolate flavor. This will compete with the best stouts you can put next to it.

MENU

None. Fulton Brewing does not serve food.

OTHER THINGS TO SEE OR DO IN THE AREA

The Fulton Brewery is part of the North Loop and Historic Warehouse District. For most of its history the surrounding neighborhood was an industrial area, including a large railroad yard, warehouses, and factories. Today, while some industrial properties remind, much of the area includes a mix of commercial, retail, and residential uses. It's also on the National Register of Historic Places.

One of the biggest neighbors is professional sports. During home games you can hear the Minnesota Twins fans cheering their hometown team from the brewery. The building containing Fulton's offices and kegging operations is within a couple of blocks from the ballpark's left field walls. Target Center, home of the Minnesota Timberwolves of the NBA, is also close by. It hosts not only basketball games, but also concerts, shows, conferences, and special events. The downtown Minneapolis Theatre District is also just a short walk to the south and east. And in the same direction you can find connections to the city's skywalk system that will take you into a maze of downtown shops, eateries, and entertainment options.

For exploring outside, the Mississippi River is located a few blocks north of Fulton. There are many walking trails and parks located along both banks of the river. About one and a half miles east you find the Mill City Museum (704 South Second Street) that tells the story of one of the largest and most technologically advanced flour mills in the world. The museum is on the site of the original A Mill, which was built in 1874 but was destroyed by a flour dust explosion. Once rebuilt it claimed it could grind enough flour to make twelve million loaves of bread a day. Visitors can tour the building and take in exhibits including a demonstration of how the explosion destroyed the first mill. While in the neighborhood, walking trails along the Mississippi River will take you to Mill Ruins Park, St. Anthony Falls and its Lock and Dam Visitor center, and St. Anthony Falls Heritage Trail will take you to the Stone Arch Bridge that once allowed trains to cross the river. Walking the bridge will take you to Hennepin Island Park on the opposite side of the river.

BREWERY RATING

	Your Rating	Shepard's Rating	General Description
Location		🍺🍺🍺	Located in downtown Minneapolis within the city's warehouse district. Shopping and entertainment is close by. Target Field and Target Center are within a few blocks.
Ease of Finding Location		🍺🍺🍺🍺	Not too difficult to find. Parking and one-way streets make advance planning important. Access to the city's light rail train is about two blocks away.
Brewery Atmosphere		🍺🍺	This is a working brewery. Fulton does kegging and bottling of 750ml bottles.
Dining Experience		n/a	Not applicable.
The Pints		🍺🍺🍺	Fulton beers are distinctive. It a brewery to watch as it grows its production and expands its fan base.

DIRECTIONS

The Fulton Brewery is located very close to the intersection between Fifth Street North with Sixth Avenue North, or roughly the north and western edge of Target Field. The Target Field Station and Rail Platform (Hiawatha Line) is just about two blocks east of the brewery. Also close by is a connection to the Northstar commuter rail line and the Cedar Lake Trail (often considered America's first bicycle freeway). When traveling in downtown Minneapolis take Fifth Street North, and once you are just past Target Field watch for Sixth Avenue North and turn right (northeast). This intersection resembles a Y-intersection. The Fulton brewery is on your left (north).

Granite City Food and Brewery

Eagan, Maple Grove, Roseville, St. Louis Park

Visit Date	*Signed*

ABOUT THE BREWERY

The Granite City restaurants began in 1999 in St. Cloud, Minnesota—a city with many quarries. All of the sister locations in the Twin Cities area have a similar look with lots of interior stonework inside and out that accentuate the name. The Granite City chain is one of the fastest growing restaurant families in the Midwest, with designs on expanding to the eastern and southern United States. The expansion is fueled not by franchising but by public stock offerings. Company president Steve Wagenheim is pretty clear that with this fast-growing chain, it is a restaurant first and foremost. That doesn't mean they neglect beer. All Granite City locations offer four to six house beers at any one time plus an additional seasonal brew or two. In 2011 Granite City started offering bottled beer in retail outlets in the Twin Cities, St. Cloud, Sioux Falls, and Fargo. Bottled beers include Northern Lager, Duke of Wellington, and Brother Benedict's Bock and are produced at he Minhas Craft Brewery located in Monroe, Wisconsin.

HISTORY

Steve Wagenheim cofounded Granite City with Bill Burdick in 1999. Wagenheim spent much of the 1980s and 1990s as chief operating officer and president of Champps Americana, a sports restaurant-bar chain. Overall, Wagenheim's experience includes executive management in restaurants, hotels and resorts. Burdick, who was trained as a brewing chemist, handled brewing operations for Granite City until he retired in 2006. A legend among fans of craft brewing, Burdick is perhaps best known for owning the popular brewpub Sherlock's Home that operated from 1989 to 2001 in Minnetonka. Like Wagenheim, Burdick has a long résumé that includes many years of experience in brewing and the hospitality industry.

The four Granite City restaurants in the metro Twin Cities use an approach to brewing called Fermentus Interruptus that was developed by Bill Burdick. This technique emerged shortly after Granite City opened its second location in Sioux Falls, South Dakota, in 2000. This trademarked process involves a wort-making facility in Ellsworth, Iowa, that prepares and then ships wort to each restaurant. Once the wort arrives at the destination restaurant it goes into a fermenter and yeast is added. That is the point at which fermentation begins and the liquid is actually considered beer. Therefore, each Granite City restaurant is technically a brewpub. And, because it makes wort and is not involved in fermentation, the Ellsworth plant is called a worthouse rather than a brewery. The family of Granite City breweries takes great pride in quality control and consistency. That means the core beers that you find in nearly all of their restaurants—such as the Northern Light Lager, Duke of Wellington, Brother Benedict's Bock, and Broad Axe Stout—should taste very similar. That is what Cory O'Neel, who trains staff and oversees onsite brewing, strives to achieve. O'Neel is the director of brewery operations and is based at the worthouse in Ellsworth. He and R.J. Nab of Granite City's Kansas City location travel to all of the locations to work with on-site managers and problem solve in the fermentation stages of making beer.

Granite City has more than two dozen restaurants in eleven states. The four locations in the Twin Cities area were opened between 2005 and 2006. The original concept for this family of restaurants is to combine craft beer with food and focus on medium-size cities, of which the Midwest has many. Many of the restaurants are located close to major highways, regional shopping centers, entertainment venues, and hotels.

DON'T MISS THIS

Granite City restaurants have similar floor plans with distinctive stone accents like flagstone pillars and walls. There's always a collection of large black and white photos, many with a Minnesota beer theme. One of the common photos in the collection is a large framed picture of a smiling bartender holding two mugs of beer. At the Eagan, Maple Grove, and Roseville locations it hangs near the entryway. A slightly different take on local artwork appears at the St. Louis Park location, where a photo showing several skiers—including company president Steve Wagenheim—hangs behind the hostess stand. Because of its proximity to the company's main office, you may even see Wagenheim himself having lunch at the St. Louis Park location.

GRANITE CITY BREWS

Broad Axe Stout　🍺🍺🍺🍺　　　　　　　*Your Ranking*_____

Medium to full bodied with creamy texture from flaked oats in its recipe. Served on a nitrogen tap. There is lots of rich roasted chocolate and caramel flavors.

Brother Benedict's Bock 🍺🍺   *Your Ranking*_____

A German-style lager with medium body, deep brown color, and a caramel malty flavor. Its recipe includes Munich and chocolate malts with Apollo and Tettnanger hops.

Burning Barn Irish Red 🍺🍺🍺   *Your Ranking*_____

A spring seasonal. Malty nose and a deep reddish amber color with a bubbly, tan head. Medium bodied and round mouth feel. Caramel malt dominates with a light spicy finish alongside a touch of hoppy bitterness. A nice meal beer that is versatile for most any entrée selection.

Duke of Wellington 🍺🍺🍺   *Your Ranking*_____

A medium- to full-bodied, copper-colored India pale ale that has a solid malty character with a hoppy nose and finish with hints of apricot. Made with Apollo, Cascade and Willamette hops.

Northern Light Lager 🍺🍺   *Your Ranking*_____

An American light lager, bubbly with a golden color. Features Apollo hops.

Oktoberfest 🍺🍺   *Your Ranking*_____

A fall seasonal. Light malty nose. Clear copper color with a marbled tan head. Medium bodied. Soft caramel maltiness. Clean finish. A light version of the Oktoberfest style.

Wag's Wheat 🍺🍺   *Your Ranking*_____

A slightly cloudy American wheat that has vivid yellow color and a thick, white head. The lightest of the Granite City beers. Made with Apollo and Glacier hops. Named after Granite City founder Steve Wagenheim.

OTHER GRANITE CITY BREWS YOU MAY WANT TO TRY

The Admiral (Two Pulls)   *Your Ranking*_____

The Admiral combines Northern Light and Duke of Wellington IPA.

The Black and Tan (Two Pulls)   *Your Ranking*_____

A blended beer made with Duke of Wellington and Broad Axe Stout.

The Blarney (Two Pulls)   *Your Ranking*_____

A combination of Brother Benedict's Bock and the Broad Axe Stout.

The Three-Headed Monster (Three Pulls)   *Your Ranking*_____

A blended beer for the adventuresome that combines Brother Benedict's Bock, Duke of Wellington, and Broad Axe Stout.

Two Pull   *Your Ranking*_____

The Granite City Two Pull is a blended beer created by mixing Northern Light and Brother Benedict's Bock.

MENU

Granite City offers a broad menu of items that are modestly priced. While the menus across the various locations look similar, there are rotating weekly specials that add variety. The restaurants commonly feature many made-from-scratch menu items. Even still, if you visit more than one location you'll still find similar menus. No matter which Granite City restaurant you are in, the meatloaf is a favorite. Just as tasty is the London broil.

Granite City always offers extensive salad selections, ranging from a basic dinner salad to grilled Asian chicken. Expect about ten different sandwiches and a half-dozen burger choices. There are also steaks, seafood, pastas, soups, and a kids' menu. Several of the house beers are integrated into menu items, such as the ale and cheddar soup.

ABOUT THE GRANITE CITY–EAGAN

Granite City Food and Brewery opened its tenth restaurant in September 2005, in Eagan. It's on the south side of the Twin Cities, only about ten minutes from Minneapolis–St. Paul International Airport. While it looks like other Granite Cities on the outside, the Eagan location is a little different inside. Formerly a Sidney's Restaurant, it has the show kitchen as a focal point for the main dining room, with a small private room on the north side. The arching bar is steel topped and seats about fifteen patrons. The four fermenters are in a room directly behind the bar. As with all of the Granite City restaurants, you can expect to choose from four to six beers, along with an additional seasonal brew or two.

OTHER THINGS TO SEE OR DO IN AREA NEAR GRANITE CITY–EAGAN

Granite City Eagan is only about five miles from the Mall of America and the Minneapolis–St. Paul International Airport. Closer to the brewpub itself is the Eagan Community Center and Central Park, a short half-block walk north. The Community Center (1501 Central Parkway) hosts many indoor events, from community garage sales to basketball tournaments. Central Park has walking trails, a pavilion and band shell for outside concerts, and events such as an art festival in June and the Fourth of July Fun Fest.

Just north is Fort Snelling State Park with an extensive network of hiking, biking, and skiing trails that link to Minnehaha Park and the Minnesota Valley National Wildlife Refuge. Trails also allow visitors to hike up to the historic Fort Snelling for a view of military life in the 1820s. One of the most scenic hikes is on Pike Island where the Mississippi and Minnesota rivers converge.

BREWERY RATING

	Your Rating	Shepard's Rating	General Description
Location		☺☺☺	Located along Pilot Knob Road near several parks.
Ease of Finding Location		☺☺☺	Easy to find because it's within a few stoplights of either I-35E or I-494. It is not visible from these major roads so a little planning is needed to efficiently navigate the interstate exits.
Brewery Atmosphere		☺☺☺	Stone accents, a show kitchen, and prominent beer fermenters provide a vibrant brewery feel.
Dining Experience		☺☺☺	Pub fare to family-style offerings. Food is well prepared and reasonably priced.
The Pints		☺☺☺	A consistent representation of the core beers is offered in all Granite City restaurants. For those looking for seasonal beers and constantly rotating brewmaster's specials, Granite City can be a little disappointing.

DIRECTIONS

From southbound I-35E, take exit 97B and turn right (west) at Yankee Doodle Road and right (north) at Pilot Knob Road (County Road 31). From northbound I-35E, take exit 97A and turn left (north) on Pilot Knob Road. From I-494, take exit 71 and go south on Pilot Knob Road for about one and a half miles.

ABOUT GRANITE CITY–MAPLE GROVE

Granite City Food and Brewery of Maple Grove was the eighth restaurant for the company. It opened in July 2004 on the north side of Minneapolis, just off I-94/694 at Hemlock Lane North (County Road 61). The Shoppes at Arbor Lakes is a well-known area landmark, and, as with many Granite City locations, ample shopping, entertainment, and hotels are close by. As you enter through the main doors there is a long steel-topped bar with about two-dozen seats. The brewpub's five fermenters are in a glass-enclosed room along the west wall of the main dining room. There's outside seating that looks northward to the Shoppes at Arbor Lakes and the busy intersection of Hemlock Lane, Main Street, and Interstate 694/94. Among the four Twin Cities locations, this Granite City often has the largest annual production, just shy of a thousand barrels.

OTHER THINGS TO SEE OR DO IN AREA NEAR GRANITE CITY–MAPLE GROVE

The Shoppes at Arbor Lake are directly across Main Street from Granite City Maple Grove. You'll find many stores and movie screens for shopping and en-tertainment. The Maple Grove farmers' market is held on Thursdays from early

June to late October at the Community Center (12951 Weaver Lake Road). The community center includes swimming pools, a skate park, and an ice arena.

Not far from the community center is the Maple Grove Arboretum (near County Road 30 and North Fernbrook Lane), a fifteen-acre park along Elm Creek with lots of walking trails. Maple Grove is also within the Three Rivers Park District and such regional parks as Elm Creek, Fish Lake, Eagle Lake, and the North Hennepin Trail Corridor. They offer many opportunities for boating, hiking, snowboarding, and skiing. The Maple Grove Art Center (7916 Main Street) offers classes, educational displays, and art exhibits.

Surly Brewing in Brooklyn Center (4811 Dusharme Drive) is about ten miles away. The original Granite City Food and Brewery in St. Cloud (3945 South Second Street) is about an hour northwest off I-94.

BREWERY RATING

	Your Rating	Shepard's Rating	General Description
Location		🍺🍺🍺	Granite City–Maple Grove is a new standalone building not far from shopping, entertainment, and major roads.
Ease of Finding Location		🍺🍺🍺🍺	Easy to find, on north side of I-94/I-694 at exit 28.
Brewery Atmosphere		🍺🍺🍺	High ceilings, lots of stone accents, a show kitchen, and prominent beer fermenters provide a vibrant brewery feel. But those looking for unique character might be somewhat disappointed in that all Granite Citys have similar décor.
Dining Experience		🍺🍺🍺	Pub fare to family-style offerings. Food is well prepared and reasonably priced.
The Pints		🍺🍺🍺	A consistent representation of the core beers is offered in all Granite City restaurants. For those looking for seasonal beers and constantly rotating brewmaster's specials, Granite City can be a little disappointing.

DIRECTIONS

Granite City in Maple Grove is located on the northwest corner of the intersection of I-94/694 and North Hemlock Lane (County Road 61). From I-94/694 take exit 28 and head north. The restaurant is only about a half-mile to the west on Main Street. The Shoppes at Arbor Lake is a major landmark.

ABOUT GRANITE CITY–ROSEVILLE

Granite City Food and Brewery of Roseville was the seventeenth restaurant for the company. It opened in November 2006 in the bustling Rosedale Center shopping mall, next door to a multiplex theater. It is actually part the mall structure, but without direct access to the shops inside. Perhaps because it its location, this Granite City feels just a bit more compact. Like most other Granite City restaurants the focal point of the main dining room is the show kitchen. There is a rectangular stainless steel topped bar that offers seating for about fifteen. Five 527-gallon fermenters are located in a room directly beyond and left of the bar. During the warmer months of the year this Granite City offers outside seating. Just to the right of the main doors are about a half-dozen umbrella covered tables between the restaurant and the movie theatre.

OTHER THINGS TO SEE OR DO IN AREA NEAR GRANITE CITY–ROSEVILLE

The Rosetown Playhouse (www.rosetownplayhouse.org) based in Roseville offers performances in the Twin Cities area. The Roseville Skating Center (2661 Civic Center Drive) claims North America's largest sheet of refrigerated ice. It also offers an outdoor skate park and multipurpose meeting facility. The Harriet Alexander Nature Center (2520 North Dale Street) is part of the community's Central Park (Lexington Avenue North and West County Road C) with boardwalks and trails through fifty-two acres of marsh, prairie, and forest habitats. Central Park also contains the Muriel Sahlin Arboretum, eight acres of gardens, paved walkways, and a fountain. And, of course, the Rosedale mall offers abundant shopping and cinema opportunities.

BREWERY RATING

	Your Rating	Shepard's Rating	General Description
Location		🍺🍺🍺	Located in the Rosedale Center shopping mall among stores and movie theaters.
Ease of Finding Location		🍺🍺🍺🍺	Easy to spot from Highway 36. Snelling Avenue North or Fairview Avenue North are the most convenient roads connecting to the mall.
Brewery Atmosphere		🍺🍺🍺	Stone accents, a show kitchen, and prominent beer fermenters provide a vibrant brewery feel.
Dining Experience		🍺🍺🍺	Pub fare to family-style offerings. Food is well prepared and reasonably priced.
The Pints		🍺🍺🍺	A consistent representation of the core beers is offered in all Granite City restaurants. For those looking for seasonal beers and constantly rotating brewmaster's specials, Granite City can be a little disappointing.

DIRECTIONS

Granite City is on Rosedale Center's southern ring of stores (you can see the restaurant from Minnesota 36). The mall is at the intersection of Minnesota 36 and County Road 51 (Snelling Avenue).

ABOUT GRANITE CITY–ST. LOUIS PARK

Granite City Food and Brewery opened its fifteenth restaurant in St. Louis Park, on the west side of Minneapolis, in September 2006. It is just a few blocks south of the company's corporate offices (5402 Parkdale Drive). It has a similar Granite City appearance from the street. Inside, however, the floor plan is a little different. Formerly a Timber Lodge Steakhouse, it has the show kitchen behind the bar rather than as a backdrop to the main dining room. You'll also notice that the ceilings are lower, and the rectangular bar is larger, seating nearly thirty. There are five fermenters behind glass along the bar area's east wall. Granite City restaurants enjoy some internal competition in sales from time to time. The restaurant that sells the most of a seasonal or special brew has the opportunity to make a second batch. The St. Louis Park location is known within the Granite City family for often winning this friendly competition among restaurant siblings, especially for the neighborhood's taste for hoppy beers. In 2009–10 the St. Louis Park location won the competition for serving the most of Batch 1,000 (the brewpub's Double IPA). That accomplishment earned its staff the ability to follow up with another batch and locals were certainly happy. And because it's near the Granite City corporate office, the St. Louis Park kitchen staff occasionally try out new items as daily specials that may get moved to the menus at other Granite City locations.

OTHER THINGS TO SEE OR DO IN AREA NEAR GRANITE CITY–ST. LOUIS PARK

St. Louis Park was incorporated as a village in 1886 and officially became a city in 1954 when residents approved a home rule charter. Today it has a population of about 45,000. The community supports fifty-one parks with bike and walking trails that connect it to downtown Minneapolis and several other suburban communities. The St. Louis Park and Recreation Center (3700 Monterey Drive) features two indoor ice areas, an outdoor aquatic park, and a skate park. Nearby Wolfe Park has many recreational opportunities for walking and biking. The park's Veterans Memorial Amphitheatre holds many public and private events throughout the year. Along Excelsior Boulevard are several golf courses, including Meadowbrook to the west and Minikahda to the east.

The neighborhood around Granite City has many venues for shopping and entertainment. About two blocks eastward are the shops at Excelsior and Grand. The Pavek Museum of Broadcasting (3517 Raleigh Avenue) has a collection of antique radio and television equipment. Next door to Granite City is a multiplex theater, Mann's Cinema 6. Directors Joel and Ethan Coen set their film *A Serious Man* (2009) in St. Louis Park.

Surly Brewing in Brooklyn Center (4811 Dusharme Drive) is about ten miles due north on Minnesota 100. Steel Toe Brewing is even closer (4848 West 35th Street).

BREWERY RATING

	Your Rating	Shepard's Rating	General Description
Location		🍺🍺🍺	Located in a thriving shopping and entertainment district.
Ease of Finding Location		🍺🍺🍺🍺	Easy to find at the northeast corner of Excelsior and Minnesota 100 intersection.
Brewery Atmosphere		🍺🍺🍺	Stone accents, a show kitchen, and prominent beer fermenters provide a vibrant brewery feel. This location has a beautiful fireplace in the main dining room.
Dining Experience		🍺🍺🍺🍺	Pub fare to family-style offerings. Food is well prepared and reasonably priced. Located near the corporate offices and company executives, this Granite City may offer occasional test items.
The Pints		🍺🍺🍺🍺	While you know what to expect with Granite City and its consistent representation of the core beers, this one gets to try new things so seasonal brews may get extra attention.

DIRECTIONS

Granite City is on Excelsior Boulevard, just east of Minnesota 100. Mann's Cinema 6, next door to Granite City, is a major landmark, as is the Park Nicolet Clinic.

Great Waters Brewing Company

St. Paul

Visit Date	*Signed*

ABOUT THE BREWERY

It almost gives one goose bumps to discover that Great Waters Brewing Company occupies part of the historic office building created by William Hamm, founder of Hamm's Brewing. Large windows along St. Peter Street have the Great Waters logo. Looking up you get a sense of the historic nature of the building with its ornate stonework and terra cotta accents.

Inside, high ceilings, stone-tile floors, and lots of openness bring out the history even more. The bar doesn't have many seats, yet that adds to the active nature of the place. The bar wraps around the glass-enclosed brewhouse, which dominates the interior. The brewhouse is open at the top, allowing the aroma of wort to filter throughout the building on brew days. The brewpub actually occupies four floors the building. The restaurant and bar is on street level while five fermenters, six serving vessels, lagering and cellar storage, office space, and the hot water boiler are far below. Also in the lowest floor of the building is a well that Great Waters uses for brewing. Outside, the pedestrian mall along Seventh Place doubles as a beer garden and outside seating for Great Waters.

Brewmaster Bob DuVernois has made beer at Great Waters since 2003. Before that he oversaw the brewing at the former Hops Restaurant and Brewery chain that was located throughout the Twin Cities. DuVernois keeps at least six to eight beers on tap and announces them on a chalkboard near the bar. Among those to watch for are the English-style St. Peter Pale Ale, the English brown called Brown Trout Brown, and the Golden Prairie Blond. A distinguish-

54

ing feature of Great Waters is the commitment to cask-conditioned beers on beer engines that make up nearly 30 percent of total beer sales. The House Ale, which is an English-style bitter, is considered the brewpub's cask flagship.

HISTORY

Great Waters Brewing Company opened in March 1997 in the northwest corner of the historic Hamm Building of downtown St. Paul. Sean O'Byrne and his former partner Mark Van Wie planned it from paper to construction. O'Byrne's first brush with selling beer came as a bartender while in college at Creighton University in Omaha, Nebraska. After graduation he entered the field of medical sales for eighteen years. In the mid-1990s while living the Twin Cities he found that his company was downsizing. So after years of traveling extensively and experiencing local restaurants firsthand, he planned his move into the brewpub business. He searched all over the metro Twin Cities for the right location, and while in downtown St. Paul looking at other spaces he happened to walk by the Hamm Building and saw a sign stating "under renovations." After a closer look at the building, he had found the ultimate home for Great Waters Brewing Company.

The Hamm Building was originally designed to be a commercial and office building with provisions for a theater. It is the only building in St. Paul with cast terra cotta structural tile on all exposed façades. Its completion is an example of the influence and philanthropy of William Hamm. The building site was acquired in 1911 by the Mannheimer family, who leased the property from the St. Paul archdiocese. Construction started in 1915, but financial problems halted the project and the building stood as nothing but a steel skeleton for nearly three years. Finally, an anxious Archbishop Ireland phoned real-estate entrepreneur (and owner of the St. Paul Saints ball club) John Norton. "I wish you could do something for these people before they go broke," said His Grace. Norton approached his close friend William Hamm and suggested that Hamm assume the lease and finish the building as a "monument to William Hamm." The idea was accepted, the frame building was enclosed, and the name Hamm was put in low relief tiles that remain over the front entrance archway. Upon its completion in 1920, the fifth and sixth floors were held exclusively for physicians and dentists, while all other floors were for general business purposes. It is believed that at one time there was a billiard hall in the basement where some of St. Paul's more notorious residents hung out. Actually, nearby on Seventh Place West the former St. Francis Hotel was a favorite stop for the Twin Cities underworld of gangsters and organized crime. For those who stayed there it was merely a short walk across the street.

In 1965 the building was completely remodeled to make room for more shops and an arcade. The Park Square Theatre, with its 350-seat auditorium, is also part of the building. The building again underwent renovations in the mid-1990s. Today the building is listed on the National Register of Historic Places.

DON'T MISS THIS

The dining room at Great Waters has a changing display of artwork. In the backbar area look for some of the original artwork from the Hamm's Bear advertising campaign. Throughout the lower floors of the Hamm Building there are old photographs of St. Paul and this actual building. Outside, near the main door on Seventh Place (in the summertime it's the Great Waters beer garden), look for the Hamm's Bear monument.

GREAT WATERS BREWS

Black Watch—on cask   🍺🍺🍺🍺   *Your Ranking*_____
This name is a tribute to the infantry battalion of the Royal Regiment of Scotland. This oatmeal stout starts with an inviting chocolate malty nose. Deep black color and a thick, soft, tan head. Medium to full bodied and slick texture. Lots of chocolate and caramel malty tones throughout. Finishes with a sweet maltiness. A great beer when the patio seems a little chilly. Finishes around 5.2 percent ABV.

Brown Trout   🍺🍺🍺🍺   *Your Ranking*_____
This English brown ale has a malty nose. Clear bronze color and thick, soft, brown head. Medium bodied and sharp texture. Clean malty flavor with a light bitter and roasted nuttiness in the ending.

Golden Prairie Blond Ale   🍺🍺   *Your Ranking*_____
A light malty nose with a clear, light gold color and soft, white head. Bubbly, light bodied, crisp, and well balanced with a dry finish. The beer list states, "Brewed for the NASCAR fan in all of us."

Hefe Weizen   🍺🍺   *Your Ranking*_____
A yeasty nose. Cloudy, yellow to golden color with a soft, white head. Light bodied, soft and creamy texture. Starts with a fruity citrus flavor and then becomes mildly dry. Eventually ends with a fruity finish with hints of sweet earthiness.

House Ale—on cask   🍺🍺🍺🍺   *Your Ranking*_____
A very fine signature beer among the cask offerings for Great Waters. Has all the qualities in body and flavor that cask beer lovers will appreciate. Begins with a light, floral hoppiness for aroma. Clear copper color with a thick, soft, creamy, off-white head. Medium bodied. Great malty flavor with a biscuit background. The hoppiness comes back in the finish, for a clean ending. Made with East Kent Golding hops. Finishes around 5 percent ABV.

Minnesota Mild   🍺🍺   *Your Ranking*_____
A clear, deep brown color, with a thick, bubbly, reddish-white head. Light to medium bodied. A light and creamy malty flavor with a slight fruitiness in the finish.

New Centurian—on cask   🍺🍺🍺   *Your Ranking*_____
Initially made as a summer-time seasonal, its popularity has made it nearly a standard offering. Mild maltiness in the nose. A clear, dark copper-bronze color and thick, soft, tan head. Medium bodied. Caramel maltiness stands out, adding some depth and overall smoothness to the taste. A mildly bitter finish.

Oktoberfest 🍺🍺🍺🍺   *Your Ranking*_____

A light, mostly clean, malty nose. Clear copper body with a thick, tan, bubbly head. Medium bodied and silky. A caramel malt start with an overall malt emphasis, yet a firm bitterness for the finish.

Piper Down Scotch Ale 🍺🍺🍺🍺   *Your Ranking*_____

Light malty nose. Deep reddish-bronze color and a thin, bubbly head. A nice sweetness with a touch of smokiness from the 2 percent of Weyermann's smoked malt. A cask-conditioned seasonal.

Pot Hole Porter 🍺🍺   *Your Ranking*_____

A strong chocolate malt nose. Clear, deep bronze and a thick, soft, brown head. Medium bodied. Starts with a malty caramel flavor and finishes with dry hoppiness.

Rye Pale Ale 🍺🍺🍺🍺   *Your Ranking*_____

This is a standard favorite at Great Waters. It's been made here since 1997. An IPA brewed with rye. A great beer on cask. Assertive hoppy nose. Hazy golden-copper color with little head. Medium bodied. Bitterness starts quiet and turns dry in the finish. Could be a great session beer, but it's a bit high in ABV.

St. Peter Pale Ale 🍺🍺🍺   *Your Ranking*_____

Overall the number one seller for Great Waters. This English-style pale ale begins with a floral nose. A clear copper color and a thick, soft, tan head. Medium bodied with some light dryness. Begins with a light malty nose, then offers a strong, firm hoppy background with a distinctive dry finish.

Skip and Go Naked 🍺🍺   *Your Ranking*_____

A seasonal beer for summer. This wheat ale is made with lemon grass and chamomile. A grassy floral nose. Hazy golden color, with a thin, soft, tan head. Light bodied. Fruity tones to the main flavor profile with a light lemon background. Finishes with chamomile and grassy qualities.

OTHER GREAT WATERS BREWS YOU MAY WANT TO TRY

Bourbon Barrel Brown Ale   *Your Ranking*_____

A brown ale aged in a bourbon barrel for an extended period before being served on cask.

Emma's Yuletide Ale   *Your Ranking*_____

A Belgian style Dubbel brewed with French and Belgian malt and hops. Fermented with a special yeast strain from the Ardennes region. Malty with hints of plum, raisin, and tart cherry. Named after the young daughter of a friend of Great Waters who is suffering from a serious illness. Introduced in Winter 2010, with proceeds from every pint helping to pay for the treatment and care of Emma.

Hooligan IPA   *Your Ranking*_____

An English-style, cask-conditioned IPA.

King Boreas Wit *Your Ranking_____*

This strong Belgian white (Wit) beer is a special seasonal, brewed to coincide with the St. Paul Winter Carnival. It's made with French and Belgian malts and hops and additions of chamomile, orange peel, and coriander.

Kölsch *Your Ranking_____*

A summertime seasonal. Some emphasis on bitterness.

O'Byrne's Irish Red *Your Ranking_____*

A copper-colored ale with firm caramel malty flavors. Obviously, a favorite of brewpub owner Sean O'Byrne.

Old Bastard *Your Ranking_____*

This is a cask-conditioned English strong ale. Deep copper color, bold maltiness and warmth. Old Bastard won a gold medal from the Real Ale Festival in Chicago.

Old Tart *Your Ranking_____*

Hazy bronze with a distinct sourness. This is a Belgian brown ale blended with a second brown ale that has been fermented with Brettanomyces yeast strain.

Patio Daddio *Your Ranking_____*

This American IPA offers firm hoppiness. Begins with a hoppy and resiny nose. Hazy copper color, along with a thin, off-white head. Medium bodied and coarse. Sharp, bitter flavor. A resiny bitter finish. A great summer beer on the Great Waters patio. Given the name, enjoy this with Dad on Father's Day!

Vulcanus Rex *Your Ranking_____*

A Scotch ale made with Scottish barley and cherrywood smoked malt. A beer that turns up for the St. Paul Winter Carnival.

Zauer Braun *Your Ranking_____*

A sour brown ale.

MENU

The Great Waters menu is very diverse for a brewpub. The appetizers include about a dozen options. The House Baked Pretzel is served with a house mustard. The Brewery Nachos feature house-made tortilla chips with cheese, lettuce, jalapeños, black olives, and salsa. There are also several vegetarian options, such as the artichoke/spinach dip and the Black & Brew Pâté of spicy black bean pâté and hummus. On the lighter side of the main menu are burger and sandwich choices. The St. Paul Burger is topped with Canadian bacon, mushrooms, and bleu cheese. A portobello sandwich is made with a marinated portobello mushroom cap, tomatoes, onion, gouda, and roasted red pepper aioli on a kaiser roll. For some, especially the out-of-towners, the Wild Rice Burger is a special local treat, consisting of a rice burger patty topped with garlic aioli, lettuce, tomato, and a choice of cheese. Main entrées offer choices of pastas, pork, fish, chicken, and steaks. Jambalaya pasta is made with penne, andouille sausage, and shrimp in a Creole sauce. The meatloaf is a hearty dish with a special brewpub blend of meats, herbs, and spices topped with a thyme brown sauce. There is also grilled duck, tuna steaks, fish and chips, shepherd's pie, and several vegetarian-oriented pastas. The desserts constantly rotate and many are made by the Great Waters kitchen staff.

OTHER THINGS TO SEE OR DO IN THE AREA

Downtown St. Paul has many cultural and entertainment opportunities. The Xcel Energy Center (199 West Kellogg Boulevard) is home to concerts and the Minnesota Wild NHL team. Nearly across the street from Great Waters, the Landmark Center (75 West Fifth Street), built in 1902 as the federal courthouse and post office, is today a national historic monument and a venue for music, dance, theater, exhibitions, public forums, and special events. The Minnesota Museum of American Art (50 West Kellogg Boulevard) focuses on important artists and cultural expressions from the mid-nineteenth century to the present. The Fitzgerald Theater (10 East Exchange Street), a Schubert theater built in 1910, is home to Garrison Keillor's *Prairie Home Companion* radio show as well as concerts and other performances. The Ramsey County Courthouse and St. Paul City Hall (15 West Kellogg Boulevard) has self-guided tours featuring the *Vision of Peace* statue by Swedish sculptor Carl Milles. The Minnesota State Capitol (75 Martin Luther King Jr. Boulevard) offers exhibits and a capitol mall walking tour. The Minnesota Science Museum (120 West Kellogg Boulevard) is a great place, especially for kids, with galleries that provide insights into the human body, dinosaurs and fossils, and the Mississippi River with an authentic climb-aboard towboat. The Minnesota History Center (345 West Kellogg Boulevard) tells the story of Minnesota through exhibits about early territorial life and Grainland, with its boxcar to climb aboard and a replica grain elevator.

One of the better-known places for breakfast is the downtown landmark called Mickey's Dining Car (36 West Seventh Street), just down the street from Great Waters. Listed on the National Register of Historic Places, this 1930s art deco diner provides an authentic experience in what "eating at the counter" is all about.

While Minnesota is notorious for its harsh winters, St. Paul celebrates the fact with its annual Winter Carnival. The event began in 1886, following a New York newspaper story that called St. Paul "another Siberia, unfit for human habitation" in winter. Offended by the characterization, the chamber of commerce decided to prove that St. Paul was not only habitable but its citizens were very much alive during winter. The St. Paul Winter Carnival now sprawls throughout the downtown each January. One of the popular components to the event is the ice carving that takes place on West Seventh Place, with one of the highlights being a twelve-foot-high throne of King Boreas that's popular for photos. The tradition of selecting King Boreas dates back to the carnival's early beginnings in the 1880s. Great Waters gets into the festive atmosphere with its lead bartender Liam Slahide, who is one of the carvers. His past contributions include an ice patio with tables and chairs and even an ice bar. The brewpub also offers a Wassail night during the event.

A great way to experience St. Paul is by taking a walking, trolley, or bus tour of the city (Down in History Tours, 215 South Wabasha Street; Capital City

Trolley, 807 East Seventh Street). Your options might take you into the historic caves of St. Paul and Stillwater, along scenic river vistas, or into haunted houses and gangster hideouts. Just about a mile west of downtown St. Paul is Cathedral Hill neighborhood with its Victorian architecture and large mansions. Novelist F. Scott Fitzgerald lived along Summit Avenue when he wrote *This Side of Paradise*. Grand Avenue is another inviting place for a walk. Its twenty-five blocks extend from the Mississippi River through the downtown, past great river views, downtown shops, and beautiful homes. A great time to visit Grand Avenue is during Grand Old Days festival in June.

North of downtown St. Paul, the Minnesota Transportation Museum's Jackson Street Roundhouse (193 East Pennsylvania Avenue) has exhibits of vintage motorcars, a rocket train, and caboose rides. The roundhouse was built in 1907 as a maintenance shop for locomotives. The Hill House (240 Summit Avenue) was the home of Great Northern Railway empire builder James J. Hill. Tours of the Romanesque mansion provide views of the skylit art gallery, crystal chandeliers, pipe organ, and elegant life in general in the 1890s.

Harriet Island on the St. Paul downtown riverfront has biking, hiking, and walking paths, picnic areas, entertainment pavilions, and the Grand Staircase that opens to the Mississippi. The Minnesota Centennial Showboat Theatre (http://showboat.umn.edu) calls the island home and in the summer months provides musical and theatrical performances. Harriet Island is also a great place to catch a paddleboat ride on the Mississippi (www.riverrides.com). Historically narrated excursions, dinner cruises, and private charters operate from the island. Each April the annual Taste of Minnesota is held on Harriet Island with food, fireworks, music, arts and crafts vendors, and a flotilla of boats.

If you're making an overnight trip, especially if your brewpub trek consists of a long weekend in downtown St. Paul, be sure to look up the Covington Inn Bed and Breakfast (www.covingtoninn.com). The Covington is a renovated towboat that is permanently moored in the Mississippi River off Harriet Island, just across the river from downtown St. Paul. The B&B offers four staterooms, each with private bath, deck access, and some of the best views of the city from the water.

BREWERY RATING

	Your Rating	Shepard's Rating	General Description
Location		🍺🍺🍺🍺	Downtown St. Paul.
Ease of Finding Location		🍺🍺🍺	Great Waters is close to major roads and intersections. Parking is available, but one-way streets can make it challenging.
Brewery Atmosphere		🍺🍺🍺🍺	Located in the historic Hamm office building, with a small beer garden on West Seventh Place.
Dining Experience		🍺🍺🍺	Pub fare to family-style offerings.
The Pints		🍺🍺🍺🍺	Perfect. Especially so for the cask-conditioned brews.

DIRECTIONS

From I-94 westbound, exit at Sixth Street (242D/Route 52), go south on Sixth Street for about eight blocks, turn right (northwest) at Wabasha Street, left at Seventh Street (west-southwest), and left at St. Peter Street (at Mickey's Dining Car). Great Waters will be within a half-block on your left. From I-94 eastbound, exit at Tenth Street, continue to St. Peter Street, turn right (south-southeast), and follow St. Peter for about four blocks to Great Waters on your left.

From I-35E northbound, exit at Eleventh Street and turn right (south-southeast) onto St. Peter Street. Great Waters Brewing Company will be within three and a half blocks on your left. From I-35E southbound, exit at Wacouta Street, turn right (south-southwest) onto Seventh Street, continue for seven blocks, and turn left (south-southeast) onto St. Peter Street. Great Waters will be within a half-block on the left.

Harriet Brewing
Minneapolis

_____
Visit Date   Signed

ABOUT THE BREWERY

Minneapolis's Chain of Lakes provides the inspiration behind this small brewery. Located south of the downtown, this wonderful parkland has miles of trails that connect a series of five lakes, including the brewery's namesake, Harriet Lake.

Jason Sowards established Harriet Brewing in 2010, releasing his first beer to the public on January 29, 2011. At the grand opening the response from the Twin Cities beer community was astonishing, if not humbling, with Harriet Brewery selling nearly five hundred growlers in a single day. Sowards had been making beer in his Linden Hills home that isn't too far from the waters of Lake Harriet. Sowards liked to brew in his garage and he discovered that the aroma of making beer captured a great deal of attention from his neighbors and even those who came to enjoy the lake and surrounding neighborhood. He developed a following for his beer with those who dropped by for a pint without actually selling a drop. That was enough to convince him to give up plans to be an engineer and start a brewery in a former garage-warehouse in the Longfellow neighborhood.

The brewery is located in a 6,000-square-foot building that had been home to a towing company for many years. The brewhouse itself occupies about 80 percent of the space. Visitors walk through the front door off Minnehaha Avenue into the main tasting room, where you can enjoy the work of local artists while you enjoy one of Sowards's brews. When Sowards was looking for images for his labels and tap handles he invited local artists to submit their

62

ideas. He was nearly overwhelmed with their response. Ultimately he chose the work of Jesse Brödd, whose acrylic paintings were turned into several Harriet labels. Brödd's work is on display in the tasting room, and there's also a separate room reserved for rotating exhibits from other artists.

Sowards also has an appreciation for music. Regulars often hang out back in the brewhouse area where a few old chairs, a sofa, and a table provide a near perfect place to enjoy a Harriet beer while listening to Sowards's collection of vinyl jazz records.

Sowards has an engineering background that motivates him to work toward a "zero carbon" footprint for his brewery. Much of his brewing equipment is electric and he has ambitious plans for installing solar energy panels to help run things. He has also developed a steam condensing system that allows him to recapture water vapor from the wort and thereby lower his water usage and save energy on heating additional water.

Harriet Brewing's core beers include a Belgian Abbey and a Belgian Dubbel and are self-distributed by Sowards to local daft accounts. Sowards expects to add special beers in 750mL bottles as the brewery grows.

HISTORY

Jason Sowards went to the University of Cincinnati to become a chemical engineer. While working on a bachelor's degree he landed a job with Marathon Petroleum in the Minneapolis suburb of St. Louis Park. He was able to complete his degree through courses at the University of Minnesota, and after graduating in 2007 he took at job at ACE Engineering in Minneapolis. Not only did he meet his wife, Tanya, in Minneapolis, but it was through work friends that he was introduced to homebrewing. By 2009 the encouragement from neighbors and all the regular visitors to his garage brewery convinced him to start a commercial brewery. Because the immediate area around Lake Harriet is mostly residential and just too expensive, Sowards had to look elsewhere for the type of property that would support his brewery. Given his rather humble beginnings as brewer in the garage of his Lake Harriet area home, he did however have a name that was a natural choice.

DON'T MISS THIS

Much of the brewing equipment came from a former brewpub in Japan called Izumo Brewing. Sowards saw it advertised for sale on the internet. It was originally manufactured by Wachsmann Brautechnik of Neu-Ulm, Germany, in 1998—as noted on a metal plaque affixed to the brewkettle's control panel. The 8.5-barrel system is copper-clad and is fired by an electric steam boiler. The brewery has a lot of room to grow from its beginnings with just two open and two closed fermenters. Harriet Brewing occupies about 5,000 square feet in a building that once housed a towing company and later an armored car business. Sowards likes to joke that his brewery can withstand big crowds and it's even "bomb proof."

HARRIET BREWS

Dark Abbey 🍺🍺🍺   *Your Ranking*_____

A Belgian Dubbel with deep dark color and bronze highlights. Thick, brown, bubbly head. Medium bodied. The flavor offers hints of raisin and plum intermingled with roasted chocolate malt.

Pilsner 🍺🍺🍺   *Your Ranking*

A light hoppy, floral nose. Bright, clear, yellow-gold color and a medium bubbly head. Light to medium bodied with a sharpness that's accentuated by the firm hoppy flavor. Finishes dry and bitter. Made with Sterling hops.

Saison Nourrice 🍺🍺🍺🍺   *Your Ranking*_____

A Belgian farmhouse ale. Begins with yeasty nose that offers hints of orange and light spicy pepper. Bright, hazy, golden-copper color with a thick, soft, tan head. Medium bodied, bubbly, and crisp. Flavor starts with a smooth yeast-fruitiness that is balanced with a malty background. Finishes clean and dry. This beer appears as a seasonal during the warmer months. It's made with two different Saison yeast strains. Sowards says he chose the name "Nourrice," which is a French term for wet nurse, because this beer has qualities that comfort and replenish the drinker.

West Side 🍺🍺🍺🍺   *Your Ranking*_____

This Belgian IPA shows off West Coast hops like Summit and Cascades, and fruitiness of Belgian yeast. A citrusy nose with bright orange copper color. A firm hoppy background with a hint of fruity grapefruit bitterness that also adds some dryness to the finish. The first beer released by Harriet Brewing and considered the brewery's flagship brew. The brewery's inaugural batch of this beer almost wasn't released. As the first beer through the system Sowards jokes that problems with his cooling system created ice-like conditions that can concentrate the alcohol and strengthen the beer. He decided it tasted fine, yet laughs that it seemed a little stronger than he planned. He went ahead and released it on opening day, but with the name "West Side Batch #1." The ultimate recipe for West Side keeps the alcohol around 6.5 percent ABV. West Side is an exceptional beer.

Wodan Weizen 🍺🍺🍺🍺   *Your Ranking*_____

A classic German Hefeweizen. The nose offers strong fruity hints of banana. A hazy, yellow-golden color and a thick, soft, white head. Light bodied, bubbly, and refreshing. The fruity tones of banana and clove, as Hefeweizen fans like to enjoy, are strong and smooth throughout. A light, crisp fruity finish. Sowards chose the name "Wodan" for its reference to the Viking god (a.k.a. Odin) who created Valhalla, the eternal beer hall for Vikings killed in battle.

OTHER HARRIET BREWS YOU MAY WANT TO TRY

Divine Oculust (Golden Strong)   *Your Ranking*_____

A bold Belgian ale with rich golden color with a restrained fruitiness, yet hints of spicy yeasty tones. This seasonal brew appears in the colder months of the year.

Doppelbock   *Your Ranking_____*

Dark and sweet with toasted caramel flavor. The beer was given a first place award in the 2010 Upper Mississippi Mashout. Its recipe includes additions of coffee from Peace Coffee, a local roaster and coffee shop that's located just a few blocks away from the brewery (south on Minnehaha Avenue near intersection with 33rd Street).

Jaguar   *Your Ranking_____*

A Baltic porter. Clean nose. Dark color and overall well balanced. Beautiful, silky, and dangerously deceptive like the big cat. Made during the summertime.

Oktoberfest   *Your Ranking_____*

A fall seasonal. Copper color and smooth maltiness. Made with a small amount of smoked malt.

MENU

None. Harriet Brewing does not serve food.

OTHER THINGS TO SEE OR DO IN THE AREA

Harriet Brewing hosts a number of events throughout the year. Check its website for days and times of special tastings and beer release parties associated with Oktoberfest, Maifest, and solstice events.

Other neighborhood attractions include the Midtown Farmer's Market (22nd Avenue and Lake Street) on Tuesdays and Saturdays through the summer and early fall. Minnehaha Falls (4801 South Minnehaha Avenue) is a 193-acre park that features a 53-foot waterfall, limestone bluffs, river outlooks, and a number of sculptures. The Minnehaha Bike Trail is a great way to find your way to this park.

The area around Harriet Brewing is very bike friendly; even brewery owner Jason Sowards bikes to work most days. Trails will not only connect you with Minnehaha Falls and points south like Fort Snelling, but you can also connect with routes to other breweries such as Herkimer, Minneapolis Town Hall, Rock Bottom, Fulton, and Flat Earth. For those without their own bike, Nice Ride rental bikes are available near the Hiawatha light rail (Lake Street/Midtown Station). The light rail runs from downtown Minneapolis to the Minneapolis–St. Paul airport on the south side near the Mall of America.

If you choose to visit the brewery's namesake, Lake Harriet is part of the Chain of Lakes, which is one of the most visited outdoor recreational areas in the Twin Cities. It's located about four miles west of the brewery. Lake Harriet was named for Harriet Lovejoy, wife of Colonel Henry Leavenworth, who founded Fort Snelling in 1819. The lake became part of Minneapolis's early park system in 1883. A pleasurable way to experience the beauty of the lake and the surrounding neighborhood is via the Como-Harriet Streetcar. This small surviving section of the trolley lines once served Minneapolis and St. Paul. Today, the trolley runs between the west shore of Lake Harriet (at Queen Avenue South and West 42nd Street) to Lake Calhoun (Richfield Road just south of West 36th Street) in the summer months. The Chain of Lakes includes more than thirteen miles of biking, walking, and jogging paths that encircle the lakes. The Lake

Harriet Bandshell (4135 Lake Harriet Parkway) is a site for summertime concerts and many special events.

Harriet Brewing is not located at the lake. Rather, it's a couple of miles to the east in the Longfellow neighborhood. The neighborhood is named after Henry Wadsworth Longfellow, the famous poet born in 1807.

BREWERY RATING

	Your Rating	Shepard's Rating	General Description
Location		🍺🍺	Located southeast of downtown Minneapolis in the Longfellow Neighborhood. Building is rather plain looking.
Ease of Finding Location		🍺🍺🍺	Not too difficult to find. Planning is important because exits from the major Interstates don't line up easily with main connecting streets.
Brewery Atmosphere		🍺🍺	This is a working brewery in the garage of a former towing company.
Dining Experience		n/a	Not applicable.
The Pints		🍺🍺🍺	Harriet Brewing reflects the dedication of a homebrewer whose hobby turned professional. Extra merit given for Jason Sowards's commitment to living his dream!

DIRECTIONS

Located southeast of downtown Minneapolis it requires a little planning to find. The brewery is about one and a half miles south of I-94, or roughly two miles east of I-35W. When traveling east on I-94 take exit 235A, and turn south on 26th Avenue South, which will eventually become County Road 48 and Minnehaha Avenue. When heading west on I-94 take exit 234A (Hiawatha Avenue) and travel south on Hiawatha for about one mile, and exit on westbound East 32nd Street. At the intersection with East Lake turn left (east) and soon thereafter turn right (south) on Minnehaha Avenue. Harriett Brewing is located on the right (west) side of Minnehaha Avenue.

When approaching from the south on I-35W, take exit 15 heading toward the north. The exit will merge onto 2nd Avenue South (heading north). Turn right (east) on Lake Street and continue about two miles to the intersection with Minnehaha Avenue and turn right (south). Harriet Brewing is just a few hundred feet ahead on the right (west) side of Minnehaha Avenue.

Herkimer Pub and Brewery
Minneapolis

Visit Date	Signed

ABOUT THE BREWERY

Located in a two-story brick building in the bustling Uptown neighborhood of Minneapolis, the Herkimer takes on a number of personalities, from cozy afternoon tavern to packed nightclub in the evening. Such personalities are reflected in its deep green colors, pressed tin ceiling, pop culture posters, and serving trays mounted on the walls. A number of custom-made pinup girl posters hang throughout the main dining and bar areas. Each visit requires a careful look around in case something was overlooked on a previous trip. There are also a number of strategically placed televisions to keep local sports fans happy. The bar is a long, rectangular central island in the main dining room.

The brewpub dedicates a significant amount of seating to an environment that encourages conversation with its large booths, a few of which have windows. The front of the building has some great views for watching passersby on Lyndale Avenue, but much of that area requires patrons to stand or lean against high tables. The best seats are actually on the sidewalk in the summertime. Portions of the brewery are behind glass and are visible from both inside and outside the building.

Brewmaster Gustavo de Toledo Vale has a strong commitment to German-style beers. While he tries to keep four to six beers on tap for most visits, his main standards include an Alt, a pilsner, and a Kellerbier. Among the seasonal and special brews to watch for are the Red Flyer Marzen in March and the Gose in late summer.

HISTORY

The Herkimer opened in December 1999. Herkimer was a childhood nickname of a friend of brewpub owner Blake Richardson, whose German grandmother liked to use the term to signify "odd or funny one." She had no idea that it would make a restaurant marquee someday.

Richardson originally partnered with Chad Jamrozy, who he met while working at the former District Warehouse Brewing Company (430 North First Avenue, which brewed from 1996 to 2002). When their business partnership in Herkimer ended a few years later, Richardson became owner of the brewpub. Richardson grew up in Sioux Falls, South Dakota, came to Minneapolis for college where he studied speech communications. His interest in beer grew after traveling around the country, including stops in craft beer states like Washington, Oregon, and Colorado. He eventually attended the Siebel Institute of Technology and World Brewing Academy in Chicago to learn brewing techniques. When the Herkimer opened Richardson took on the brewmaster duties. He was also one of the original brewers for Shannon Kelly's, a brewpub that operated in St. Paul from 1995 to 1997.

The Herkimer's current brewmaster, Gustavo de Toledo Vale, was hired in 2008. Vale, originally from Brazil, lived in the U.S. while his father worked for IBM. In 1991 Gustavo decided to study art in the U.S. He received a bachelor's degree from the Pratt Institute in Brooklyn, New York. After graduation he went to work at the New York Post and later the Wall Street Journal as a graphic designer. In the early 2000s he picked up the hobby of homebrewing. By 2007 he was growing restless in his job, and that's when he and his wife Erin decided to move to Germany for a year so he could study brewering and apprentice in Berlin and Munich, including a job at the Paulaner Brewery of Munich. During that year in Germany Gustavo says he fell in love with brewing lagers. When he and his wife came back in late 2007 he wasn't in a hurry to find work but noticed an opening for a brewmaster at the Herkimer, so he applied. By the following February Gustavo was living in Minneapolis.

The Herkimer's building was constructed in 1929. Its sixteen-inch-thick floors once supported a neighborhood laundromat for many years. It has also housed a clothing store. The brewing equipment was salvaged from a former brewery in West Virginia. It's an 8.5-barrel brewing system with the brew kettle and five fermenters on the restaurant level. Because the building is rather massive, four additional storage tanks, seven serving vessels, and grain storage are located downstairs.

DON'T MISS THIS

Walk down the block a few doors and stop in at moto-i (2940 Lyndale Avenue South), a sake brewpub also owned by Blake Richardson. Opening in 2008, moto-i lays claim to being America's first sake brewpub. For around twelve dollars you can order a tasting flight of three different sakes, a perfect introduction to sake. Moto-i is also great for those who crave Japanese food. Even if you don't like sake, moto-i has one of the best overall Minnesota beer selections in town with over a dozen on tap. In summer the rooftop is open with a great view of the Minneapolis skyline. Richardson also does the brewing at moto-i.

HERKIMER'S BREWS

Alt Bier   *Your Ranking*_____
Begins with a malty nose. Clear copper body and a thin, bubbly, tan head. Medium bodied. Malty flavor dominates despite a light hoppy finish. Made with Magnum and Hallertau Mittelfrüh hops. A gold medal winner at the 2007 Great American Beer Festival.

Daily Pils 🍺🍺🍺🍺   *Your Ranking*_____
This traditional Bohemian pilsner has a wonderful floral nose that offers an inviting hoppiness. Clear golden color and a thin, soft, white head. Medium bodied and round texture. A light malty start with a citrus background that lends some sharp crispness. Finishes with a light, dry bitterness.

Dunkel Weiss 🍺🍺🍺   *Your Ranking*_____
Lots of yeast and fruity tones to the nose. Its color is cloudy brown to rich mahogany, with a thick, marbled, rocky looking head that is tan colored. Medium bodied and soft texture. Sweet fruity and yeast tones come in fast and very assertively, followed by a spicy sweet finish.

Handy's Lager 🍺🍺   *Your Ranking*_____
An American premium lager. Malty nose. Clear, light yellow-golden color, and a thin, soft, off-white head. Light bodied. A fruity sweetness dominates.

High Point Dunkel 🍺🍺🍺   *Your Ranking*_____
A very light malty nose. Dark body with bronze highlights. The head is thin, bubbly, and tan. Full bodied and creamy. A light, dry start with a fruity malty body. Light malty sweetness in the finish with a hint of warmth.

Red Flyer Marzen 🍺🍺   *Your Ranking*_____
A light floral nose. Clear, reddish-bronze color and a thick, soft, tan head. Medium bodied and very bubbly. A citrus beginning with a soft sweet caramel background. Finishes with a light dryness. A year-round Oktoberfest that offers strong balance.

Schwarz 🍺🍺🍺🍺   *Your Ranking*_____
A malty nose, very dark black color, and a thick, soft, tan head. Medium bodied and soft. Smooth tones of chocolate malt. Clean and well balanced.

Sky Pilot 🍺🍺🍺🍺   *Your Ranking*_____
A Kellerbier with a light hoppy nose and hazy golden color. Medium bodied with a sharp hoppineess and long-lasting bitterness. Made with Magnum and Czech hops. This unfiltered pilsner is a gold medal winner at the 2006 Great American Beer Festival.

Vienna Country Lager 🍺🍺🍺🍺   *Your Ranking*_____
My favorite among the Herkimer brews. A light malty nose, but overall very clean. Hazy golden copper color with a soft, off-white head. Medium to light bodied and crisp texture. Solid crisp maltiness. Malty finish with just a light smoky accent.

OTHER HERKIMER BREWS YOU MAY WANT TO TRY

Glitchen Rye　　　　　　　　　　　*Your Ranking*_____
A traditional German-style Roggenbier. Brewed with 50 percent rye and 15 percent wheat malts.

Gose　　　　　　　　　　　　　　　*Your Ranking*_____
This is a special treat at the Herkimer. Gose is a cross between a Belgian Wit and a Berliner Weisse. If offered at all, look for it in late summer. Its recipe includes coriander seeds and sea salt. Fermentation involves both Hefeweizen yeast and lactobacillus. Expect a dominating sourness, but a very refreshing beer.

Kölsch　　　　　　　　　　　　　　*Your Ranking*_____
A summer seasonal. Light golden color and crisp.

Maibock　　　　　　　　　　　　　*Your Ranking*_____
This late winter, early spring beer offers a light malty flavor and smooth, warm finish.

Oktoberfest　　　　　　　　　　　*Your Ranking*_____
Deep reddish amber color with rich maltiness. Brewed for the fall.

Smoked Doppelbock　　　　　　　*Your Ranking*_____
Full bodied and lots of malty flavor. This beer is aged for two months before it is released. Brewmaster Gustavo de Toledo Vale considers this one of his favorite beers to make. Look for it in winter.

Tooler's Weiss　　　　　　　　　　*Your Ranking*_____
A German-style wheat beer. Unfiltered with strong hints of banana and cloves.

MENU

The Herkimer food ranges from pub sandwiches and soups to more hearty entrées like steaks, chicken, and pasta. On the lighter side, Herkimer has about ten appetizers that include calamari, crab cakes, sweet potato fries, baked Brie, and the famous Herkimer Wings made with a sweet ancho chile glaze. The Dunkel Onion Soup is made with Herkimer's High Point Dunkel. There are about a half-dozen sandwiches, such as the HerkiBurger, a hamburger patty coated with a raspberry barbecue sauce. But the house special Custom Burger is a build-your-own with more than twenty choices of toppings. Unique dishes feature vegetable cannelloni, halibut filet, and plum chipotle pasta. A great finish to the meal brings a choice of Sticky Pecan Pie or the Chocolate Pepper Cake topped with ancho chile chocolate sauce.

If you're there mainly for the beer and find yourself hungry, try the Herkimer Mini Burgers and choose among Mini Macs, Chicken, Veggie, and the Classic, made with ground beef, bacon, and cheddar cheese. When ordering a Mini you'll want to glance to the far wall leading into the kitchen where the Herkimer Mini Burger Meter registers the current number that have been sold. The sign changes weekly.

OTHER THINGS TO SEE OR DO IN THE AREA

Herkimer is located in the southern part of Minneapolis's Uptown neighborhood on the northern edge of the Lyn-Lake neighborhood, often referred to as Uptown's edgier cousin. In these neighborhoods you'll find a vibrant entertainment industry with nightclubs and unique stores and shops. Within walking distance of the Herkimer is the Jungle Theater (Lake and Lyndale), which offers plays year-round. Intermedia Arts (2822 Lyndale Avenue South) is one of the best galleries in the city. And a fun stop is the Bryant-Lake Bowl (810 West Lake Street), a 1930s-era eight-lane bowling alley and ninety-nine-seat theater.

In August the area near Herkimer hosts several art fairs. The Uptown Art Fair is held in the middle of Uptown (Thirty-first to Twenty-eighth streets); the Powderhorn Festival of Art takes place in Powderhorn Park (Thirty-fourth Street and Fifteenth Avenue South); and the Loring Park Art Festival, a juried event, is in downtown Minneapolis in Loring Park. All three occur in early August. The Lyn-Lake Street Fair is an annual art, music, and food festival in August. In January, the annual Lake Harriet (southwest of Herkimer) Winter Kite Festival is colorful and fun. Winter also offers opportunities for cross-country skiing or snowshoeing at Theodore Wirth Park (northwest of Herkimer).

In the fall the Herkimer attracts fans for Sunday afternoon NFL games. Despite being home turf for the Minnesota Vikings, the Herkimer is known to cater to rival Green Bay Packers fans (www.packerbar.com).

BREWERY RATING

	Your Rating	Shepard's Rating	General Description
Location		🍺🍺🍺🍺	This is a bustling entertainment district and neighborhood center with many opportunities to enjoy walking about, shopping, and dining.
Ease of Finding Location		🍺🍺	Driving this area presents a few challenges; parking, traffic, and one-way street can be problematic. It requires some planning for out-of-towners.
Brewery Atmosphere		🍺🍺	Herkimer's personality seems to change with the time of day: nightclub, college bar, sports bar, neighborhood tavern.
Dining Experience		🍺🍺🍺	Mostly pub fare to up-scale casual.
The Pints		🍺🍺🍺	A good experience. The brewmaster's commitment to German style beers adds a lot to the Herkimer beer experience. Watch for seasonal and special beers.

DIRECTIONS

Finding the Herkimer takes a little planning and especially an understanding of the one-way streets and the brewpub's location with respect to the freeway. The Herkimer is located south of downtown Minneapolis, and one option is to follow Lyndale Avenue South from the central city.

From southbound I-35W, take exit 14 (Thirty-sixth to Thirty-fifth streets), then head west on Thirty-fifth Street to Lyndale Avenue, and turn north; Herkimer will be five or six blocks north from the intersection of Thirty-fifth and Lyndale. From northbound I-35W, take exit 15 (Lake), turn west, and travel to Lyndale Avenue, then turn north on Lyndale and Herkimer will be about a half-block further on the left (west) side of Lyndale.

Lift Bridge Brewery
Stillwater

Visit Date   Signed

ABOUT THE COMPANY

What might be the odds that a simple conversation over beer leads one to start a brewery? There's little doubt that many beer enthusiasts, especially home-brewers, have had "I can do that" conversations. Lift Bridge Brewery is an ex-ample of acting on one's dream—in the case of this Stillwater beer maker, it was the dreams of five local homebrewing buddies who came together to share recipes and try different approaches to making beer. So, it was inevi-table that at some point the idea of owning a brewery would surface from the beer-filled minds and hearts of Jim Pierson, Steve Rinker, Dan Schwarz, Trevor Cronk, and Brad Glynn.

While founded two years earlier, the first Lift Bridge brews were released in 2008. The company actually began as a contract brewer with the help of beer-making colleagues like Flat Earth Brewing in St. Paul. After establishing its brands, Lift Bridge opened its own working brewery in Stillwater in 2011. (Before opening its own working brewery, it used the name Lift Bridge Beer Company.)

The brewery is located just south and west of downtown Stillwater. It fea-tures a new 15-barrel brewing system made by the Canadian company New-lands Systems. Additional components include three 30-barrel fermenters; and one 30-barrel bright tank. Given the 11,000 square feet of space in their build-ing there is plenty of room to expand. When trying to locate the building, the local water tower makes for a great landmark.

Lift Bridge is a growing brewery with unique signature beers that are easy to find in bottles. Among those to seek out include Farm Girl Saison, Crosscut Pale Ale, Chestnut Hill, and the Belgian tripel called Minnesota Tan that is made with lingonberries. The brewery also makes several other brews that are available on tap in Stillwater and the Twin Cities. One of the draft beers to watch for is the complex Biscotti with a malty depth and vanilla and honey tones. Lift Bridge's brewery in Stillwater supplies draft beer, growlers, and special limited release brews. It also has an onsite tasting room.

HISTORY

Brad Glynn and Steve Rinker had been making beer together for several years before founding the company in 2006. Glynn and Rinker actually met as co-workers at a local construction company. It wasn't long before fellow home-brewing buddies Schwarz, Cronk, and Pierson had signed on as partners. Glynn says the group is very close, like brothers, and over the course of a few years had pushed themselves to devise large-scale recipes and collaborate on a business plan for Lift Bridge. Before the company was firmly established and its brews were launched, the group tinkered with recipes for at least a couple of years to come up with just the right beers they would offer.

By September 2008 they had made their first commercial batch of beer with the help and equipment of St. Paul's Flat Earth Brewing, a calculated business move to create an early presence in the market. Glynn had actually worked part-time at Flat Earth, so the brewing partnership was easy. Contracting for beer production allowed Lift Bridge to get its draft beer on area taps, establish name recognition, and build a list of accounts. In May 2009 Lift Bridge released its first bottled beer, Farm Girl Saison; by the end of that year its second beer, Crosscut Pale Ale, appeared on local store shelves. As the popularity of Lift Bridge grew so did demand. By 2010, to keep up, it had transferred most of its brewing and all of its bottling to Wisconsin's Stevens Point Brewery, and in 2011 Lift Bridge shifted its bottle production to the Cold Spring Brewing Company.

Each of the partners has his own role in the brewery. Dan Schwarz is the chief executive officer. Brad Glynn serves as the chief operating officer and oversees the brewery and its functions. Jim Pierson is the chief financial officer. Steve Rinker is in charge of sales, and Trevor Cronk takes care of marketing issues. In 2011 Matt Hall joined Lift Bridge as brewmaster. Hall grew up in St. Paul but left home to work on a degree in environmental biology at the University of Montana in Missoula. After graduating in 1995 he returned to take a position with the Stoh Brewery. That job was actually in the old Hamm's Brewery facility in east St. Paul. When Stoh closed in 1997, Hall decided to go back to school; this time at the Siebel Institute of Technology and World Brewing Academy where he completed a diploma course. He worked at the Stevens Point Brewery in Wisconsin from 1997 to 2005 before taking a position at Keoki Brewing Company in Hawaii on the island of Kauai. He returned to the mainland in 2008 for a job at Firestone Walker in Paso Robles, California. Having grown up in Minnesota, Hall was always interested in returning to Minnesota. So when the Lift Bridge Brewery offered him a job in November 2010 it was an opportunity he felt he couldn't pass up.

DON'T MISS THIS

When taking a tour at Lift Bridge there is a small but very relevant historical display of Stillwater's brewing past that includes several articles, antiques, and relics from the city's beer making past.

LIFT BRIDGE BREWS

Chestnut Hill 🍺🍺🍺   *Your Ranking*_____

A fall seasonal. A malty and spicy nose. Deep, dark bronze color with ruby tints and a thick tan head. This brown ale is roasted, nutty, and spicy. That spiciness really lingers in the finish adding to its distinctive and assertive flavor. The name is a reference to Chestnut Hill, the middle hill in Stillwater. Chestnut Street is the main roadway that leads to the lift bridge.

Crosscut Pale Ale 🍺🍺🍺   *Your Ranking*_____

This beer showcases Cascade hops. A light citrusy, hoppy nose. Clear amber-copper color with a bubbly, off-white head. Medium bodied and round texture. A resiny hoppiness with a firm, malty background. Finishes dry and citrusy. This is a very well balanced pale ale. Grapefruit peel is added to the boil for additional citrus tones that blend well with the Cascade hops. This beer's name recognizes Stillwater's early logging history.

Farm Girl Saison 🍺🍺🍺🍺   *Your Ranking*_____

Lift Bridge's first beer is a tribute to Brad Glynn's wife, Gwen, who asked that the Lift Bridge boys make a beer that was more of a session beer. Gwen grew up in rural southwestern Minnesota. This Farm Girl has a sweet, fruity, yeasty nose. Cloudy yellow color with a thick, soft, white head. Light, soft, bubbly texture. A yeasty, spicy, fruity flavor. Finishes with dry spiciness and yeasty. Made with Belgian yeast, Belgian pils malt, wheat malt, and candi sugar.

Hop Prop IPA 🍺🍺🍺🍺   *Your Ranking*_____

This is an aggressive American IPA with an orange-copper color and a thick tan head. Strong citrus aroma and piney flavor. A sharp resiny lingering finish. Made with Centennial, Citra, and Amarillo hops. First brewed in 2011 as a limited release and most likely found at the brewery or on select tap accounts.

Minnesota Tan 🍺🍺🍺🍺   *Your Ranking*_____

A summer seasonal. This is a Belgian tripel made with lingonberries. Each keg of beer has about five pounds of puréed lingonberries from Canada that leave the beer with a faint pink tint. Minnesota Tan begins with a fruity nose. It has some fruity and yeast flavors you expect from a Belgian tripel, yet an assertive tartness from the lingonberries. Medium to full bodied. The berries are strongest in the beer's finish. Head brewer Brad Glynn says that this beer is made for the Scandinavians who call Stillwater home. Its name does cause one to wonder what this beer would be called if the Lift Bridge Brewery were located on the other side of the river—Wisconsin Red?

OTHER LIFT BRIDGE BREWS YOU MAY WANT TO TRY

Belgian Biscotti   *Your Ranking_____*

There's a lot going on in this beer, inspired by a biscotti recipe of Steve Rinker's grandmother. It's made with several malts (including wheat, oats, and local honey), European hops, Grains of Paradise, Madagascar vanilla bean, whole star anise, and a Belgian yeast strain. Deep copper color and complex spicy flavor. Serve this beer around 50 degrees to accentuate the malt and spices. It also has some strength at 7 percent ABV.

Chestnut Hill ala Nutsack   *Your Ranking_____*

A cask-conditioned version of Chestnut Hill that is aged on roasted hazelnuts. Given a gold medal as the People's Choice Awards during the 2009 Firkin Fest held at St. Paul's Happy Gnome. This beer is only available at special events.

Harvestör Fresh Hop Ale   *Your Ranking_____*

This hoppy ale is made with fresh Cascade and Willamette hops from the hops garden of Lift Bridge co-owner and chief operating officer Brad Glynn.

MENU

None. The Lift Bridge Brewery does not serve food.

OTHER THINGS TO SEE OR DO IN THE AREA

Lift Bridge refers to Stillwater's historic river crossing. The bridge and the town's name are reflected in many of the beer names, their labels, and descriptions. The iconic lift bridge that gives the brewery its name spans the St. Croix River and connects downtown Stillwater to Houlton, Wisconsin. A section of the bridge rises when ships approach. Built in 1931 to replace a swing bridge, it was constructed for a cost of $460,000, which Minnesota and Wisconsin split evenly.

Stillwater is often referred to as the birthplace of Minnesota because in 1848 it hosted a convention that helped establish it as a territory in 1849 and eventually a state in 1858. The river front and downtown are must stops on any visit. The downtown offers many unique shops, galleries, restaurants, and antique stores that occupy older historic buildings. The community holds a number of festivals throughout the year. The Brewers Bazaar and Rivertown Art Festival is held in May. Lumberjack Days are held in July. The Fall Colors, Fine Art and Jazz Festival occurs in early October. Many of the community festivals and associated activities occur in Lowell Park that is adjacent to the St. Croix River.

Stillwater has also been the home of several breweries over time. At least four existed in the nineteenth century until Prohibition. As you enter downtown Stillwater from the south you pass by the former site of the Joseph Wolf Brewery (402 South Main Street), which operated from 1869 to 1919. What is left of the brewery is now a restaurant (Luna Rosa), but the brewery's lagering caves are available for tours.

BREWERY RATING

	Your Rating	Shepard's Rating	General Description
Location		🍺🍺🍺	Located on the western edge of Stillwater. The building originally belonged to a local construction company. From the outside it resembles more of an office building than a brewery.
Ease of Finding Location		🍺🍺🍺	Not too difficult to find. Watch for the Stillwater water tower.
Brewery Atmosphere		🍺🍺🍺	This is a working brewery with new equipment.
Dining Experience		n/a	Not applicable.
The Pints		🍺🍺🍺	Lift Bridge brews are unique in the market. The Belgian Biscotti and Minnesota Tan are among their most distinctive.

DIRECTIONS

Lift Bridge is located on Stillwater's western edge. Highway 36 heading east from the Twin Cities is an easy way to find the brewery. Just watch for the Stillwater water tower as you are approaching town. You'll turn north at the intersection with Washington Avenue, then after about a quarter-mile you'll want to turn right (east) on Tower Drive.

From Interstate 94, take exit 253 and travel north on County Road 17 (Lake Elmo Avenue North). After about three miles turn to the right (northeast) on Stillwater Boulevard North. After approximately three miles you'll arrive at Highway 36, and then turn right (east). Highway 36 intersects with Washington Avenue in about a half-mile (watch for the Herberger's Department Store). Turn right on Washington Avenue North, then right again at Tower Drive.

Lucid Brewing Company
Minnetonka

ABOUT THE BREWERY

Eric Biermann and Alyssa Dwyer met in 2004. Their dream was to start a business together. They also enjoyed homebrewing. So it was inevitable that the couple would share their creations with friends, and those friends undoubtedly provided the encouragement to turn their dream into a "lucid" reality. By late summer 2011 Lucid Brewing was a company, and Biermann and Dwyer's homebrew recipes were the basis of its product line.

Lucid Brewing is located in an industrial park in Minnetonka, roughly the southwest corner of the metro Twin Cities area. At the heart of the brewhouse is a 15-barrel brewing system, composed of a mash tun, brew kettle, hot liquor tank, fermenters, and a bright tank. After looking around for used equipment, Biermann settled on new elements that he purchased from Zhongde Systems of China. Lucid is set up for about 2,500 barrels per year, and Biermann's initial goal is around 1,500 barrels annually. It took a fair amount of volunteer labor from some of those homebrewing friends — with Biermann and Dwyer's beer as a reward — to help get it all up and running. Lucid occupies about 6,000 square feet of the 27,000-square-foot warehouse that has contained a variety of businesses over the years, including a woodworking company, a food distributor, and a gymnastics studio. Renovations to the interior included the building of a grain milling room and a cooler for beer storage. Most of the space remains open to allow for the brew kettle, fermenters, and keg cleaning and filling. From the outside the building looks to be part of a common industrial park. It's a one-level tan concrete block exterior with burgundy trim near the roofline.

Lucid Brewing's first beers included an American Wheat and a Double IPA. Initially the brewery focused on local draft accounts and will self-distribute its beers. Special and seasonal brews in 750mL bottles are expected to be added as the brewery grows.

HISTORY

The partnership behind Lucid Brewing consists of Eric Biermann, his wife, Alyssa Dwyer, fellow homebrewer and close friend Jon Messier, plus a silent investor. Biermann is the brewmaster, Alyssa helps in recipe development and marketing, and Jon handles sales and promotion. Biermann grew up on a farm near Belgrade northwest of the Twin Cities. Both of his great-grandparents were from northern Germany. While he doesn't know about any brewmasters in his family, with a name like Biermann there's a good chance that someone in the family made beer at some point.

Initially, Biermann's path wasn't headed toward brewing. He attended St. Cloud State and in 1994 earned a degree in accounting and micro-computing. After several years of working for different Minnesota companies in accounting and finance he eventually discovered a strong interest in making beer. As that continued to become more important to him he found himself volunteering at breweries across the country. Biermann's travels took him to Cigar City Brewing of Tampa, Florida, and Odonata Beer Company of Sacramento, California. In 2009 Biermann signed up for the American Brewers Guild Training Program based in Salisbury, Vermont. His six months of coursework included a residency at the Hoppy Brewing Company in Sacramento, California, followed by an apprenticeship at Flat Earth Brewing in St. Paul. Eric met his partner Jon Messier, a native of Rhode Island, through a shared love of homebrewing and as members in the Minnesota Home Brewers Association. Messier originally came to the Twin Cities to obtain a degree in aerospace engineering from the University of Minnesota. After college he went to work for Medtronics in Mounds View, Minnesota.

DON'T MISS THIS

For those taking a tour ask about Biermann's early pilot brewing system that he used as a homebrewer. Biermann used the 20-gallon system at home, and that experience eventually led to some of the brewery's initial recipes. He purchased it from MoreBeer of Concord, California, in 2008 and keeps it around for test brews.

LUCID BREWS

Air 🍺🍺🍺   *Your Ranking_____*
This is the lightest beer in the Lucid lineup. It was also the first beer offered commercially by the brewery. It starts with a light citrus aroma. Its body is golden and hazy with a medium soft white head. A light bubbly mouth feel. The flavor offers a light but firm citrus hoppiness with a hint of mango fruitiness. Finishes crisp and lightly dry. Initially this beer was made with Galaxy and Summit hops and later batches feature Citra hops.

OTHER LUCID BREWS YOU MAY WANT TO TRY

Camo   *Your Ranking*_____

An Imperial, or Double, IPA with lots of citrus, floral, and piney bitterness. Made with Cascade, Amarillo, Summit, and Simcoe hops. Some warmth in the finish from its 9 percent ABV.

Saison   *Your Ranking*_____

Lucid Brewing will offer a range of seasonal brews and this is one to watch for in the summer time. Made with a French yeast strain. Expect crisp flavor with some tartness and a dry finish. Biermann considers this an old school beer and takes pride in the fact that there are no special spices in the recipe.

MENU

None. Lucid Brewing Company does not serve food.

OTHER THINGS TO SEE OR DO IN THE AREA

The annual Minnetonka Summer Festival is held the last Saturday in June with events that include a fun run, a children's tot trot race, and fireworks. The Burwell Art Fair is another late June event. It is held at the Charles H. Burwell House (13209 East McGinty Road). On Tuesday evenings during June and July the Music in the Park concert series is held at the outdoor amphitheater at the Minnetonka Civic Center Campus (14600 Minnetonka Boulevard). The amphitheater also hosts community theater productions. The Minnetonka Farmers' Market is another summer time attraction. It is held near the amphitheater on Tuesdays just before Music in the Park concerts. The Excelsior Farmers' Market is held on Thursdays from May through October in Lyman Park (Water Street between George and Third).

Lake Minnetonka is a 14,500-acre lake that is seven miles west of Lucid. With its numerous bays and islands the lake is a resort destination. The Museum of Lake Minnetonka operates the steamboat *Minnehaha*, which provides narrated lake tours. Just north of Lake Minnetonka, Long Lake hosts a summerfest celebration in late June. Most of the events take place at Nelson Park in Long Lake.

For those who enjoy nature walks and the beauty of local plants, the University of Minnesota's Landscape Arboretum is located in Chaska about ten miles west of Lucid Brewing. The Arboretum (3575 Arboretum Drive) was created in 1908 as the University's Fruit Breeding Farm. Today it includes more than one thousand acres of gardens, forests, parries, and marshes. You can tour the Arboretum on more than twelve miles of garden paths and hiking trails or drive the three-mile scenic route through the gardens and collections.

BREWERY RATING

	Your Rating	Shepard's Rating	General Description
Location		🍺🍺🍺	Located in an industrial business park on the southwest corner of the Twin Cities Metro area. The restaurants and taverns in the area around Lake Minnetonka provide lots of opportunity for this young brewery to find tap accounts.
Ease of Finding Location		🍺🍺🍺	Easy to find off of Interstate-494.
Brewery Atmosphere		🍺🍺	Lucid occupies about 6,000 square feet of space. Lots of room to grow.
Dining Experience		n/a	Not applicable.
The Pints		🍺🍺	Still a brewery/work in progress. Lucid is bound to grow on Minnesota beer enthusiasts.

DIRECTIONS

From Interstate 494 take exit 13 (Highway 62) and turn west. At the first stop light past I-494 turn right (north) on Baker Road. Travel about a quarter of a mile and Culligan Way will be on your left (west). After turning off of Baker Road onto Culligan Way, Lucid Brewing is located about three driveways in, on the right.

Minneapolis Town Hall Brewery

Minneapolis

Visit Date	Signed

ABOUT THE BREWERY

The Town Hall Brewery is on the west bank of the Mississippi River in the Seven Corners area of Minneapolis, not far from the Humphrey Metrodome and the University of Minnesota campus. This is a brewpub with a speakeasy attitude, as reflected in the neighborhood, the building, and the aggressive brewing of brewmaster Mike Hoops. On any visit you'll find a range of styles, cask ales, and brewmaster's specials that make this brewpub a must-visit, whether you're a returning local or an out-of-town beer enthusiast. This brewpub offers an amazing number of beers throughout the year, some thirty to fifty different brews that commonly include barrel-aged brews. It's anniversary week in (closest to October 24) and its barrel-aged week in February schedule daily releases of very special beers that rival the best of any brewpub in the country.

Town Hall has a beautiful custom-made back bar and a pressed tin ceiling with tints of green, burgundy, red, and turquoise. The ceiling isn't original; it was purchased second-hand by the building's owner in the 1960s. Before it was assembled, it had to be laid out on the sidewalk along Fifteenth Avenue so workers could determine how to make it fit.

Throughout Town Hall are lots of deep wood accents, old photos, and large murals. On the outside of the building along Washington Street a large mural offers an impression of what to expect when you walk through the brewpub's door and into the main barroom. It makes for a fun backdrop to the summer beer garden.

Town Hall is basically divided into two large rooms, each with its own bar. The main bar, with its black and white tile floor, has some great window seats that look out to the intersection of Washington and Fifteenth avenues. The second bar, in the western half of the building, offers additional seating for dining, as well as a fireplace, large cushy chairs and sofa, pool table, and dart boards. The brewhouse with its stainless steel equipment is located behind glass in this part of the building. The serving tanks and cold storage of casks are all downstairs.

Town Hall will commonly have five to seven beers on tap with at least one cask-conditioned beer on a hand pump. It also offers several taps to guest breweries. Among the standard Town Hall beers are the Black H_2O Oatmeal Stout, the Hope and King Scotch Ale, Dortmunder Local Export Lager, West Bank Pub Ale, and the Masala Mama India Pale Ale. Town Hall has added to its reputation as a Twin Cities beer haven with its special seasonal releases like Thunderstorm and the Russian imperial stout called Czar Jack.

HISTORY

Minneapolis Town Hall Brewery — better known as just Town Hall — was established in 1997. Brewpub owner Pete Rifakes and a middle school buddy, Scot McClure, opened the doors of Town Hall on October 24 that year. Both remember it well because it was the day of a home football game for the Minnesota Gophers, who were playing the Wisconsin Badgers. Rifakes and McClure grew up in suburbs of Madison, the city that is home to the Badgers. Actually, the name of the brewpub goes back to when the pair played baseball nearly every day in summer at the nearby Middleton Town Hall fields.

In 1998 the partnership dissolved on good terms, and Pete took over the business. Pete earned a bachelor's degree from the University of Illinois and then became a financial consultant in Chicago for a few years. But his taste for craft beer was honed when he returned to school to attend the University of Washington in Seattle, where he earned an MBA. After graduation, he joined the finance department of Northwest Airlines and worked up his business plan for a brewpub on the side.

Town Hall was almost located in the Minneapolis Warehouse District, but leasing obligations and signage limitations prevented a final deal. The building that today houses Town Hall was constructed in 1906 as a trolley station. Originally there were three buildings until they eventually were joined into one. You get a sense of this as you walk from the brewpub's bar area into the dining room. The checkered tile floor in the main bar almost carries you back to a time when you could purchase a ticket for travel throughout the Twin Cities.

After the trolley left the station for good, the building sat vacant for several years. In the pre-Prohibition years it served as a Gluek's tied house (a tavern affiliated with Gluek Brewing Company). It eventually even contained a liquor store — perhaps a harbinger of the brewpub. In the 1950s and 1960s it became an important part of the local theater district; Hay City Stage was here until it moved downtown. But probably the most recognizable name on the building was Dudley Riggs E.T.C. (Experimental Theater Company). Dudley Riggs, a local comedian, hosted a number of shows, events, and even well-known entertainers like John Belushi and Louie Anderson. It was Riggs who purchased the pressed tin ceiling and had it installed in what is now the main bar room. The building sat vacant in the mid-1990s, until Town Hall opened in 1997.

Brewmaster Mike Hoops is as famous as any local actor. His brewing talents are well known by local beer aficionados and well respected regionally in the beer world. After beginning his brewing career at Fitger's Brewhouse in Duluth, Mike took some time off to live in Michigan's Upper Peninsula. Following a chance meeting with Pete Rifakes at the Great Taste of the Midwest beer festival in Madison in 1998 and the departure of Town Hall's first brewmaster, John Haggarty, Hoops found himself back in brewing in 2000. If the name sounds familiar, it might be because when Mike left Fitger's, his brother Dave Hoops took over the brewing operations there. Those who enjoy Town Hall and Fitger's like to watch for when the brothers collaborate on special brews like versions of the popular Grand Cru and other barrel-aged beers.

In 2010 Pete Rifakes opened up Town Hall Tap (4810 Chicago Avenue South) in south Minneapolis. It's operated under a separate bar license and does not have a working brewery. However, you can find Town Hall beers on tap. Rifakes likes to keep at least seven to ten of his brewpub's beers on pushed lines, plus a few cask-conditioned beers are likely to be found. You'll also find nearly a dozen other draft beers that combine with an extensive bottled selection. The building was once home to the restaurant L'Ecosse. Extensive renovations occurred both inside and out. In the summer large garage doors open to the sidewalk. Inside, Town Hall Tap occupies about 2,700 square feet, which makes it smaller and yet cozier than the brewpub. Inside you'll also find Pete Rifakes's personal beer sign collection. There is also an antique bar that Rifakes found during his midwestern travels; the bar is thought to have been originally built in the nineteenth century for a tavern in Peoria, Illinois.

In the fall of 2011 Rifakes's business partner in the Town Hall Brewery, Paul Dzubnar, opened the Crooked Pint Ale House. Locals consider it somewhat of an offshoot of the Town Hall Tap theme. Dzubnar also owns Green Mill Restaurants, with almost thirty locations across the Upper Midwest. The Crooked Pint offers a strong commitment to local craft beers, a pub style menu, and live music. It's located in the South Washington Avenue district of downtown Minneapolis, just a few blocks from the Guthrie Theater.

DON'T MISS THIS

Look around the brewpub for the old beer-related photos that Pete Rifakes found when he dug through the local historical society archives. Near the kitchen you'll see Orth's Brewery. Another photo shows the building when it housed Bright Spot Tavern and Liquors (but you'll have to really look hard to find this one).

TOWN HALL'S BREWS

Anniversary Ale 🍺🍺🍺🍺   *Your Ranking*_____
Begins with a very floral, resiny aroma. Hazy, deep bronze color and a thick, bubbly, tan head. Full bodied. A light malty start with a warm mix of caramel and hoppiness. Finishes warm and sharp. There is a lot of flavor in this beer, similar to a Celebrator Doppelbock. Look for this beer around October 24.

Black H₂O Oatmeal Stout 🍺🍺🍺🍺 *Your Ranking_____*

A warm, roasted chocolate malt stout. Dark, translucent color with a thick, soft, brown head. Full bodied and silky. Sweet caramel and chocolate flavors. A lingering sweetness in the finish. Great creamy, thick qualities and lots of flavor. Watch for this beer on a nitrogen tap. A bronze medal winner at the 2000 Great American Beer Festival.

Broken Paddle ESB 🍺🍺🍺 *Your Ranking_____*

This extra special bitter begins with a hoppy nose. Clear, deep golden color and a thick, soft, off-white head. Medium bodied and somewhat slick texture. Malty beginning that quickly turns hoppy and sharp. Mildly bitter finish. Great flavors, just a bit confusing with the texture and body. When this beer was first brewed, Mike Hoops broke his brewer's paddle while stirring the mash and thus the inspiration for its name.

Chocolate Porter 🍺🍺🍺 *Your Ranking_____*

A firm, malty nose. Dark with ruby highlights. A thin, off-white, bubbly head. Medium bodied and soft texture. Smooth, sweet chocolate flavors dominate. A lightly warm, malty finish. This is a very pleasant porter, and you just want to keep the pints coming because it'll really grow on you.

Czar Jack (Bourbon Barrel)
Russian Imperial Stout 🍺🍺🍺🍺 *Your Ranking_____*

If you like big and rich barrel-aged brews, this is one to watch for. It is usually released during the brewpub's anniversary week in late October and again as part of the lineup during Barrel-Aged Week in February. A gold medal winner at the 2001 Great American Beer Festival.

Dortmunder Local Export Lager 🍺🍺🍺 *Your Ranking_____*

A German-style golden lager. Light, earthy nose. Light bodied and soft texture with a mild, malty flavor and crisp, light, bitter finish. Brewed with classic German malt, along with American Sterling and Czech Saaz hops. Owner Pete Rifakes says that this beer was designed to take the place of Town Hall's Bright Spot Golden Ale as his customers' tastes evolved toward the light but flavorful German lager styles.

1800 🍺🍺🍺 *Your Ranking_____*

This is a strong English IPA. A floral nose. A clear golden color, with a medium soft and marbled white head. Full bodied and soft. Begins with a sweet, somewhat perfume-like fruitiness before the hops come in at the end for a dry finish. Made with British Maris Otter malt and hopped with over seven pounds of East Kent Golding and Fuggles per barrel. A bronze medal winner at the 2005 Great American Beer Festival.

Grand Cru 🍺🍺🍺🍺 *Your Ranking_____*

An assertive fruity nose. Clear, reddish-copper color and a soft, off-white head. Medium to full bodied and round texture. A sweet fruity body with hints of grape, apricot, and vanilla. Fruitiness really shines in the finish. Might be a little sweet for those who enjoy this style, but it's well worth trying for the flavor of grapes! Finishes at around 9.5 percent ABV. This beer is offered only about every other year. One of brewmaster Mike Hoops's favorites. A silver medal winner at the 2004 Great American Beer Festival. Also watch for this beer aged in oak barrels.

Hope and King Scotch Ale 🍺🍺🍺🍺   *Your Ranking*_____

A very light malty nose. A hazy deep bronze color and a thin, soft, tan head. Full bodied and soft texture. Malty sweet flavor with light toasted notes in the background. A light caramel finish. Brewed with both English and American barley and many specialty malts for deep color and hints of roasted chocolate, caramel, and raisins with little hop presence. This beer was recognized at the Great American Beer Festival with gold medals in 2001 and 2011, a bronze medal in 2002, and a silver medal in 2004.

Macaroon 🍺🍺   *Your Ranking*_____

One of Town Hall's infused line of brews. Not a beer for everyone. However, some will find the unique nuttiness of a macaroon combined with pineapple to be a great summertime brew. Lots of coconut and nutty aroma and flavor. Clear copper color with a soft tan head. Medium bodied. There is lots of macaroon flavor in every pint, thanks to aging this beer with large chunks of coconut.

Mango Mama 🍺🍺🍺🍺   *Your Ranking*_____

A citrus twist on the brewpub's IPA. Fresh mango in a cheesecloth bag is dropped into the fermenter and left for a week or two to create a distinctive fruity edge to the Masala Mama. You can smell it in the beer nose. Hazy orange color with a thick, soft, white head. Full bodied and somewhat thick. Assertive mango fruitiness, yet blends incredibly well with the resiny hoppiness. Finishes bitter, even a little dry. A great complement to seafood. This is an exceptional beer.

Marmalade Sky 🍺🍺🍺🍺   *Your Ranking*_____

An American pale ale brewed entirely with Amarillo hops and additions of both sweet and bitter orange peel, making this somewhat of an American orange pale ale. Rich gold-copper color and a bubbly, tan head. Light but firm citrus notes in the nose and main flavor profile. Considered the house pale ale at Town Hall Tap.

Masala Mama India Pale Ale 🍺🍺🍺🍺   *Your Ranking*_____

An aggressive hoppy nose. Hazy golden to copper color and a bubbly, tan head. Full bodied and bubbly texture. Lots of bitterness and dryness, especially in the finish. Great flavor and smooth body. Overall, a controlled and firm IPA, with a bit of malt. There are great qualities in this IPA without the hops overwhelming you. Considered an American IPA. Made with four different hop varieties and five additions during the brewing process. Hops include Amarillo, Cascade, Centennial, and Mt. Hood.

Oktoberfest 🍺🍺🍺   *Your Ranking*_____

A floral hoppy nose. Clear bronze color with a soft tan head. Medium bodied and round mouth feel. Begins with a firm caramel maltiness. Hops come in midway through the taste and linger throughout the finish. Some pleasing hoppy character to this fall seasonal.

Parkway Java Porter 🍺🍺🍺   *Your Ranking_____*
Made especially for the Town Hall Tap. Lots of roasted coffee aroma that creates a very pleasing finish. Very dark color and a medium, soft, brown head. Brewed with beans from Sovereign Grounds (813 East 48th), a coffee roaster located in the same neighborhood as the Town Hall Tap.

Pot O Gold Potato Stout 🍺🍺🍺🍺   *Your Ranking_____*
Okay, normally a beer with potato in its name might not sound appealing. But this stout has a light malty nose, dark color, full body, and exceptionally smooth texture. It has a caramel and chocolate body with a clean finish. It really offers great flavor, despite a not-so-appetizing name. This beer makes an occasional appearance, usually around St. Patrick's Day.

Raspberry Porter 🍺🍺🍺   *Your Ranking_____*
A mild, fruity nose. Deep, dark color and full body. A light fruity beginning with some firm malty flavors before the raspberries eventually win the flavor battle in the end.

Russian Roulette 🍺🍺🍺🍺   *Your Ranking_____*
This imperial stout is aged with Belgian dark chocolate. A sweet, robust, chocolate malty nose that is very inviting. Dark brown to black color, full bodied, and lots of rich chocolate malt. A warm and spicy finish. A wonderful winter beer! A gold medal winner at the 2008 Great American Beer Festival.

Thunderstorm 🍺🍺🍺🍺   *Your Ranking_____*
Made with lemon grass, orange peel, and Minnesota honey. A sweet, malty nose. Deep golden-copper color and a thick, soft, tan head. Full bodied and bubbly. Smooth and sweet from malt and hints of honey. Finishes with caramel and honey sweetness. This beer won a silver medal at the 2004 Great American Beer Festival.

Wee Heavy 🍺🍺🍺🍺   *Your Ranking_____*
A big beer lover's beer. Made with a touch of peat-smoked malt that comes out in the aroma and finish. Dark bronze color with a bubbly, tan head. Full bodied. Lots of smooth caramel maltiness. Finishes smoky and warm. Served in a 10-ounce goblet.

West Bank Pub Ale 🍺🍺🍺   *Your Ranking_____*
A traditional English bitter, named for Town Hall's side of the river. A light floral nose. Clear golden color and a thick, soft, off-white head. Medium bodied and somewhat round texture. A nice malt and hop balance. This beer is often referred to as Town Hall's house or session beer.

OTHER TOWN HALL BREWS YOU MAY WANT TO TRY

Abominable   Your Ranking_____
A rich American porter made with Yeti Cold Press coffee from Peace Coffee of Minneapolis. The coffee is found in the nose and finish. This is a dark beer with bronze highlights and a creamy, white head.

Blue Label Barrel Aged Blend   Your Ranking_____
An unfiltered English strong ale made with a blend of imperial porter that is aged in an oak whiskey barrel. A limited release beer. Also referred to as Jester's Reserve Imperial Porter.

Eye of the Storm   Your Ranking_____
A boldly rich and flavorful golden beer. Full bodied and round mouth feel. Made with Minnesota Orange Blossom, Basswood, and Canola honey. Finishes smooth, sweet, and warm at more than 9 percent ABV. A silver medal winner at the 2008 and 2011 Great American Beer Festivals.

LSD   Your Ranking_____
A crisp herbal brew with lavender, sunflower honey, and dates. A silver medal winner at the 2011 Great American Beer Festival.

(Port) Odin   Your Ranking_____
A Baltic porter that is aged for eighteen months in an oak barrel that once stored French port wine.

Three Hour Tour Coconut Milk Stout   Your Ranking_____
A milk stout made with raw coconut added during secondary fermentation. When this beer was first released in October 2010 the brewpub sold twenty growlers in just fifteen minutes!

Twisted Jim   Your Ranking_____
The barrel-aged version of the pub's barley wine called Twisted Reality. The difference is that the beer is aged in barrels once used to make Jim Beam bourbon.

Twisted Reality   Your Ranking_____
This barley wine is a deep bronze color and full bodied with lots of caramel tones. Also offers plenty of warmth.

West Bank Pale Ale   Your Ranking_____
This is an American pale ale. An evolution of the West Bank Pub Ale.

MENU

The menu at Town Hall has a combination of pub and eclectic offerings. There are about a half-dozen salads to choose from. The Raspberry Spring Chicken Salad features grilled Cajun chicken with raspberry vinaigrette. The appetizers list is extensive, but most are fried options and sinfully unhealthy, such as chili cheese fries, beer-battered onion rings, quesadillas, and the original Town Hall nachos, which feature a homemade salsa and green onions.

There are about six to eight burgers and six to eight sandwiches. One of my favorites is the Rachel, a turkey Reuben with swiss cheese and sauerkraut. There's also a hearty meatloaf sandwich with beef, pork, and veal mixed with onions, peppers, spices, and Black H_2O Oatmeal Stout. Entrée choices include steaks, fish, and pasta. A specialty dish worth strong consideration is the Jamaican Rum Tenderloin with mashed potatoes, gravy, and vegetables. The Mediterranean Linguini features sautéed chicken breast and sun-dried tomatoes. For vegetarian options, the Asparagus and Spinach Alfredo tops the list.

OTHER THINGS TO SEE OR DO IN THE AREA

Town Hall Brewery is located on the northeast edge of downtown Minneapolis. Nearby the Hubert H. Humphrey Metrodome serves as the home of the Minnesota Vikings. There are tours of the Metrodome Monday through Saturday. There are also several museums, theaters, and scenic attractions within a few blocks of Town Hall.

The Minneapolis Riverfront District spans both banks of the Mississippi River in downtown Minneapolis and provides numerous opportunities for shopping and entertainment.

A great way to view the Mississippi River is from the Stone Arch Bridge. Made with native granite and limestone, it has twenty-three arches and spans the river below St. Anthony Falls. The bridge is a key link in the St. Anthony Falls Heritage Trail, which has pedestrian walkways and bicycle lanes. The Heritage Trail is a two-mile trail with an extensive system of interpretive and directional signs and kiosks.

Also nearby on the banks of the Mississippi is the Mill City Museum (704 South Second Street). It offers insights into the impact of flour milling on the history of Minneapolis, as well as some great views of the river.

For fans of the performing arts, the Mixed Blood Theatre (1501 South Fourth Street) is a professional multiracial company that offers performances that promote cultural pluralism and equality. The Theatre in the Round (245 Cedar Avenue) developed from expanded visions of the Guthrie Theatre (725 Vineland Place) and University of Minnesota theaters.

The Frederick Weisman Art Museum (333 East River Road) on the university campus contains over 16,000 works of art. The restored Milwaukee Road Depot (225 Third Avenue South) now is home to a seasonal indoor figure skating park, exhibition space, indoor water park, restaurant, and bar.

Bell Museum of Natural History (10 Church Street Southeast) offers excellent displays of natural habitat, from woods to the Great Lakes. A touch-and-see room offers kids the chance to stare down a grizzly and even try on a pair of antlers.

Making it easy to find a place to stay, the Holiday Inn Metrodome is next door to the Town Hall Brewery, complete with parking ramp. There's also a Nice Ride bike station near Town Hall's main door.

BREWERY RATING

	Your Rating	Shepard's Rating	General Description
Location		🍺🍺🍺🍺	Location near the University of Minnesota and the theater district makes for lots of activity.
Ease of Finding Location		🍺🍺🍺🍺	Close to major roads and intersections. Parking ramp and hotel are next door.
Brewery Atmosphere		🍺🍺🍺🍺	Great local feel and atmosphere.
Dining Experience		🍺🍺🍺🍺	Pub fare to family-style offerings.
The Pints		🍺🍺🍺🍺	Solid year-round offerings; special seasonal and cask-conditioned ales make nearly every visit perfect.

DIRECTIONS

From northbound I-35W, take exit 17 and turn east. Town Hall Brewery is about one block east at the intersection of Washington and Fifteenth avenues.

From southbound I-35W, take the Washington Avenue exit to the first set of stoplights and then turn left (crossing over I-35W). At the next stoplight, turn left in front of Town Hall Brewery.

Town Hall Brewery is a modest walk from the Hiawatha light rail line. The Cedar/Riverside Station (613 15th Avenue, South) is located about a half-dozen blocks south of the brewpub. The Hiawatha Line connects to Target Field at its northern end and to the Minneapolis–St. Paul Airport and Mall of America at its southernmost point. The Hiawatha has stops near several Minneapolis beer venues, including Fulton Brewery (414 6th Avenue, North), Rock Bottom Restaurant and Brewery (800 LaSalle Plaza), and Harriet Brewing (3036 Minnehaha Avenue).

Pour Decisions Brewing Company

Roseville

Visit Date   Signed

ABOUT THE BREWERY

Pour Decisions Brewing was created based on the dreams of St. Paul home-brewers Kristen England and B. J. Haun who hope their decision to create a brewery together will be anything but a "poor" choice. The partners met through the St. Paul Homebrewers Club, each having won a number of brewing awards for their recipes. Both have advanced graduate degrees and laugh about their decision to stay in school so long as one of the inspirations behind the name.

In 2008 Haun proposed the idea to England about working together on a brewery concept. Together they spent about two years developing a business plan, raising the necessary funding, and making decisions about equipment and brewery construction. They chose Roseville for its location in the greater Metro Twin Cities area.

England and Haun occupied their building and announced their plans publically on April 1, 2011. The timing of the announcement was speculated as an April Fool's joke by many blog and Twitter sites that debated the authenticity of the brewery for several days. England, who even describes himself as a bit "cheeky," liked the idea of creating interest fueled by initial speculation as to whether or not his brewery was real.

By summer 2011 England and Haun had started installing brewing equipment in a 7,500-square-foot warehouse building that was formally used by the St. Paul *Pioneer Press*. The brewery relies on a 20-barrel brew kettle that was custom made by a stainless steel fabricator in California. The system is decoction capable and based on English, Italian, and German design elements. The initial layout of the brewery included two 40-barrel fermenters and one 40-barrel bright tank. The tasting room greets you as you enter, but remains open to the larger interior of the building so you can watch the activity on brewing days.

The debut of this Roseville-based brewery in fall 2011 showcased two beers. The Patersbier is crisp with spiciness from its Belgian yeast, and the sessionable Pubstitute is low in strength but distinctive with its mahogany color and light dryness. Pour Decisions' brews are available on draft in the Twin Cities area. England and Haun hope to add a 16-ounce canning operation in the future.

HISTORY

Pour Decisions Brewing Company was established in 2011 by B. J. Haun and Kristen England. England is originally from Michigan and moved to the Twin Cities for graduate school at the University of Minnesota. After earning a PhD in pharmacology in 2007 he landed a position as a post-doctoral medical researcher at the university. England's home brewing hobby emerged in 2003, not long after arriving in the Gopher State. He also draws upon his travels to to Germany and Belgium. He even lived for over a year in Sweden. Before starting Pour Decisions England and his wife, Orsolya, had dreams of starting a brewery in her native Hungary. It's a dream that's been put on hold but one they hope to make happen someday.

England is very involved in the local home brew scene as a certified Beer Judge. That passion for understanding beer styles and their origins led him to volunteering as continuing education director for the Beer Judge Certification Program where he's made many contributions to style definitions and the professionalism of homebrewing. He even contributed to beer writer Stan Hieronymus's 2010 book *Brewing with Wheat*.

B.J. Haun, a Wisconsin native with a PhD in agronomy from the University of Wisconsin, came to the Twin Cities to work at a biotech company. An avid homebrewer since 2002, Haun has a number of brewing awards to his credit. In 2010 he took Best of Show at the Minnesota State Fair. That recipe is the basis for the brewery's Patersbier.

DON'T MISS THIS

The tasting room's bar is made from Minnesota cedar wood and was hand constructed by England and Haun. For those taking a tour, be sure to look around for the brewery's 2.5-barrel pilot system that allows England and Haun to make small batch specialty brews that you'll only find at the brewery.

POUR DECISIONS BREWS

Patersbier 🍺🍺🍺   *Your Ranking*_____

A Belgian golden ale. Begins with mild bready and spicy nose. An orange-golden color, very bubbly, and a soft off-white head. Medium bodied. Flavor offers some yeasty character with hints of orange fruitiness that combines with the spiciness of the Styrian Golding hops and a Belgian yeast. Finishes with a distinctive spiciness that give this beer a crisp overall impression. This beer was inspired by Kristen England's trips to Belgium where he toured the Brewery Der Trappisten Van Westmalle and was able to taste Westmalle Extra, a special beer made only for the monks. The term "Patersbier" is a reference to the "brothers" of the monastery.

The Pubstitute 🍺🍺🍺🍺   *Your Ranking*_____

This is a Scottish light ale, or approximately a 60 schilling Scottish ale. A very light malty nose. Mahogany color with reddish hues and a marbled tan head. Light to medium bodied. A mild but firm maltiness with hints of figs and plums. Finishes with light toffee tones and just a hint of hops in a faint dryness. A very sessionable brew at around 2.8 percent ABV. This beer is based on B. J. Haun's 2010 Best of Show winner at the Minnesota State Fair.

OTHER POUR DECISIONS BREWS YOU MAY WANT TO TRY

The Actress and the Bishop   *Your Ranking*_____

A bitter golden ale. The nose has hints of floral hoppiness and citrus tones. Clear golden color and a soft white head. Light to medium bodied and crisp. Initially the flavor begins with a malty sweetness that gives way to a mild, but firm, spicy and dry bitterness from the Brewers Gold hops. That spicy dry bitterness continues through the finish. The name is a reference to the common joke punchline, "Said the actress to the bishop."

Pour Decisions' Cask Beers   *Your Ranking*_____

England and Haun constantly have ideas about using oak barrels to age their beers, including, barrels that previously stored rum and gin. Ask about their limited release and special brews, especially the experiment batches created with their 2.5-barrel pilot brewing system.

MENU

None. Pour Decisions Brewing Company does not serve food.

OTHER THINGS TO SEE OR DO IN THE AREA

Roseville and Pour Decisions Brewing are just north of the Minnesota State Fairgrounds (1265 Snelling Avenue). The fair runs for twelve days from late August into early September. Other local activities include the Harriet Alexander Nature Center (2520 North Dale Street), which is part of the community's Central Park (Lexington Avenue North and West County Road C). It offers boardwalks and trails through fifty-two acres of marsh, prairie, and forest habitats. The Central Park also contains the Muriel Sahlin Arboretum, eight acres of gardens, paved walkways, and a fountain.

The Guidant John Rose Oval (2660 Civic Center Drive) is a unique outdoor recreation facility with 110,000 square feet of refrigerated ice from November to March. The Oval has a 400 meter speed skating track surrounding an infield area used for hockey. In the summer it's also popular among inline skaters and skateboarders. And, of course, the Rosedale Center offers abundant shopping and cinema opportunities.

The neighborhood surrounding Pour Decisions offers a number of great near-by beer venues. A few minutes east and north of Pour Decisions is Grumpy's Bar and Grill (2801 Snelling Avenue), which is frequented by local beer enthusiasts and is a place to look for a Pour Decisions brew along with a meal. Granite City Food and Brewery is located about a mile south at the Rosedale Center (Snelling and Highway 36). And Barley John's Brewpub (781 Old Highway 8 in New Brighton) is north and west about three miles.

BREWERY RATING

	Your Rating	Shepard's Rating	General Description
Location		🍺🍺	Located in a warehouse building in an industrial park.
Ease of Finding Location		🍺🍺🍺	Brewery is in an industrial neighborhood, just north of Rosedale Center. Following Snelling Avenue makes it pretty easy to find.
Brewery Atmosphere		🍺🍺🍺	A working brewery with lots of room to grow. The tasting room has a hand-made bar that adds personality and character to an otherwise nondescript warehouse.
Dining Experience	n/a		Not applicable.
The Pints		🍺🍺🍺	Not many beers initially, but expect new beers to be introduced as the brewery gains acceptance and fans. Small batch and special releases at the brewery make this a great stop on a Twin Cities brewery expedition.

DIRECTIONS

When traveling north on Snelling Avenue, watch for County Road C, which is approximately three quarters of a mile north of Highway 36 (Rosedale Center). Turn left (westward) on West County Road C at Rosebrook Park, and then take the first right (northward) on Lincoln Drive. After about a quarter of a mile, turn left (westward) on Terrace Drive. Pour Decisions is located about one-quarter of a mile west of the Lincoln Drive and Terrace Drive intersection on the south side of Terrace in a warehouse looking building. The brewery is the second from the last business space in the building. The Roseville water tower is another visible landmark that is located about a half-mile west of Pour Decisions Brewing Company.

Rock Bottom Restaurant and Brewery
Minneapolis

Visit Date	*Signed*

ABOUT THE BREWERY

Rock Bottom arrived in downtown Minneapolis in 1993, the third brewpub in the national chain that now numbers more than thirty. It is located on the ground floor of LaSalle Plaza, a skyscraper that also contains the Palomino restaurant, the downtown YMCA, several retail shops, and professional offices. One of the best seats in the house is actually outside the house; in the summer, Rock Bottom's sidewalk beer garden offers a place to eat and drink while enjoying all the sights and sounds of Hennepin Avenue and the Minneapolis theater district.

At Rock Bottom–Minneapolis, a striking long bar and two floors of brewhouse greet you as you walk through the main doors. The cold storage and serving vessels can be seen through windows, behind the main bar. Be sure to look up to see the second level of stainless steel fermenters. That mezzanine level is actually a hanging floor that required special modification to the building to support the weight of the fermenters. The restaurant has two areas of seating. In the main entry are the long bar, tables, and booths, along with various video games and pool tables. To the right of the bar is the dining room, with some window tables that look out over bustling Hennepin Avenue.

Rock Bottom has brewpubs in several other midwestern states: Illinois, Indiana, Iowa, Nebraska, Ohio, and Wisconsin. There is also a nonbrewing Rock Bottom at the Minneapolis–St. Paul International Airport. While you're likely to see some common themes in beer and food as you visit other Rock Bottoms, each one has its own chef and brewmaster who take local interests and flavors

95

seriously, so you'll find some unique approaches too. Rock Bottom also operates restaurants that go by other names, such as Old Chicago, ChopHouse, and Sing Sing dueling piano bars.

Almost all Rock Bottoms seem to offer a red ale or lager, a brown ale, a wheat, and a version of premium lager. Despite misperceptions among beer enthusiasts, Rock Bottom brewmasters are given the freedom to make brews unique to each location. Rock Bottom–Minneapolis will regularly have eight or more beers on tap. The North Star Lager is a big seller for the brewpub, but the Itasca Extra Pale Ale is a hoppy beer with just as serious a following. Brewmaster Bob McKenzie also offers a line of seasonal and cask-conditioned brews unique to this Rock Bottom. McKenzie makes stopping at this Rock Bottom special. His seasonal beers have included Belgians, pilsners, and hoppy American ales. The cask-conditioned hand pumps almost always feature a hoppy brew or two, and the brewpub offers special release beers in 750mL bottles.

HISTORY

The Rock Bottom restaurant chain is based in Colorado. Building on his successful brewpub formula at the Walnut Street Brewery in Boulder, owner Frank Day came up with the name Rock Bottom as he began the business venture in downtown Denver. The first Rock Bottom opened in 1991 in Denver's Prudential Insurance Company building (1001 Sixteenth Street). Playing on Prudential's slogan, "Own a Piece of the Rock," Day figured "Rock Bottom" was appropriate, given the brewpub's location on the ground floor of a building in the Mile High city.

Bob McKenzie, long-time brewer for the Minnesota-based Granite City chain of restaurants and brewpubs, took over the brewmaster responsibilities in April 2011. He replaced Bryon Tonnis who had been the Rock Bottom brewmaster since 2005. McKenzie is a native of Kirriemuir, Scotland, and his early brewery training includes schooling at Heriot-Watt University. He learned firsthand about Minnesota beer making and the taste preferences of local beer enthusiasts during six years of brewing with Bill Burdick at Sherlock's Home in Minnetonka. McKenzie left Sherlock's in 1999 to take the head brewer position with Granite City in St. Cloud (a business venture between Burdick and Granite City founder Steve Wagenheim). Much of McKenzie's work at Granite City involved making site visits and training local staff in quality control. That meant he rarely had the chance to directly brew in the St. Cloud brewhouse. After taking his new position at Rock Bottom McKenzie said, "I'm just lovin' it, it's great to be back in the brewery again, and making my beer!" What's more, if you listen closely you might just hear music coming from Rock Bottom's brewhouse — McKenzie is also known for his ability to play the bagpipes.

DON'T MISS THIS

Looking around the Minneapolis Rock Bottom you notice outdoor landscape photos and murals that are familiar from other Rock Bottom brewpubs. Interspersed among those pictures in its Minneapolis location, however, you'll want to look closely at the hanging T-shirts. The articles of clothing are signed by performers who have come into Rock Bottom for a beer after one of their shows in the nearby theatre district.

Also, as you walk up to Rock Bottom's main doors inside LaSalle Plaza, you can't help but notice an old hot liquor (water) tank that sits just outside the brewpub's main entrance. No one seems to know the background of this distinctive brewing artifact, but brewers admit that they have borrowed more than a few pieces of it when their equipment in the brewhouse has failed.

ROCK BOTTOM–MINNEAPOLIS'S BREWS

Bighorn Nut Brown 🍺🍺🍺🍺   *Your Ranking*_____
This is a good beer to watch for at Rock Bottom. A firm, inviting, malty nose. Beautiful chestnut color and a thick, soft, tan head. Medium to full bodied and soft. Nice caramel and chocolate malt tones. Finishes malty with a light roasted accent. Brewed with Belgian aromatic chocolate malt and Willamette hops.

El Jefe Hefe Weizen 🍺🍺🍺   *Your Ranking*_____
This Bavarian-style Hefeweizen has a strong banana aroma. Cloudy yellow color and a thick, soft, white head. Light bodied and crisp. Nice citrus and yeasty flavors with a subtly sour finish that builds. A light and crisp Hefeweizen. Rock Bottom–Minneapolis offers several different Hefeweizens throughout the year.

Erik the Red Lager 🍺🍺🍺🍺   *Your Ranking*_____
This Vienna-style lager is very clean. No nose. Brilliant, clear, reddish-amber color with a thick, bubbly, white head. Medium bodied and crisp. Firm caramel tones dominate with a light and slightly sweet, spicy finish. Made with Santiam hops. This is just a nice all-around choice.

Fantôme Wheat 🍺🍺🍺🍺   *Your Ranking*_____
This American wheat is aged in a Chardonney barrel. A light, sweet, grape-like nose. Clear, deep yellow color with a thin, off-white head. Medium bodied and smooth mouth feel. A sweet, fruity, and yeasty flavor. Finishes with a wine-like sweetness and some warmth. Sold in 750mL bottles.

Intoxicator Doppelbock 🍺🍺🍺🍺   *Your Ranking*_____
Its nose lets you know there will be a lot of caramel and chocolate malt. This Doppelbock is rich with a spicy underpinning of intense malt. A full-bodied beer. Malty sweetness dominates, with a light hint of roastedness in the finish. Made with 30-40 percent smoked German malts. A very flavorful big beer for Rock Bottom and one worth watching for in February. A smoked version of this beer goes by the name Intoxicator Rauchdoppelbock. Over the years it has also turned up as an oak-aged Intoxicator Rauchdoppelbock.

IPA 🍺🍺🍺🍺   *Your Ranking*_____
Resiny and piney nose. Yellow-golden and clear body with a thin, soft, tan head. Medium bodied and round texture. Strong piney bitterness from beginning to end with a firm malty backbone that gives some complexity to the bitterness. Bob McKenzie has redefined this hoppy Rock Bottom–Minneapolis brew and made its character very assertive if not aggressively bitter.

Itasca Extra Pale Ale 🍺🍺🍺   *Your Ranking_____*
A light hoppy nose. Cloudy copper body and a thick, soft, white head. Medium to full bodied and soft texture. Begins with a firm maltiness and very light fruity background. The hops build throughout. Finishes with light bitterness and some subtle smokiness. Brewed with pale and crystal malts. Itasca is a reference to Minnesota's oldest park.

Itasca Extra Pale Ale (dry hopped) 🍺🍺🍺🍺   *Your Ranking_____*
Assertive hoppy nose. Hazy, copper body and medium, soft, tan head. Medium to full bodied. More pronounced hoppiness from aroma throughout the finish.

Kölsch 🍺🍺🍺🍺   *Your Ranking_____*
A light grainy nose. Very clear golden color with a medium-soft white head. Light and bubbly mouth feel. A smooth, malty, grainy flavor. Clean finish with a light dryness. A light and refreshing Kölsch. Introduced by Bob McKenzie in summer 2011.

Modern Monk Dubbel 🍺🍺🍺   *Your Ranking_____*
This Belgian Dubbel is aged in Pinot Noir barrels for four months before it is tapped. Oak and vanilla nose. Brilliant bronze color with ruby tints, and a thin, off-white head. Full bodied and round mouth feel. Malty start to the taste, then sweet and grape-like fruitiness to the background and finish. Hints of plum, rasin, and oak in the end. Sold in 750mL bottles.

Newbiew Belgian IPA 🍺🍺🍺🍺   *Your Ranking_____*
The first Rock Bottom beer that brewmaster Bob McKenzie released after taking over the brewhouse in April 2011. The beer features all American hops with Centennial, Cascade, and Simcoe. It is fermented with a Belgian yeast. It begins with a light hoppy nose. The color is a hazy copper with a soft, tan head. Medium bodied and round mouth feel. A yeasty sweetness comes in early, but the hops win in the end with a sharp resiny crispness.

North Star Premium Lager 🍺   *Your Ranking_____*
This beer falls somewhere between an American lager and a European pilsner. No nose or aroma. Clear straw color and no head. Light body. Earthy sweetness. This beer just didn't seem to have enough flavor or body to taste and will challenge even light beer fans.

Piper's Finger Scottish Ale 🍺🍺🍺🍺   *Your Ranking_____*
A light roasted nose with just a hint of smoky-roasted malt. Deep clear bronze color and a soft, tan head. Medium bodied. Firm malty flavor with smooth caramel body. A faint smokiness to the malty finish. Served on a nitrogen tap line. The name reflects brewmaster Bob McKenzie's bagpipe playing abilities.

Rye Saison (dry hopped) 🍺🍺🍺   *Your Ranking_____*
Served on cask. A light yeasty nose with a faint hint of banana. Hazy golden color and a soft white head. Medium bodied, round and soft. A light fruity start to the flavor that slowly transitions to a dry bitterness that lingers into the finish. The dry ending really compliments the spicy yeasty beginning.

OTHER ROCK BOTTOM BREWS YOU MAY WANT TO TRY

Bastogne Blonde Ale   *Your Ranking*_____
Light golden color and very effervescent. This beer won a silver medal at the 2010 Great American Beer Festival in the Belgian- and French-Style Ale category. A limited release beer for Rock Bottom–Minneapolis.

Belgian Tripel   *Your Ranking*_____
One of Rock Bottom–Minneapolis's Signature Series sold in 750mL corked bottles. Deep golden color and full bodied. A smooth fruity sweetness with a light warmth in the finish.

Coconut Chai Stout   *Your Ranking*_____
An American stout with its own Zen-like character. Made with additions of coconut milk and spiced with a blend of chai (tea) spices.

Euro Trash Brunette   *Your Ranking*_____
An amber-brown ale. Malty and medium bodied.

Stillwater Stout   *Your Ranking*_____
Dark and full bodied with strong chocolate malt flavors. Made with 15 percent flaked oats that add roundness to the mouth feel. This oatmeal stout turns up three or four times a year.

White   *Your Ranking*_____
A hazy straw color Belgian Wit beer. Crisp and light.

MENU

The Rock Bottom menu features a full complement of salads, brick-oven pizzas, pub favorites, burgers, sandwiches, and pastas. Many selections offer a range of tastes, from hearty pub food to family-style choices. The menu features an "originals" section with mac and cheese, southwestern shrimp and chicken dishes, and short ribs. If you are in the mood for a steak, Rock Bottom has several methods of preparation. The Texas Fire Steak gets a dose of smokin' jalapeño butter, while the rib eye is seasoned and grilled to your preference. The ten or twelve appetizer choices include quesadilla rolls, Ball Park Pretzels brushed with brown ale, and Titan Toothpicks (tortillas stuffed with smoked chicken, Monterey Jack, and southwestern seasonings). Rock Bottom's Brewery Nachos can be a meal by itself. Elsewhere in the menu you'll find about a half-dozen salad choices, ranging from a Brewer's Cobb to the Chicken Waldorf with its sun-dried cranberries, grapes, and candied walnuts — a wonderful match for one of Rock Bottom's Hefeweizens. To finish off your visit to Rock Bottom don't overlook the dessert menu. The Triple Chocolate Stout Cheesecake is made with Rock Bottom beer.

OTHER THINGS TO SEE OR DO IN THE AREA

The Minnesota Twins call nearby Target Field home. The stadium opened in 2010 on Twins Way (formerly Third Avenue North). The area between Target Field and the Mississippi River is known as the Warehouse Entertainment District with bars, restaurants, and music venues. Another anchor of the Warehouse District is the Target Center, which is host to the Minnesota Timberwolves of the NBA. The NFL's Minnesota Vikings play in the Hubert H. Humphrey Metrodome (900 South Fifth Street), east of Rock Bottom.

Just walking in this area offers many possibilities for shopping and entertainment. And in poor weather, the skywalk system connects many things, including LaSalle Plaza (of which Rock Bottom is part), so you need not ever venture outside. One of the major landmarks for shopping is Nicollet Mall, a twelve-block pedestrian and transit mall in the heart of downtown Minneapolis with many restaurants and shops. As you walk the mall outside be sure to look for the legendary hat-tossing statue of Mary Tyler Moore, made famous in the opening scene of the 1970s television show that was set in Minneapolis.

The Hennepin Theatre Trust operates the historic State, Orpheum, and Pantages theaters, which entertain more than half a million people each year. The Hennepin Center for the Arts (528 Hennepin Avenue) provides offices and performance space for many local arts organizations, including Ballet Arts Minnesota, James Sewell Ballet, Minnesota Dance Theatre, and the Minnesota Chorale. The Minneapolis Institute of Arts (2400 Third Avenue South) has exhibits from all over the world. Nearby, the award-winning Hennepin History Museum (2303 Third Avenue South) focuses on the diverse range of cultures and social histories of the area. If you enjoy art, the Walker Art Center (1750 Hennepin Avenue) and Minneapolis Sculpture Garden also make an excellent day trip.

BREWERY RATING

	Your Rating	Shepard's Rating	General Description
Location		🍺🍺🍺🍺	A great location in downtown Minneapolis offers ample opportunities for shopping and entertainment.
Ease of Finding Location		🍺🍺🍺	Traffic and parking can be problematic. One-way streets add to the challenge. But scoping out the parking ramps ahead of time reduces the stress. However, this is an area where public transportation options exist and should be considered.
Brewery Atmosphere		🍺🍺	Located in the LaSalle Plaza. Lots of space for dining. Parts of the brewery can be seen behind and above the bar.
Dining Experience		🍺🍺🍺	Pub fare to family-style offerings.
The Pints		🍺🍺🍺	A good experience. The core beers here are well done and there's always a special seasonal that makes repeat visits very rewarding.

DIRECTIONS

From I-94/35W, take exit 233, then turn left (northwestward) merging onto Eleventh Street South. After about a half-mile (eight blocks), turn right (northeastward) onto Hennepin Avenue. Rock Bottom will be about two blocks ahead at the corner of Hennepin and Ninth Street South in the Palomino Building (LaSalle Plaza). Several parking lots are close by, between Ninth and Tenth streets on Hennepin, and the nearby Target Center.

If you want to use commuter rail, the Hiawatha line has stations close by. Just walk up to Fifth Street and you'll have choices of platforms in the Warehouse District, along Nicollet Mall, or west to Target Field. All are within a half-mile. The Target Field station also connects to the Northstar commuter rail service, which reaches northern and western parts of the city.

Rock Bottom is also just a few blocks away from Fulton Brewery (414 6th Avenue, North).

Steel Toe Brewing
St. Louis Park

ABOUT THE BREWERY

Steel Toe Brewing is the dream of a former machinist turned brewmaster. Jason Schoneman, an Iowa native who was a tool maker for the John Deere and Caterpillar companies making custom parts and running automated machines. In the late 1990s he discovered homebrewing and a love of beer that only grew stronger with skiing and snowboarding trips to Colorado where he also experienced the craft brew culture of the Rocky Mountains. By 2001, he had left his job in heavy equipment manufacturing and taken a job at brewery in Montana.

After working his way through different brewery jobs Schoneman eventually decided to create his own brewery. To make his dream come true he turned to the skills he had gained from a career in custom machining and fabricated much of his own brewery equipment. Then, when it came time to name his brewery he remembered that feeling he got at the end of a long day when he was able to shed the heavy steel toe boots, grab a beer, and just kick back. And that became the inspiration behind the name—Steel Toe Brewing.

Schoneman released his first beers in late summer of 2011. Most of his distribution is through local draft accounts. However, he sells growlers and special limited releases at the brewery's small tasting room. Steel Toe's core brews include a Golden Ale, Double Red, Oatmeal Stout, and IPA. Schoneman also offers occasional seasonals and bourbon barrel–aged beers.

HISTORY

While owner Jason Schoneman has lots of experience as a machinist he also has an impressive brewing résumé. Before opening Steel Toe Brewing in 2011 Schoneman had accumulated more than a dozen years of experience in making beer. When his wife Hannah's job took them to Montana, Jason first found work at the former Lightening Boy Brewery in Belgrade. Seeing the potential for a career, Schoneman then took a diploma brewing course at the Siebel Institute of Technology in 2005. As part of that work he spent two weeks learning brewing techniques firsthand from German brewers in Gräfelfing near Munich. From 2005 to 2009 he worked at the Pelican Pub and Brewery in Oregon, beginning as a cellar man and rising to head brewer. After leaving the Pelican in 2009 Schoneman arrived in the Twin Cities and began planning his own brewery.

Steel Toe began taking shape in summer 2011. Schoneman relied on many of his skills as a tool maker to build what he needed and to assemble the brewhouse in the 6,000-square-foot building that was once used by a metal fabricator. His brewkettle was once a culture tank used in cheese processing, the mash tun is a former bulk milk tank, and his hot and cold liquor tanks are also former dairy equipment. He did find three fermenters and a bright tank in a brewpub called Otto's Pub and Brewery in State College, Pennsylvania. Once he saw them advertised on the internet, Schoneman didn't waste any time because he knew they wouldn't be for sale long. Taking some chance on the cold February weather he arrived in Pennsylvania on a Wednesday, immediately made an offer, and three days later the tanks were in Minnesota.

While Schoneman is the first "commercial" brewer in his family, he's not the first to make beer. He says his father likes to tell stories of his mother (Jason's grandmother, August Schoneman) who would make beer in the 1930s on the family farm near Aplington, Iowa, for the field hands. Perhaps not too surprisingly, Jason's grandmother was of a German descent.

Schoneman's ancestory combined with his time studying in Germany motivates him to showcase German beer styles in his own brewery. Before opening Steel Toe, a friend whose father owned a brewery in Pennsylvania gave Jason several old pre-1900 beer recipes that were written in German. Schoneman figures they may have been handed down from German brewers. So as his own brewery grows he plans to translate them so he can incorporate them into his own brews.

DON'T MISS THIS

Steel Toe Brewing is a metal worker's dream. Much of the equipment came from dairy farms in Wisconsin. The brew kettle was once a bulk tank used to make cheese, and the mash tun was a former bulk milk tank that was used on a dairy farm.

STEEL TOE BREWS

Dissent 🍺🍺🍺 *Your Ranking_____*

This dark ale has a roasted nose and deep dark bronze to black color. Full bodied with a light silky mouth feel from additions of flaked oats to the grist. Lots of chocolate maltiness and roasted flavors. Named because it doesn't easily fit into a standard style and sets its own standard for what you might perceive a dark beer should be. A special find for a dark beer that is flavorful but with some balance.

Provider 🍺🍺🍺🍺   *Your Ranking*_____
This golden ale begins with a light graining nose. A hazy light golden color. Bubbly and light bodied. Clean, crisp and well balanced flavor. The first commercial beer released by Steel Toe.

Size 7 🍺🍺🍺   *Your Ranking*_____
An IPA with a pale golden color and strong hoppy character. Made with three different hops. Starts with a piney hoppiness aroma. Medium to full bodied. An assertive resiney flavor from start to finish. Gets its name from its 77 IBUs and 7 percent ABV. The second beer made by Steel Toe.

OTHER STEEL TOE BREWS YOU MAY WANT TO TRY

Bourbon Barrel Barley Wine   *Your Ranking*_____
Bold and assertively malty. Watch for this beer as a special release.

Rainmaker   *Your Ranking*_____
A double red ale. Assertive hoppy aroma, medium bodied and moderate bitterness. Hints of roastedness in the background and finish. Brewmaster and owner Jason Schoneman named this beer out of his love for a Colorado mountain bike trail with the same name.

MENU

None. Steel Toe Brewing Company does not serve food.

OTHER THINGS TO SEE OR DO IN THE AREA

St. Louis Park is immediately west of downtown Minneapolis. The community has been home to such notable figures as movie directors Joel and Ethan Coen along with Joe Nussbaum. New York Times columnist Thomas Friedman, Senator Al Franken and baseball announcer Halsey Hall also called this Minneapolis suburb home. By the way, the Coen brothers set their 2009 film, *A Serious Man*, in St. Louis Park.

The Pavek Museum of Broadcasting (3517 Raleigh Avenue) is located in St. Louis Park. It contains one of the world's finest collection of antique radios, televisions, and broadcasting equipment. Also nearby is the Bakken Museum (3537 Zenith Avenue, South) that offers electrifying exhibits and artifacts on the history of electricity.

If you enjoy biking the Cedar Lake Regional Trail connects St. Louis Park with downtown Minneapolis. It's considered America's first bicycle freeway with three lanes for most of its length that allows two lanes for bikes and a third lane for two-way pedestrian traffic. The trail is located less than a block north of Steel Toe Brewing. Also nearby is Wolfe Park that provides great walking, hiking and picnicking opportunities. The park has an amphitheater that hosts plays and concerts in the summer.

St. Louis Park is also home to Granite City Food and Brewery (5500 Excelsior Boulevard). Another excellent beer venue is McCoy's Public House (3801 Grand Way) in the Excelsior and Grand Development neighborhood. Local homebrewers will also recognize the neighborhood as home to Midwest Homebrew Supplies (5825 Excelsior Boulevard) and the Four Firkins (8009 Minnetonka Boulevard), a specialty beer store.

BREWERY RATING

	Your Rating	Shepard's Rating	General Description
Location		🍺🍺🍺	Located in a multiuse building. The proximity to Midwest Homebrewing Supplies makes for a great combo-stop!
Ease of Finding Location		🍺🍺🍺🍺	Easy to find.
Brewery Atmosphere		🍺🍺	Located in basic industrial warehouse with high ceilings.
Dining Experience		n/a	Not applicable.
The Pints		🍺🍺🍺	To sample beers in the brewery is a special treat. One can't help but appreciate the hand-crafted nature of the beer and the metal fabrication skills of owner/brewer Jason Schoneman.

DIRECTIONS

When traveling north or south on Highway 100 take the West 36th Street exit and travel eastward on West 36th Street. A couple of lights past Highway 100, turn left (north) on Raleigh Avenue. Raleigh Avenue will become West 35th Street. Steel Toe Brewery will be located on the left (north) side of the road in a small tan building with green awnings. The St. Louis Park water tower is a visible landmark to watch for.

Stillwater Brewing Company
Stillwater

STILLWATER BREWING COMPANY

ABOUT THE BREWERY

This small brewery is located on the northern edged of the Stillwater's historic downtown. Beer enthusiasts Zachary Morgan and Justin Stanley started the brewery in 2011 in a building that contributes to that local history. The Stillwater Brewing Company is located in the Isaac Staples Sawmill Building. The structure dates back to the mid-nineteenth century and is one of the oldest buildings in Stillwater. It was once at the center of a thriving lumber business belonging to Staples, who at the time was one of the area's most successful businessmen. Staples purchased a local mill for just $15,000, and from there he grew his business to include the saw mill, lumberyard and later a flour mill along the St. Croix riverfront. Isaac Staples was one of Minnesota's first millionaires.

The Stillwater Brewing Company is a little different than most of Minnesota's beer makers. Morgan and Stanley have an agreement with a retired brewmaster who makes wort for them at a faculty in North Carolina. About once a week the wort is prepared and shipped overnight in four 50-pound containers. Once it arrives at the brewery it goes into one of two tanks and then, depending upon the style, specific yeast and hops are added. When the yeast gets added, that's when it actually starts turning into beer.

Morgan and Stanley don't consider themselves direct competitors with larger commercial brewers; rather they take pride in being small, efficient and supplying the local Stillwater community. Their brewery's location being in the downtown, and in the Isaac Staples Building, makes it part of the local tourism and shopping draw that Stillwater is well known for.

Stillwater Brewing Company offers about a half-dozen regular beers that are sold in half-gallon growlers, and 7.5-gallon KeyKegs. The Keykeg system is a one-way disposable keg that the brewery distributes to local bars and taverns. Once empty, the used KeyKeg can be disposed of with other plastic recyclables. The KeyKegs used by Stillwater Brewing are about the size of a quarter-barrel.

HISTORY

The Stillwater Brewing Company made its first beer in 2011. It joins a list of historic beer makers in Stillwater's past. During the nineteenth century there were last three breweries located around today's downtown district. Norbert Kimmick is recognized as one of the earliest Stillwater brewers. Kimmick started his brewery around 1851, and it later became the Frank Aiple brewery that operated until 1896. Gerhard Knips also started brewery in the late 1850s and it would become the St. Croix Brewing Company until it closed in 1877. The Wolf Brewery operated from 1869 until Prohibition.

At today's Stillwater Brewing Company Zachary Morgan is part owner and head brewer. Morgan who grew up in Milton, West Virginia moved to Minnesota in 2005 when he met his wife, Anne, who is a Minnesota Native. When not making beer, Zachary works for the Archdiocese and Cathedral of St. Paul. In addition to helping with the brewery's record keeping Anne is an oncology nurse. Zach and Anne live in nearby White Bear Lake. Co-Owner Justin Stanley also helps with brewing and with distribution. Stanley is also originally from Milton, West Virginia where he and Zach grew up less than a mile from each other as were boyhood friends. In 2010 Stanley moved to Minnesota from Florida where he had been working as the Executive Director for the Deaf and Hard of Hearing Services.

DON'T MISS THIS

When touring Stillwater Brewing take note of a couple of features. The brewery's bar is actually made from a former grain bin. You might also notice artwork from local artists on some of the brewery's walls. But an even closer observation of the brewery's two fermentation tanks revels that they are labeled with names from Greek Mythology—Charybdis and Scylla, a reference to the poem Odyssey. The legend tells of a narrow channel of water off the coast of Sicily where on one side was a giant whirlpool caused by a sea monster named Charybdis. On the opposite side of the straits lived another creature called Scylla who was also was recognized for an equally deadly whirlpool. Sailors navigating the challenging waters had to choose their fate, or poison, between Charybdis and Scylla. Ironically, that a story greatly appreciated by brewery owners Justin Stanley who happens to have an undergraduate degree in classic literature, and Zachary Morgan who has a degrees in English literature, theology and philosophy.

STILLWATER BREWS

Annie's Honey Bier 🍺🍺   *Your Ranking*_____
A seasonal beer offered in March through May. Based on the Czech Pilsner style of beer, and made with clover honey. A light floral nose. Hazy yellow-straw color with a thick, soft, white head. Light bodied. Named after Anne Morgan, the wife of owner Zachary Morgan.

Betram's Pale Ale 🍺🍺🍺🍺   *Your Ranking*_____
This is an American pale ale made with Hallertau, Crystal, and Cascade hops. A citrus and spicy nose with a bright golden color. Medium to full bodied. Citrus bitterness with a light malty finish offer some balance to the beer. Named after Zachary Morgan's father.

Big Mike D's Nut Brown 🍺🍺🍺   *Your Ranking*_____
Light malty nose with an amber to bronze color. Medium bodied and session-like. A malty finish. Made with toasted oats and also additions of vanilla extract that provides a light toasty aroma and finish. A beer named after Zachary Morgan's Father-in-Law.

Black Tie Ale 🍺🍺🍺   *Your Ranking*_____
A light earthy-malty nose. Hazy copper color with a thin, bubbly, off-white head. Medium bodied. Smooth caramel maltiness. A light malty finish. This amber ale is made just one time each year. All of the proceeds go to Valley Outreach Food Shelf, a local food pantry serving the Stillwater area.

James T's Red Wheat 🍺🍺   *Your Ranking*_____
This was the first beer made by Morgan and Stanley when they opened Stillwater Brewing in 2011. The beer is named after Justin Stanley's father. It's made with 50 percent red wheat that adds to the beer's malty nose and medium body. It's dry hopped with Mt. Hood hops. A floral nose. Vivid reddish amber color with a thin tan head. Medium bodied and bubbly. Finishes with a light yeasty sweetness.

OTHER STILLWATER BREWS YOU MAY WANT TO TRY

Estafeta IPA   *Your Ranking*_____
An IPA made with seven different hops, include Centennial, Millennium and Warrior that go into the drop hopping process. This beer is named for the street in Pamplona, Spain where the running of the bulls takes place. The beer's label features Justin Stanley watching the bulls.

Frat Boy Pilsner   *Your Ranking*_____
A light bodied golden beer. Based on the Czech Pilsner style, and very similar to Annie's Honey Bier in its appearance. A hint of malty aroma, golden-straw color, and crisp light flavor.

Hoptoberfest   *Your Ranking*_____
A fall seasonal made with eight different hops.

Mountaineer's Summer Wheat   *Your Ranking*_____

A Belgian Wit beer released for summer. It offers hints of apricot and raspberry in the flavor profile. The beer pays homage to the mountains of West Virginia where company founders Zach Morgan and Justin Stanley grew up.

Padre's Porter   *Your Ranking*_____

A bold, dark porter made for winter. The beer is a tribute to the Franciscan Friar that married Zach and Ann Morgan. On the label you'll find a picture of the Priest smoking to cigars at once while drinking a black ale.

MENU

None. Stillwater Brewing Company does not serve food.

OTHER THINGS TO SEE OR DO IN THE AREA

The river front and downtown Stillwater offer many shops, galleries, restaurants and antique stores. Stillwater holds a number of festivals throughout the year. Especially of interest to the beer enthusiasts is the Brewers Bazaar held in conjunction with the Rivertown Art Festival in May. Other community events include Lumberjack Days in July, and the Fall Colors Fine Art and Jazz Festival in early October. Many of the community festivals occur in Lowell Park that is adjacent to the St. Croix River. If you enjoy taking in public parks, just across the street (to the north) from Stillwater Brewing Company is Pioneer Park that was once part of the Isaac Staples' estate.

Stillwater is sometimes referred to as the birthplace of Minnesota because in 1848 it hosted a territorial convention that helped establish it as a territory in 1849 and eventually a state in 1858. For those who enjoy retracing the history of the area, the Washington County Courthouse is well worth exploring. It's a two-story structure was built in 1867-70, that served as the judicial center of the county for more than a century. In 1971 the building was placed on the National Register of Historic Places as the oldest standing count house in Minnesota. Also, the Washington County Historical Society maintains the Warden's House Museum (602 North Main) that was once living quarters to the 13 wardens who ran the territorial prison. Inside, visitors will see examples of tools, clothing and Civil War artifacts. The Stillwater Deport, Logging and Rail Museum (601 Main Street) features a twenty-eight foot tall atrium with logging railroad exhibits.

Stillwater was home to several breweries in the nineteenth century. You can get an idea what beer making was like before Prohibition by visiting the Joseph Wolf Brewery (402 South Main Street), which operated from 1869 to 1919. What is left of the brewery is now a restaurant (Luna Rosa), but the brewery's lagering caves are available for tours.

BREWERY RATING

	Your Rating	Shepard's Rating	General Description
Location		🍺🍺🍺🍺	Located on the northern edge of downtown Stillwater's historic district. Near lots of shops, antique stores, places to eat, and lodging. Also near the St. Croix River.
Ease of Finding Location		🍺🍺🍺🍺	Easy to find.
Brewery Atmosphere		🍺🍺	Located in the Isaac Staples Sawmill Building. The brewery itself is very small by all standards.
Dining Experience		n/a	Not applicable.
The Pints		🍺🍺	Stillwater Brewing reflects the hearts and minds of a pair of dedicated homebrewers. While their beers are good, their system is small and presents some challenges in keeping up with demands. Very much worth a tour and a growler. While one can sample and buy on site, to fully enjoy you'll have to take home a growler or KeyKeg.

DIRECTIONS

Stillwater is located about twenty-five miles east of downtown St. Paul. When approaching from I-94, take exit 258 (Minnesota 95). Travel northward for about seven miles into downtown Stillwater. When approaching from Highway 36, the brewery is about one and a half miles north of where Highway 36 intersects with Highway 95. Stillwater Brewing is located in the Isaac Staples Sawmill Building, approximately four blocks north of the city's iconic lift bridge.

Summit Brewing Company
St. Paul

Visit Date _____   Signed _____

ABOUT THE BREWERY

Summit Brewing is the bastion of Twin Cities brewing. Founded in 1984 by Mark Stutrud, the first beers established the company in the local market-place in 1986. Initially, Summit beers were all self-distributed by Stutrud himself. Through those early years Summit Brewing persevered at a time when many bigger breweries consolidated or gave up. The personal determination of Stutrud set a Midwest standard for craft brewing and it showed many smaller brewers success was possible — but it wasn't easy. Today, Summit is viewed as a regional leader in the industry and produces over 100,000 barrels annually.

After a dozen years of slow and steady growth Stutrud broke ground on a new facility in 1997 in a business park south of downtown St. Paul along the banks of the Mississippi River. Its distinctive three-story building stands out with its green arched roof and Summit logo. The first floor has large windows, some of which illuminate the brewhouse at night for an inspiring view of the copper-clad brew kettles that Stutrud rescued from a German brewery.

The reception area of the building offers great views of the brewhouse controls and the brewhouse itself. This area is often the site of public gatherings and special events at Summit, and a wonderful old bar serves as a focus for tours and tastings. The gift shop is in a small room to the right of the main entry.

Summit turns out more than a dozen different beers throughout the year. While it distributes to a number of Midwest states, over 90 percent of its beer stays in Minnesota and most of that right in the Twin Cities. Among the very popular year-round offerings are the Pilsner, Great Northern Porter, Horizon Red Ale, and India Pale Ale. A few of Summit's seasonal releases consist of well-done German-styles such as Maibock, Hefeweizen, and Oktoberfest. In 2009 the brewery started its Unchained Series of limited release beers. Each brew is a unique signature of one of the Summit brewers who get to choose the style and recipe themselves and get to put their name on the label. The brewery only releases a few of these each year. The first in the series was a Kölsch, followed by a Scottish-style ale, then an India rye ale. Others have included a Belgian-style golden ale and an imperial pumpkin porter. There's no promise that what's been made will be made again. The beers that become part of the Unchained Series reflect the choices and creativity of the brewers themselves and as such are often looked upon as one-time brews.

HISTORY

Summit owner Mark Stutrud, a native of North Dakota, moved to St. Paul in 1980 and worked as a clinical social worker for St. Mary's Hospital. By the mid-1980s he started thinking about other career options. As a homebrewer at the time he admits he had fantasized about building a brewery. After spending vacations volunteering and getting to know a number of brewers personally, his dream started to become reality. By 1984 he was developing a business plan and doing market research, and soon he left his day job at the hospital.

In building Summit, Stutrud was mentored by such industry insiders as Charlie McElevey, who worked as a master brewer and engineer for Seattle's Red Hook Brewery; Bill Newman from the William S. Brewing Company in Albany, New York; and Fred Thomasser, who first got into brewing in 1934 and went on to work for a number of New York breweries. Thomasser is well-known locally because he was the last brewmaster for the Jacob Schmidt Brewing Company; his grandson Tom is the chief officer of operations for Summit.

Stutrud started Summit with advice from McElevey, Newman, and Thomasser, but he also took a number of short-courses from the Siebel Institute of Technology and World Brewing Academy in the 1980s. He completed Siebel's diploma course in 1991.

As a company, Summit's constant growth is reflected in dramatic expansions. When it began, its first brewhouse relied extensively on second-hand brewing equipment from a small brewery called Brauerei Zum Hirsch of Heimertingen, Germany. That brewery had made beer for more than three hundred years. Stutrud traveled to Heimertingen and personally oversaw the deconstruction of the equipment and had it shipped to St. Paul.

The original location of Summit was at 2264 University Avenue in a building that had once been used as an auto parts warehouse. With some financial assistance from St. Paul's Home Grown Economy Project, much of 1986 was spent renovating that building. In the summer of that year Stutrud was making test batches and working on recipes. His first release on September 25 was Summit Extra Pale Ale, and his first keg was sold to Johnny's Bar, which was located directly across the street. Today, Extra Pale Ale remains the company's bestseller and flagship brew.

Within a year business was good enough for the brewery to add its first bottling line. By 1993 its original location on University Avenue was expanded to a nearby dwelling—which required the construction of a 250-foot pipeline for transfer of beer between buildings. It was in 1998 that Summit moved to the Montreal Circle location. In 2001 and 2002 more equipment was added, including included a whirlpool water system, three fermenters, and a 300-barrel bright tank. Another round of expansion happened in 2010 when three new fermenters were also added, bringing the total of fermentation and bright vessels to over thirty tanks in the cellar area of the brewery. Until one takes a walking tour it's difficult to have a true understanding of the brewery's size and it's potential for growth.

Visitors taking brewery tours gather in the hospitality area where the large copper-clad brew kettles provide an inspirational starting point. Like Summit's first smaller brewery, these kettles also came from Germany. They were once used by the Hurnerbraü Brewery of Ansbach. Stutrud had to have them cut into sections so they could be loaded onto a container ship and brought to the U.S. They remained in storage for nearly two years while the new brewery was being built.

When asked how he came up with the name "Summit" for his brewery, Stutrud laughs, "It's a helluva lot easier for people to pronounce that my last name!" The brewery's name not so coincidentally relates well to St. Paul's Summit Avenue, which connects to the downtown and has a four-mile stretch that claims to have more restored Victorian homes than any other boulevard in the U.S.

DON'T MISS THIS

The ornate old bar in the corner of the reception area that serves as a starting and ending point for Summit tours. Company founder and president Mark Stutrud discovered the bar in a Minnesota antique store. It's believed to have originated in southern Minnesota.

SUMMIT'S BREWS

Extra Pale Ale  *Your Ranking*_____

Summit's flagship beer. Begins with a light hoppy nose. A deep copper color and a thick, bubbly, white head. Medium bodied and soft texture. The firm, mild, hoppy beginning grows into a long-lasting bitter finish. This British-style pale ale has been brewed at Summit since 1986 and was Summit's first commercial beer. Made with Horizon, Fuggle, and Cascade hops. Malts include Harrington and Caramel. Winner of a bronze medal at the 2007 and 2008 Great American Beer Festivals, a silver medal at the 2010 Great American Beer Festival, and a gold medal at the 2010 World Beer Cup.

ESB (Extra Special Bitter) 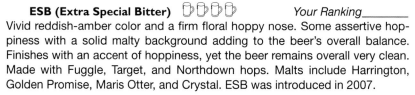 *Your Ranking*_____

Vivid reddish-amber color and a firm floral hoppy nose. Some assertive hoppiness with a solid malty background adding to the beer's overall balance. Finishes with an accent of hoppiness, yet the beer remains overall very clean. Made with Fuggle, Target, and Northdown hops. Malts include Harrington, Golden Promise, Maris Otter, and Crystal. ESB was introduced in 2007.

Great Northern Porter 🍺🍺🍺🍺   *Your Ranking*_____

A light malty nose. Deep, dark color and a thick, bubbly, brown head. Medium bodied and sharp texture. Light caramel start with a firm but mild chocolate background. A light, sweet, roasted ending. This porter is well done and matches especially well with a cold Minnesota winter. The second beer made by Summit, introduced in 1987. Made with Horizon, Fuggle, and Cascade hops. Malts include Harrington, Caramel, and a dehusked Carafa malt that intensifies the aroma and dark color. A gold medal winner at the 1987 Great American Beer Festival and a bronze medal winner at the 2002 World Beer Cup. This is an exceptional beer.

Hefe Weizen 🍺🍺🍺🍺   *Your Ranking*_____

This German-style Hefeweizen has an aromatic, fruity nose. Cloudy golden color with a thin, white head. Light bodied. The body offers a fruity citrus flavor. A slightly spicy ending. Made with Willamette, Fuggle, and Tettnanger hops alongside Harrington and wheat malts.

Horizon Red Ale 🍺🍺🍺   *Your Ranking*_____

Introduced as a regular Summit beer in 2010. Made with two-row pale, caramel, cara-red, wheat, and black malts and Horizon, Amarillo, Cascade, and Summit hops. Assertive, hoppy nose. Deep reddish-amber color with a thick, tan head. Medium bodied. A sharp, somewhat spicy combination of malt and hops. Medium bitter finish.

India Pale Ale 🍺🍺🍺   *Your Ranking*_____

A year-round beer with a distinctive, assertive, hoppy nose. Reddish-amber color with a tan, bubbly head. Medium to full bodied and crisp, even sharp texture. A distinctive, strong, dry bitterness throughout the main body of taste, coupled with a long-lasting hoppy finish. Brewed with Northern Brewer, East Kent Golding, Warrior, and U.S. Golding hops, then dry-hopped with whole flower East Kent Golding.

Maibock 🍺🍺🍺🍺   *Your Ranking*_____

A spring seasonal for Summit. Malty nose, a clear copper body with a thin, soft, white head. Medium bodied and soft texture. Sweet, warm, caramel flavors dominate. Finishes with a smooth warmth. Overall, smooth and malty. Brewed with Czechoslovakian Saaz and Mt. Hood hops, along with Harrington and Munich malts. Fermented with German lager yeast. This beer has also been called Heimertingen Maibock, for the town in Germany that Summit's original brewing equipment came from.

Oatmeal Stout 🍺🍺🍺🍺   *Your Ranking*_____

Also called "Boadicea." Begins with a light roasted malty nose. Rich dark black color and a thick, marbled, brown head. Medium to full bodied and soft. Smooth chocolate maltiness from beginning to end. This is a sweet stout with caramel, chocolate, and coffee accents. A limited release beer found on a beer engine. A beer worth seaking out for those who enjoy a wonderful oatmeal stout.

Oktoberfest 🍺🍺🍺   *Your Ranking_____*

A fall seasonal brew for Summit. This is a caramelly Oktoberfest. Initially has a light roasted nose that gives way to a firm maltiness. A clear reddish-bronze color with a thick, soft, white head. Medium bodied and smooth texture. Firm, strong caramel flavors. Finishes malty with a hint of warmth from its 7.2 percent ABV. The beer gets its great balance from Harrington and Caramel Munich malts and Northern Brewer, Tettnanger, and Saaz hops. A bronze medal winner at the 2003 Great American Beer Festival.

Pilsner 🍺🍺🍺🍺   *Your Ranking_____*

A Czech-style pilsner with a firm hoppy aroma and rich golden color that showcases Horizon, Vanguard, and Saaz hops. Malts include Moravian 37 and Caramel. Medium bodied, crisp with a light hoppy finish. The Moravian malt comes from barley grown on the North Dakota farm of brewery owner Mark Stutrud's cousin.

Silver Anniversary Ale 🍺🍺🍺🍺   *Your Ranking_____*

A special brew made in 2011 to celebrate Summit's twenty-fifth anniversary. The beer was inspired by Summit's Extra Pale Ale (EPA), the first beer offered by brewery owner and brewmaster Mark Stutrud. It's hoppy, even a touch more so than the EPA, with a crisp and sharp bitterness. It's made with Cascade, Centennial, and Citra hops that provide the basis of its 80 IBUs. Malts include 2-row Harrington and Crystal. A hoppy-floral nose. Clear copper color and a thick, soft, white head. There is a sharp citrus hoppiness throughout, with a firm malty backbone. The finish is dry and crisp. Also watch for this beer on cask, which softens and rounds out the flavor while still offering that crisp hoppy bite and dry finish.

Winter Ale 🍺🍺🍺🍺   *Your Ranking_____*

A great winter warmer for those cold Minnesota nights. Malty nose. A burgundy-colored body with a thick, bubbly, tan head. Full bodied. Malty with a spicy background and finish. Winter Ale is 6.2 percent ABV. Made with Willamette, Fuggle, and Tettnanger hops. Malts include Harrington, Caramel, and Carafa.

OTHER SUMMIT BREWS YOU MAY WANT TO TRY

Düsseldorfer-style Alt Bier   *Your Ranking_____*

A fall seasonal. Copper colored, rich, malty, and somewhat dry.

Scandia Ale   *Your Ranking_____*

A summer-time seasonal. A cloudy, light golden color. Spicy notes of cardamom, coriander, and bitter orange make this a refreshing beer. Made with Saaz hops. Added to the Summit lineup in 2007.

Scottish Style Ale—Unchained Series   *Your Ranking_____*

A smooth earthy and smoky nose. Deep rich mahogany color with a soft, tan head. Lots of caramel malt body with a light herbal background and finish. Made with Target and Willamette hops, along with heather. This was the second beer in the Unchained Series, a 90 shilling Wee Heavy from brewer Eric

Blomquist. The first in the series was a Kölsch from the hands of Mike "the Miz" Miziorko.

MENU

None. Summit Brewing does not serve food.

OTHER THINGS TO SEE OR DO IN THE AREA

The Mississippi River channel is just beyond the Summit brewery (southward). Along the river are a number of parks and hiking and biking opportunities. About five miles southwest of Summit is Fort Snelling State Park (junction of Minnesota highways 5 and 55, just east of the Minneapolis–St. Paul International Airport). At the restored 1820s military outpost you'll experience the sights of the fortress, the sounds of musket fire and cannons, and military drills and crafts demonstrations by costumed guides. Also in the park is Pike Island, named for Lieutenant (later General) Zebulon M. Pike, who here in 1805 purchased from the Dakota Indians the tract on which the fort was built in 1820–24.

Fort Snelling is at the confluence of the Minnesota and Mississippi rivers, an area called Mendota (the Sioux word for "meeting of the waters"). You can visit the Sibley House and take a ninety-minute walk through the historic village of Mendota. One of Minnesota's oldest towns, Mendota emerged from an early nineteenth-century fur-trading center. The Henry H. Sibley house (1357 Sibley Memorial Highway) was built in 1838 for Minnesota's first governor (1858–60). Sibley was also a manager of the American Fur Company between 1825 and 1853. Next door is the Jean Baptiste Fairbault house, built in 1839. Both houses offer tours.

Less than half a mile up the Mississippi River is Hidden Falls–Crosby Farm Regional Park (Shepard Road and Mississippi River Boulevard) with hiking and biking trails, picnic areas, nature center, and marina. Across the river on the west bank is Minnehaha Park Falls (intersection of Hiawatha Avenue and Minnehaha Parkway). This is one of the oldest parks in Minneapolis, and it includes a fifty-three-foot waterfall, limestone bluffs, and river overlooks. Near Minnehaha Park is Mississippi River Lock and Dam No. 1, where you can watch large boats and barges navigate the river. Some of the best views of the area are found at Cherokee Park (Cherokee Heights Boulevard and Smith Avenue), which offers a panoramic view from the bluffs overlooking the river. Riverboat captains used the confluence of the Minnesota and Mississippi rivers as a major landmark and called it Pilot Knob. That point of land nearly became the site of the territorial capital.

If you enjoy golf, Highland National Golf Course (Montreal Avenue and Edgcumbe Road) is nearby. A few miles south of Summit Brewing, the Minnesota Valley National Wildlife Refuge (3815 American Boulevard East, Bloomington) offers insights into the Minnesota River and its valley. The refuge has many options for tours and interpretive exhibits, an art gallery, and a short trail loop for walking.

If you are looking for indoor activity, a landmark if not iconic attraction just five miles southwest of Summit is the Mall of America. This 4.2-million-square-foot shopping center has more than five hundred stores and is considered the nation's largest combined retail and entertainment center. Within the mall is

Nickelodeon Universe, the largest U.S. indoor theme park with more than thirty rides, including a seventy-four-foot Ferris wheel.

If you enjoy historic architecture, head north of Summit Brewing to the Ramsey County Courthouse (15 West Kellogg Boulevard), built in 1932 as an early skyscraper in St. Paul. Self-guided tours of this civic building offer interesting insights into architecture and interior design. Its eighteen floors are finished in different woods from around the world. It also contains a thirty-six-foot onyx statue, *Vision of Peace*.

Summit Brewing is one of four breweries within just a few miles of each other. Flat Earth Brewing (2035 Benson Avenue) is less than a mile eastward. Heading northward on Seventh Street into downtown St. Paul you'll go right by Vine Park Brewing Company (1254 Seventh Street West). Further downtown, but only about three miles from Summit, is Great Waters Brewing (426 St. Peter Street).

BREWERY RATING

	Your Rating	Shepard's Rating	General Description
Location		🍺🍺🍺	Located not far from the historic Joseph Schmidt brewery. Neighborhood is mostly commercial and industrial, but homes and busy Seventh Street West are nearby.
Ease of Finding Location		🍺🍺🍺🍺	The brewery is close to major roads and intersections.
Brewery Atmosphere		🍺🍺🍺🍺	Building was constructed in 1998. Former brewery equipment from Heimertinger, Germany, adds a touch of history with a modern brewery look.
Dining Experience		n/a	Not applicable.
The Pints		🍺🍺🍺🍺	Perfect. Great tour, great tasting room, and great beer selections.

DIRECTIONS

From downtown St. Paul, take Seventh Street West (also Minnesota 5). Just before reaching I-35E turn south (left) into the Crosby Lake Business Park.

From I-35E, take exit 103B and go east on Seventh Street West (Minnesota 5). Approximately one block east of I-35E, turn south (right) into the Crosby Lake Business Park. The brewery will be ahead less than a quarter of a mile.

From Minneapolis–St. Paul International Airport, follow Minnesota 5 directly into St. Paul and while crossing over I-35E immediately watch on the right (south) for Crosby Lake Business Park and turn at the sign. The brewery will be straight ahead.

Surly Brewing Company
Brooklyn Center

ABOUT THE BREWERY

Surly beers were born in 2006 at the hands of Omar Ansari, who became interested in brewing when a friend gave him a homebrewing kit. A few years later during a flight to Portland, Oregon, Ansari and his wife, Becca, were joking about where they should go to find a beer as soon as their plane landed. Becca told Omar, you become "surly" when you walk into a place that doesn't have any good beer — thus the name!

Ansari's commercial brewery is located in a nondescript brick building that's part of an industrial-business park in Brooklyn Center, on the near northwest side of Minneapolis. The building has been a longtime home to Ansari's family business called Sparky Abrasives. It is a company that makes grinding wheels and materials for the metal industry. When Omar graduated from college he worked in the family company from 1992 to 2005.

At the heart of the Surly Brewing Company is a 30-barrel Sprinkman system that was obtained from a failed brewery in the Dominican Republic called Barley's. The brewery also consists of stainless steel fermenters and even some components that where once used by Wisconsin dairy farmers. Surly beers stand out on local store shelves because they are packaged in large 16-ounce cans. Brewmaster Todd Haug brought the canning idea to Ansari, who at first thought it was an awful idea. But when Ansari further explored canning he determined it would be a more stable way of packaging his beer while also giving the product a distinctive appearance on store shelves.

Surly's difference from other brands isn't just the can. Its edgy names and unconventional approaches to aggressive recipes add to the Surly image. Haug says he resists it when beer enthusiasts try to tie his beers too closely to a specific style. Bold assertive beers with names like Furious, Bender, CynicAle, Hell, and Darkness attract the cult-like following of a heavy-metal band — after all, the brewery shares a building with an abrasives company. All this has helped propel the brewery to stardom among Minnesota craft beer drinkers. Its annual production has skyrocketed. In 2006 it turned out just 883 barrels of beer; in 2010 it surpassed 12,000 barrels. In 2011 Surly unveiled plans for a new $20 million brewery that includes an attached restaurant, bar, and rooftop deck. That expansion could take Surly beyond 100,000 barrels per year. The plan requires changes to state law to allow a brewery of that size to sell beer on site. If those changes are approved, Surly hopes to move forward on the plan by 2013. The mayors of both Minneapolis and St. Paul have expressed interest in the project and have tried to entice Ansari to consider their cities with talk of riverfront locations.

In 2007 Surly Brewing was named the Best Brewery in America by *Beer-Advocate* magazine, and Ansari was named Artist of the Year by *City Pages*. In 2010 Ansari was selected as an Ernst & Young Entrepreneur of the Year for Minnesota.

HISTORY

Brewing for Omar Ansari began in 1994 when a friend gave him a homebrew kit. However, his taste for beer began much earlier when, at the age of fourteen, he had his first beer at Munich's Hofbrauhaus. Later, the homebrew kit inspired a hobby that brought out the artist in Ansari. For nearly ten years prior to starting Surly, Ansari expanded his homebrewing equipment, recipes, and beer-making skills. At one point he even considered opening a homebrew supply store. Eventually, his burgeoning homebrewing hobby outgrew his home and garage so he moved it into the building where his family's abrasives company was located. Ansari is a graduate of Macalester College in St. Paul with a degree in economics. When he graduated in 1992 he went to work in his family's business, Sparky Abrasives, where he remained until he started Surly Brewing in 2005.

Head brewer Todd Haug started homebrewing when he was nineteen. His landed his first commercial position with the Summit Brewing Company of St. Paul, where he started on the bottling line. He eventually worked his way into helping in the brewhouse. When he left Summit he landed a job at the then new Rock Bottom in downtown Minneapolis, where he worked for eight years. In 2004 he was hearing rumors about a new brewery opening in the Twin Cities area. That year at the Craft Brewers Conference in San Diego he met Ansari. In reality it was more a case of getting reacquainted since both had attended the same junior high school but hadn't seen each other since.

But before Surly Brewing could make a drop of beer, there was a big hurdle to overcome. Since the 1950s Brooklyn Center has had a dry ordinance that prohibited brewery operations within its boundaries. Ansari set out to change the city's regulations, and along the way he was surprised by the proposal's more-positive-than-expected reception. One of the local town commissioners was even a homebrewer who could identify with Ansari's dream. Soon after the local ordinance was changed, Surly became more than just a flash on the kitchen stove that heated Ansari's homebrew kettle. By 2005 Surly was officially founded, and in the spring of 2006 it sold its first beer.

In 2011 Ansari joined other brewers to get a state law changed to allow breweries to sell beer by the glass.

DON'T MISS THIS

Take a close look at Surly's tap handles the next time you reach for a pint. The distinctive shiny aluminum pulls come from the Carley Foundry of Blaine, Minnesota. Once shipped to the brewery, each one is hand-ground by Ansari or Haug before it leaves the brewery to grace the taps at your favorite local tavern.

SURLY BREWS

Bender 🍺🍺🍺   *Your Ranking*_____

Lots of hops and malts in a complex aroma. Deep, hazy mahogany color with a thick, marbled tan head. Full bodied. The taste is malty yet spicy with hints of raisin, cocoa, and toffee. Finishes with a spicy bitterness. An example of how Surly likes to play outside the common beer style definitions, Bender displays a combination of characteristics from an oatmeal stout or a brown porter with a hoppy edge. This is an exceptional beer.

Bitter Brewer 🍺🍺🍺   *Your Ranking*_____

A hoppy and fruity nose. Hazy orange color with a thick, soft, tan head. Medium to full bodied and round mouth feel. The maltiness has a biscuity or lightly roasted background. Finishes with a firm bitterness. Similar to an English bitter, made with a British ale yeast. Malts in the recipe include pale ale, Optic, medium crystal, roasted barley, and oats. Hopped with Columbus and Glacier. A seasonal beer available from May through July.

Coffee Bender 🍺🍺🍺🍺   *Your Ranking*_____

An rich American brown ale made with a cold coffee extraction process that gives this brew an intense coffee aroma and flavor. Features Guatemalan Finca Vista Hermosa coffee. Hopped with Columbus and Willamette. Dark bronze color and a thick, rocky, tan head. Medium to full bodied. A gold medal winner at the 2007 Great American Beer Festival and a bronze medal winner at the 2009 Great American Beer Festival.

CynicAle 🍺🍺🍺   *Your Ranking*_____

A Belgian-style saison. A light floral, sweet nose. Light copper color, hazy, with a thin, tan head. Medium bodied and bubbly. Begins with a sweet maltiness up front, but tones of apricot and peach come through in the background and finish. Overall, some hoppiness, similar to a pale ale with hint of peach. Made with Slovenian hops. This was Surly's first seasonal beer. It offers great versatility as a meal beer.

Furious 🍺🍺🍺🍺   *Your Ranking*_____

An American version of an India pale ale, a beer that Ansari describes as a West Coast reddish pale ale. Made with Warrior, Ahtanum, Simcoe, and Amarillo hops. Its base malt comes from Scotland and contributes to strong malty backbone that adds to its flavor complexity. Wonderful hoppy nose. Medium to full bodied. A hazy, rich copper color and marbled tan head. Sharp, assertive hoppy flavor and lingering bitter finish. Furious was recognized with the Best of the Fest Award at Arborfest in 2006 and 2007. Arborfest is held in late spring on the Macalester campus in St. Paul.

Hell 🍺🍺🍺🍺 Your Ranking_____

This Munich Helles lager is a summertime seasonal from Surly. Unfiltered and light golden color. Light golden, slightly hazy, and bubbly. Brewed with Pilsner and Carahell malts. Hopped with Sterling. A nice alternative to Surly's other brews when looking for a beer that is a little light, yet still flavorful.

Surlyfest 🍺🍺🍺 Your Ranking_____

Inspired by the Oktoberfest celebrations, but this fall seasonal is a hoppy, dry rye lager. Made with imported malted barley, rye and a German lager yeast strain. Features Sterling hops. A light earthy nose and clear golden color with a reddish tint. Medium bodied and soft. Firm caramel maltiness throughout. Watch for this beer in September and October.

OTHER SURLY BREWS YOU MAY WANT TO TRY

Abrasive Ale Your Ranking_____

This is a double IPA made with oats. Watch for it in winter. First made in 2008, it joined the seasonal Surly lineup in 2010. Begins with a citrusy hoppiness in the nose. Cloudy orange color and a thin, white, soft head. Full bodied and bubbly. Main flavor profile offers strong hoppiness with citrus and grapefruit tones. That citrus hoppiness lingers into the finish. The name is a reference to Sparky Abrasives, Ansari's family business that shares the building with Surly Brewing. It was originally called 16 Grit, a size of grit used at the abrasive factory.

Darkness Your Ranking_____

This Russian imperial stout creates quite a buzz in the Twin Cities the day of its release. Its faithful following of fans camp out at the brewery and stand in line for hours on "Darkness Day," when the brewery holds a festival-like event to hand out tickets for purchasing limited quantities of 750mL bottles. It's robust with flavors of chocolate, cherries, raisins, coffee, and toffee.

Jesus Juice Your Ranking_____

A limited released braggot made in 2010. Sweet and fruity with hints of raisin and plum.

Mild Your Ranking_____

A British mild ale made with Pale, Golden Promise, Brown, Crystal and Roasted malts. Hopped with Columbus. This was Surly's first session beer. Available in early Spring.

Pentagram Your Ranking_____

A beer that commemorated Surly's fifth Anniversary. A brown ale fermented with Brettanomyces yeast. Strong cherry tartness with hints of raisin.

Smoke   *Your Ranking_____*

This is an oak-aged, smoked Baltic Porter. There's certainly a lot of complexity in this beer. At the heart of its flavor is smoked malt from Bamberg, Germany. Lots of roastedness with hints of raisin, plus, figs and licorice. First brewed in 2008. Look for this beer as a fall seasonal in 750mL bottles.

Tea Bagged Furious   *Your Ranking_____*

Limited availability but one to watch for at beer fests where Surly is present. Double dry hopped (reference to tea bagged) and cask conditioned. Surly has also been known to produce a Tea Bagged version of Bender.

Wet   *Your Ranking_____*

This IPA is a fall seasonal featuring fresh picked (wet) hops. Recipes for this beer have featured as much as 2,400 pounds of Citra and Simcoe hops that are picked in Oregon and then shipped to Surly so than can be added to the brew within three days.

MENU

None. Surly does not serve food.

OTHER THINGS TO SEE OR DO IN THE AREA

The area today that is Brooklyn Center was opened to settlement in the 1850s. But the politics of organizing the modern city began in a farmer's garage. Brooklyn Center's community Web site describes a Valentine's Day election in 1911 to approve the incorporation papers for the village. Voting was evidently held at Earle Brown's garage at the old Martin Farm on Hopper Road. Brown later willed his farm to the University of Minnesota in what became the Brooklyn Center Industrial Park. Brooklyn Center celebrates Earle Brown with a festival in June with a parade, crafts, concert, and fireworks.

Brooklyn Center has over five hundred acres of parkland and nature centers. The Eugene H. Hagel Arboretum (Sixty-first and Major avenues) is seven acres of gardens and natural habitat. On the eastern border of Brooklyn Center, the North Mississippi Regional Park offers picnic areas, shelter houses, trails, and river access.

The serious (or Furious) Surly fan will want to watch for Darkness Day. The annual event is tied to the brewery's release of its imperial stout called Darkness. A limited number of bottles are released on a Saturday (usually in October), and hundreds will line up in the early morning hours for a ticket to purchase one or more of the bottles to be released that afternoon. It's actually a full day similar to an open house at the brewery with food, music, and, of course, Surly beer.

BREWERY RATING

	Your Rating	Shepard's Rating	General Description
Location		🍺🍺🍺	Surly is not hard to find, but it is located in an industrial business park.
Ease of Finding Location		🍺🍺🍺	A short distance from Minnesota 100, but a little planning helps, especially once inside the business park. Watch for the Surly sign on the old oil tank on Dusharme Drive.
Brewery Atmosphere		🍺🍺🍺🍺	This is a working brewery that feels like one. There is a small tasting area and gift shop, but Surly's location and no-frills buildings are all part of its character, if not charm.
Dining Experience		n/a	Not applicable.
The Pints		🍺🍺🍺🍺	Great line of flavorful and distinctive beers. Nontraditional Surly beers (like the name) are brews with an attitude.

DIRECTIONS

Surly Brewing Company is on the western side of Minneapolis, most easily accessed via Minnesota 100. Exit at France Avenue and travel southeast, then turn left (east) on Forty-seventh Avenue North. At the next intersection with Drew Street, turn left (north). Travel one block to the next intersection and turn right onto Forty-eighth Avenue North and continue through the business park to Dusharme Drive, which angles left (north). At the end of the road is Surly Brewing.

Theodore Fyten Brewing Company and St. Croix Brewing Company

St. Paul

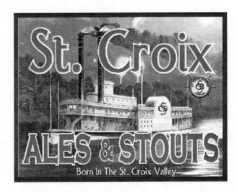

ABOUT THE BREWERY

Theodore Fyten Brewing Company and the St. Croix Brewing Company are part of a family of three breweries owned by Tod Fyten of St. Paul. Fyten's third brewery is the Mantorville Brewing Company in the small Minnesota town of Mantorville, located about seventy-five miles south of St. Paul. While all are federally licensed as breweries, Fyten has used his Mantorville brewery, the home to the Stagecoach brands, for some draft production of all three breweries. He has an agreement with the Lake Superior Brewing Company of Duluth for 12-ounce bottling and packaging of all three brands.

Tod Fyten has been carefully planning the buildup of both Theodore Fyten Brewing and St. Croix Brewing. He started purchasing and storing equipment in the 1990s with the plan to eventually have three functioning breweries. Tod Fyten is positioning the Theodore Fyten Brewing Company for opening in west St. Paul some time after 2011. Equipment for his St. Croix brewery is likely to remain in storage for some time longer. Eventually, the Theodore Fyten Brewing Company will make draft beer and growlers and specialty bottles of both Fytenburg and St. Croix brands at its historic St. Paul location. Fyten hopes that the St. Croix brewery eventually will become a standalone operation somewhere in the St. Croix valley.

Because both breweries are owned by Fyten and since they currently share the same office location, they are listed as one entry for now. However, both are established as individual companies with unique product lines.

Tod Fyten is well known in the Minnesota brewing industry. His first job after college was as an intern at the Minneapolis Grain Exchange where he became acquainted with maltsters and how they judged grains. After a short time in Germany, where he took part in a program that allowed him to study at a brewery in Wittenburg, he came back to Minnesota and went to work in sales as a distributor. He later worked for James Page Brewing (now closed) and was one of the creators of the trade publication *Midwest Beer Notes*. Fyten also learned directly from some of the region's legendary beer makers. He served as a sales representative for the Jacob Leinenkugel Brewing Company of Chippewa Falls, Wisconsin, where he met company president Jake Leinenkugel. And, while at James Page Brewing, Fyten's experience in co-packaging agreements with the August Schell Brewing Company of New Ulm helped him get to know company president Ted Marti.

The Theodore Fyten Brewing Company and St. Croix Brewing Company have offices in the shadow of St. Paul's historic Joseph Schmidt brewery. Tod Fyten chose to locate his companies just about a block away, in a limestone and gray stone building that had served as Schmidt's horse stables. The building dates back to the late 1850s, and much of its original brick and wood remains. When Fyten moved in, he says, it still had the smell of horses and it required some extensive sand-blasting and cleaning. The building isn't Fyten's only link to Minnesota's brewing past. Three generations of his family worked for the Schmidt brewery.

HISTORY: THEODORE FYTEN BREWING COMPANY

This is the third brewery under the ownership of Tod Fyten. He founded the company in 1999. Theodore was Tod's great-great-grandfather, a harness maker who worked with the draft horses for the Joseph Schmidt brewery. His son John and later his grandson George Jr. (Tod's grandfather) all worked for Schmidt.

Tod Fyten's brewery represents another generation of brewing in this neighborhood. Fyten was able to purchase a copper-clad brew kettle from a failed brewery in Louisville, Kentucky, in 1997. The equipment was new and never used. The 10-barrel system was made by Vendome Copper and Brass Works of Louisville as a modern replica of a pre-Prohibition brew kettle. It's one of only four such systems that were made by Vendome.

The Fytenburg brands have been available in limited quantities for several years, mainly through special tastings and events. But the brewery's identity is emerging as Tod Fyten renovates the building that formerly played a very important supporting role in the Schmidt brewery empire. The Fytenburg products are best described as Dutch Belgian and European styles of beer, a reflection of the Fyten family as emigrants from Belgium and Holland in the 1860s. The flagship brew of the company is its Fytenburg Grand Cru. It also produces Teddy's Root Beer.

DON'T MISS THIS

If you have the opportunity to tour Fyten's offices, be sure to look around for signs of the building's brewery past. Even after extensive renovation much of the original walls and ceilings remain, right down to the hitching posts.

THE BREWS OF THEODORE FYTEN BREWING

Fytenburg Grand Cru 🍺🍺🍺   *Your Ranking*_____
Dutch Belgian amber ale made with six different types of malt and European noble hops with a Belgian yeast strain. Considered the flagship of the Theodore Fyten brews. Offers an assertive fruity-yeasty nose up front. Hazy brown color with a thin, soft, tan head. Medium bodied, round to slick texture. A yeasty sweetness dominates with a spicy background. A crisp fruity finish. Ends up at 6.2 percent ABV. Based on a homebrew recipe that Tod Fyten developed for his wedding in 1989.

OTHER FYTENBURG BEERS YOU MAY WANT TO TRY

Fytenburg Grand Cru Blanche   *Your Ranking* _____
A strong white beer. "Blanche" is sometimes used to describe the French version of wheat beer.

Fytenburg Reserve   *Your Ranking* _____
A dark and strong Belgian ale. This is a beer to watch for in special packaging.

HISTORY: ST. CROIX BREWING COMPANY

The original St. Croix brewery was founded in Stillwater sometime around 1860 by Gerhard Knipps. It wasn't called St. Croix Brewing Company until 1877, when it was under different ownership, and even then for about only a year. In 1995 the St. Croix Brewing Company name was used once again, this time by Lakeland resident Karl Bremer. Based upon Bremer's homebrew recipes, Maple Ale emerged as the company's first flagship brew, with assistance from Briese Malting of Chilton, Wisconsin. Early in the company's history, the beers were made by August Schell Brewing of New Ulm.

In 1997 St. Croix added Serrano Pepper Ale to the lineup and laid claim to the first pepper ale in the United States. In 2002 Tod Fyten became a partner in the brewery and by 2003 he owned all of the company. Fyten has had equipment for this brewery in storage since 2003 when he purchased it from the failed Watertower Brewing (brewpub) of Eden Prairie.

THE BREWS OF ST. CROIX BREWING

Cream Stout 🍺🍺🍺   *Your Ranking*_____
Made with six varieties of malt and a combination of American and British hops. Deep, dark, and smooth with hints of roastedness in the background and finish. This beer has some body and warmth from its 7 percent ABV.

Creamy Brown Ale 🍺🍺   *Your Ranking*_____
Made with six varieties of malt, along with American and British hops. No nose. A hazy amber-copper color. The head is thin, soft, and tan. Medium bodied and soft. A caramel maltiness dominates the flavor. Finishes with a light sourness. This beer was introduced in 2010, inspired by the settlement history of

the St. Croix River valley and the early brewing pioneers who made beers for the thirsty loggers.

Maple Ale *Your Ranking*_____
Begins as an amber ale that is made with pure maple syrup. Made with three different malts and hops that include Cascade and Northern Brewer. Strong, assertive maple nose. Dark brown color with a soft, tan head. Medium bodied. Strong malt and maple flavors. A seasonal beer for St. Croix. In 2011 this beer celebrated its fifteenth year as a brew from St. Croix.

OTHER ST. CROIX BEERS YOU MAY WANT TO TRY

Creamy Brown Ale *Your Ranking*_____
Made with six varieties of malts, along with American and British hops. This beer was introduced in 2010. Its recipe was inspired by the settlement history of the St. Croix River valley and the early brewing pioneers who made this style of beer for the thirsty loggers.

Double Barrel Smoked Porter *Your Ranking* _____
As the brewery celebrated its fifteenth anniversary 2011, Tod Fyten developed this special version of a porter aged in oak barrels that were used to make bourbon.

Serrano Pepper Ale *Your Ranking*_____
A pale ale made with serrano peppers. Hopped with Chinook and Willamette hops. The serrano peppers offer an herbal character that leaves some spicy heat without overwhelming the beer. As of 2011 this beer was temporarily retired as Tod Fyten reassessed all of his brands (St. Croix, Fytenburg, and Mantorville). Because of its hot peppery character the southwestern theme, watch for this beer to reappear as part of his Mantorville Brewery's stagecoach line of beers.

MENU

None. Theodore Fyten Brewing and St. Croix Brewing do not serve food.

OTHER THINGS TO SEE OR DO IN THE AREA

Just a few blocks north of the breweries' offices is the Summit Hill neighborhood, which will lead you to Cathedral Hill (roughly centered at the intersection of Summit Avenue and Dale Street). Victorian mansions along Summit Avenue recall the Gilded Age, especially the home of railroad tycoon James J. Hill (240 Summit Avenue). A few blocks east-northeast of the Hill house on Summit Avenue you'll get impressive overlooks of downtown St. Paul and the Mississippi River. One the area's best-known landmarks is the Cathedral of St. Paul and National Shrine of the Apostle Paul. Tours of the cathedral are offered weekdays.

Continuing on Summit Avenue, the road changes to John Ireland Boulevard and it will take you right by the Minnesota History Center (345 West Kellogg Boulevard). Inside there is a chance to explore the state's past through exhibits and hands-on experiences (www.minnesotahistorycenter.org).

A major landmark for the Twin Cities beer enthusiast is the Muddy Pig (162 North Dale Street). This is a brew haven, offering one of the most diverse beer lists in the Twin Cities. It's also a place to grab a meal while exploring this historic neighborhood. Three other breweries (Flat Earth, Summit, and Vine Park) are in this neighborhood, and just a little farther to the east in downtown St. Paul is Great Waters Brewing Company.

BREWERY RATING

	Your Rating	Shepard's Rating	General Description
Location		🍺🍺🍺🍺	Great sense of history, in the former footprint of the Joseph Schmidt Brewery.
Ease of Finding Location		🍺🍺🍺	Not difficult, just requires some planning.
Brewery Atmosphere		🍺🍺🍺	It's best to call ahead if you want to meet Tod Fyten and take a tour of the building. A great location and building will be even better when Fyten establishes it as a working brewery.
Dining Experience		n/a	Not applicable.
The Pints		🍺🍺🍺	Beers are good. Overall experience and history associated with these breweries are wonderful. Watch for Fyten firing up as a full-scale brewery.

DIRECTIONS

Theodore Fyten and St. Croix Brewing offices are located at the corner of Webster Street and West Jefferson Avenue. Both streets intersect with West Seventh Street, which will take you into downtown St. Paul (driving northeastward). Just look for the old Joseph Schmidt brewery buildings, a landmark that is visible above nearly all other buildings in the neighborhood.

Vine Park Brewing Company
St. Paul

ABOUT THE BREWERY

Vine Park is a brew-your-own business where customers can be hands-on in making of beer or just treat themselves to the great beers of brewery owners Andy Grage and Dan Justesen. While there are house beers and sodas, Vine Park really speaks to the local homebrewer. It's a place where you get to be the brewmaster, or, for some, the wine maker. This brew shop has more than fifty beer recipes for you to follow or you can bring your own. Brewers also get direct assistance from staff in helping refine their ideas or solve problems in their beer or wine making.

As you walk through the door, you come face-to-face with lots of copper, similar to what you see in large commercial breweries only on a much smaller scale. There are six 25-gallon kettles for customers to use. There is also a slightly larger 3-barrel, copper-clad brew kettle, visible through the windows, when you're ready to step up the size of your batches. Vine Park offers a range of options for the do-it-yourselfer, from extract to all-grain brewing in 12-gallon batches. You can come in and brew, have your beer stored while it ferments, and then return on bottling day. You can have Vine Park staff get involved in helping with your brewing and bottling. Vine Park also offers classes on how to brew your own. Groups and companies often come here for team-building events.

But overall, this is just a great place to be exposed to the local homebrew culture and learn for yourself what making beer is about. Grage and Justesen purchased the business in 2004 and established it at its current location. They are often in the shop, personally helping customers or even making their own batches of beer, which you can purchase in half-gallon growlers. Vine Park almost always has two to four of its own brews for sale, plus root beer and cream soda.

HISTORY

Vine Park is the first brew-your-own beer shop in Minnesota. It began in 1995, just a little farther north, up West Seventh Street in the Irvine Park neighborhood — from which its shortened name was derived. The original concept began as the father-and-son business venture of David and Scott Thompson. David, himself a homebrewer, had retired from the family lumber business and spent a few years sailing in the Caribbean before coming back the Twin Cities. One day while having lunch with a friend, David saw on the bar's television a story about a brew-your-own establishment in Philadelphia. He was so taken by the idea he flew to Philly to see the actual shop. When he returned to St. Paul he found he had to work on changing state law to allow such a business. But by 1995 he was working in his own brew-your-own shop.

During the months of construction that led to the opening of Vine Park, Thompson got to know Andy Grage quite well as he came into Grage's Northern Brewer homebrew supply store asking for advice. Thompson asked Grage to manage the brew-your-own operations while he focused on expanding the business to include a brewpub. The restaurant part of Vine Park began in 2001, and it even got recognized by *Mpls.St.Paul* magazine as having "the best brewpub fare in town."

Grage grew up in Duluth and earned a degree in hotel-restaurant management from the University of Wisconsin–Stout. When David Thompson decided he wanted to sell in 2003 (perhaps to return to sailing), he first offered the business to his son Scott and part-ownership to Grage. But Scott decided it was time to pursue other opportunities so an interested Grage found another partner, Dan Justesen. Justesen, a longtime Twin Cities resident, had very important credentials on his own résumé — that of a longtime Vine Park customer. Both Grage and Justesen have completed brewing certificate programs from the World Brewing Academy of Munich.

One of their first challenges was to find a different building. After months of searching they found their present location at 1252 West Seventh, about ten blocks from the original location. Once a commercial bakery, the building needed extensive remodeling, but Grage and Justesen's experience managing and patronizing the former location had taught them a lot about how to use space and make a brew-your-own shop customer friendly. Grage looks back and laughs about finding the location. He says before they moved in the windowless building was in bad shape. It was more like a barn with a plywood door that forced you to turn sideways to get inside. Grage spent weeks scraping years worth of bakery grease from the metal rafters. Renovations on the 4,500-square-foot building took about five months. When Vine Park reopened in June 2005 it did not continue the brewpub side of business that Thompson had founded. The larger equipment used when it was a restaurant was sold to the Angry Minnow Brewpub in Hayward, Wisconsin. The present location is roughly in the old brewery row that was once home to the Jacob Schmidt and, later, Minnesota Brewing Company. The modern Summit brewery isn't far, just about five blocks to the south and west.

DON'T MISS THIS

While Vine Park is a brew-on-premise establishment, it's also a licensed microbrewery. Because both exist in the same space, there are strict rules about keeping the two business entities separate. That's one reason why Andy Grage and Dan Justesen close the brew-your-own store on Mondays and brew "their" own beer, which is available for sale in growlers. The Vine Park owners are also strong supporters of the Upper Mississippi Mashout, an annual homebrew contest that draws hundreds of entries. The Mashout's best-of-show winner gets to brew their winning entry in Vine Park's larger 3-barrel system.

You may also want to ask Grage and Justesen about beer trips and travel opportunities. Each year Vine Park hosts a trip to a great beer destination. Past trips include Germany, the Czech Republic, Belgium, and South Africa.

VINE PARK BREWS

Munich Helles 🍺🍺🍺🍺   *Your Ranking*_____
This light-colored lager begins with a light floral nose. Brilliant copper color with a thick, soft, tan head. Medium bodied and smooth texture. Great caramel malt balance with a firm, hoppy background from German noble hops. Clean finish.

Pale Ale 🍺🍺🍺   *Your Ranking*_____
Light hoppy nose. Light copper color and a soft, tan head. Sharp hoppy flavor and lingering bitterness.

Stout 🍺🍺🍺   *Your Ranking*_____
Malty nose with a rich, thick-looking black color. Medium bodied with a solid chocolate malty flavor.

Stump Jumper 🍺🍺🍺🍺   *Your Ranking*_____
An amber ale made with Belgian Pale, Crystal, and Biscuit malts. Hopped with Northern Brewer and Fuggles. Starts with a light floral nose. Clear amber color with a medium, bubbly, tan head. Medium bodied. Great overall balance with a slight emphasis to the hops. A nice session beer.

OTHER VINE PARK BREWS YOU MAY WANT TO TRY

Belgian Abbey   *Your Ranking*_____
A rich malty brown ale with flavors of chocolate and caramel.

Big Tex IPA   *Your Ranking*_____
Bold ruby-amber color, full bodied, and hoppy. Made with Amarillo hops.

Evil IPA   *Your Ranking*_____
A West Coast–style India pale ale made with Centennial hops. Offers an assertively hoppy nose. Deep copper color with a thick, soft, tan head. Medium

bodied with a roundness. Strong bitterness with a firm malty background. Finishes bitter.

Oktoberfest   *Your Ranking*_____
A light amber-colored lager with smooth malty flavor. Some warmth in the finish. Look for this beer in the fall.

Rabid Penguin Porter   *Your Ranking*_____
The name of this dark and full-bodied porter just makes you want to hop home with a growler.

Walnut Brown Ale   *Your Ranking*_____
A traditional English brown ale with tones of coffee.

Winter Ale   *Your Ranking*_____
A deep bronze American strong ale.

Cream Soda and Root Beer   *Your Ranking*_____
You can find Vine Park's cream soda and River City Root Beer in six-packs and kegs. It also offers private label root beers for groups, companies, or private parties.

MENU

None. Vine Park does not serve food.

OTHER THINGS TO SEE OR DO IN THE AREA

All along West Seventh Street you can find numerous places to eat. Downtown St. Paul is about two miles north and east up Seventh Street. One such place that gets high marks, and frequent referrals from Grage and Justesen, is the German restaurant Glockenspiel (605 Seventh Street West). It's hard to describe, but after a full afternoon of brewing your own beer there's nothing like the Brötzeitteller sampler plate of summer sausage, Jagdwurst, ham, Leberkase, salami, and herring. And a good beer, of course.

If you are looking to explore, the Mississippi River channel is just a few blocks south of Vine Park. Along the river are a number of parks and hiking and biking opportunities. About five miles southwest of Vine Park is historic Fort Snelling (junction of Minnesota highways 5 and 55, just east of the Minneapolis–St. Paul International Airport). Fort Snelling State Park is named for Lieutenant (later General) Zebulon M. Pike, who in 1805 purchased from the Dakota Indians the tract on which the fort was built.

Fort Snelling is at the confluence of the Minnesota and Mississippi rivers—an area known as Mendota (the Sioux word for "meeting of the waters"). You can visit the Sibley House and take a ninety-minute walk through the historic village of Mendota. As one of Minnesota's oldest towns, Mendota emerged from an early nineteenth-century fur-trading center. The Henry H. Sibley House (1357 Sibley Memorial Highway) was built in 1838 for Minnesota's first governor. Sibley was also a manager of the American Fur Company. Next door is the Jean Baptiste Fairbault House, built in 1839. Both houses offer tours.

Vine Park is one of four breweries within a few miles of each other. Summit Brewing (910 Montreal Circle) is only about five blocks west. Flat Earth Brewing (2035 Benson Avenue) is just a little farther eastward. Farther downtown but only a couple miles north and east is Great Waters Brewing (426 St. Peter Street) in the historic Hamm's building. The offices of Theodore Fyten and St. Croix Brewing (363 Webster Street) are also just west of Vine Park.

BREWERY RATING

	Your Rating	Shepard's Rating	General Description
Location		🍺🍺🍺	Vine Park is in the bustling Seventh Street West neighborhood. The location offers a variety of restaurants and other businesses. Its proximity to other beer makers adds to this being a fun stop on a Twin Cities brew tour.
Ease of Finding Location		🍺🍺🍺🍺	Location along Seventh Street West (Minnesota 5) off I-35E makes it easy to find. Street parking can be a little challenging.
Brewery Atmosphere		🍺🍺🍺🍺	This is a brew-your-own shop so there really is no comparison for those who enjoy making beer. There's always something interesting going on, from watching customers to talking with Andy and Dan. You'll need to call ahead if you want to brew yourself.
Dining Experience		n/a	Not applicable.
The Pints		🍺🍺🍺	Great fun with a good beer, and very enjoyable watching and talking to local homebrew enthusiasts. This is a great stop for those just wanting to experience beer, making it, or learning how to brew your own.

DIRECTIONS

From I-35E, take the West Seventh Street exit and go east on West Seventh for about four blocks. Vine Park on the right side of the road. You can also get there very easily from downtown St. Paul by following West Seventh Street (Highway 5). Vine Park is approximately two and a half miles from the entertainment district surrounding the Xcel Energy Center.

Brady's Brewhouse
New Richmond, Wisconsin

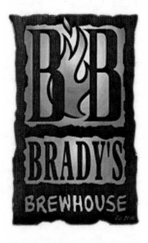

_____   _____
Visit Date   Signed

ABOUT THE BREWERY

Brady's Brewhouse in New Richmond, Wisconsin, is found about fifteen miles directly east of Stillwater, or roughly forty-five minutes from St. Paul. This brewpub is located in one of the oldest buildings in town that was constructed in 1895 as an opera house. It later served as home to an auto dealership for nearly fifty years. Following that it became the residence of an electrical company and appliance store. When owner Chris Polfus opened his brewpub in 2010 he brought attention to the building's and the community's heritage through various historical artifacts and old photos.

The building containing Brady's is long and narrow, about three times longer than it is wide. The main bar is oak and is also long and narrow. It calls attention to the brewpub's commitment to craft beers by showing off the large number of taps and bottle selections. There's a second-floor mezzanine that offers additional seating and some basic bar amusements like dart boards and video games. The restaurant side of the business is very family-friendly, while the bar area can be a little more outgoing with occasional musical performers ranging from acoustic to bands and even an open jam night.

Polfus chose the name Brady's because it was an old family name. Most locals will associate Polfus with the John Deere implement business that Chris's grandfather started in 1941. Chris grew up in the area and continues to be part of that family business. He started looking into opening his own business in 2009 with the intent to run a restaurant and bar. However, during the early stages of writing his business plan he took a trip north to Fitger's

Brewhouse. Chris Polfus says as soon as he walked into the Duluth brew-pub he knew he was going to add a brewery to his dream of owning his own business.

BEERS

The brews of Brady's are made by Rick Sauer, a well-respected and long-time Wisconsin brewer who helped create a number of Badger-land brewer-ies. Before taking the brewmaster job at Brady's, Sauer helped create Twin Ports Brewing (now home to the Thirsty Pagan) in Superior, Wisconsin. Prior to that he made beer for Rail House Brewing Company of Marinette, Wisconsin. At Brady's the light bodied Golden Ale 🍺🍺🍺 lives up to its name as a nice local alternative to big brewery bottled beers. Brady's Pale Ale 🍺🍺🍺🍺 is a solid choice for its rich golden-copper color and assertive hoppiness. The Big Muskie Pale Ale 🍺🍺 is still hoppy but it's a much lighter version of Brady's Pale Ale. The Vagabond Irish Red 🍺🍺🍺 has a reddish-amber color and a firm malty character. The very first batch of the Irish Red was made with smoked malts that were roasted in the brewpub's wood-fired oven. The Hop Tornado IPA 🍺🍺🍺 is dry hopped with Willamette hops and it is well worth a pint. The Midnight 🍺🍺🍺🍺 is a chocolate porter and is one of the best Brady brews. This brewpub will keep six to eight house beers on tap, including a seasonal or two. In addition, the bar has over forty other beer selections on tap and in bottles.

MENU

Brady's menu features a variety of family-friendly entrées like burgers, salads, soups, meatloaf, chicken, steaks, and trout from a local fish farm. At the heart of the kitchen is a wood-fired oven and grill. With that in mind, pizzas are one of the staples at Brady's and are prepared in the wood-fired oven. There are a half-dozen choices made on hand-tossed sourdough. The Mr. Meaty Pizza has smoked bacon, pepperoni, salami, and caramelized onion. The vegetarian-pleasing Farmers Market is made with red sauce, wild mushroom ragout, roasted garlic, caramelized leeks, artichoke hearts, spinach, and grape tomatoes. Dinner entrées feature some tough choices. The house-made Beer Cheese Soup is always for consideration either on its own or as a side. Steaks include a Sirloin, a New York Strip, and a hearty 14-ounce rib eye called "The Windsor." Brady's also offers a special selection of stuffed burgers that fea-ture two quarter-pound patties stuffed with a variety of ingredients. The Brady Burger is stuffed with Ellsworth cheese curds and topped with hop-honey mustard. The Silly Good Burger is filled with crunchy peanut butter and spicy jalapenos.

Das Bierhaus
Menomonie, Wisconsin

Visit Date   Signed

ABOUT THE BREWERY

For those who enjoy the influence of German beer-making culture, a drive to Menomonie, Wisconsin, and a visit to the Das Bierhaus is a rewarding trip. Menomonie is located about forty-five minutes east of the Twin Cities along Interstate 94. This small brewpub is suggestive of a Bavarian beer hall. Located just west of the downtown area, Das Bierhaus occupies a small brick building that once served as a local meat locker.

Das Bierhaus is owned Lee Quale of nearby Glenwood City. Years earlier Quale had struck up a friendship with brewer Robert Wilber, who was at the time making beer for William Kuether Brewing Company of Clear Lake, Wisconsin. Wilber was giving Quale the spent grains from the brewery to feed to his cattle. As they got to know one another over beers, thoughts of creating their own brewery emerged. So in 2006, when William Kuether Brewing closed, Quale and Wilbur decided it was time to make their shared vision a reality.

As the business plans took hold and the building renovations began, Wilber and Quale located a brewing system in Colorado Springs, Colorado. It once made beer at the Arctic Craft Brewery that operated from 2002 to 2004. The market for used brewing systems is very competitive, so when Wilber found the equipment on a website he immediately flew to Colorado Springs to personally close the deal and begin packing up the system so it could be transported to Wisconsin.

The brewhouse is mostly located behind the bar in its own room. Wilber is often seen through glass windows working on his latest batch. If you look closely, you can see beer being transferred through clear plastic tubing on its way to fermentation and conditioning tanks in the front of the restaurant.

Wilber is a native of Germany and was trained at the Technical University of Munich. Das Bierhaus is actually the tenth brewery that he has worked at, and his third in the U.S. He takes great pride in his German heritage and traditional approaches to making beer. To those seriously interested, Wilber likes to explain, "I am not trying to make microbeer. These are traditional German beers that have been made for years. I don't experiment with them because they have already been perfected and my goal is to recreate them to the best of my abilities."

Wilber keeps about three to five beers on tap for most visits. You'll find a pilsner, Dunkel, and Hefeweizen. A few of his seasonal brews to watch for include an Oktoberfest, Altbier, Kölsch, Doppelbock, and Weizenbock.

BEERS

Robert Wilber makes beers following the German traditions of Reinheitsgebot. His beers have plenty of body and unique characteristics that make this brewpub worth more than just one visit. The Pilsner 🍺🍺🍺🍺 has bright golden color and a medium soft white head. It's a medium bodied, assertive pilsner with lots of flavor. The Hefeweizen 🍺🍺🍺 is hazy golden with a thin, off-white head. It offers a light spiciness with a crisp fruity finish. The Altbier 🍺🍺🍺 offers a chance to taste Wilber's German heritage. It's a hazy bronze-colored beer with a thin, tan, bubbly head and an emphasis more on malt than hops. Another favorite is the dark bronze-colored Schwarzbier 🍺🍺🍺🍺. It has some smooth chocolate maltiness, yet overall it's clean and balanced with a light roasted background. The Oktoberfest is a special treat, but it doesn't stay around long. A few other beers to watch for include the Munich Dunkel, Gambrinator Doppelbock, and a Rauchbier.

MENU

The German-style beers are not the only reason for making the trip to the Das Bierhaus. The brewpub's menu features a range of authentic German foods, with a focus on handmade sausages. Some of the most popular include the Jaegerschnitzel, which is the special house Schnitzel covered in mushroom gravy. The Fleischkaese is a Bavarian pork loaf grilled and topped with a fried egg. Don't overlook is the German Sampler. It's a platter of bratwurst, kaeseknacker, and frankfurter sausages alongside sauerkraut, red cabbage, spaetzle dumplings, and rye bread. You can also find a variety of chicken schnitzel specials and a Friday night fish. And what self-respecting German eatery would not have Apfelstrudel à la mode — and Das Bierhaus is to be respected for it.

Dave's BrewFarm
Wilson, Wisconsin

Visit Date   Signed

ABOUT THE BREWERY

This is one brewery not to blow off! Dave's BrewFarm of Wilson, Wisconsin, is attempting to take the Twin Cities beer market by storm—in a manner of speaking. This small farmstead brewery gets nearly all of its electricity from wind power. And one of its most popular beers is a Belgian strong ale called Matacabras, a reference to the legendary north wind in Spain that's so strong it is famed for killing goats.

Owner and brewmaster David Anderson grew up in St. Louis Park in suburban Minneapolis. In 1996 Anderson attended the Siebel Institute of Technology and World Brewing Academy. His first job was brewing at the former Ambleside Brewing Company that operated in Minneapolis in the mid-1990s. He also sold specialty beers for the Wine Company of St. Paul for a short time until a consulting job working with start-up breweries took him to Italy and Vietnam, as well as several U.S. states. But Anderson eventually found himself back in the Twin Cities area with the dream of opening up his own brewery. After what he calls "months of looking at dirt," he finally found a place that spoke to him near the Wisconsin village of Wilson (population 180). Anderson says the thirty-five-acre farm where he built his brewery appealed to him because it had rural beauty and a great location for wind-generated power.

Not long after closing on the property in 2008, he built a 2,200-square-foot brewery and, on top of that, 1,500 square feet of living space. Yes, he and his wife, Pamela Dixon, actually live above the brewery, giving special meaning to the term "brewhouse." On brew days, Anderson says, the aroma of wort reminds him of all the hard work that went into building the brewery and it "smells like victory."

Before they could move in they needed to obtain a federal exemption from the Alcohol and Tobacco Tax and Trade Bureau (TTB), which oversees breweries. Regulations dating back to the 1950s prohibit a commercial brewery being located in a home or houseboat. The houseboat wasn't the issue for Anderson, but he did have to install specific walls and doors that clearly separate his living space from the brewhouse.

By February 2009, Anderson had installed a 120-foot tower with a 20-kilowatt generator to supply electricity to the house and brewery and any excess power to the local power company. A year later, his February electric bill was just eighty-one cents. Anderson says the windmill should pay for itself in about ten years.

David Anderson is active with area homebrewers and their clubs, often serving as a volunteer judge in local homebrew competitions. He's also been a judge for the Great American Beer Festival in Denver and internationally at events in Italy.

BEERS

Dave's BrewFarm has a 7-barrel brewing system that is used for developing recipes before scaling up to full commercial production. Anderson also uses his rather small system for draft beer, growlers, and special releases of brews in 22-ounce bottles. He gets help with bottling from Sand Creek Brewing of Black River Falls, Wisconsin, and assistance with canned products from Wisconsin's Stevens Point Brewery.

BrewFarm's Matacabras and Select were the first commercial beers that Anderson released. Matacabras 🍺🍺🍺🍺 is a beer that doesn't fit neatly within the common beer styles, and is best described as a strong ale due to its 8 percent ABV. It's made with a strain of Belgian Trappist yeast, rye malt, and brown sugar, along with Millennium, Perle, and Amarillo hops. Matacabras has a hazy amber color, tan head, and spicy, malty flavor that is complex and distinctive. The label of Matacabras has an upside-down goat being pulled into a tornado, along with the obligatory subtext: "No goats were harmed in the production of this ale."

BrewFarm Select 🍺🍺🍺 is a golden lager packaged in twelve-packs of aluminum cans. Select has a bright golden color, malty body, and crisp, light, bitter dryness from Perle and Cluster hops. It has a hint of warmth at 5 percent ABV.

Anderson makes a Wind Series of brews, which include a Weizen Doppelbock called Kotura, a term for Lord of the Wind. The sweet stout is called Mocha Diablo, made with additions of three different hot peppers. A Diablo wind is a hot, dry offshore California wind from the northwest. Harukaze (a Japanese word meaning "spring wind") is based on an ancient brew called "gruit" that, instead of hops, has spices like white pepper, ginger, cardamom, rose hips, and heather tips.

Anderson's creativity isn't limited to his windy brews. The McAnderson is a complex Scottish ale that is made with Palisade hops and molasses. The Aubexxx is a golden strong ale made with Belgian yeast and Vanguard and Northern Brewer hops. At beer festival appearances Anderson occasionally shows of a bit of whimsy with special limited batches. His Dandy Saison is made from dandelions that he picks on his Wilson farm property. And his Breakfast Lager is made with Grape-Nuts cereal right out of the box, giving new meaning to having beer for breakfast.

Anderson's brewery license permits a tasting room. When he's not attending brew festivals he's open on weekends for visitors and tours. (Keep in mind if you travel there to call ahead for hours.)

MENU

None. Dave's BrewFarm does not serve food.

Lucette Brewing Company
Menomonie, Wisconsin

ABOUT THE BREWERY

The legend of Paul Bunyan is familiar to many Minnesotans. So next time you're having a few beers with friends and someone challenges you in Paul Bunyan trivia, see if anyone knows a brewery named after Paul's significant other. While Babe might create a chuckle, Lucette was his sweetheart. It's that softer side of Paul Bunyan that gives this small brewery in Menomonie, Wisconsin, its name.

Lucette Brewing opened in October 2010 on the south edge of Menomonie's downtown. Logging and lumber has been a longtime part of the local economy, so the owners of Lucette Brewing chose a name that reflects that heritage and is also clearly a conversation starter for those versed in Minnesota folklore. Lucette Brewing was created by Mike Wilson and Tim Schletty, both Minnesota natives who met while they were working in beer distribution and retail sales in the Menominee area. Wilson grew up in Chisholm, in the heart of Minnesota's Iron Range, and Schletty is originally from St. Paul. Lucette's head brewer, Jon Christiansen, grew up in Milwaukee and is a graduate of the Siebel Institute of Technology and World Brewing Academy. Christiansen's professional training took him to Germany for five weeks, where he studied at the Doemens Academy in Munich. He also did a four-month apprenticeship in 2004 at the De Koninck Brewery in Antwerp, Belgium. From 2006 to 2008 he worked at Water Street Brewery in Delafield, Wisconsin. From 2009 to 2010 he was head brewer for Joseph James Brewing in Henderson, Nevada. Christiansen was hired by Lucette in November 2010.

Lucette Brewing is located just west of downtown Menomonie along Highway 29 (Hudson Road) where it crosses the Red Cedar River. The brewery building is on the west bank of the river near Riverside Park. It's an area of town that was once part of the city's railroad neighborhood. The building containing Lucette was constructed in the 1970s. While it has served several uses, area residents may remember it best as a local bicycle shop.

Much of Lucette's brewing equipment came from a former brewpub in Kansas City, Missouri. Schletty and Christiansen traveled there to check out the equipment and oversee shipping of the 15-barrel brew kettle, which was delivered during a typical Midwest snowstorm in the late winter of 2010. There was so much snow the day the delivery truck arrived that the driver was reluctant to bring it close to the building. The equipment had to be off-loaded at the main highway, where a Bobcat brought it down the brewery's main driveway and into the building.

For those who are curious about Lucette and Paul's relationship, Hackensack, Minnesota, claims to be her home and a local park there actually has a statue of Lucette and their son, Paul Jr.

BEERS

Lucette Brewing has three standard beers. The Easy Rider Pale Ale 🍺🍺🍺 shows off Centennial hops. It has a floral aroma from dry hopping that is balanced with some firm caramel maltiness. The Slow Hand 🍺🍺🍺🍺 is a dark, full-bodied, smooth and silky American stout that offers lots of malty flavor with hints of coffee, chocolate, caramel, and roastedness. It's made with five different malts, including a type called Blackprinz that is intensely roasted from hulless barley. And Shinning Dawn 🍺🍺🍺🍺 is a bright and bubbly, medium-bodied Belgian-style golden ale. It offers an overriding sweetness from Pilsner malt, yet there is still some wonderful spiciness in the background from Columbus hops in combination with a yeast strain from Antwerp, Belgium. The name Shining Dawn comes from the Latin derivation for gold. Lucette also offers several seasonal brews including the Farmer's Daughter 🍺🍺🍺, an American blonde ale that is made with coriander and Grains of Paradise, which provide a distinctive spiciness alongside a light fruity aroma. And a special treat is Christiansen's honey wine. Lucette beers are found on draft in the Twin Cities. In the future the brewery may start distributing its beers in 16-ounce cans. If you're in Menomonie and are looking for Lucette on tap with a meal, try the Log Jam Bar (709 South Broadway Street). It's owned by Tim Schletty's father.

MENU

None. Lucette Brewing Company does not serve food.

Rush River Brewing Company
River Falls, Wisconsin

_____   _____
Visit Date   Signed

ABOUT THE BREWERY

Rush River takes its name from a small creek that winds its way around the Wisconsin farm of one of the brewery's owners. The brewery actually began in 2004 on a Maiden Rock, Wisconsin, farm in the hills overlooking Lake Pepin, just across the Mississippi River from Red Wing, Minnesota. Brewer and co-owner Dan Chang describes the initial Rush River brewery as less than a thousand square feet in a pole shed with a gravel floor where they had to put in walls, plumbing, and heating themselves. That first brewery was so small that it could fit in the current brewery's walk-in cooler. It was a brewery that was soon outgrown.

In 2007 Rush River open a new production brewery on the northern edge of River Falls, just a few minutes from Interstate 94 with direct access to the Twin Cities, where over half of its beer is sold. The new building now includes a 1,200-square-foot drive-in cooler. The heart of the brewery is a 20-barrel brew kettle and six stainless steel fermenters.

Nick Anderson and Dan Chang met while the two were working for Mac and Jack's Brewery in Seattle, Washington. Both started as keg washers, or, as Chang describes it, at the bottom rung of the brewing ladder. In 2000 their friendship brought them back to the Midwest, where Anderson worked for an uptown Minneapolis bar and Chang took a position at Summit Brewing in St. Paul. After four years they had saved enough for the basic equipment and developed a business plan. Robbie Stair joined their partnership in the beginning because it was on his farm that the brewery started. From the brewery's begin-

143

ning in 2004 until 2007, when it moved to the new facility in River Falls, Rush River Brewing was mostly just draft beer. When the new 10,000-square-foot brewery opened it included several pieces of equipment that were being given a second change. Chang, Anderson, and Stair found a bottler in New Jersey and their packager came from Michigan's New Holland Brewing Company, which had actually purchased it years earlier from St. Paul's Summit brewery. Rush River focuses its distribution on the Twin Cities and some cities in western Wisconsin.

BEERS

The Unforgiven Amber Ale 🍺🍺🍺🍺 is considered the flagship brew for Rush River. It was the first beer released by the brewery. Rich amber-bronze color with a soft, tan head and about 6 percent ABV. Carefully designed by Dan Chang, it is dry hopped and fermented using special yeast. Small Axe Golden Ale 🍺🍺🍺 is a wheat beer made with about 40 percent wheat malt. Light and crisp, it was originally a summer seasonal but grew popular enough to become part of the regular year-round lineup. Lost Arrow Porter 🍺🍺🍺🍺 is very dark with soft texture and a solid maltiness; it finishes around 5 percent ABV. It's made with chocolate and black patent malts that provide a mild yet firm roastedness that stays in balance with the beer's overall flavors. Among Rush River's hoppy beers is an India pale ale called Bubble Jack 🍺🍺🍺, which was the brewery's first seasonal brew and is among the brewery's bestsellers in the Twin Cities. An even hoppier version is the imperial IPA known as Double Bubble 🍺🍺🍺 that's made with twice the hops of Bubble Jack and three pounds of honey per keg. It finishes around 9 percent ABV and is most commonly found as draft beer. Late season Winter Warmer 🍺🍺🍺🍺 is a rich, hazy, amber-colored Scotch ale that's perfect for a snowy evening by a roaring fire. Rush River also makes chocolate oatmeal stout and Uber Alt. The alt was introduced in 2010 and is stronger than the traditional Altbiers, ending up around 4–5 percent ABV. The hazy, copper-colored Uber Alt is made with large amounts of German pilsner malt along with German noble hops before finishing at 8.5 percent ABV. The chocolate oatmeal stout is called Nevermore and it usually turns up in late winter. It's made with additions of rolled oats that give it smooth mouth feel and also white cocoa that offers some semi-sweetness to the overall flavor profile.

Special limited batches of Rush River beer turn up in select Twin Cities bars and popular beer hangouts. The brewery also occasionally gets asked to work with area restaurants on brewmaster dinners. A Minneapolis neighborhood favorite that appears in small batches is the brewery's Lyndale Brown Ale, made as a tribute to the neighborhood where Robbie Stair once owned a bar and where Nick Anderson and Dan Chang met.

MENU

None. Rush River Brewing Company does not serve food.

Northeast Region

BOATHOUSE BREWPUB AND RESTAURANT (ELY)

CARMODY IRISH PUB AND BREWING (DULUTH)

CASTLE DANGER BREWERY (TWO HARBORS)

DUBH LINN IRISH BREWPUB (DULUTH)

DUBRUE (DULUTH)

FITGER'S BREWHOUSE (DULUTH)

LAKE SUPERIOR BREWING COMPANY (DULUTH)

SOUTH SHORE BREWERY (ASHLAND, WISCONSIN)

THIRSTY PAGAN BREWING (SUPERIOR, WISCONSIN)

Often referred to as the Arrowhead region, northeastern Minnesota is a very special place. Along its border with magnificent Lake Superior are wilderness lakes and the Boundary Waters Canoe Area Wilderness. The woods and water make for a great destination for not just beer but outdoor recreation. The landscape features beautiful scenery and incredible opportunities for hiking, biking, canoeing, kayaking, camping, fishing, boating, skiing, snowshoeing, and even golf. Its many artisans are represented in numerous art galleries, heritage museums, and local craft shops.

BoatHouse Brewpub and Restaurant

Ely

Visit Date _____   Signed _____

ABOUT THE BREWERY

Ely, in the far northern reaches of Minnesota, is perhaps best known as an entry point into the Boundary Waters Canoe Area Wilderness (BWCAW). This protected area of nearly 1.1 million acres is a renowned for its hiking, canoeing, camping, and fishing opportunities where access is limited and solitude becomes a way of life. It borders Canada, in the Arrowhead region of Minnesota. For the beer enthusiast, one of the most rustic aspects of the wilderness experience can be time in the woods, or on the water, without a beer. Canned and bottled products are forbidden inside the boundaries of the BWCAW. The area has strict rules prohibiting nonbiodegradable food and packaging. However, BoatHouse Brewpub and Restaurant in the heart of Ely makes for a great place to check the maps over that last beer before heading in or to toast the completion of a successful trip and return to civilization and fresh brewed beer.

Ely, a town of about 3,700 people, is located in the Vermilion Iron Range. From the nineteenth century it supported several iron ore mines, but the last closed in 1967. There is still some logging of forests in the area, but large tracts of protected wilderness surround Ely.

The BoatHouse is located at the intersection of Sheridan Street (Minnesota 1) and East First Street. The locals know it for good beer and food and occasionally live music. The BoatHouse has a bar on one side and main restaurant seating on the opposite side of the building. There's a small stage for bands and performers. You'll also find a pool table and an electronic dart board, which can be handy when settling disagreements over the best Boat-

House beer or just how long that last portage was that made you so thirsty! The bar itself is about twenty-five feet long and seats about a dozen. The custom-made brewery for the BoatHouse is a 3.5-barrel brew kettle designed by Allied Beverage Tanks of Chicago. The copper-clad brew kettle and six fermenting tanks sit inside their own room and can be seen through large windows. The serving tanks are located behind the bar. On the walls hang typical décor of the north woods: deer heads, trophy fish, and snowshoes.

On most visits to the BoatHouse you'll find five to seven house beers on tap. The Eelpout Stout is a great brew, especially in the colder months. But brewer Joel Carlson is partial to Belgian beers so it's worth paying attention to his seasonal and special batches.

HISTORY

The BoatHouse Brewpub and Restaurant opened in August 2007, but brewing didn't happen until March of 2008. Those in-between months, during the slower winter season, allowed time to install brewing equipment with minimal impact on business. The owner of the BoatHouse, Mark Bruzek, grew up in southern Minnesota. After college his travels in Europe introduced him to German beer and his interest in U.S. craft brewing arose from those experiences. For twenty years he practiced pediatric dentistry in Wisconsin, but throughout that time he and his family maintained ties to the area with a cabin and boathouse on Lake Vermilion near Ely. That boathouse inspired the brewpub's name.

Bruzek's nephew, Andy Sakrison, and a friend, Jake Carlson, used to hang out in the boathouse and were initially involved in getting the BoatHouse Brewpub up and running, but both have since left. Jake Carlson's younger brother, Joel, took over the brewmaster responsibilities in spring 2010.

Joel Carlson grew up in Virginia, Minnesota, about fifty miles southwest of Ely. He started homebrewing in 2004 while a student at North Dakota State University in Fargo. After getting a degree in construction management and business administration, he landed a job in water and wastewater management in Brainerd. But Carlson's love of beer led him to enroll in a brewing short-course at Chicago's Siebel Institute of Technology and World Brewing Academy. He worked for Great Waters Brewing Company in St. Paul from 2008 to 2010, when he left to become brewmaster at the BoatHouse.

Carlson is very much at home in the area, having taken his first trip into the Boundary Waters with his family when he was fourteen. As if it's possible to mix business, pleasure, and passion, Carlson seems to have accomplished it here in Ely, as evidenced by the beers that he makes and the local references found in their names.

DON'T MISS THIS

Be sure to just look around inside this building. On the east wall is a large map of the Superior National Forest for settling bets over the distances of canoe portages. Above the entry door to the bar hangs a monster muskie caught by Tim Duff of Manaki, Canada, in 1998.

Before the building became home to the BoatHouse it served Ely for over a hundred years. The walls of this structure certainly have their own stories to tell. Most recently it was a popular bar called Cranberries, and before that it had been used for a couple of different auto-parts stores. A few locals say they remember that a mortuary was centered on the area of the building where the brewhouse is located.

BOATHOUSE BREWS

Eelpout Oatmeal Stout   🍺🍺🍺🍺   *Your Ranking*_____
Dark with bronze highlights and a thin, soft, white head. Full bodied and slick texture. Lots of caramel malty tones with a roasted, biscuit-like finish. Gets its silky body and fruity character from additions of whole naked oats that are added to the mash. A very nice stout for its color and texture, and especially its chocolate and caramel flavor. The beer gets its name from the eelpout fish, caught locally, which is eel-like in appearance with an elongated body.

Entry Point Golden Ale   🍺🍺🍺🍺   *Your Ranking*_____
Considered the flagship among BoatHouse brews. Just a perfect name for a beer offered at the entry to the BWCAW. Clear, light golden color, bubbly, and mild but firm malty flavor. It finishes with a light, smoky ending. Give this beer and the BoatHouse credit for creativity and naming rights!

Hasselhopp Rye Pale Ale   🍺🍺🍺🍺   *Your Ranking*_____
An American pale ale made with additions of malted rye that give it spicy and peppery notes. A hoppy citrus nose. Copper color with a thin, soft, tan head. Medium bodied. Lots of hops flavor that includes citrusy and piney bitterness. Spiciness and peppery tones are found in the finish. This beer was originally called Rye Fish at All and was created by Joel's brother Jake, who preceded him as brewmaster. Jake and a few friends were at a cabin on Eagle's Nest Lake, just outside of Ely, to do some ice fishing in the dead of winter. They brought along homebrewing equipment to make beer out on the frozen lake. The fishing wasn't all that great but the brewing provided the inspiration for the original name of this warm dry-rye ale.

Little White Lie   🍺🍺   *Your Ranking*_____
A Belgian Wit beer. Light citrus nose with hints of orange. A hazy golden color with a thin, soft, white head. Light and bubbly. Orange and citrus flavors stand out. Crisp, slightly sour finish.

Pilot Pub Ale   🍺🍺🍺🍺   *Your Ranking*_____
An English pale ale that makes for a great BoatHouse session beer. A light copper-colored beer that is light bodied and well balanced with a light overall biscuit and toasted malt sweetness. This beer was the first batch brewed at the BoatHouse, thus the name Pilot.

OTHER BOATHOUSE BREWS YOU MAY WANT TO TRY

Basswood Brown   *Your Ranking*_____
Amber color with rich malty flavor.

Blueberry Blonde Ale *Your Ranking*_____

This is a big fruity ale with ABV over 6 percent. A crisp, light-bodied blonde ale that is infused with blueberry purée and then kegged in small quantities.

Call of the Mild *Your Ranking*_____

A dark mild ale.

Infra-Red Belgian Saison *Your Ranking*_____

A brewmaster's special from Joel Carlson. It finishes around 5.4 percent ABV and 20 IBUs.

Pitch-a-Tent IPA *Your Ranking*_____

Just a great hoppy brew for those headed into or out of the boundary waters.

Stuart's Portage 🍺🍺🍺 *Your Ranking*_____

A seasonal brew at the BoatHouse. This is an IPA with lots of citrus hoppiness upfront. A clear copper color with a thick, soft, off-white head. Medium bodied and bubbly. The hoppiness lingers in the finish. It's made with Summit and Dwarf hops for a bitterness of 100 IBUs. The beer gets its name from a very tough, one-mile-plus portage off the Echo Trail.

MENU

The BoatHouse Brewpub and Restaurant serves breakfast, lunch, and dinner. You might find a "breakfast" menu a bit different for most brewpubs, but consider where it is and the significant number of canoeists and campers who get up early and stop in before heading into BWCAW. Breakfast selections include a variety of egg combinations, breakfast sandwiches, and wraps. The lunch menu offers wraps, sandwiches, and burgers, along with chili and hot wings and such Mexican options as fajitas, burritos, chimichangas, and quesadillas. There are a number of vegetarian options in wraps.

The BoatHouse dinner menu features nightly specials along with roasted chicken, a Porter-glazed rib eye, pan-seared trout, and meat loaf. Dinners come with choices in salad, soups, potatoes, and vegetables of the day. Give extra consideration to the signature beer-battered specialties with walleye and shrimp.

Here's a winning combination: the jalapeño "gunboat" poppers, stuffed with cream cheese and Italian sausage, and an Eelpout Oatmeal Stout.

OTHER THINGS TO SEE OR DO IN THE AREA

Ely is an entry point for the Boundary Waters Canoe Area Wilderness and Canada's Quetico Provincial Park. There are thousands of miles of canoe routes, pristine lakes, hiking trails, and beautiful campsites.

The town itself offers much more than just outfitters. There are museums, galleries, craft stores, and clothing shops, including the Steger manufacturer of Mukluks. There are also many other eateries and taverns to consider. Ely hosts a number of music events and festivals. Among the most popular are the Blueberry Art Festival in July and the Harvest Moon Festival in September.

The Dorothy Molter Museum (2002 East Sheridan Street) is a memorial to the legendary last permanent resident to live inside the boundaries of the BWCAW. Molter died in 1986 on Knife Lake. She was known as the root beer lady for offering root beer to thirsty hikers and canoeists. The North American Bear Center (one mile west of Ely on Minnesota 169) and the International Wolf Center (Minnesota 169 on Ely's eastern edge) provide learning opportunities about wildlife and habitat preservation.

In the 1930s the Civilian Conservation Corps (CCC) left a lasting mark on many states, especially Minnesota, which had more CCC camps than any other state. Many of those camps were in the Ely area. One example of CCC work that Ely residents and visitors still enjoy is the pavilion at the South Kawishiwi River Campground. Still used for its original purpose, the pavilion hosts weddings, receptions, and reunions. The stone pathways that curve around the pavilion and all the furniture inside were made by CCC crews.

This region is also known for being the traditional homeland of the Ojibwe people. The Bois Forte Heritage Center and Cultural Museum (1500 Bois Forte Road, Tower) is an opportunity to better understand Ely's first inhabitants. This area of Minnesota is also known for mining. The Ely-Winton History Museum (1900 East Camp Street), on the Vermilion Community College campus, offers a glimpse of how mining and logging shaped the area. The Soudan Underground Mine State Park (twenty miles west of Ely on Minnesota 169) offers guided tours that travel over a half-mile to the bottom of the state's first iron mine.

There are a number of ways to enjoy the scenic beauty of Minnesota's north woods. Many guide services offer dogsled excursions, floatplane adventures, hunting and fishing advice, and a host of canoe and camping outfitters.

BREWERY RATING

	Your Rating	Shepard's Rating	General Description
Location		🍺🍺🍺🍺	Minnesota's northern outpost to the BWCAW is the perfect spot for a craft beer maker.
Ease of Finding Location		🍺🍺🍺	Easy once you are in Ely, but it involves a drive for most of us.
Brewery Atmosphere		🍺🍺🍺🍺	A local tavern with brewhaus. While not spacious, it has its own unique character.
Dining Experience		🍺🍺🍺	Basic bar and tavern food. This brewpub serves breakfast!
The Pints		🍺🍺🍺🍺	Wait till you've done a trip in the BWCWA and you'll be surprised how good these beers taste.

DIRECTIONS

Ely is about 110 miles north of Duluth, and roughly ten miles from the Canadian border. You are likely to arrive in Ely on Minnesota 1. Upon arriving, stay on Minnesota 1, which becomes Sheridan Street. The BoatHouse Brewpub and Restaurant is at the intersection of East Sheridan and North First Avenue East.

Carmody Irish Pub and Brewing
Duluth

308 E Superior St.
carmodyirishpub@yahoo.com

Visit Date   Signed

ABOUT THE BREWERY

There's something about the Irish influence that creates a smile on the face of a beer drinker. Perhaps it is the thought of Arthur Guinness or the image of fun-loving Irish people hanging out in pubs, hoisting a few pints or sipping whiskey and singing to the beat of a bodhran with the accompaniment of a fiddle. That certainly should be part of the atmosphere found in any self-respecting American version of the Irish pub — and that's what you'll find in Duluth's Carmody. This Irish "brew" pub makes its own beer in the basement.

Carmody opened as an Irish pub on Duluth's Superior Street in 2005. In the fall of 2009 a very small brewery was fabricated in the basement of the building and the regulars were treated to house brews. It wasn't for another six months, in May 2010, until the pub actually held a grand opening for the brewery side of the business and officially announced its Irish brewpub status.

The building has some history, beginning with its construction in 1888. It once even served as a local livery stable. Its dimensions are long and narrow with a few window booths that overlook busy Superior Street. The dark wood bar has more than a dozen seats. You'll find not only Carmody house beers but more than two dozen other brews on tap with one of the best assortments of whiskeys in town. The back part of the pub has space for live entertainment or a meal.

Visitors can expect to find three to six Carmody beers for most visits. Tipplers Golden is a light ale with lots of flavor. The stout selections will range from a light, dry Irish original–style to a fuller bodied and sweeter potato stout. The signature beer for Carmody's is its Irish red.

HISTORY

Carmody is owned by Duluth residents Ed and Liz Gleason with Rick Boo. The Gleasons were once co-owners in the former Twin Ports Brewing Company in Superior, Wisconsin (now Thirsty Pagan). They were partners with Rick Sauer in the venture, and Sauer even helped them set up their brewing equipment in Carmody.

The small 2.5-barrel brew kettle is tucked away in the basement of the pub, almost hidden one floor below the bar. That tends to give the place the the attitude of a "blind pig" establishment of the 1930s. Much of the equipment is small scale and was fabricated on site. It consists of just two 4-barrel fermentation vessels and a single conditioning tank. The beers are transferred from conditioning to serving tank, where they are carbonated, then moved into kegs and stored in the pub cooler. The brew kettle was actually cobbled together from an old distiller's mash tun. The entire system is electric, but Carmody has a new steam-jacketed mash tun and kettle that it plans to hook up to city steam sometime in the future.

The brewing at Carmody is handled by Mike Miley, who also occasionally helps brew at the Thirsty Pagan in Superior. Miley grew up in St. Paul and attended the University of Minnesota–Duluth, earning a degree in communications in 2006. While hanging out with college friends in 2003 he started homebrewing. A roommate at the time, Nathan McAlpine, happened to be working part-time at the Thirsty Pagan. When McAlpine left temporarily to attend a brewing course at Chicago's Siebel Institute of Technology and World Brewing Academy, Miley filled in for him. It turned into a part-time position that he kept even after McAlpine returned. Those who stop by the Thirsty Pagan might even find Miley tending bar.

DON'T MISS THIS

The pub and its flagship brew, Agnes Red, is named for the owner's cousin Agnes Carmody. Agnes was born in County Clare, Ireland, in 1892 and died in Duluth in 1978. A photo of Agnes hangs near the pub's fireplace.

CARMODY BREWS

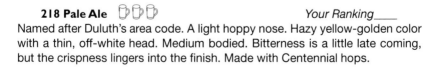

218 Pale Ale   *Your Ranking____*
Named after Duluth's area code. A light hoppy nose. Hazy yellow-golden color with a thin, off-white head. Medium bodied. Bitterness is a little late coming, but the crispness lingers into the finish. Made with Centennial hops.

Agnes Red   *Your Ranking_____*
This standard Irish red ale is indeed a brilliant ruby-red color. A light caramel nose with a solid malty flavor with a bitter background from Cascade hops.

Famine 47 Stout 🍺🍺🍺🍺   *Your Ranking*_____

Made with potatoes, this stout recalls the Great Famine of the 1840s, during which thousands died when Ireland's potato crop failed. Assertive chocolate, malty nose. Famine 47 is very dark with a soft, off-white head. Full bodied and soft with smooth chocolate and caramel flavors and a rich roasted background and finish. It's served on a nitrogen tap that helps give it a smooth texture and finish.

Jona's Pale 🍺🍺🍺   *Your Ranking*_____

Not a regular beer, but one to ask about. This pale ale begins with a light hoppy nose. Hazy copper color and a soft, tan head. Medium bodied. Its somewhat piney and resiny bitterness lingers in the finish. Named after one of Carmody's regular bartenders.

Nancy's 5K English Ale 🍺🍺🍺🍺   *Your Ranking*_____

This American Red begins with a malty nose. A clear reddish-bronze color with a medium bubbly, off-white head. Medium bodied. Assertive resiny and piney bitterness. Dry finish. One of Carmody's most flavorful beers. First brewed in summer 2011 for the Nancy English 5K run. A dollar from each pint sold went to the Dr. Nancy I. English Memorial Foundation, which assists nontraditional women students who are interested in local community service continue their education.

Scanlon IPA 🍺🍺🍺🍺   *Your Ranking*_____

Made with three hops: Cascade, Glacier, and Amarillo. Brewer Bob Blair considers this an imperial IPA because of its big malt-to-hop flavor complexity and its nearly 10 percent ABV. The beer gets its name from local football legend Dewey Scanlon, who played for Duluth's Denfeld High School in the 1920s before becoming head coach of the Chicago Cardinals.

Tipplers Golden 🍺🍺   *Your Ranking*_____

The name of this golden ale refers to someone the Irish author James Joyce often wrote about, a tippler who drinks to excess. It's made with British malt and Glacier hops. Begins with a light, fruity nose. Its color is light and hazy with a medium soft and marbled white head. Light bodied and a sweet malty flavor, followed by an earthy finish.

OTHER CARMODY BREWS YOU MAY WANT TO TRY

Eamon's Amber Ale   *Your Ranking*_____

A medium-bodied amber ale made with U.S. Goldings and Cascade hops.

Highway 61 Pale Ale   *Your Ranking*_____

An occasionally appearing pale ale. Made with sweet and bitter orange peel, along with coriander, which you can detect in its nose and finish. The beer is hazy and light orange-copper with an off-white head. Light to medium bodied with a fruity, slightly edgy maltiness. Finishes with a hint of dryness. The name is a tribute to a local musician who became a big star—Bob Dylan and his song and album *Highway 61 Revisited* (a.k.a. the scenic North Shore Highway).

Whatever Ale   *Your Ranking_____*

Most likely this beer appears as a seasonal Weizen. However, with such a name it could apply to any newly tapped brew!

MENU

The food selections are limited. The pub offers a basic pizza and a variety of toppings with which patrons can custom-build to suit their preferences. Appetizers include platters of smoked fish and crackers from Northern Waters Smokehaus (located in the Dewitt-Seitz Marketplace building in Duluth's Canal Park).

OTHER THINGS TO SEE OR DO IN THE AREA

Just a few doors up the street from Carmody is the office of Lake Superior Port Cities, Inc. (310 East Superior Street), where you can find tourism and travel guides and copies of *Lake Superior* magazine. It's a great place to discover things that might be of interest.

Canal Park is a must visit with its shops, galleries, hotels, and Lake Superior attractions, such as the Great Lakes Aquarium and the SS *William A. Irvin*, and the Lake Superior Maritime Museum. A walk of about ten to twelve blocks will get you into the heart of activity there.

Also not far from Carmody is the Lake Superior Railroad Museum (506 West Michigan) in the historic Union Depot. Here you can catch a ride on the North Shore Scenic Railroad, which will take you along the big lake's rugged coast. From the water, the sightseeing excursions and dinner cruises of the Vista Fleet (323 Harbor Drive) offer wonderful views of the Duluth skyline and harbor.

Carmody itself offers several reasons for another pint. It's quite common to hear local musicians playing in the pub. A must-see event includes the occasional Pinewood Derby races. You can buy your car kit at the bar, build it at home, and come back a few weeks later to race against others. These competitions vary, so you'll need to inquire at the bar for dates and times.

Carmody is just three blocks from Fitger's Brewhouse (600 East Superior Street) and Dubrue (211 East 2nd Street). As already mentioned, it has ties to the nearby Thirsty Pagan (1623 Broadway) in Superior.

BREWERY RATING

	Your Rating	Shepard's Rating	General Description
Location		🍺🍺🍺	Old brick building along Duluth's Superior Street, not far from boardwalk leading to Canal Park or sidewalks into the heart of Duluth. Also, three blocks from Fitger's Brewhouse.
Ease of Finding Location		🍺🍺🍺🍺	Very easy. Street parking or a parking ramp two blocks up Superior Street at the Fitger's Brewery Complex.
Brewery Atmosphere		🍺🍺	The pub has lots of brick and wood accents, and even a fireplace. Nice Irish pub feel. Brewery is downstairs and tours are both guided and self-guided. This is a very small brewery, like adding a brewery to your favorite pub.
Dining Experience		🍺🍺	Limited menu of build-your-own pizzas and smoked fish platters.
The Pints		🍺🍺🍺	A half-dozen house beers along with two dozen other tap brews.

DIRECTIONS

From Interstate 35, exit at Lake Street. Travel northwest (left) about one block and turn north onto Superior Street. Carmody is located about four blocks north of the Lake and Superior intersection on the lake side of Superior Street.

Castle Danger Brewery
Two Harbors

ABOUT THE BREWERY

Finding the perfect pint is a combination of good beer and the journey associated with its discovery. Minnesota's north country and especially the magnificent vistas and raw natural beauty of Lake Superior make for an incredible beer trip if not an expedition. Castle Danger Brewery is unlike any metropolitan venue, mostly because of the natural venue it offers.

Castle Danger Brewery reflects the heart of a local homebrewer who allowed his hobby to flourish almost uncontrollably. Brewery owner and brewmaster Clint MacFarlane opened it in 2011 following about five years of homebrewing and creating fans for his beer among friends and family members. MacFarlane's Castle Danger Brewery is a 3-barrel brewing system with just a couple of fermenters that are housed in a small outbuilding that's so close to Lake Superior you can feel the spray of the lake on breezy days. That shed is actually part of a long-standing family-owned vacation resort that serves travelers along Minnesota's Historic North Shore Drive of Highway 61, making it somewhat of a bed, breakfast, and brewery.

The 700-square-foot shed containing the brewery is connected to the resort's laundry facility, making it small by anyone's standards. MacFarlane says his brewing system, as initially installed, will make about 150 barrels annually. Among the beers that you can expect to find in growlers at the brewery or on tap in a handful of local North Shore taverns include Danger (Pale) Ale, Gale Force Wheat, and George Hunter Stout, which is named after MacFarlane's great-great-grandfather who operated the pre-Prohibition Iron Range Brewing Company in nearby Tower, Minnesota.

HISTORY

The term "castle" is a reference to the high points and cliffs that rise above the Lake Superior coastline. Early ship captains saw these land forms as resembling castles and the waters between them were considered very dangerous. Thus the local unincorporated town took Castle Danger as its name in 1890. Clint and Jamie MacFarlane chose the name for their brewery in 2011.

Castle Danger Brewery is about forty miles north of Duluth, between Two Harbors and Beaver Bay. The small building containing the brewhouse is part of the Castle Haven Cabins Resort that Clint and Jamie took over from Jamie's mother and father, Dwight and Debbie Lind, in 2005. Jamie's great-grandfather, Daniel Lind, emigrated from Norway in the late 1890s and actually homesteaded the land in 1902. The first cabin was built in 1933 by Jamie's grandfather Marcus and his brother Edgar Lind, both of whom also operated the family's commercial fishing business at the time. Today the resort has thirteen cabins, all with spectacular views of Lake Superior. Both Jamie and Clint grew up in Two Harbors and attended high school there. As for Castle Danger Brewing, Clint does the brewing and distribution and Jamie handles the brewery's accounting and bookkeeping.

DON'T MISS THIS

When traveling to Castle Danger Brewery be sure to make plenty of time to experience the majesty of Lake Superior—by surface area the largest freshwater lake in the world.

CASTLE DANGER BREWS

Castle Cream Ale 🍺🍺🍺🍺   *Your Ranking_____*

A light malty nose. Clear copper color and a medium, soft tan head. Light to medium bodied and smooth texture. Great balance and clean throughout. Made with Hallertau Mittelfrüh and Tettanger hops. It also has additions of Honey Malt and Red Wheat for light sweetness and a more rounded mouth feel. This beer was originally made by Zach Padellford who interned with Castle Danger from October 2010 until May 2011. Padellford graduated from the University of Minnesota–Duluth with a degree in chemical engineering and after leaving Castle Danger he took a job with Anheuser Busch (In-Bev) in Los Angeles, California.

Danger Ale 🍺🍺🍺🍺   *Your Ranking_____*

Begins with a light hoppy nose. Light golden color and a medium soft tan head. Medium bodied. A hoppy start but overall great balance between the hops and malts. A crisp, bitter finish. Made with Hallertau Mittelfrüh, Hersbrucker, and Tettanger hops.

Gale Force Wheat 🍺🍺🍺🍺   *Your Ranking_____*

This Hefeweizen has a sharp hoppy bite. MacFarlane calls it a Hopiweizen. Starts with a light, spicy nose. Bright hazy golden color with a thick white head. Light bodied and crisp. The hoppiness is assertive up front, with some wonderful balance with the yeasty esters of banana and cloves that kick in at the end. Made with Hallertau Mittelfrüh, Tettnang, and Amarillo hops. This is an exceptional beer.

George Hunter Stout 🍺🍺🍺   *Your Ranking_____*

Dark color with a medium to full body. Rich chocolate maltiness. Made with a small amount of wild rice that provides a light nutty background with sweetness in the finish. The recipe features Cascade, Northern Brewer, and Cluster hops. Malts include Pale Ale, Crystal, Chocolate, and Black and a touch of wild rice. George Hunter was Clint MacFarlane's great-great-grandfather who lived in Tower, Minnesota, where he ran the Iron Range Brewing Company from the 1890s until Prohibition.

OTHER CASTLE DANGER BREWS YOU MAY WANT TO TRY

Camp Depression Lager   *Your Ranking_____*

This California common is a light to medium-bodied, smooth and clean lager. Made with California ale yeast. Its name is a reference to a Depression-era logging camp located near the Andrews area of Gooseberry State Park. Brewery owner and brewmaster Clint MacFarlane's father once stayed there as a young boy.

Nester Grade Amber Ale   *Your Ranking_____*

An amber ale with some hoppiness. Finishes with spiciness and hints of raisin-like warmth. Its name is a reference to an old rail line that connected logging camps in the woods above Gooseberry Falls to the shore of Lake Superior. Much of the woods and land belonged to Thomas Nester, who had as many as four hundred men working for him when logging was at its peak.

MENU

None. The Castle Danger Brewery does not serve food.

OTHER THINGS TO SEE OR DO IN THE AREA

The journey getting to Castle Danger Brewery is clearly part of the experience. Minnesota's North Shore Scenic Drive (Highway 61) stretches more than 150 miles along Lake Superior coastline, winding northward from Duluth to Grand Portage near the Canadian border. Along the way you'll have impressive vistas of Lake Superior as the roadway dips and turns through ancient rock formations and forests while passing over waterfalls.

The area is a nature lover's dream, especially for those who enjoy biking, hiking, camping, canoeing, picnicking, hunting, and skiing. Also, many of the small towns along the scenic North Shore Dive have local shops, art galleries, great food, and historical attractions. There are also a number of festivals and celebrations throughout the year in these communities. Just about all of the towns along Highway 61 have well-informed visitor information and Chamber of Commerce offices that can help you find whatever you need for the perfect trip. Don't be shy about stopping and asking for advice.

Castle Danger is located about forty-five minutes north of Duluth. Between Duluth and Two Harbors you'll have the choice of taking the Old North Shore Road or the new Highway 61. If you choose the old roadway you'll be traveling a little closer to the shoreline; however, be prepared to slow down for walkers, joggers, bikers, and roller-bladers. There are also some great opportunities for views, picnic areas, and great food. A wonderful way to experience the trip is with a lunch of smoked fish atop a rocky outcrop along the lake. Russ Kendall's Smoke House near Knife River (about fifteen miles north of Duluth) is a source of smoked whitefish or trout for just such an adventure. Kendall's has been a local source of fresh fish since Russ's father W. T. opened it in 1908. Russ died in 2007, but his son and grandson are involved with the business today, marking four generations of Kendalls to smoke fish on the North Shore.

Two Harbors can be more than just a day trip with its shops and galleries. And while there are many community events throughout the year, the summertime highlights include Heritage Days in July and the August Kayak Festival. For kids the tugboat *Edna G.*, which once helped ore carriers navigate the waters of Two Harbors, is docked there. The Lake County Historical Society uses the tug as an interpretive center during the summer months.

As you leave Two Harbors continuing northward to Castle Danger watch for Betty's Pies (1633 Highway 61) on the left. This restaurant and coffee shop has been part of the area since 1956 when Betty Lessard's father, Aleck Christiansen, built a fish shack by the Stewart River on Highway 61. Betty thought it would be a good idea to have some baked goods for the fishermen when they stopped in. That business has been a mainstay of the area and a major landmark along the North Shore Drive for a half-century. Today, during the summer months, it's not uncommon for more than three hundred pies to be sold in a day.

Along Highway 61 there are several beautiful state parks. Just a few minutes north of the Castle Danger Brewery is Gooseberry Falls State Park. And a little further north is the historic Split Rock Lighthouse State Park, which offers some of the most spectacular views of Lake Superior. The Superior Hiking Trail connects Duluth with towns all the way north to the Canadian border — nearly 275 miles of walking path. The trail, which lies just east of Highway 61, takes hikers through forests and along rivers and waterfalls as it winds its way through the bluffs to the Sawtooth Mountains.

If you're making Castle Danger Brewery part of a larger exploration of Minnesota's Arrowhead region, continuing north on Highway 61 will take you to picturesque and welcoming small coastal villages like Grand Marais. The natural beauty of the region has long attracted artists to the area, and Grand Marais is haven to many. No visit would be complete without a stop at the harbor area and a peek into local shops like Sivertson Gallery (14 West Wisconsin Street). Just a short walk down the street is the Gunflint Tavern, which is sure to offer several Minnesota brews from beer makers like Surly, August Schell, and Lake Superior Brewing. Grand Marais is a well-known entry point to the Boundary Waters Canoe Area Wilderness with its connection to the Gunflint Trail.

BREWERY RATING

	Your Rating	Shepard's Rating	General Description
Location		🍺🍺🍺🍺	Located north of Two Harbors, along Minnesota's North Shore Drive (Highway 61) with stunning views of Lake Superior. Also part of the Castle Haven Cabins.
Ease of Finding Location		🍺🍺🍺🍺	About twelve miles north of Two Harbors on Highway 61. Located just before Gooseberry Falls State Park. A great vacation destination.
Brewery Atmosphere		🍺🍺🍺🍺	A small three-barrel brewhouse that from the outside appears to be a small storage building that's part of any cabin-resort. It's an inspiring brewery not only for its ability to turn out small batch brews but also for its view of Lake Superior. Neither can be overlooked.
Dining Experience		n/a	Not applicable. However, when renting a cabin, grab a growler of Castle Danger and head to your personal deck that looks out at the water. The setting will enhance an already great beer.
The Pints		🍺🍺🍺🍺	When enjoying a growler while staying in one of the resort's cabins overlooing Lake Superior—it can't be anything but perfect.

DIRECTIONS

Castle Danger Brewery is located twelve miles north of Two Harbors on Highway 61. Watch for turnoff to the Castle Haven Cabins on the lake side of the highway, between mile markers 37 and 38.

Dubh Linn Irish Brewpub
Duluth

Visit Date   Signed

ABOUT THE BREWERY

Outside of Ireland, few Irish pubs are as sincere about their heritage as the Dubh Linn in Duluth. As you walk in the main door from Superior Street you are confronted with the various flags and crests of Ireland alongside a collection of mementos that the Maxim family has brought back from numerous trips there as they explored the roots of their ancestors. The family matriarch, Elizabeth Murphy, immigrated to the U.S. from County Cork in the 1930s.

The Dubh Linn Irish Brewpub is owned by Mike Maxim and his father Mike (Senior). But the entire family, including three brothers and a sister and a few of their spouses, seems to turn up behind the bar from time to time. The pub is long and rectangular with enough space for several pool tables, two shuffle boards, and several dart boards. The added touches of Ireland include various antiques that have significant meaning to the Maxim family members. Hanging from the ceiling as you enter is a four-by-fifteen-foot Jameson Whiskey sign from Ireland in the shape of an arrow that reads "Only 15 Miles — The Old Jameson Distillery On The Right." In the game room side of the brewpub is an even larger custom-made sign that was given to the Dubh Linn Brewpub by the Guinness Brewery. One can't help but notice the red phone booth in the main bar area, which some might associate as more British décor. Just look closely above it and you'll find a touch of traditional Irish humor from the Maxims. Painted on the wall in Gaelic is the Irish curse translated as, "May your enemies roll their ankles so your know them by their limping." Just off the main bar a fireplace and some large soft chairs add a touch of intimacy, as if that's truly possible in a boisterous Irish pub that's well know as a local sports bar and comedy club. The Dubh Linn is really anything but quiet and secluded with its large-screen television that helps to create a haven for world soccer fans. And on Saturday evenings the back room, also called the Murphy room in honor of Elizabeth Murphy, is transformed into a live entertainment venue for comedy and musical performers.

For most visits you can expect three to five house beers, which change frequently. You can also find a range of other Minnesota craft brews and hard cider on tap. The bar is also well known for Irish whiskeys and single malt scotches — Maxim lays claim to the state's most extensive collection, with more than 130 varieties. For those who look closely beyond all those bottles, there's another touch of local history with the shelves they sit upon. The metal supports were once book shelves, recycled from Duluth's Carnegie Building, which was once the city's public library.

HISTORY

In old Irish Dubh Linn means "The Dark Pool." At the confluence of the rivers Dodder and Liffey a pool was formed and that was where the city of Dublin arose. But in northern Minnesota the Dubh Linn Irish Brewpub has only been a fixture of Duluth since 2006. However, the building that is its home is much older, dating back to the early twentieth century. Locals probably remember it as a Snyders Drug Store and before that it was home to a dry goods business for many years. It has even survived at least two extensive fires. The first in the 1920 nearly destroyed the building. The second in the 1970s left it heavily damaged by smoke and water.

Before opening the Dubh Linn, Mike Maxim (Junior) ran a pool hall called Sharks just a few blocks west on Superior Street. After closing that business in 2004, Mike and his father were looking for other business opportunities when they discovered the building that they would transform into a little bit of Dublin. In its first five years they ran it as a pub before adding the brewery to the building's basement in 2011. Mike (Junior) discovered much of the brewing equipment by happenstance. While striking up a typical over-the-bar conversation with a customer he learned about some equipment in private storage in northern Wisconsin. The equipment is believed to be from a failed brewery in Michigan's Upper Peninsula. But all that remained rather vague, even as Mike worked through a middle man to make the purchase. In the end, Maxim was able to buy the primary components to a 4-barrel system, including several stainless steel fermenters in 2010. Maxim then stored the equipment until he could find the time to start reassembling it in the summer of 2011. The Dubh Linn Irish Brewpub served its first house beers that July by the hands of brewer Clint Collins. New house brews are announced on a board at the end of the bar, and the tap handles have small square chalkboard-type heads where the name of the beer is written in colored chalk.

DON'T MISS THIS

Of the beers offered by the Dubh Linn, the one to seek out is its Irish stout, which truly is a Guinness clone. In traveling across Ireland, the Maxim family discovered an old book that contained comments and brewing details from a Guinness family member about the original recipe used to create the well-known brew at the St. James Gate Brewery in Dublin. The assumed authentic recipe from the 1860s is at the heart of this Duluth brewpub's flagship beer.

DUBH LINN BREWS

IPA 🍺🍺🍺   *Your Ranking*_____

It might not exactly be an Irish brew, but the local hoppy beer fans should enjoy it. Starts with a light floral hoppiness. Clear copper color and a thin, off-white head. Medium bodied and round mouth feel. A malty beginning but the hops find their own in a pint and continue to linger in a dry bitterness for the finish. Some firm pleasant resiny tones. While it might be a little tame for some, it still offers firm bitter character.

Maple Ale 🍺🍺🍺🍺   *Your Ranking*_____

A brown ale made with Minnesota maple syrup. The Maxim family also owns about eighty acres of maple forest in northern Minnesota, which may from time to time generate the syrup that goes into this beer. It's one of the most distinctive Dubh Linn brews and is likely to become one of the brewpub's signatures, especially in the colder months of the year because of its sweeter tones and medium body that is round and smooth. The beer has nice balance with malty sweetness and the maple that is more of an accent in the latest stages of the flavor profile, even lingering lightly into the finish.

Pêche (peach radler) Ale 🍺🍺   *Your Ranking*_____

A summer seasonal. Assertive peach nose. Clear golden color with a thin, bubbly, off-white head. Light bodied and round. The sweetness some in early and really lingers on the palate.

OTHER DUBH LINN IRISH BREWPUB BREWS YOU MAY WANT TO TRY

Dubh Linn Irish Stout   *Your Ranking*_____

Based on an original Guinness version. This is a medium- to light-bodied dark ale. Malty, smooth, clean, and balanced.

MENU

The Dubh Linn Irish Brewpub offers a traditional pub menu. Many of its food selections are based on Maxim family recipes and locally available ingredients. The Maxims utilize the local farmers' market and local fish and meat shops. The smoked fresh Lake Superior trout makes for a great meal starter or afternoon snack with the pub's Irish Stout. The hearty shepherd's pie is made with lamb and sausage mixed with carrots, parsnip, and potatoes. The fish in the fish and chips is made with beer batter. The Reuben is uniquely Dubh Linn, with corned beef that is prepared in a special pub brine and then braised with Smithwick's Irish Ale before it is topped with Swiss cheese and sauerkraut and served on rye bread made fresh by a local Duluth bakery. For appetizers the Dubh Linn offers eight different versions, if not levels of heat, in its Celtic Wings. There is also a range of sandwiches, burgers, soups, and salads. For dessert there's nothing like the Maxim family recipe for cheesecake!

OTHER THINGS TO SEE OR DO IN THE AREA

The Dubh Linn is in the heart of downtown Duluth. Canal Park is just a short walk away with its shops, galleries, and attractions. The Great Lakes Aquarium, SS *William A. Irvin*, and Lake Superior Maritime Museum are family oriented stops in Canal Park that will complete a day or weekend trip to Duluth. The area includes the Duluth Entertainment and Convention Center complex (350 Harbor Dive) and the Amsoil Arena, which is home ice to the University of Minnesota–Duluth men's and women's hockey teams. DECC also hosts other major entertainment events, conventions, and the Duluth Superior Symphony Orchestra.

Also a short walk to the west of the Dubh Linn is the Lake Superior Railroad Museum (506 West Michigan) in Duluth's Historic Union Depot. This is where you can catch the North Shore Scenic Railroad train. It was an active depot from 1892 to 1969, and today its Great Hall hosts special exhibits, performances, and receptions. The Old Depot is also home to the Duluth Art Institute, the Duluth Playhouse, the Duluth Children's Museum, and the Lake Superior Ojibwe Gallery.

It is also a pleasant walk (at least in the summer time) from the Dubh Linn to Caramody (308 East Superior), Fitger's Brewhouse (600 East Superior), and Dubrue (211 East 2nd Street).

BREWERY RATING

	Your Rating	Shepard's Rating	General Description
Location		🍺🍺🍺🍺	Downtown Duluth along Superior Street puts it in the middle of the city and in close proximity to many other things to see and do.
Ease of Finding Location		🍺🍺🍺🍺	Close to major roads and intersections. Parking is easy to find.
Brewery Atmosphere		🍺🍺	The pub itself has its own distinctive character and personality. Lots of Irish accents gives you the feel that you've taken a trip to Dublin. The brewery is down in the building's basement with very limited access for beer enthusiasts. This venue is all about the Irish pub (which does have an authentic feel), but the brewery is out of sight and you might miss the local beer altogether if you don't look for the beer menu board.
Dining Experience		🍺🍺🍺	Irish pub fare to family tavern-style offerings.
The Pints		🍺🍺	Based on its success as just a pub before it installed a brewery, one should expect Dubh Linn to evolve and grow for the better.

DIRECTIONS

From Interstate 35 exit at Lake Street in downtown Duluth. Turn northwest (left) on Lake Street, and in just about a block you'll be at the intersection with Superior Street. Again, turn left (westward) onto Superior and the Dubh Linn Irish Brewpub will be on your right within a block and a half.

Dubrue
Duluth

ABOUT THE BREWERY

Dubrue stands for Duluth Brewing. From rather humble beginnings its first beer was released in July 2011 from a small garage-like building near the Duluth Clinic and Essentia Health facility. The structure was once used by the Gold Cross Ambulance Company. Dubrue's brewhouse doesn't occupy much space. However, on warm days in Duluth the building's large garage doors can be opened to expose the inner workings of the brewery and make it seem much larger than it is.

Inside, the brewing system is mostly assembled from former dairy equipment. Owners Bob Blair and Nick Cameron are no strangers to the local Duluth beer scene. Both came up through the brewing ranks at Fitger's Brewhouse.

Blair and Cameron planned their brewery over a couple of years. They evaluated various concepts from bar to brewpub, then eventually decided upon a production brewery. Along the way to making that decision the need for financial capital pointed out the importance of being frugal. That led them to the utility and cost savings they could get by turning former dairy equipment into a brewery. They also choose to do much of their own building renovations, including the installation of a steam boiler and the piping network needed to support it. They also built their own beer cooler and storage area. All of that is found inside the 2,000-square-foot space they lease. For those visiting Dubrue, this is a small brewery in a very small space with minimal evidence from the outside that the building contains a production brewery. Blink at the wrong time and you might just walk, ride, or drive by without noticing it.

Dubrue's core beers include a Pub Ale modeled after the well-known English beer Boddingtons as well as a dark, bitter India Black Ale that will rival more common hop monster IPAs. Dubrue's start-up phase focused mainly on draft beer for local pubs and taverns with bottled products to be added in 2012 or later.

HISTORY

Owners Bob Blair and Nick Cameron grew up in Duluth and attended high school together. After going different ways to attend colleges and start their careers, they eventually found themselves back in town as brewers at Fitger's Brewhouse. Nick actually worked his way up from bartending, to cleaning kegs, and then eventually helping out in the brewing process. He also worked for a short time at Kona Brewing in Hawaii. When Nick isn't making beer he is a financial analyst for Essentia Health in Duluth.

Bob Blair likes to joke that he actually started homebewing while in high school. After a few years in the army he came back to Duluth and worked part-time for a summer at Lake Superior Brewing Company. That experience helped him to decide that he wanted to be a professional brewer. So at the age of twenty-two he enrolled at Oregon State University, eventually receiving a degree in fermentation sciences. While living in the Pacific Northwest he had an opportunity to work at McMenamins-Edgefield (Troutdale, Oregon). In 2005 he came back to Duluth and took a job at Fitger's. He also brewed part-time for Carmody Irish Pub and Brewing in Duluth from 2009 to 2010 before he and Cameron opened Dubrue.

DON'T MISS THIS

The 15-barrel brewing system is worth a close look. It's composed of a variety of used pieces of dairy equipment that Blair and Cameron found from Pulaski, Wisconsin, to Chicago, Illinois. It's not uncommon for former dairy equipment to be retrofitted, especially in start-up breweries. It's just that an examination of this brewhouse provides an understanding as to why brewers often call them "Frankenstein" systems, since they are made up of milk and cheese bulk tanks and a maze of stainless steel pipes. When looking around this small brewery you might also see the brewery's first sample bar, which will likely be sitting just inside the large garage doors. It's small — seating only a couple of people — and can be used for festivals. It has the look of a household bar that might have once been used in a 1970s rec room. The bar was a gift to the brewery from Nick Cameron's mother-in-law. Also hanging on the wall is a plaque showing the four members of the 1998 Duluth East swim team. If you look closely you'll see a young Bob Blair, who was involved in several record-setting performances while in high school.

DUBRUE BREWS

India Black Ale (IBA)   *Your Ranking_____*
This a very dark and hoppy beer, made in the spirit of a Cascadian black ale; some also refer to these beers as a Black IPA. Dubrue's version features Centennial and Amarillo hops. You find those hops in the very beginning with a

strong resiny nose. Its color is deep black with bronze highlights and a medium soft, brown head. It's full bodied, round, and somewhat bubbly. There is a light smokiness to the flavor alongside assertive citrus hoppiness. Finishes sharp and dry with a light roastedness.

Pub Ale   *Your Ranking*_____
A very pleasant crisp session beer. A light earthy-malty nose. Hazy golden to amber color with a bubbly tan head. Medium bodied. A malt forward flavor profile with a light fruity, even grassy hoppiness in the background. Bitterness comes out stronger in the finish with a dryness. Made with Centennial hops. A touch of lemon peel is added in a process like dry hopping to give the beer a crisp fruity edge. Dubrue encourages local accounts to put this beer on a nitrogen tap line to soften its mouth feel and bring out more of the smooth malty tones.

OTHER DUBRUE BREWS YOU MAY WANT TO TRY

Black and Tan   *Your Ranking*_____
A combination of the Pub Ale and the India Black Ale. The Pub Ale actually floats on top of the Black Ale making this more of a "reverse" Black and Tan.

MENU

None. Dubrue does not serve food.

OTHER THINGS TO SEE OR DO IN THE AREA

Dubrue is located about a block and a half north of Duluth's Superior Street. There are shops and numerous bars along this busy thoroughfare. The Fond-du-Luth Casino (129 East Superior Street) is a major attraction nearby. Checking out the performances at the Renegade Theater Company (222 East Superior Street), home to Duluth's only resident sketch comedy team, could be good for a laugh.

Canal Park is about six blocks away. You can actually catch a glimpse of the main channel leading to and from the Ariel Lift Bridge. Canal Park contains numerous shops, galleries, and attractions like the Great Lakes Aquarium, SS *William A. Irvin*, and Lake Superior Maritime Museum. Canal Park sits just east of the Duluth Entertainment and Convention Center complex (350 Harbor Dive) and the Amsoil Arena, which is home ice to the University of Minnesota–Duluth men's and women's hockey teams. DECC also hosts other major entertainment events, conventions, and the Duluth Superior Symphony Orchestra.

Dubrue is a short walk to three other brewpubs: Carmody (308 East Superior), Fitger's Brewhouse (600 East Superior), and Dubh Linn Irish Brewpub (109 West Superior).

BREWERY RATING

	Your Rating	Shepard's Rating	General Description
Location		🍺🍺	Dubrue adds its own character to the thriving overall Duluth beer industry. It's just a few blocks north of the main downtown area. The immediate neighborhood is a little rundown, but generally it's composed of residential apartments. Also close to Duluth Clinic/Essentia Health.
Ease of Finding Location		🍺🍺🍺	Not difficult to find. Finding street parking close by can be a challenge. Minimal signage adds somewhat to the challenge of finding this brewery.
Brewery Atmosphere		🍺🍺	The brewery occupies a building that was once a garage for a local ambulance company and still shows some of that character. There really is nothing too special about the building itself, but inside it definitely has the look and feel of a small working brewery.
Dining Experience		n/a	Not applicable.
The Pints		🍺🍺🍺	With a limited number of beers initially, Dubrue is a brewery to watch as it grows and becomes more of the local beer scene.

DIRECTIONS

From Interstate 35 exit at Lake Street in downtown Duluth. Continue straight ahead (northwest) on Lake Street, crossing through its intersection with Superior Street. In two blocks Lake Street intersects with 2nd Street, where your turn right (northeastward) onto what becomes East 2nd Street. Dubrue is located about two blocks ahead on the left (north) side of the street, near the intersection of East 2nd Street and North 2nd Avenue East.

Fitger's Brewhouse
Duluth

Visit Date _____ Signed _____

ABOUT THE BREWERY

Fitger's Brewhouse is located on a seawall high above Lake Superior in the historic Fitger's Brewing Company building. There are many visual architectural reminders of Fitger's storied history, none more striking than the brewery's smokestack and water tower, which carry the Fitger's name and star logo. Together they contribute a distinctive and historical landmark to the Duluth skyline.

Old brick and heavy warehouse beams add atmosphere to what was, and is today, a sprawling Fitger's Brewery Complex. Throughout the building, including the Fitger's Hotel, are a number of black-and-white photos showing the old Fitger's brewery and many wonderful scenes from the late 1800s and early 1900s. One artifact that beer aficionados will not want to miss is found in the lobby of the Fitger's Hotel—a larger than life drawing of King Gambrinus. Drawn by international artist Arthur Fitger, it was originally intended to be a model for a large statue for a rooftop beer garden, which was never built.

The present-day Fitger's Brewhouse is highly regarded in the Minnesota brewing industry and nationally among peers. By volume of beer produced, it is Minnesota's largest brewpub. Fitger's opened as a bar in 1995 and started brewing beer in 1997. The first brewmaster, Mike Hoops, began as a bar manager. He then helped oversee the transition to brewpub and remained as brewmaster with Fitger's until 1999. After taking a little time away from professional brewing, Mike eventually ended up at Minneapolis Townhall where he continues as brewmaster. However, when he left Fitger's his brother Dave

171

was called to take over. At the time, Dave was working at Pyramid Breweries in Berkeley, California. Prior to that he had completed brewer's programs at the University of California–Davis and the Siebel Institute of Technology and World Brewing Academy in Chicago. Despite living in California, Dave had become good friends with Fitger's Brewhouse owners Rod Raymond and Tim Nelson. So when his brother left, it was with some comfort that Dave was able to step into the brewmaster's rubber boots. Dave is considered a local kid, having grown up and lived in Duluth until his was ten years old. He had picked up homebrewing while living in San Francisco, and the hobby had grown so much he found himself volunteering at microbreweries to learn about brewing. Dave Hoops continues to hone his brewing skills and periodically takes trips to Germany to develop his lager brewing skills.

Inside Fitger's Brewhouse (the actual brewpub) on the first floor, an old Fitger's sign invites you into the main dining room. A small loft is located virtually in the rafters of the pub but it provides an excellent venue for watching people down below at the main bar. The current brewhouse is composed of a 10-barrel brewing system, with more than fifty fermentation and conditioning vessels. Among those are several wood-clad vessels and copper-colored English grundy tanks that you can see from the brewhouse windows on the first floor of the Fitger's Complex. When exploring the larger building, you'll find additional fermenters, along with a gift shop and a beer store, one floor below the brewpub, with T-shirts, hats, other clothing, and growlers. Fitger's may look small, but it's spread out over two floors.

The Fitger's Brewhouse crowds a lot into the restaurant space, giving it the vibrant feeling you want in a neighborhood tavern. A vast array of postcards stuck to the barroom's support posts show how much customers appreciate Fitger's. While some are rather risqué, many offer humorous insights into just how far Fitger's reputation and beer have traveled. For the fortunate few, the best seats in the house are at a table for six by windows offering views of Superior Street.

Fitger's Brewhouse always has an impressive and abundant lineup of beers. It is common to find up to ten beers on tap, including three or four seasonals that change every few weeks. The list below reflects only a small sampling of Fitger's brews, and some may not return to their taps. The beer menu at Fitger's is one of the most dynamic among Minnesota brewpubs, and that is what makes it such a great stop. Among the beers that seem to have stood the test of time on tap are Big Boat Oatmeal Stout, Witchtree ESB, Starfire Pale Ale, El Niño Double Hopped IPA, Lighthouse Golden, and Apricot Wheat. Beyond those, the rotation makes this place fun and always worth a pint or two. In 2011 the brewpub started selling hand-corked 750mL bottles in a "Great Lakes Series" of beers. These well-aged limited release brews are named after individual Great Lakes, followed by a style description, and carry the name of brewer who designed each. Only about two hundred bottles were initially offered. The styles have included a Belgian Strong Ale (Erie), an Imperial German Schwartzweizen (Superior), a Smoked Doppelbock (Huron), and a Brettanomyces aged Belgian Pale Ale (Ontario). You can also expect to find one to two cask ales served on the beer engine (hand pump).

HISTORY

Sidney Luce opened Duluth's first brewery in 1857, less than two blocks away from the present Fitger's site (approximately North Seventh Avenue East and the lakeshore). Not just a brewer, Luce also made candy bars, pop, and champagne. He was more an early investor, and Gottlieb Busch ran an early brewery on his land. In 1865 Luce sold the operation to Nicholas Decker, who grew the business with advertising campaigns that capitalized on the area's natural resources with phrases like "mountain-brook water."

In the 1870s Decker sold a share of the brewery to Michael Fink. When Decker died in 1875, Fink leased the brewery for two years until he could purchase it from the Decker family. By 1881 Fink expanded operations to the present Fitger's brewery site. Fink chose the name Lake Superior Brewing Company, and he hired a twenty-eight-year-old German named August Fitger. Within a year August Fitger was half-owner of the brewery. In 1885 Fink sold his half of the brewery for $18,000 to Percy Anneke, who had been working as an auditor for the Joseph Schlitz Brewing Company. The brewery under Fitger and Anneke saw tremendous expansion in the 1890s and early 1900s. In 1902 Fitger hired German-trained John Beerhalter to be his masterbrewer. In 1904 the brewery became incorporated and was renamed Fitger Brewing Company. By 1910 it had become one of the largest breweries in Minnesota.

During Prohibition the business relied on its candy making with such products as Fitger's Flapper, the Fitger's Spark Plug, and the five-cent Fitger's Nut Goodie. The brewery facility was also used to bottle Lovit Pop. After Prohibition, Fitger's went back to brewing and by 1940 it was producing a hundred thousand barrels annually. Four years later the brewery was bought by the Beerhalter family, who ran it until 1972 when industry competition and consolidation forced it to close.

After sitting vacant for several years, the brewery building got a new life as Fitger's Brewery Complex when it reopened in September 1984. Today, you find a forty-eight-room hotel, two restaurants, and several retail shops. Fitger's Brewhouse Brewery and Grille opened in 1997 and has brewed almost continuously since (an electrical fire in 2001 destroyed a brew kettle and caused Fitger's to shut down for several months while it underwent remodeling and equipment improvements).

In 2006 Fitger's Brewhouse owners Rod Raymond and Tim Nelson opened the Red Star, a nightclub-style bar that is across the hallway from Fitger's Brewhouse in the old brewery complex. In 2007 Burrito Union (1332 East Fourth Street) joined the Fitger's family. And in 2011 Tycoon's Zenith Alehouse, a bar in Duluth's old city hall (132 East Superior Street), opened as the third venue affiliated with Fitger's. All serve Fitger's beer, and each location occasionally has something special made just for it. Tim Nelson and Rod Raymond purchased Duluth's old Carlson Bookstore Building (206 East Superior Street) in 2010 with long-term plans to expand Fitger's beer production with a larger brewery. However, that would require modification to current state law to allow a production brewery and brewpub to operate under the same ownership.

DON'T MISS THIS

With its distinctive smokestack, the Fitger's Brewery Complex is easy to spot along the Duluth skyline. Just walk around inside and you're likely to notice a display or photo you didn't see before. The building is conducive to self-guided tours (a small walking tour pamphlet is usually available from the hotel), and an audiovisual presentation continuously runs on the lower level of the lakeshore side of the complex. Near the entrance to the brewpub, a set of stairs will take you to a small brewery museum that contains many artifacts from the early days of Fitger's, including one of the original copper kettles.

FITGER'S BREWS

Apricot Wheat 🍺🍺🍺   *Your Ranking*_____
This American Wheat has a strong apricot aroma. Cloudy golden and light bodied. Lots of fruity flavors, with a light hoppiness that tries to come through the taste. The apricot tones are firm, but not overwhelming. Made with about three gallons of apricot per 10-barrel batch of beer. A beer that you almost always find on tap at Fitger's.

BWCA Alt 🍺🍺🍺🍺   *Your Ranking*_____
A light yet firm malty nose. Hazy bronze color with a soft, off-white head. Medium bodied and round texture. Firm caramel maltiness and moderate bitterness with a light nutty finish.

Big Boat Oatmeal Stout 🍺🍺🍺🍺   *Your Ranking*_____
An American version of an English oatmeal stout. A dark body, soft, white, creamy head, and silky texture. The initial sweet flowery flavor turns to a strong coffee taste. Finishes with roasted tones. Made with four different malts and 18 percent oats. Name is a tribute to the local shipping industry. This is one of those beer that seems great anytime. Lots of flavor and body. Served on a nitrogen tap line.

Blonde on Blonde 🍺🍺🍺   *Your Ranking*_____
A special lighter bodied pale ale brewed for summer and the Duluth (Bob) Dylan Fest. A light floral nose. Clear, light golden color with a medium soft, off-white head. Medium bodied and crisp. Some maltiness up front in the flavor, then a mild but firm dry bitterness throughout and into the finish. Some of the barley malt that goes into this beer comes from Ashland, Wisconsin, and the farm of Bo Belanger, the owner and head brewer at South Shore Brewery.

Brewhouse Brown 🍺🍺🍺🍺   *Your Ranking*_____
Pleasant, inviting malty nose. Hazy amber color with a medium bubbly tan head. Lots of firm maltiness in the flavor and finish. A well-rounded beer and great with food. Rotates with Witchtree ESB on a dedicated amber beer tap.

Decadence 🍺🍺🍺🍺   *Your Ranking*_____
A bold, warm, and flavorful imperial stout. Aged on a bed of raspberries and cocoa nibs. Strong chocolate maltiness in the nose. Very dark color with a soft brown head. Full bodied with a creamy and soft mouth feel. The main fla-

vor features a rich and spicy chocolate maltiness with a raspberry-fruity background. Finishes warm with assertive semi-sweet raspberry tones that linger. A wonderful cold weather brew to be enjoyed in front of an open fire.

Duluth Steam 🍺🍺🍺   *Your Ranking*_____

A light malty nose. Clear copper color and a white, rocky head. Medium bodied. Smooth, clean malty tones of caramel dominate. A crisp, lightly hopped finish with just a hint of fruitiness in the background. Its name refers to the plant in Duluth that supplies steam to the brewery.

El Niño Double Hopped IPA 🍺🍺🍺🍺   *Your Ranking*_____

Six types of hops are used to make this IPA. A very flowery, hoppy nose. Cloudy, dark golden color with a thick, bubbly, off-white head. Medium to full bodied with a soft texture, when served on a nitrogen tap. Strong, dry, hoppy flavors dominate. Finishes with a long, lingering, dry bitterness. This is among Fitger's best sellers and a favorite of those who enjoy assertively hopped beers.

Finn's Finest #1 🍺🍺🍺🍺   *Your Ranking*_____

A West Coast pale ale originally made to mark the birthday of Dave Hoops's son. Great hoppy nose. Clear, rich golden color and a thin, bubbly, off-white head. Medium bodied with a dry texture. Strong, firm bitterness throughout. A memorable hoppy beer.

French River Hefeweizen 🍺🍺🍺🍺   *Your Ranking*_____

Firm banana nose. Cloudy, bright yellow-golden color with a thick, soft, white head. Light bodied and crisp. Strong banana and clove flavors. A great German Hefeweizen.

Frühling Lager 🍺🍺🍺🍺   *Your Ranking*_____

A marzen-style beer with brilliant color and smooth malty flavor. Begins with a light but very solid malty nose. Vivid reddish-copper color with a marbled tan head. Medium bodied and somewhat soft. Rich and smooth caramel malt flavor with a light roasted to nutty background. Finishes with that same smooth maltiness and a light smokiness in the end.

Huron—Smoked Doppelbock 🍺🍺🍺   *Your Ranking*_____

The "Huron" member of Fitger's Great Lakes Series of beers. Created by Frank Kuszuba. An inviting firm smoky aroma. Deep bronze color with a soft, brown head. Full bodied and round mouth feel. Lots of caramel and chocolate maltiness along with the smokiness. A light fruity background. Finishes malty, warm, and somewhat sweet. Gets its smokiness from additions of cherry-smoked malt. Aged for seven months before it is released.

Lighthouse Golden Ale 🍺🍺🍺🍺   *Your Ranking*_____

The number two seller at Fitger's. A standard beer, so its nearly always on tap. A bright straw to golden-colored ale brewed with two-row barley and American and Czech hops. Floral nose and clear, light straw color. The head is soft, creamy, and white. A light bitterness dominates with a mild smoky finish. Lots of flavor makes this a distinctive light brew.

Mariner Mild 🍺🍺🍺   *Your Ranking*_____

A strong caramel nose. Dark bronze color with a thick, soft, white head. Light to medium bodied and soft texture. Overall, light and soft malty flavor. Nicely accented with light toasty finish.

Northern Waters Smoked Helles 🍺🍺🍺   *Your Ranking*____

Assertive smoky nose. Clear golden color with a soft, off-white head. Light to medium bodied and round. A burnt type of smokiness in the body of the malty flavor. Smoke lingers into the finish. Overall the smoke is a nice accent that adds to this light- to medium-bodied beer without distracting.

Park Point Pilsner 🍺🍺🍺🍺   *Your Ranking*_____

A German style pilsner hopped with Czech Saaz and Hallertau hops. Begins with a light malty nose. Light to medium bodied. Clear, bubbly golden color and a thin, soft white head. Clean flavor with a crisp hoppy background and fin-ish. This is a signature beer for Fitger's brewmaster Dave Hoops. Its name is a tribute to Park Point in Duluth, a seven-mile-long sandbar joined to Canal Park by the Ariel Lift Bridge. When included with Wisconsin Point, which stretches three miles from the opposite side of the bay, Park Point makes up the longest freshwater sandbar in the world. This is an exceptional beer.

Petroglyph Porter 🍺🍺🍺   *Your Ranking*_____

This porter looks very dark with a bronze body and soft, tan head. No nose leaves a very clean and fast-tasting impression. There is a strong burst of roasted nuttiness, almost a slight musty flavor.

St. Stephen's Abbey 🍺🍺🍺🍺   *Your Ranking*_____

A Fitger's favorite that is a must-try beer. A light yeasty aroma offers a warm, inviting introduction to this Belgian-style abbey. Clear bronze with a light hazi-ness, and a thick, bubbly, tan head. Full bodied and round. The firm, musty, yeasty qualities are well balanced and smooth. Finishes with a light, fruity sweetness.

Starfire Pale Ale 🍺🍺🍺🍺   *Your Ranking*_____

Fitger's number one seller. Firm, strong, assertive hoppiness makes this a great pale ale. A floral, hoppy nose. Clear copper color and a thin, bubbly, off-white head. Full bodied with a sharpness. Bitterness is constant with a dryness that builds in the finish. A well-done pale ale that could easily pass for a very clean IPA with its 70 IBUs and 6 percent ABV. When offered on cask, this is an even more outstanding brew. This beer is based on brewmaster Dave Hoops's love of bitter beers that he developed during his time on the West coast.

Superior—Imperial German
Schartzweizen 🍺🍺🍺🍺   *Your Ranking*_____

The "Superior" member of Fitger's Great Lakes Series of beers. Created by brewmaster Dave Hoops himself. An assertive yeast, banana, and plum nose. Deep dark brown color, almost black, with a thick brown head. Full bodied and warm. Strong spicy tones of cloves combined with toffee-like maltiness that all linger well into the finish.

Superior Trail IPA 🍺🍺🍺   *Your Ranking_____*

This IPA is made with all American hops. Lots of piney aromas. Clear copper color and a thick, soft, off-white head. Medium to full bodied. Aromas turn to resiny flavor that lingers through the finish. Some warmth in the end.

Trampled by Hops 🍺🍺🍺🍺   *Your Ranking_____*

This imperial IPA is as assertive as the local band Trampled by Turtles, for which it is named. Brewmaster Dave Hoops sat down with the band and designed this hoppy brew to their liking. Its nose offers a strong floral hoppiness. The color is a clear copper with a marbled tan head. It's medium to full bodied with a sharp mouth feel. There is a strong piney hoppy flavor that matches the nose. It finishes with a lingering resiny bitterness. Not the strongest imperial IPA you'll find, but complex and spicy. In the band's early days, until their following grew too large, Trampled by Turtles occasionally performed at Fitger's. In 2011 they opened for Willie Nelson at the Bayfront Festival Park in Duluth and were topping *Billboard* magazine's national bluegrass chart.

Witchtree ESB (Extra Special Bitter) 🍺🍺🍺🍺   *Your Ranking_*

The flagship beer for Fitger's. Brewed with English noble hops and English-style pale malt. Served on a nitrogen tap. Almost no nose, just a light floral aroma. Clear copper color with a thick, soft, off-white head. Medium bodied. A light malty start with a firm but mild bitterness. A light hoppy ending. A great ESB, and the nitrogen tap helps accentuate the bitter qualities. Rotates with the Brewhouse Brown on a dedicated amber beer tap.

OTHER FITGER'S BREWS YOU MAY WANT TO TRY

Black Currant Brown   *Your Ranking_____*

Made with local black currants. A fruity nose with sharp, fruity-sour flavors.

Black-eyed Lager   *Your Ranking_____*

Lots of flavor in this beer. An assertive malty nose. Dark colored with ruby-red hues and a thick, soft, white head. Full bodied. Strong chocolate malty flavors with a firm, bitter background. A dry finish.

Breakwater Wit   *Your Ranking_____*

A wheat ale brewed with unmalted wheat, coriander, and orange. Hopped with Cascade hops. Fermented with a Belgian yeast strain.

Collaboration Cherry Grand Cru   *Your Ranking_____*

A collaboration by the Hoops brothers Dave (Fitger's) and Mike (Minneapolis Townhall Brewery). This copper-colored beer offers semisweet cherry flavor and a modest background of caramel and toffee from the malt.

El Diablo   *Your Ranking_____*

A Belgian strong ale. Light golden color. Rich and inviting floral flavors. A light dry finish.

Farmhouse Special Reserve   *Your Ranking*_____
A light-bodied and light-colored Belgian Saison. Made with coriander, ginger, Grains of Paradise, and sweet orange peel. A bronze medal winner at the 2004 Great American Beer Festival.

Lester River Hefeweizen   *Your Ranking*_____
A light golden to yellow, light-bodied Hefeweizen. Offers tones of banana and bubble gum.

Old Redbeard Barley Wine   *Your Ranking*_____
Begins with a malty nose. Deep hazy copper to bronze color. Minimal bubbly head. Fully bodied and round. Lots of caramel maltiness in the flavor and finish. Some warmth in the end. Watch for a version of this beer that's been aged in bourbon barrels.

Wheat Wine   *Your Ranking*_____
A light but firm fruity nose. Deep amber to brown color with a thin, bubbly, off-white head. A light malty beginning with a lingering sweetness and a grainy finish.

Wildfire Lager   *Your Ranking*_____
This beer features the heat of seven different types of hot peppers. It begins with a strong jalapeño nose that doesn't let up. Its clear copper color and soft, tan head are deceiving. The heat and spicy character continues to build over the course of a pint. You'll want to keep some chips or something cool on hand just to put this wildfire out.

MENU

The Fitger's menu really specializes in pub food with an eclectic twist. Appetizers range from onion rings to three types of nachos, beer-battered french fries, and a hummus plate. A favorite addition to any plate are the blue corn chips dipped in pub sauce reminiscent of Thousand Island dressing. They're a standard favorite with any of the Fitger's beers.

Burgers and sandwiches make up a large part of the menu. The brewhouse favorite is called the Pub Burger, with sautéed mushrooms and onions. The Jalapeño Burger is for those who like a truly "hot" meal. The signature pick for a light lunch is the smoked salmon wrap. Other specialty sandwiches are the Lakefront Turkey with sprouts and red pepper chutney, the grilled tuna steak sandwich, and the black bean burrito with tomatoes, onions, and fresh cilantro.

The brewhouse also caters to vegetarians with a burger made with fresh wild rice from northern Minnesota; the grilled portobella mushroom sandwich stacked with fresh field greens, tomatoes, and melted swiss cheese; black bean vegetarian chili; or an order of hummus and sprouts with fresh garlic, olive oil, and lemon.

There are often several choices for satisfying a sweet tooth. The Big Brewhouse Cookie works well with a Big Boat Oatmeal Stout. But for a real treat try the flavor-of-the-day gourmet cheesecake.

OTHER THINGS TO SEE OR DO IN THE AREA

Duluth has a number of festivals that can coincide with a visit to Fitger's. And the brewery often makes special beers for such occasions. Among the highlights is Dylan Fest, a week in late May that marks the birthday of singer and Duluth native Bob Dylan. In 2011 Fitger's made Blonde on Blonde for the event. In late September Duluth holds its Oktoberfest festivities. A large number of activities are held at Bayfront Festival Park. You can expect Fitger's to offer an Oktoberfest for that one. And if you enjoy beer festivals the annual Gitchee Gumee Brewfest happens in April in nearby Superior, Wisconsin.

Throughout the year Duluth's harbor is full of attractions for adults and kids. A boardwalk allows one to follow the Lake Superior shoreline from Fitger's Brewhouse all the way to the Aerial Lift Bridge and Canal Park. The Great Lakes Aquarium is a wonderful way to explore and learn about the big lake. Nearby, shipping exhibits such as Barker's Island and the S.S. *William A. Irvin* ore boat are also great for kids.

Traveling north from Duluth, follow scenic Minnesota Highway 61 (the North Shore Drive route). It follows the rugged Lake Superior coast all the way to Canada. Along the way there are pull-offs for enjoying the views and many cascading rivers that create beautiful waterfalls. One well worth the drive is Gooseberry Falls State Park with its scenic overlooks and hiking trails. Just a little farther up the road is the famous Split Rock Lighthouse.

A great way to see the north shore is by train. The North Shore Scenic Railroad leaves the Union Depot in downtown Duluth (506 West Michigan Street) and travels right by Fitger's. There are several different excursions lasting up to six hours for a round trip to Two Harbors. The Duluth Art Institute, also housed in the Union Depot, has rotating exhibitions.

For a glimpse into what life might have been like in the early days of Duluth, the Glensheen Mansion (3300 London Road) offers tours. Built in 1908, the thirty-nine-room house and grounds cover seven acres of land along the lakeshore.

Fitger's itself can be a destination for music by local performers. Other local beer stops nearby include the Carmody Irish Pub (308 East Superior), Dubrue (211 East 2nd), Dubh Linn Irish Brewpub (109 West Superior Street), and Lake Superior Brewing Company (2711 West Superior).

BREWERY RATING

	Your Rating	Shepard's Rating	General Description
Location		🍺🍺🍺🍺	Central city location along the shore of Lake Superior offers wonderful views and walks.
Ease of Finding Location		🍺🍺🍺🍺	Close to major roads and intersections, along the bike path that connects to Canal Park. Parking in an attached parking ramp.
Brewery Atmosphere		🍺🍺🍺	The working brewery is somewhat cramped in this historic brewery building. However, there is certainly an old brewery feel that's like no other working brewery in the state.
Dining Experience		🍺🍺🍺🍺	Brewpub itself offers a tavern atmosphere. Pub fare to family menu, somewhat eclectic. Restaurant seating is rather limited and cramped. A pleasant yet small beer garden along the front of the building on Superior Street is great for summer days.
The Pints		🍺🍺🍺🍺	A perfect experience

DIRECTIONS

From Interstate 35, exit at Lake Street. Travel northwest (left) about one block and turn north onto Superior Street. Fitger's is located about five blocks north of the Lake and Superior intersection. Watch for the brick smokestack that says Fitger's and the building's red water tower with the black star bearing the letter "F" signifying Fitger's.

Lake Superior Brewing Company
Duluth

Visit Date   *Signed*

ABOUT THE BREWERY

You can't help but chuckle over the fact that Lake Superior Brewing shares a building with the Minnesota Department of Revenue. Just think—you can come in to get your tax questions answered and then go next door for a brewery tour and beer. Depending upon the answers to your tax issues, that brewery tour might be even more fun!

Lake Superior Brewing moved into Duluth's Lincoln Park neighborhood, just west of the downtown, in 1998. There's almost no evidence that a brewery might be somewhere in this one-story brick building, except for the shared sign above the door. Perhaps this just adds to the irony that a brewery should be quietly, almost secretively, operating behind the backs of the revenuers at their desks!

Inside the brewery there's a lot more to greet the eyes. This is a very active brewery packed in about 4,000 square feet of warehouse space, which makes for crowded conditions for making beer. Lake Superior relies on a 16-barrel system, some half-dozen fermenters, a bottler, and a large cooler. There's also a variety of specialized equipment that could be described as in its second life or even as a collegial hand-me-down from another brewery, like the steam boiler once used by Summit Brewing of St. Paul. And if you look closely you might be able to identify a few refurbished dairy tanks.

Head brewer Dale Kleinschmidt is very hands-on in nearly every step. If you call and ask for a tour, don't be surprised if he answers the phone and even meets you at the door to personally give the tour. He is somewhat humble about his brewing talents, referring to himself as a head brewer, rather than a brewmaster.

Kleinschmidt discovered homebrewed beer in the early 1970s while a student at Eastern Arizona College when a friend offered him some of what he'd made. At the time he considered it interesting but he didn't make his own beer until after returning home to Duluth for the summer. After leaving college Kleinschmidt became a transportation contractor for the local school district. For much of the 1980s and early 1990s he worked in Duluth with the Community Action Program, helping low-income citizens find assistance in meeting their utility bills and improving their home energy conservation practices. During that time he also became involved in the local homebrew club, the Northern Ale Stars, where he met Lake Superior Brewing's early founders and owners, Bob Dromeshauser, Don Hoag, and John Judd. The Northern Ale Stars are the state's oldest homebrew club.

Dromeshauser had previously been a University of Minnesota–Duluth research scientist working on hypothermia related issues when he decided to change careers and purchase a local homebrew supply store in the early 1990s. He expanded it to a full-fledged commercial brewery in 1994. In 1995 Kleinschmidt started volunteering at the brewery and within three weeks he was offered an apprenticeship. As Kleinschmidt describes it, he showed up one day and never left—and eventually Bob Dromeshauser just hired him!

Lake Superior Brewing Company produces four year-round beers, about a half-dozen seasonals, and High Bridge Root Beer. It also has made beer for others, including Mantorville Brewing, St. Croix Brewing, and Brainerd Lakes Brewing, and it supplies a house beer for the Clyde Park Bakery, Restaurant, and Brewery in Duluth.

HISTORY

Lake Superior Brewing was established in 1994. It was the first commercial brewery to open in Duluth since the original Fitger's brewery closed in 1972. It started in the Fitger's Brewery Complex, occupying only about two hundred square feet and amounting to not much more than a walk-in cooler for Dromeshauser's homebrewing supply store. Dale Kleinschmidt laughs when thinking about it being so small he could stand in one place and nearly touch all of the equipment without moving. Lake Superior Brewing was originally located just inside the first floor main entry doors of the Fitger's Complex. It has been home more recently to the Lake View Coffee House and subsequently the clothing store Andi's Closet.

When Dromeshauser was in the early dreaming stage of opening Lake Superior Brewing in the early 1990s, he made a trip with a few Duluth homebrewers to meet Siegfried Plagens, the well-known master brewer at the former Minnesota Brewing Company in St. Paul. Plagens, a German-trained brewer, had more than forty years of experience when he met Dromeshauser. During that visit to the brewery Dromeshauser mentioned to Plagens that he was considering starting up a brewery. As that conversation unfolded Plagens suggested that Dromeshauser come to St. Paul for a month for an apprenticeship at the brewery. After that month Dromeshauser asked Plagens how he could repay him for the experience, to which Plagens responded, "Just pass on the experience to someone else."

That's exactly what Dromeshauser did when he offered Kleinschmidt an apprenticeship in 1995. Kleinschmidt was part of an initial class of brewery apprentices that included Mike Hoops, who became the first brewer at Fitger's Brewhouse and now is brewmaster at Minneapolis Town Hall Brewery, along with Dromeshauser's son Erik who lives in Duluth.

That tradition passed down from Siegfried Plagens continues today under Kleinschmidt's mentorship. Lake Superior Brewing has been the early training ground that has inspired a number of brewers who have gone on to breweries such as Summit and Great Waters in St. Paul, Brewery Ommegang (Cooperstown, New York), the Harpoon Brewery (Boston, Massachusetts), Kona Brewing Company (Kailua Kona, Hawaii), the New Belgium Brewing (Fort Collins, Colorado), and Upland Brewing (Bloomington, Indiana).

In the early days, Lake Superior had a brewing capacity of only about three hundred barrels a year. By 1996 it expanded to about nine hundred square feet and increased production by about five times. In 1998, badly needing more space and wanting to expand bottling operations, the brewery moved to its current location on West Superior Street. It occupies a building that was originally built for a Red Owl Supermarket. Prior to Lake Superior Brewing occupying the building, it had been home to a company that supplies and services vending machines. In 2010 Lake Superior Brewing added three additional fermenters that expanded its capacity by nearly 40 percent.

Lake Superior Brewing operates in the historic shadow of the old Duluth Brewing and Malting plant that was once in operation less than two blocks away. On that site (231 South Twenty-ninth Avenue West) now is a building supply company.

DON'T MISS THIS

All of Lake Superior's regular year-round beers have won awards in the World Beer Championship competition organized by the Beverage Testing Institute.

LAKE SUPERIOR'S BREWS

Kayak Kölsch ꒰꒱꒰꒱   *Your Ranking*_____
A traditional-style German Kölsch made with five different malts and two varieties of hops. Light golden, mostly clear with a light haze. A thick, soft, white head. Light, malty aroma and a medium, soft body. Light fruity sweetness and citrus finish. Won a silver medal at the World Beer Championships in 2002 and was named *Draft* magazine's number one Kölsch in 2010. Kayak Kölsch was inspired by a trip to Germany by the brewery's founders Bob Dromeshauser and John Judd who enjoyed Kölsch in its namesake city of Cologne (Köln).

Lake Superior Special Ale ꒰꒱꒰꒱   *Your Ranking*_____
This was the first beer made by Lake Superior Brewing and it remains the company's flagship brew. A North American style of the classic British pale ale. Made with imported English ale yeast and only Cascade hops that offer a distinctive sharp citrus aroma and flavor. Copper colored and hazy. A me-

dium, bubbly, white head. Medium to full bodied with a round texture. Assertive malt and hoppy flavors give this beer a complex and spicy flavor profile. Won a silver medal at the World Beer Championships in 2002. It should be the first beer to come to mind when you think of Lake Superior Brewing. An exceptional beer!

Mesabi Red 🍺🍺🍺   *Your Ranking*_____

A great red ale. Light, malty nose, a vivid copper color, and a thick, bubbly, tan head. Medium bodied with a crisp texture. Light but firm bitterness helps bring out the crispness. Made with five different malts and a blend of three different hops. Won a silver medal at the World Beer Championships in 2002. The Mesabi Iron Range is a vast deposit of ore and the largest of four major deposits that make up Minnesota's Iron Range.

Old Man Winter Warmer 🍺🍺🍺🍺   *Your Ranking*_____

A barley wine–style beer. Complex fruitiness that changes with aging. First brewed in 1999 and released in 2000. There are some aggressive malty aromas and sweetness in this brew. Very dark color with a thick, soft, tan head. Full bodied and creamy texture. This beer gets brewed in later winter and usually isn't available until after Thanksgiving. A great beer to buy and age even longer. Try storing a few bottles away for the holidays the following year. A silver medal winner at the World Beer Championships in 2002.

Seven Bridges Brown Ale 🍺🍺🍺🍺   *Your Ranking*_____

Made from the second filings of the Old Man Winter Warmer. Clear, deep bronze color and a thick, creamy, tan head. Medium bodied and soft. Some great caramel malt sweetness. A light roasted finish. Overall, smooth and lots of flavor. A late winter seasonal beer. This beer is offered only on demand and isn't seen every year.

Sir Duluth Oatmeal Stout 🍺🍺🍺🍺   *Your Ranking*_____

Very dark color and a thick, soft, brown head. Full bodied and creamy texture from the oatmeal. Rich roasted coffee and chocolate overtones from English and Belgian dark malts. A great oatmeal stout! This beer won a gold medal at the World Beer Championships in 2002. In 1679 the explorer Daniel Greysolon Du Lhut (Duluth) raised a French flag at the westernmost point of Lake Superior in the area that became the city that would bear his name and eventually provide identity to this beer.

St. Louis Bay IPA 🍺🍺🍺   *Your Ranking*_____

Brewed with more than a pound of hops per barrel. Made with East Kent Goldings. Great floral nose. Deep copper color with a thin, soft, tan head. Full bodied. Hoppy start with a light malty middle. The hops continue to build into a long-lasting dryness. A mild oak flavor in the middle helps bring out a mild maltiness. Some nice hoppy flavors yet the beer still has some overall balance from the malt, making it a little tame for the hop heads looking for more intensity. A summer seasonal. The St. Louis River enters Lake Superior at Duluth, forming St. Louis Bay.

OTHER LAKE SUPERIOR BREWS YOU MAY WANT TO TRY

Bueno Blanco   *Your Ranking*_____
This specialty brew shows off Cascade hops. The hops compete with a variety of Mexican flavors, like cilantro and habañero peppers.

Clyde (Ale)   *Your Ranking*_____
A beer made for the Clyde Park Bakery, Restaurant, and Brewery in Duluth. A light malty nose. Clear, deep bronze color with reddish tints. A medium, off-white head. Medium bodied and bubbly. Lots of malt up front that tapers off in flavor into a dry and clean finish. This is a very nice brown ale and goes great with a range of food choices.

Negra Noche   *Your Ranking*_____
A very dark Vienna lager style beer. Made with five different malts and German hops.

Oktoberfest   *Your Ranking*_____
A great seasonal (fall) favorite. Brilliant copper color and marbled tan head. Made with German hops and rich caramel malt. Won a gold medal at the World Beer Championships in 2009.

Split Rock Bock   *Your Ranking*_____
This is a hearty, dark mahogany–colored beer, malty with chocolate overtones. A late winter into early spring seasonal. Based on a homebrew recipe of Bob Dromeshauser from the early 1990s that won a gold medal in an American Homebrewers Association competition.

Trusty Old Brew   *Your Ranking*_____
A beer formerly produced on contract for Grandma's Saloon and Grill Restaurant (Canal Park).

Windward Wheat   *Your Ranking*_____
A true German Hefeweizen. Made with 55 percent wheat malt, a blend of German hops, and imported German wheat beer yeast to impart fruity and spicy overtones. It is left cloudy to remain authentic. A summer seasonal released in June. An earlier version of this beer was called Marathon Wheat, a reference to the annual running of Grandma's Marathon.

MENU

None. Lake Superior Brewing Company does not serve food.

OTHER THINGS TO SEE OR DO IN THE AREA

Duluth's downtown harbor area is especially great in summertime. A favorite for families is the Great Lakes Aquarium in Canal Park. There are also a number of shipping exhibits, such as Barker's Island and the S.S. *William A. Irvin* ore boat. The U.S. Coast Guard visitor center and the Aerial Lift Bridge are fun.

The bridge itself is an icon for the area. There are many shops and galleries to explore.

Traveling eastward from the brewery you will come to four other Duluth beer venues: Dubh Linn Irish Brewpub (109 West Superior Street), Carmody Irish Pub (308 East Superior Street), Dubrue (211 East 2nd Street), and Fitger's Brewhouse (600 East Superior Street).

You might want to venture across the harbor and St. Louis River into Superior for a visit to Thirsty Pagan Brewing (1623 Broadway Street). This small brewery located in a former creamery building is well known for a range of beer styles, pizza, and live music. Superior was also home to the Northern Brewing Company, which operated from 1890 until 1967. The brewery (702 North Eighth Street) stood vacant for several years; the office building and taproom were torn down in the mid-1980s. The bottling house and a portion of the brewhouse still remain. Locally, the brewery's Northern Blue Label beer was a mainstay in the early twentieth century. The label and its distribution were sold to the Cold Spring Brewing Company, which brewed the beer by that name until 1995.

Grandma's Marathon draws thousands of runners to Duluth every June. It was created in 1977 when a local running club called the North Shore Striders partnered with Grandma's Restaurant (in Canal Park) to host the marathon along Highway 61 from Two Harbors to Canal Park. It has grown to become the thirteenth-largest marathon in the United States.

The walking and biking paths along the shore of Lake Superior are truly special. You can rent a bike if you are caught without your own. Enger Park and Hilltop Park, located on the bluff overlooking the harbor, offer excellent views.

Traveling north, Minnesota Highway 61 (the North Shore Drive route) will take you to Gooseberry Falls State Park, about thirty miles from Duluth. There you find spectacular waterfalls, scenic overlooks, and eighteen miles of hiking trails. Just a little farther up the road is the famous Split Rock Lighthouse.

About fifteen miles southwest from Lake Superior Brewing is Jay Cooke State Park. The park is situated on the St. Louis River, which enters Lake Superior through the Duluth-Superior Harbor. It offers several miles of hiking and biking trails with scenic overlooks of the St. Louis River and Twin Ports area. Bike trails connect the park to Duluth.

Also in this area southwest Duluth is Spirit Mountain (9500 Spirit Mountain Place), known mostly as a ski and snowboarding recreational area. One of the many highlights at Spirit Mountain is the Timber Twister, a year-round roller coaster that races along a 3,200-foot track through trees and down the mountain. It's a six-minute ride that offers views of Lake Superior, and it has a unique control system that allows riders to vary their own speed.

BREWERY RATING

	Your Rating	Shepard's Rating	General Description
Location		🍺🍺	A commercial area of Duluth.
Ease of Finding Location		🍺🍺🍺	Easy but requires some planning.
Brewery Atmosphere		🍺🍺🍺	Commercial/industrial, warehouse. A cramped but real brewery feel, and very friendly tours.
Dining Experience		n/a	Not applicable.
The Pints		🍺🍺🍺	A great experience, especially when brewer Dale Kleinschmidt conducts the tour himself.

DIRECTIONS

From Interstate 35, exit at North Twenty-seventh Avenue West (exit 254). Travel two blocks west to the intersection of Minnesota 23 (West Third Street) and Twenty-seventh Avenue. Lake Superior Brewing is in the King Building, which sits back to the north and west from the intersection.

South Shore Brewery
Ashland, Wisconsin

ABOUT THE BREWERY

The South Shore Brewery is a destination for those who truly enjoy the "journey" of finding good food, scenic drives, and the adventure of locating the perfect pint. Located in Ashland, Wisconsin, this brewery is about seventy miles
east of Duluth. Getting there involves a scenic drive through state and national
forests that make up Wisconsin's untamed northwoods charm. The city of Ashland sits on Chequamegeon Bay, along Lake Superior's south shore, and thus
the name of this small brewery that is attached to two restaurants. The brewery shares a building with the L.C. Wilmarth's Deep Water Grille and The Alley,
so altogether it's a brewpub atmosphere.

Originally, South Shore opened in 1995 in Ashland's old Soo Line Depot,
a building constructed in 1893 that helped the city become a focal point for
travel and shipping on Lake Superior. But a fire in 2000 destroyed much of the
historic depot (its remaining shell still stands on the southern edge of town).

Soon after, the South Shore Brewery relocated to its present location. The
three-story brick and brownstone building along Ashland's Main Street was
built by Louis Cass Wilmarth as a grocery store and apartments in 1895. The
Wilmarth Building dates from the era when Ashland was the center of the thriving Lake Superior brownstone industry that had a long-lasting architectural impact on much of the Upper Midwest.

South Shore's owner and brewmaster Bo Bélanger is well known among
Wisconsin and Minnesota beer makers. He also believes strongly in using local
ingredients in his beers. Many of the South Shore brews feature barley that he

grows on his own farmland near Ashland. He's also been active in assisting farmer cooperatives in growing local hops. To keep up with the popularity of his beers in both six packs and 22-ounce bombers, Bélanger hopes to expand brewing and distribution. His plans call for a new brewery on Ashland's east side possibly in 2012.

BEERS

The South Shore Brewery will offer six to eight beers on tap for most visits. The Nut Brown Ale 🍺🍺🍺🍺 is exceptional and should be on anyone's short list of overall favorites. It's a vivid bronze-colored beer with a light toasty nose and biscuit flavor that is smooth and clean. The Rhoades Scholar Stout 🍺🍺🍺🍺 is a dark brown to black sweet English stout that has assertive chocolate tones and malty finish. In the coldness of winter, a mint-flavored, bourbon barrel–aged version of this beer is ideal for the holiday season. South Shore Pale Ale 🍺🍺🍺🍺 offers a strong floral nose and citrus bitterness that is memorable. In the early spring Honey Double Maibock 🍺🍺🍺🍺 is a clear golden-amber colored beer with malty flavor and a light smoky sweetness from the honey. The ESB 🍺🍺🍺🍺 is another standout beer with a clean maltiness that remains in balance from a light hoppy finish. This is even more special when it's served on a nitrogen tap. On the lighter side, the Northern Lights Ale 🍺🍺🍺 is an herbal cream ale that makes for a good choice for those seeking a clean and incredibly balanced experience. The Inland Sea Pilsner 🍺🍺🍺 is light and crisp with just a hint of honey in the background. Applefest Ale 🍺🍺🍺, a fall seasonal, is one of the brewery's most popular specialty brews. It's a very bubbly brew made with apples from nearby Bayfield County.

MENU

The restaurant side of this brewpub is called L.C. Wilmarth's Deep Water Grille. There is also an attached second bar and dining room called The Alley. The Deep Water Grille offers fine and casual dining with a variety of traditional pub dishes, burgers, and entrees. A few of the signatures from the Deep Water Grille menu include top sirloin and ribeye steaks, jambalaya, fettuccini Alfredo, and Stout Barbeque Pork Ribs. If you enjoy fish, the Lake Superior whitefish sandwich is an excellent choice. The cream of wild rice soup is another favorite. There are also Friday night fish specials and weekend prime rib dinners. The Alley offers a more focused and relaxed menu that features appetizers, soups, salads, burgers, and pizza. As you might gather from the name, The Alley was once an alleyway between the brewpub and its next-door neighbor. Pizza choices in The Alley are excellent, with at least eight different selections on the menu. The South Shore pizza is not to be overlooked with its chorizo sausage, onions, peppers, tomatoes, cheddar jack cheese, and cilantro.

Thirsty Pagan Brewing
Superior, Wisconsin

Visit Date	Signed

ABOUT THE BREWERY

The Thirsty Pagan began when Steve Knauss and his wife, Suzan, purchased the former Twin Ports brewery from Rick and Nancy Sauer in 2006. The ownership change reflected a new chapter for brewing in Superior. The Thirsty Pagan is located in the former Russell Creamery building, a two-story structure with cream-colored brick and terra cotta designs. Throughout the interior, old beer signs hang from the ceiling, and much breweryana on the walls offer a glimpse of local brewing history. The advertisements from Northern Brewing of Superior, along with Hamm's and Fitger's, are a tribute to previous generations of brewers. All that certainly adds to the charm of the place and makes for a memorable visit. A large mural of Miller Highlife's Lady in the Moon takes up nearly an entire wall and provides a backdrop for the local musicians who perform here several nights a week.

The building itself was constructed in 1920 and has its original tile walls and floors. While the Thirsty Pagan is charting its own course, locals have fond memories of Twin Ports Brewing Company when it occupied the same space. That former owner, Rick Sauer, also ran the Choo Choo Pub from 1996 to 1999, where he served his brews in the old railroad dining car that is now the Choo Choo Bar and Grill (5002 East Third Street, Superior).

Thirsty Pagan brewmaster Nathan McAlpine manages a 3-barrel system and brews three or four times each week in an effort to keep up to nine beers on tap. Inside the brewhouse, a collection of small 2- and 4-barrel fermenters are on wheels, which allow them to be moved to and from the brewing area and the brewpub's walk-in cooler. McAlpine is a University of Minnesota–Duluth graduate with a degree in chemical engineering. He also has gone through the master brewer program at the Siebel Institute of Technology and World Brewing Academy in Chicago, which took him to Munich for nearly a month of hands-on brewing and then brewery tours through Germany, Belgium, and Luxembourg.

The Thirsty Pagan isn't a large venue. It makes only about four to five hundred barrels annually. It does, however, manage to offer nearly three dozen different beers over the course of a year. The Gitchee Gummi Gold, North Coast Amber, Derailed Ale, and Burntwood Black are beers to expect on any one visit.

BEERS

The Thirsty Pagan has four to five main beers on tap for any visit, with another three to five small-batch seasonal and one-time beers. The White Cap Wheat 🍺🍺🍺 is a light golden ale with mild but firm hoppiness. The North Coast Amber 🍺🍺🍺 is a nice session beer that is copper in color with a caramel, malty profile from the Munich and Caramel malts. Those looking for a hoppy beer might try the Derailed Ale 🍺🍺🍺, a medium-bodied American pale ale made with Cascade, Glacier, and Columbus hops. Derailed Ale is the number one seller for Thirsty Pagan. The Wisconsin Point Cream Ale 🍺🍺🍺 is light bodied and soft with a firm, grainy type of maltiness. It was inspired by McAlpine's interactions with local homebrewers. Burntwood Black 🍺🍺🍺🍺 is a dark, medium-bodied ale with a malty complexity, made with seven different type of barley. The Hammer of the Gods 🍺🍺🍺 is a bold, malty English barley wine with lots of warmth that's nice on a cold day with the wind blowing in from Lake Superior. One beer to plan your visit around is the Capitalist Pig Russian Imperial Stout 🍺🍺🍺🍺. This bold brew has deep maltiness with rich caramel and chocolate tones and lots of warmth from an alcoholic strength that deserves respect. This brewpub also has a beer engine for special releases. The hand pump is commonly dedicated to English styles brews.

Seasonal brews to watch for from the Thirsty Pagan include the springtime Spruce Wheat, which is made with pine needles. In the fall, a similar version called Spruce Willis is a Scotch ale spiced with pine needles. The Padma is a double (imperial) IPA that has been cellar aged for up to a year before its release. The Smokey the Porter is an English style porter that is brewed with smoked malt. On the lighter side of the seasonal beer menu, in 2010 the Thirsty Pagan introduced Celiac Saison, a gluten-free beer with light color and body. It's made with sorghum and honey rather than barley or wheat.

MENU

The Thirsty Pagan specializes in pizza and toasted deli sandwiches. The pizzas are made to order with your choice of a dozen or more toppings. Signature sandwiches include a toasted sub with ham, salami, pepperoni, and shredded mozzarella cheese. The Mediterranean is a favorite with its pepperoni, salami, olives, spinach, and feta. There's also a veggie sub. But it's hard to beat just a Derailed Ale with a round loaf of fresh-baked brewhouse bread.

Northwest Region

LEECH LAKE BREWING COMPANY (WALKER)

GRANITE CITY FOOD AND BREWERY (FARGO, NORTH DAKOTA)

Northwestern Minnesota is home to a large number of lakes and the headwaters of the Mississippi River. It represents a transition from midwestern prairie landscape to the great north woods. Among the forests and the lakes are lots of things to enjoy, including fishing, boating, biking, golfing, and bird watching in a variety of environmental habitats. Many towns have specialty shops, art galleries, and community festivals to reward yours visits throughout the year.

Leech Lake Brewing Company

Walker

Walker, MN

ABOUT THE BREWERY

The town of Walker is in the heart of the Chippewa National Forest and it sits on the western arm of Leech Lake, the third largest lake in Minnesota with over 120,000 surface acres of water. That makes it one of the state's most popular vacation destinations. Actually, if it weren't for Greg Smith's dream to live where he and his family vacation, Leech Lake might not have the brewery it has.

Leech Lake Brewing Company opened in 2010 on the western edge of Walker, nestled in a grove of pine trees. The building was once a pole shed that served as a storage barn for a local landscaper. However, the dream of making a vacation home a permanent residence and, on top of that, owning a brewery, proved so compelling that Greg Smith quit his day job as a computer programmer with IBM, cashed in his retirement funds, and literally bought the barn.

Much of the brewery was assembled by Smith, who also handled a significant amount of the building's renovations. The small tasting room is a great place to sample beer and look out through windows into the brewhouse. You just might find Smith there, hard at work on his latest creation. His brewing system is one of the smallest being used among Minnesota's brewers. Each brew is just fifty-eight gallons, so Smith must brew three times to fill two 3-barrel fermenters that make up one complete 7-barrel batch. So, depending on the style, Smith's days can be filled with up to eighteen hours of brewing.

Smith's beer has developed quite a following. On days when the tasting room is open you'll find it packed with locals and tourists alike, all standing shoulder-to-shoulder in the small sampling room waiting for a refill of their tasting glass as they decide what growler they'll take back to their resort, cabin, or camper. In the summer the line for growler fills will extend out the door and into the parking lot—most likely rivaling the line at any of Walker's local ice cream shops.

Leech Lake Brewing Company supplies beer to several local restaurants and taverns in and around Leech Lake. It is available in kegs, growlers, and 22-ounce bottles. The brewery's core beers include a porter, Scottish ale, ESB, pale ale, IPA, and an imperial IPA.

HISTORY

Greg Smith grew up in Denver, Colorado, where he learned about craft beer. In college he met his wife, Gina, who had been coming to Walker all her life on family vacations. In 1992 his sister-in-law gave him Charlie Papazian's *Complete Joy of Home Brewing*, which sparked his interest in the hobby. As he got better with every batch, his beers started turning up at family gatherings and on vacations at Leech Lake. While working at IBM as a computer programmer, he started thinking about how to telecommute from the Leech Lake area. By 2008 the Smiths, with their daughter and twin sons, were residents of South Walker Bay.

Upon arriving to Leech Lake, Smith was able to dedicate more time to developing a business plan for what he initially envisioned as a part-time brewery. However, by early 2010 his plans began moving ahead at a much faster pace than he expected. Smith found a 3-barrel mash tun and brew kettle that had been in use in a brewpub in Mexicali, Mexico. He purchased the equipment and had it shipped to Walker even though he didn't have a building for it. By April 2010 he decided to change his business plan from one that focused on weekend brewing and keeping his weekday job to one in which he brewed full time. He left IBM and used some of a severance package with retirement funds to purchase and remodel the building that today is Leech Lake Brewing Company. More specifically, his former 401(k) plan helped pay for his two-headed bottling machine.

DON'T MISS THIS

It's easy to drive past the brewery because Leech Lake Brewing sits off Walker Industries Boulevard, somewhat concealed in a grove a trees. Don't drive too fast or you just might miss it.

LEECH LAKE BREWS

3 Sheets 🍺🍺🍺🍺   *Your Ranking_____*
This is an imperial IPA with a complex blend of hoppy and spicy flavors. Its nose is piney and resiny. Cloudy copper-bronze color with a thick, soft, tan head. Medium bodied and round. Strong piney bitterness. Finishes with a spicy bitterness and warmth.

47° North 🍺🍺🍺🍺   *Your Ranking_____*
This IPA is hopped with hefty additions of English Fuggles, which gives the beer an assertive hoppy nose. Rich orange-golden color with a thick, tan, soft

head. Medium to full bodied. Strong bitterness from its 90-plus IBUs. A light, but firm, dry finish. Its name reflects the geographic latitude of Walker, Minnesota, at 47 degrees north of the equator (to be exact, the brewery is located at N 47°06.168′ and W 94°36.788′).

Batch 10-56 🍺🍺🍺 *Your Ranking*_____
A light floral nose. Cloudy copper color and a thin soft head. Light to medium bodied and sharp. A mild bitterness with a fruity background and finish. Made with two-row, Crystal, and Caramalt. Its bitterness is from Fuggle hops. This is a local drauft beer offered in late summer. Its name is from law enforcement's code for an intoxicated pedestrian.

Driven Snow 🍺🍺🍺🍺 *Your Ranking*_____
A robust porter. Malty nose with a hint of roastedness. Dark black with a thick, soft, brown head. Full bodied and silky smooth mouth feel. Finishes with assertive roasted chocolate malty tones and is smooth and not burnt. This beer has lots of color from additions of Black Patent, Chocolate, and dark Crystal malts. It also has roasted barley and molasses in the recipe.

Loch Leech Monster 🍺🍺🍺 *Your Ranking*_____
This Scottish ale has a light malty nose. Its color is hazy brown with a thin, bubbly head. Medium bodied and round mouth feel. Lots of caramel tones up front with just a light fruity-citrus background. Finishes with light roasted tones to the caramel maltiness and some warmth. Made with a blend of Golden Promise, Brown, Dextrin, and Black Patent malts, and hopped with Fuggles. A light amount of roasted barley offers a hint of smokiness.

Maris the Otter 🍺🍺🍺🍺 *Your Ranking*_____
A summer seasonal for Leech Lake. Starts with a very light fruity nose. A cloudy, orange-copper color and a medium, soft, tan head. Medium bodied and sharp mouth feel. The malt dominates but the Fuggle hops come through for a crisp finish. Made with Maris Otter Malt, hence the name. This beer is most likely to be found only on local tap accounts, or you can get it in a growler from the brewery. It is not expected to be bottled product.

Minobii 🍺🍺🍺 *Your Ranking*_____
An ESB with nice balance. A clean nose with just a hint of maltiness. Orange-copper color and a medium, marbled, tan head. Medium bodied and sharp. A smooth malt beginning that builds throughout the main flavor profile. Just a light accent of hops and some warmth come out in the finish. Its recipe includes two-row Pale, medium Crystal, and Dextrin malts with flaked maize and dark brown sugar. Hopped with Fuggles. Its name is an Ojibwe word meaning "drink and be merry." This is a very nice all-around meal companion type of beer.

OTHER LEECH LAKE BREWS YOU MAY WANT TO TRY

Blindside *Your Ranking*_____
A pale ale with some balance. Made with two-row Pale malt along with light and medium Crystal malt. Hopped with English Fuggles.

Burbot Brown Ale *Your Ranking_____*

This brown ale is a seasonal release, made just for the International Eelpout Festival that is held in Walker each February.

MENU

None. Leech Lake Brewing does not serve food.

OTHER THINGS TO SEE OR DO IN THE AREA

The Leech Lake area has many vacation resorts and countless opportunities for water recreation, cycling, hiking, skiing, snowmobiling, and golf. Fishing brings many visitors to the area, especially for its renowned walleye fishery.

Walker hosts the International Eelpout Festival the second weekend in February. The annual event features fishing tournaments and a fishhouse parade. (The eelpout resembles an eel, with its elongated body. A flathead freshwater cod, it also goes by the names "burbot" and "lawyer.") If you want to experience the lake without a fishing pole, Coborn's Leech Lake Cruises offer a scenic way to take in the lake and its various bays. In late summer, Walker Bay Days features many live activities for all members of the family, including games for the kids, a talent contest, musical performances, sea plane and sailboat rides, a traditional pow-wow exhibition, a history tent, and boat-in movies shown on the water. For fans of Leech Lake beer there's also a beer and brat tent.

To the west of Walker is Itasca State Park (off Minnesota 200 and U.S. 71), which marks the source of the Mississippi River. Established in 1891, Itasca is Minnesota's oldest state park. As the headwaters to the Mississippi River, it contains more than a hundred lakes. Shingobee Recreation Area is about five miles southwest of Walker (off Minnesota 34) and is a favorite place for cross-country skiing. The Shingobee River is known as an easy canoe trail, as is the Boy River, which stretches over twenty miles between Leech Lake and Iguadona Lake. On land, cyclists will find that Walker is roughly the midpoint of the Heartland State Trail, a paved path that connects Park Rapids to Cass Lake. If you enjoy bird watching, go to the federal dam where the lake empties into the Leech River to see eagles feeding.

The Leech Lake area has many shopping opportunities and activities for the entire family. The Moondance Ranch and Adventure Park (five miles south of Walker on Minnesota 371) offers miniature golf, go-karts, and horseback riding. The Northern Lights Casino (6800 Y Frontage Road NW) offers not only gaming but a hotel and several dining options along with an arcade and swimming pool for the kids. Big name entertainers regularly perform.

BREWERY RATING

	Your Rating	Shepard's Rating	General Description
Location		🍺🍺🍺🍺	Walker is a popular vacation destination, and a brewery is a great amenity for the area. Brewery itself is located outside of town. This really is a destination brewery for the Minnesota beer enthusiast who enjoys the travel and exploration of finding the state's breweries.
Ease of Finding Location		🍺🍺	Finding Walker is easy, but finding the brewery is a bit challenging. Located north of town. It's best to have map or GPS.
Brewery Atmosphere		🍺🍺🍺🍺	This is a small but active working brewery. Visit on a summer Saturday during tasting room hours and you'll see how this brewery is part of the Walker's attraction.
Dining Experience		n/a	Not applicable.
The Pints		🍺🍺🍺🍺	Great beer, but the search and the journey make this a perfect experience.

DIRECTIONS

Located on the northern edge of Walker. Travel about three-quarters of a mile north from downtown Walker to the intersection with Sautbine Road NW and turn left (west). Continue west on Sautbine Road for approximately a half-mile to Townhall Road. After turning left (southeastward) onto Townhall Road watch for an immediate right turn (south) onto Walker Industries Boulevard. The brewery will be located on your left (east side) in a grove of trees.

Granite City Food and Brewery

Fargo, North Dakota

Granite City
FOOD & BREWERY®

Visit Date	Signed

ABOUT THE BREWERY

Granite City Food and Brewery of Fargo was the third restaurant for the company. It opened November 20, 2001, on Fargo's southwest side on the edge of the West Acres Shopping Center near the intersection of Interstates 94 and 29. Several hotels and a multiscreen theater are all within a very short walk.

Granite City operates more than two dozen restaurants in the Midwest, with plans for expansion in the northeast and south. Prior to opening in Fargo, Granite City had locations in St. Cloud, Minnesota, and Sioux Falls, South Dakota. Granite City president Steve Wagenheim spent much of the 1980s and 1990s as chief operating officer and subsequently president of Champps Americana, a sports restaurant-bar chair. In 1999 Wagenheim cofounded Granite City with Bill Burdick, who handled brewing operations for Granite City until he retired in 2006. Burdick owned the popular brewpub Sherlock's Home from 1989 to 2001 in Minnetonka and was active in the brewing, restaurant, and hospitality industry for many years.

The Fargo Granite City was the first in the chain of restaurants to take advantage of the trademarked Fermentus Interruptus system developed by Burdick. The process involves a central wort-making facility in Ellsworth, Iowa, which prepares and then ships wort to each store where yeast is added and fermentation begins.

BEERS

Granite City offers four to five standard beers and special seasonals at all of its locations. The Northern Light Lager 🍺🍺 is an American light lager with a bubbly golden color. Wag's Wheat 🍺🍺 is a slightly cloudy American wheat that has vivid yellow color and a thick white head; it is the lightest of the Granite City beers. The Duke of Wellington 🍺🍺🍺 is a medium- to full-bodied, copper-colored India pale ale that has a solid malty character with a hoppy nose and finish. Brother Benedict's Bock 🍺🍺 is a German-style lager with medium body, deep brown color, and a caramel malty flavor. On a darker note, the Broad Axe Stout 🍺🍺🍺🍺 is medium to full bodied with creamy texture and lots of rich roasted chocolate and caramel flavors. Granite City also does beer blending with its Two Pull brew, which combines Northern Light and Brother Benedict's Bock. The Admiral Two Pull combines Northern Light and Duke of Wellington IPA. Among special seasonals at the Fargo Granite City location are a Belgian Wit, Burning Barn Irish Red, and Ostara's Ale.

MENU

The Granite City menu is broad and modestly priced (the company's internal slogan is: Give the customer a twenty-five dollar experience for thirteen dollars). It features many made-from-scratch items, and if you visit more than one Granite City you'll find quite a few similarities. Among the most popular items no matter which Granite City restaurant you are in is the open-faced meat loaf sandwich. Just as tasty is the London broil.

Granite City's extensive salad selection ranges from a basic dinner salad to grilled Asian chicken. Expect about ten different sandwiches and a half-dozen burger choices. One of the signature burgers is the Bleu Peppercorn, a half-pound of Angus beef seasoned with black peppercorns and topped with creamy bleu cheese. There are also steaks, seafood, pastas, soups, and a kids' menu. Several of the house beers are integrated into menu items, like the Ale and Cheddar Soup. Granite City also is well known for its Sunday brunch.

Southern Region

AUGUST SCHELL BREWING COMPANY (NEW ULM)

BACKWATER BREWING COMPANY (WINONA)

BRAU BROTHERS BREWING COMPANY (LUCAN)

MANKATO BREWERY (MANKATO)

MANTORVILLE BREWING COMPANY (MANTORVILLE)

OLVALDE FARM AND BREWING COMPANY (ROLLINGSTONE)

TOPPLING GOLIATH BREWING COMPANY (DECORAH, IOWA)

WORTH BREWING COMPANY (NORTHWOOD, IOWA)

DEMPSEY'S BREWERY, RESTAURANT, AND PUB (WATERTOWN, SOUTH DAKOTA)

GRANITE CITY FOOD AND BREWERY (SIOUX FALLS, SOUTH DAKOTA)

CITY BREWING COMPANY (LA CROSSE, WISCONSIN)

PEARL STREET BREWERY (LA CROSSE, WISCONSIN)

POTOSI BREWING COMPANY (POTOSI, WISCONSIN)

SAND CREEK BREWING COMPANY (BLACK RIVER FALLS, WISCONSIN)

This region is bordered by the Mississippi River on the east, the Dakotas on the west, and Iowa to the south; the Minnesota River flows within its midsection. It's known for its quiet streams and beautiful forest-lined bluffs and scenic valleys. Here the Minnesota prairies and grassland can still be observed in splendor and wonder. It also contains many historical sites important to Dakota Indians and early pioneers. Many communities on the western edge of this region maintain cultural connections to early American Indian heritage through museums, historical markers, and community events. The Mississippi River provides spectacular views, riverboat rides, and unique small towns along the Great River Road. There are also prairies, rivers, and lakes that provide outstanding opportunities to enjoy the outdoors.

August Schell Brewing Company

New Ulm

ABOUT THE BREWERY

August Schell is Minnesota's oldest working brewery and the second oldest continuously operating family brewery in the United States. In 2010 it celebrated its 150th anniversary. This should be a stop on anyone's Minnesota brewery tour, especially to learn about not only the history of August Schell but Minnesota's overall brewing past. Tours offer a walk around the brewery into several of its facilities. Many of the original red-brick buildings are still standing. There is also a small museum on the grounds that makes a tour truly a walk back in time to what this brewery and its hometown of New Ulm were like.

Founder August Schell had a strong desire to create a beautiful setting for his brewery. He also loved flowers and wildlife, so he created his home with gardens, an aviary for his pigeons, and a deer park — all to remind him of his native Germany. August and his wife, Theresa, built the Schell mansion in 1885 for $5,000. The home is listed on the National Register of Historic Places. It is not open to the public, but you can tour the grounds that include a fenced deer park, sunken gardens, and fish ponds. Visitors may even see peacocks roaming freely around the brewery compound. Peacocks were used in Schell's advertising in the early twentieth century. The company has a strong commitment to history, and the Schell museum is a wonderful start to a tour.

Schell makes about a dozen different brews under its own labels along with several other well-known brands, such as Grain Belt and Hauenstein. When Schell acquired the Grain Belt label in 2002, it nearly doubled its total beer production. To make room for the demand for Grain Belt, Schell cut back on its contract brewing. Schell's soft drink line includes Buddy's sodas in orange, strawberry, and grape flavors. It also produces 1919 Classic American Root Beer—1919 being the year Prohibition began.

HISTORY

Born in 1828, August Schell grew up in the Black Forest region of Germany. He left home at age twenty for America, arrived in New Orleans, and began working his way up the Mississippi and Ohio rivers, eventually stopping in Cincinnati where he worked as a machinist in a locomotive factory. By 1856 he arrived in New Ulm and took a job as a machinist in a flour mill. Schell started work on his brewery in 1860 and soon began a partnership with Jacob Bernhardt, a former brewmaster at the Benzberg Brewery in St. Paul. Together they established what would eventually become the August Schell Brewing Company. It was one of five New Ulm breweries to operate during the years before Prohibition.

Schell and Bernhardt chose a site for their brewery near the Cottonwood River because its natural spring would provide ideal water for brewing and the river itself would provide transportation in summer and ice in winter. In the first year they produced about two hundred barrels of beer (today the annual figure is well over one hundred thousand barrels).

Just two years after the brewery was started, the city of New Ulm and many other towns in the region were burned and ransacked during the Sioux Uprising. Schell's brewery was spared, however, left untouched, largely because Mrs. Schell was well liked by the native people for her generosity and kindness.

In 1866 Jacob Bernhardt became ill and decided to sell his interest in the brewery. August Schell agreed to place the entire brewery up for sale to the highest bidder. When the sale was completed, Schell had purchased the brewery for $12,000.

By the time August Schell was fifty years old he had begun to suffer from severe arthritis. This ultimately caused him to hand over management of the brewery to his oldest son, Adolph, and the brewing to his youngest son, Otto, who had studied brewing in Germany. Adolph eventually left the brewery and moved to California, leaving the brewery to Otto and a brother-in-law, George Marti. Founder August Schell died in 1891. Otto Schell died suddenly in 1911 and Marti took over the brewery. During Prohibition the Schell brewery survived by making near beer and soda, but unofficially the locals claim a little moonshine didn't hurt the company's bottom line. Schell's 150th anniversary series of draft beers featured "Not Guilty" 1924 Deer Brand Beer, a reference to product discovered during a raid of the brewery by federal agents in 1923 (the case was dropped a year later in 1924).

George Marti oversaw the brewery through the dry years, but he died in 1934 soon after Prohibition ended and his wife, Emma, became company president. Not long after, their son Alfred Marti took charge. Alfred loved music as much a beer and sponsored a group called Schell's Hobo Band that was known for its brass, drum, and oom-pah sounds. Schell's Hobo Band continues to be a fixture of the brewery today.

When Alfred retired in 1965, his son Warren took over the brewery and expanded the styles of beer produced, including soft drinks and the ever popular 1919 Root Beer. Fifth generation descendent Ted Marti, the son of Warren, became company president in 1986 and has done nearly every job at the brewery, from brewmaster to Mr. Fixit with his trusty pocketknife. Schell's is the oldest operating Minnesota brewery and is America's second-oldest family-run brewery, behind Pennsylvania's Yuengling.

In the late 1990s and early 2000s the Schell brewery underwent extensive remodeling and expansion. Part of those modifications involved updating the brewhouse and removing the 110-barrel copper brew kettle that Otto Schell had put in place in 1900 for $25,000. Recent renovations have called for new fermentation and aging tanks. In 2006 the brewery opened a new gift shop and hospitality room. Much of the current growth at Schell has been due to the acquisition of the Grain Belt brands.

Schell Brewing was named one of the top ten breweries in the nation in 2009 and again in 2010 at the U.S. Open Beer Championships. The brewery brought home six medals in 2009 and five medals in 2010. In 2010 Minnesota Business Magazine recognized Schell Brewing with a Legacy Award, which honors a family-run company with more than three generations of family governance. Schell's Ted Marti represents a fifth generation of descendants from founder August and Theresa Schell. Ted and his wife, Jodi, have three sons—Jace, Kyle, and Franz—and all have indicated some interest in the brewery. The oldest, Jace, currently works at the brewery and plans to attend brewing school in Germany. By the way, Jodi manages the brewery's gift shop so it's not uncommon to see her before or after a tour.

DON'T MISS THIS

Schell's is packed with history, from the museum to the buildings. A tour will take you to the doors of the brewery office that was built in 1860 as the original family residence. The museum is in the brewery's former carriage house. In summer be sure to explore the grounds, especially the gardens. You'll be impressed with the vineyards and deer park, as well as a resident family of peacocks, any of which you might find perched atop the brewery's former boardinghouse.

AUGUST SCHELL BREWS

Bock 🍺🍺🍺   *Your Ranking*_____

A malty nose. Clear, bubbly, ruby-bronze body with a thick, soft, tan head. Medium bodied and soft. A firm caramel maltiness that is smooth and lingering. This is a long-standing brew for the company dating back to the 1860s; however, its recipe was reformulated in 2009. In recent years it carried the name Caramel Bock. It's made with ten different types of malts, alongside noble hops. A late winter seasonal beer offered in January and February.

Dark 🍺🍺🍺🍺   *Your Ranking*_____

This American dark lager has deep amber color and firm malty flavor. Light malty nose. Medium bodied. A clean, caramel flavor with a light roasted finish. Look for this beer to be sold in a clear bottle to show off its dark color.

Deer Brand 🍺🍺🍺   *Your Ranking_____*

Look for the deer antler tap handle at your local tavern. This American lager offers light golden color and clean flavor. Crisp flavor and texture. Deer Brand is a pre-Prohibition beer for the brewery. It was originally called simply Schell's Lager Beer. In more recent times it has gone by the name Schell's Original. However, in 2010 its name was changed back to Deer Brand. This beer won gold medals in 2009 and 2010 at the U.S. Open Beer Championships.

Doppel Bock 🍺🍺🍺   *Your Ranking_____*

Rich with lots of caramel malt flavor and very smooth. Heavy malty nose. Deep bronze color with a thick, soft, tan head. Full bodied and very round. Strong caramel tones with hints of chocolate malt that linger through the finish. Made with five different specialty malts and three distinct hop varieties. Lagered for twelve weeks before it is released. Available in early spring.

FireBrick 🍺🍺🍺   *Your Ranking_____*

This Vienna-style amber lager is smooth and well balanced. A light malty nose. Clear copper to reddish-amber color with a medium, soft, bubbly, off-white head. A caramel malty start that eventually gives way to light hoppy finish. Made with four different malts and three types of hops. FireBrick was introduced in 1999 and is named after the bricks that line Schell's old boilers. A bronze medal winner in the 2002 Great American Beer Festival.

Hefeweizen 🍺🍺🍺   *Your Ranking_____*

A firm fruity nose with hints of banana and clove. Straw colored with a thick, soft, white head. Light bodied and very crisp. Yeasty flavor with a citrus background. Yeasty tones of banana in the finish. Made to the Bavarian wheat style. A silver medal winner in 1993 and a gold medal winner at the 1998 Great American Beer Festival. It won a gold medal in the 2009 U.S. Open Beer Championships.

Hopfenmalz 🍺🍺   *Your Ranking_____*

A floral hoppy nose. Hazy golden-copper color with a thick, soft, tan head. Medium bodied and soft. A hoppy start with a malty backbone and a return of dry bitterness in the finish. Hopfenmalz was originally part of the Schell's 150th Anniversary Draft Series, a collection of single-batch, limited-release brews based on the vote of brewery fans. The brewery describes it as an amalgamation of the pilsner's drinkability, the malty breadiness of the Vienna lager, and the crisp bitterness of Cascade and Tettnang hops that are often found in a pale ale—which all seem to be reflected in syllables of its name.

Maifest 🍺🍺🍺   *Your Ranking_____*

This springtime seasonal is a blonde double bock with lots of flavor. A firm malty nose. Deep copper to amber color with a thin, soft, off-white head. Medium bodied and soft. Strong yet smooth caramel malty flavors throughout the flavor profile. Brewed with a blend of three specialty malts and three varieties of hops. A bronze medal winner at the 2010 U.S. Open Beer Championships.

Oktoberfest 🍺🍺🍺🍺   *Your Ranking*_____

Schell's best selling seasonal beer. A sweet, malty nose. Clear, deep copper color with a thin, soft, tan head. Medium to full bodied and round texture. Strong, firm, smooth caramel tones with a warm and light bitter accent for the finish. Brewed with four different malts with additions of Cascade and Nugget hops. A silver medal winner in 1991 and again in 2010 at the Great American Beer Festival. Available in the fall.

Pils (Pilsner) 🍺🍺🍺🍺   *Your Ranking*_____

A great example of a Bavarian pilsner. An aggressive floral nose. Clear golden body with a medium-soft, off-white head. Medium bodied and crisp texture. A firm, malty, slightly grainy beginning with a firm, crisp bitterness in the background and finish. This pilsner has some great flavor and nice bitterness. Brewed with 100 percent barley malt and German Hallertau hops. First brewed by Schell in 1984. This beer has won multiple medals at the Great American Beer Festival, including a silver in 2006, a gold in 1988, and a bronze in 1987. It also won a silver medal in 2010 and a gold medal in 2009 at the U.S. Open Beer Championships.

Schell Light 🍺🍺   *Your Ranking*_____

No nose. Clear straw color with a thin, white head. Light grainy flavors and mild, hoppy finish. A lighter, low-calorie version of Deer Brand that doesn't sacrifice any of the taste. A bronze medal winner at the 2010 U.S. Open Beer Championships.

Schell Stout 🍺🍺🍺   *Your Ranking*_____

Begins with a firm malty nose. Deep dark black color with a medium bubbly and rocky brown head. Medium to full bodied and very round. A smooth maltiness with a semisweet chocolate malty background that lingers into the finish. There is some roastedness, but overall a smooth malty beer. Schell Stout won a silver medal in 2009 and again in 2010 at the U.S. Open Beer Championships.

Schmaltz's Alt 🍺🍺🍺🍺   *Your Ranking*_____

A light malty nose. A hazy bronze color with a very thick and soft tan head. Medium bodied. Rich sweet maltiness with a light hint of spicy licorice in the background and finish. Also an underlying roastedness with hints of chocolate malt. Overall, still a very clean finish. A wonderful seasonal beer offered from November to February.

Snowstorm 🍺🍺🍺🍺   *Your Ranking*_____

A tradition that began in 1994, this is the Schell beer to watch for. As the brewery states, just like snowflakes, no two Snowstorm seasons are alike. Each year the brewmasters select a secret recipe for this winter warmer. Some versions have gone on to become regular beers like FireBrick and Schell Stout. With each annual installment expect a big beer with aggressive malty flavor, sometimes fruitiness, with lots of warmth. Available in November and December while the supply holds out. The concept for this beer was originally called Blizzard, but Dairy Queen Corporation objected so Schell changed the name. The beers in this series always seem to be exceptional and worth looking forward to even if your're not wanting winter to return anytime to soon.

Zommerfest 🍺🍺   *Your Ranking_____*

One of the lighter Schell beers. This Kölsch-style beer is available in early summer. A light grainy nose. Golden and slightly hazy with a thin, soft, white head. Light bodied and crisp texture. Light to mild malty flavor dominates. Made with 90 percent barley malt and 10 percent wheat malt. Originally introduced for Memorial Day weekend in 1998. Zommerfest won a gold medal at the 2010 U.S. Open Beer Championships.

OTHER SCHELL BREWS YOU MAY WANT TO TRY

Grain Belt Nordeast   *Your Ranking_____*

This American amber lager has a light malty body with a crisp hoppy aroma and mild bitterness. It's named after the neighborhood where the original Grain Belt brewery was established in 1893 and the northern and eastern European immigrants who helped to shape northeast Minneapolis.

Grain Belt Premium   *Your Ranking_____*

A light, clear golden beer, found in the clear bottle with the traditional red and white label. This beer follows in the long tradition of Grain Belt beer. Part of that past is still reflected by the old bottle cap sign overlooking the Mississippi River in northeast Minneapolis. Minneapolis Brewing Company introduced Golden Grain Belt Beer in 1893. During Prohibition the brewery produced near beer and soft drinks as the Golden Grain Juice Company. Grain Belt Premium was introduced in clear bottles, to show its golden color and emphasize its pureness. By the 1950s, the industry was consolidating with large breweries like Pabst and Miller but Minneapolis Brewing also grew, in part because of the success of Premium. In 1967 Minneapolis Brewing Company changed its name to Grain Belt Breweries. The industry continued its consolidation and fierce competition, and by 1975 Grain Belt was sold to G. Heileman Brewing Company of La Crosse, Wisconsin. When Heileman began to experience financial difficulties in the early 1990s, Minnesota Brewing purchased Grain Belt Premium. Minnesota Brewing went out of business in 2002, but August Schell picked up Grain Belt Premium in 2002. That year, on October 25, at a party at Grain Belt Brewing in Minneapolis, a few hundred people signed a keg into which the original Grain Belt Premium recipe was inserted. The keg was then sealed and transported to New Ulm where it is part of the Schell Museum of Brewing.

Grain Belt Premium Light   *Your Ranking_____*

A lighter version Grain Belt Premium.

Schell's 150th Anniversary Draft Series   *Your Ranking_____*

The brewery marked its sesquicentennial by dusting off a book of old German brewing recipes believed to have been given to the brewery during the time of Prohibition. These resulting beers are only found in draft. Schell started offering these special beers two years before its 150th birthday in 2010. Each beer in the Draft Series has been distributed to a very select number of accounts. And each beer has been released on a specific date that relates to an important time in the history of Schell Brewing. A few of the beers in this series have included: the 1878 Einbecker Doppelbock (released on the birthday of August Schell); 1890 Schwarzbier (released on the birthday of Warren Marti); Not

Guilty 1924 Deer Brand (marks the year charges were dropped against the brewery when it was accused of selling alcoholic beer during Prohibition); and 1905 V.T./Vacuum Tonic (released on the birthday of current Schell president Ted Marti).

Stag Series   *Your Ranking_____*

A series of specialty and experimental beers that are limited editions. Some of the beers in the series have included Barrel Aged Schmaltz's Alt, Wild Rice Farmhouse Ale, and a Rauchbier.

MENU

None. August Schell does not serve food.

OTHER THINGS TO SEE OR DO IN THE AREA

The city of New Ulm was founded in 1854 by a German land company from Chicago. Its name references the original settlers, who were from the province of Wurttemberg, Germany, of which Ulm is the principal city. The 2000 Federal Census Report listed New Ulm as the most German city in America. Its German heritage is celebrated through the city's events, festivals, architecture, and monuments.

The community's largest celebration is Heritagefest, which occurs over two weekends each July. The New Ulm Concord Singers are one of the most popular groups during Heritagefest, singing traditional German music. As you walk through the crowds, you might catch glimpses of unusual characters, the Heritagefest Narren or the Heinzelmännchen Garden Gnomes.

If you miss Heritagefest, on Monday evenings during summer there is a series of free concerts in German Park (Second North and German streets). Friday lunchtime features Picnic in the Park with different food vendors.

Touring the city of New Ulm you find a great number of monuments, such as Hermann the German (Center and Monument streets), that pay tribute to all New Ulm citizens of German heritage. The 102-foot monument honors Hermann, the Cherusci, a German warrior who defeated the Romans in battle and freed the German people from oppression. Other well-known landmarks include the Melges Bakery Building (213 South Minnesota Street) and the Waraju Distillery Chimney (Center and Linden streets). One of the most recognizable is New Ulm's 45-foot Glockenspiel (Fourth North and Minnesota streets), whose bells weigh two tons. The bells chime the time of day in Westminster style.

Historic walks are a great way to enjoy New Ulm. The John Lind House (622 Center Street) is an 1887 Victorian that was the home of Minnesota's four-teenth governor. It is on the National Register of Historic Places. You can learn about Minnesota music, including classical, big band, blues, and old time, at the Minnesota Music Hall of Fame Museum (27 North Broadway). The historic Keisling House (Third North and Minnesota streets) is home to the Council for the Arts, where area artists are featured monthly in the art gallery and gift shop. New Ulm has a Civil War horse-drawn civilian artillery unit that performs for parades, Memorial Day, July Fourth, and throughout Heritagefest. Its forty-two members dress in period uniforms and are well known for their cannons, caissons, and sabers.

The New Ulm Bike Trail follows an old railroad line, winding alongside the Minnesota River. The trail offers some great secluded natural habitat, spectacular views, and excellent potential for an up-close experience with wildlife. The river valley itself is a great way to explore many small towns, historic sites, and scenic vistas of southern Minnesota.

Flandrau State Park (1300 Summit Avenue) is a 1,000-acre recreational park along the Cottonwood River with picnic areas, playgrounds, and opportunities for canoeing, kayaking, fishing, and camping. Flandrau Fest in June emphasizes water fun, with activities ranging from dunk tanks and beach ball hunts to tubing and rubber duck races.

Schell's Annual Bock Fest occurs in early February. In addition to great beer, the local food favorites are the Bock Brats made with pork and spices, all steeped in Schell's Caramel Bock. One ritual at the festival is "poking" the beer, where a hot iron rod is thrust into a container of beer, creating a caramelization of the malt and more malty flavors or even light roasted tones. Another fun time to visit New Ulm is for Oktoberfest, the first two weekends in October. It's another great opportunity for German food and Schell's Oktoberfest is part of a community-wide celebration with music and festival atmosphere.

The Morgan Creek Vineyards (www.morgancreekvineyards.com), about fifteen minutes southeast of New Ulm, offers tours, tastings, and special events with live music. But pamper yourself after touring Schell and/or Morgan Creek Vineyards with a weekend at one of the B&B inns along German Street. Among the best is the Deutsche Strasse Bed and Breakfast (404 South German Street), built in 1884. Its breakfast menu is awesome and the special house coffee so memorable you'll want to take some home.

BREWERY RATING

	Your Rating	Shepard's Rating	General Description
Location		🍺🍺🍺🍺	The brewery buildings and grounds are in a wooded setting near the Cottonwood River.
Ease of Finding Location		🍺🍺🍺	Not difficult to find, just watch for the signs that point your way. When approaching the brewery, the narrowness of Schell's road beyond South Park can be challenging—especially when meeting beer trucks!
Brewery Atmosphere		🍺🍺🍺🍺	Tours around the grounds point out the historical nature of the buildings and the Schell Gardens.
Dining Experience		n/a	Not applicable.
The Pints		🍺🍺🍺🍺	The history and setting put August Schell on the list of any Minnesota beer tour. Also, with so many beers you are bound to find something you'll like.

DIRECTIONS

New Ulm is located about ninety miles southwest of the Twin Cities. The August Schell brewery isn't too difficult to find. When approaching from the east on U.S. Highway 14, turn south on Broadway once you cross the Minnesota River. Continue on Broadway for approximately four miles to Eighteenth South Street and turn right (west) toward South Park and follow the signs to the brewery. August Schell Brewing is located on Schell Road, which winds through the woods and follows the meandering Cottonwood River. Beer travelers might note that the brewery's address of 1860 corresponds to the year it was established.

Backwater Brewing Company
Winona

ABOUT THE BREWERY

A brewery in a bowling alley might not seem appealing to beer enthusiasts at first. But from the long bar, watching bowlers and their moments of hysterics can be quite entertaining. Many other amusing observations can be made in a place where the brewery seems, well, out of place. The brewhouse is tucked in a room next to the bathroom. And on more than one visit, the Backwater beer offerings were written on white tape and stuck on the front of tap handles. Maybe the tape is more of a statement on behalf of small breweries to the macros than an effort to cover up another brewery's logo.

Backwater Brewing Company has local flair all its own and deserves a special place on any brewery tour of southeast Minnesota. Don't overlook the signs in the parking lot that read Backwater Brewing Company or you might just write this off as the local bowling alley. Just inside the front door are the main bar, restaurant, and a small enclosed room where you'll find the brewery. That room, now the Backwater brewhouse, was once just a storage closet for the bowling alley. Brewmaster Chris Gardner makes his beer with a 1-barrel system that produces about twenty-five gallons of beer per batch. His approach to brewing is much like large scale homebrewing, so his recipes can, and often do, change subtly based on what type of ingredients he has on hand or can get when he's ready to brew. The back bar, with its mostly soundproof windows, overlooks a sixteen-lane bowling alley.

Backwater Brewing has four standard beers: pale ale, nut brown, red ale, and stout. Seasonals often include a red ale and an ESB. Backwater also makes its own root beer.

HISTORY

Backwater Brewing Company was established in 1995 as a brewpub. "Backwater" refers to the land on which the brewpub sits because it was once the actual backwater of the Mississippi before it was filled in during the nineteenth century. Local residents know it as Wellington's Backwater Brewing Company, the name it originally used. "Wellington" was the first name of brewmaster Chris Gardner's grandfather. The bowling alley connection to the brewery was started by Chris's father, Paul Gardner, who built Westgate Bowl in 1961. The Gardner family still owns and runs the overall business. The brewery was added in 1995 and Chris took on brewmaster responsibilities. In the early 1990s Chris became interested in homebrewing and he even ran a small homebrew supply shop as part of a liquor store that was attached to the bowling alley. When he and his family became serious about adding a brewery, Chris attended a short course on brewing at Chicago's Siebel Institute of Technology and World Brewing Academy in 1995. Before Backwater got going, Chris also did some collaborative brewing with Pete Henderson of the Clubhaus Brewpub, which operated in Rochester from 1994 to 1999.

Winona has been home to as many as eight breweries dating back to the 1850s. Until the Backwater brewery arrived, this community had not experienced local beer since the 1960s, when the Peter Bub Brewery closed.

DON'T MISS THIS

If you don't look closely you just might miss the actual brewery. This brewhouse is small, if not the smallest working brewery in the state at only about 125 barrels per year. The brew kettle, which is located in a small room off the main bar, was once used for small test batches by Bell's Brewery of Kalamazoo, Michigan. Chris and his brother Geoff traveled to northern Michigan to purchase the kettle and haul it back to Winona on a flatbed trailer. The kettle had been in the hands of a homebrewer who had bought it from Bell's years before. Other parts of the Backwater brewery could also be considered hand-me-downs. The fermenters and a bright tank came from the Maritime Pacific Brewing Company in Seattle.

BACKWATER BREWS

Bullhead Red   *Your Ranking*_____
Light malty nose. A clear, reddish-amber body. Malty start and dry finish. This is a seasonal brew for Backwater.

Cat Tail Pale Ale   *Your Ranking*_____
An American-style pale ale. Light, faint, hoppy nose. Clear, light copper to golden color and a thick, off-white head. Medium bodied and a round mouth feel. A distinctive bitter flavor. A light bitterness, but overall a clean finish.

River Town Nut Brown Ale 🍺🍺   *Your Ranking_____*

A favorite among the locals and the brewery's best seller. A light malty nose. Reddish-amber color and a thin, tan head. Sweet malt bodied. Made with five different malts.

Steamboat Stout 🍺🍺🍺   *Your Ranking_____*

This is an oatmeal stout. Light, roasted nose. Medium bodied. Deep dark color with caramel and chocolate malty tones and a mild dryness. A light coffee-roasted finish.

Wing Dam Wheat 🍺   *Your Ranking_____*

This is a Kölsch-style ale. A light yeasty nose. Hazy golden color with a thick, bubbly, off-white head. Light bodied. A grainy maltiness with a fruity background. Sour finish.

OTHER BACKWATER BREWS YOU MAY WANT TO TRY

ESB   *Your Ranking_____*

A seasonal brew at Backwater.

MENU

The image of a bowling alley doesn't always conjure up complimentary images of food selections. However, Backwater Brewing does a good job of providing a range, from basic burgers and tavern food all the way to smoked ribs, brisket, and pulled pork. You'll find an extensive appetizer and finger food menu with potato wedges called Texas fries, nachos, cheese curds, and the popular Hodge Podge, which is an assortment of fried and grilled starters. Backwater Brewing has about a dozen sandwiches and about that many burgers. The signature Wellington Burger is made with bacon, cheese, and sautéed mushrooms. You'll also find chicken, seafood, salads, soup, and seasonal chili. The BBQ Smokehouse side of the menu shouldn't be overlooked for the ribs and brisket.

OTHER THINGS TO SEE OR DO IN THE AREA

Winona is located on the west side of the Mississippi River, between the river itself and limestone bluffs that rise upwards of five hundred feet. The experience of getting to Winona (for nonresidents) is a large part of enjoying a pint at Backwater Brewing Company. The Great River Road (U.S. 35) on the Wisconsin side of the river makes for a superb drive, but U.S. 61 on the Minnesota side also has spectacular views. The Upper Mississippi River Wildlife Refuge is a 261-mile stretch of the river that extends through Winona. If offers inspirational scenery and ample opportunities for water sports, hunting, and fishing. Great River Bluffs State Park (43605 Kipp Drive) is just south of Winona, where U.S. 61 connects with I-90. The park contains two scientific and natural areas and breathtaking views of the Mississippi River valley.

There are many shopping and antiquing opportunities in Winona and other communities along the river. Exploring and even seeking out bed-and-breakfasts can be a rewarding experience for weekend or longer vacations. The community of Red Wing is an excellent place to visit. Located on the river about an hour north of Winona, it has many architecturally interesting buildings, shops, and antique stores.

If you enjoy art, the Minnesota Marine Art Museum (800 Riverview Drive) features four galleries in a unique building on the banks of the Mississippi. The Performance Center on the Winona campus of St. Mary's University is a venue for music, theater, and dance, with performances at several locations throughout Winona. The Winona Symphony Orchestra has a rich history dating back to its founding in 1907. Its home is the Winona State University Performing Arts Center (175 Mark Street).

In the hills behind Backwater Brewing (to the south and west) is one of the area's most significant landmarks, Sugar Loaf Bluff (roughly the junction of U.S. 61 and Minnesota 43). The rocky pinnacle overlooks Winona and the river, extending eighty-five feet above the top of the bluff. Limestone from the surrounding hills was used for many of the town's buildings.

Over the years more than a few local businesses have incorporated "Sugar Loaf" into their names. The former Sugar Loaf Brewery (a.k.a. Peter Bub Brewery at Sugar Loaf Road and East Lake Boulevard) began in the 1850s and used the name Sugar Loaf from the 1870s until Prohibition. It reopened in 1933 as the Peter Bub Brewery and closed in 1969. The brewery used caves that were excavated in the hillside for aging its beer.

Backwater Brewing in Winona is centrally located among several other breweries in the southeast corner of the state. It's also only about nine miles from Olvalde Farmhouse Ales in Rollingstone (16557 Country Road 25). But remember if you are considering a tour of Olvalde you must call ahead to see if owner and brewer Joe Pond is in town. The brewery is on his in-laws' family farm and he commutes from the Twin Cities when he needs to brew. Somewhat further west is Mantorville Brewing, about seventy miles to the east in Mantorville (101 East 5th Street). Again, it's another brewery that requires advanced planning and scheduling because owner Tod Fyten also commutes from the Twin Cities on brew days. Another stop to consider when planning a larger beer tour to the area is La Crosse, Wisconsin, where you'll find Pearl Street Brewery (1404 St. Andrew Street) and City Brewery (925 South 3rd).

BREWERY RATING

	Your Rating	Shepard's Rating	General Description
Location		🍺🍺🍺🍺	Part of the fun is finding this brewpub. The drive along the Mississippi River makes it an enjoyable destination.
Ease of Finding Location		🍺🍺🍺	On a frontage road of U.S. highways 14 and 61 on Winona's southern edge. Signage doesn't make its identity as a brewpub obvious. Rather, look for Westgate Bowl.
Brewery Atmosphere		🍺🍺	The brewery itself is in a small enclosed room at the south end of the bar. Sights and sounds of the bowling alley are abundant. The beer is a welcome "add-on" to this business.
Dining Experience		🍺🍺	A wide range of choices, from tavern and supper club to bowling alley bar food.
The Pints		🍺🍺	It rarely gets more local than these small batch beers. Always variety in new and old, and worth a stop when traveling the Mississippi valley.

DIRECTIONS

Backwater Brewing Company is on the southern edge of Winona. It makes for a great weekend getaway from the Twin Cities or from various points in Wisconsin and northern Iowa. It's roughly 110 miles southeast of St. Paul on U.S. 14/61. Rochester is about fifty miles west, and La Crosse, Wisconsin, is only about thirty miles southeast.

From the south on Interstate 90, take exit 252 (Minnesota 43) directly into Winona. When Minnesota 43 intersects with U.S. 14/61, turn left (north) and within a few miles you'll see Backwater Brewing on your left (west).

From the southeast and Wisconsin on Interstate 90, exit 269 (U.S. 14/61) will take you directly into Winona and Backwater Brewing.

From the north, Backwater Brewing is on the right (west) side of U.S. 14/61, about a quarter-mile from the intersection and stoplights of Pelzer Street (U.S. 14 heading west) and U.S. 61 (U.S. 14 east).

From St. Paul, U.S. 61 follows the Mississippi River on the Minnesota side, while Wisconsin 35 (Great River Road) follows the river in Wisconsin. Either way, traveling the river between Red Wing and Winona makes for a beautiful drive, especially for the fall colors. You might even consider taking the Amtrak.

Brau Brothers Brewing Company

Lucan

Visit Date	*Signed*

ABOUT THE BREWERY

With a name like Brau how could you not become a brewer? In German the word means "to brew," and that is just what the Brau siblings do in the small (population 220) southwest Minnesota town of Lucan. Although their family is actually three generations removed from Germany, with their last name, owning a brewery seems almost like a birthright to the Braus.

Brau Brothers Brewing began in 1998 when Dustin Brau and his wife, Mary, purchased a tavern in Lucan and called it the Brauhaus. By 2000 Dustin was creating beers for his customers. By 2006 he decided he wanted to focus more on brewing so he sold Brauhaus; however, he kept his local ties to Lucan by locating his commercial brewery just a few blocks away. His brothers offered their help and each lent important expertise to the brewery. The oldest, Trevor, does inventory, ordering, and bookkeeping. Younger brother Brady is a computer programmer, so he helps with software needs and he designed many of the brewery's automated programs, which include a bottling line and pasteurizer. In 2011 they added additional fermenters to increase the brewery's capacity by nearly 60 percent.

From the outside, the Brau Brothers brewery resembles a red pole barn or farm shed. But a closer look around the property reveals this to be more than a working brewery. The Braus have about six adjacent acres planted with about a dozen varieties of hops. Some of those get used in the fall brewing season for "wet" hop beers. They also dug a 400,000-gallon pond next to the brewery that is used to irrigate those hop vines. On a few acres a little farther out of town, the Braus are growing barley that gets malted at the brewery. In a small town that has its own meaning of locally made, the Brau brothers needed few other reasons for growing their own hops and barley. Brau Brothers Brewing is entirely family owned. Even their father, Dale (a.k.a. Mr. Fixit), helps out around the brewery when needed.

Dustin Brau has made an impressive number of different beers and styles since beginning at the Brauhaus. After the transformation to a production brewery, the focus was on about a half-dozen beers as year-round bottled products. Brau Brothers distributes throughout Minnesota, Iowa, Wisconsin, North and South Dakota, and even parts of Michigan. The main brews include Pale Ale, Pilsner, Cream Stout, and Strawberry Wheat. In 2010 Brau Brothers began a line of cask-conditioned beers that have found their way into Twin Cities and Sioux Falls tap accounts. Brau Brothers has even started growing its own rye barley for a special batch of brew that is fermented in Prohibition era whiskey barrels obtained from the Templeton Rye distillery in Templeton, Iowa. Among those beers that merit special attention is the Bohemian Pilsner for its traditional use of Czech Saaz hops in the recipe. The Scotch Ale also appeals to beer aficionados.

HISTORY

The Brau brothers all grew up in Lucan. Dustin was the brother who became the catalyst for creating the family brewery in their hometown, but they all seem to share in the brewery operations. Mary was born in nearby Wabasso and actually met Dustin in grade school. But it was much later in college that Dustin got a taste of homebrewing with the purchase of a beer making kit. Dustin and Mary graduated from Southwest State University (now Southwest Minnesota State University) in nearby Marshall with degrees in hotel and restaurant management. Their strong desire to stay in the area and the opportunity of running their own restaurant convinced them to open the Brauhaus in 1998. By 2000, Dustin's continued love of homebrewing had led him to constructing a small 2-barrel brewing system that he used to make beer for Brauhaus patrons. Most of the current recipes at his current commercial brewery originated to some extent from his experiences running the Brauhaus.

In 2006, Dustin formed Brau Brothers Brewing with Trevor and Brady. The first beers from their production brewery appeared later that year. At the center of their brewery is a 15-barrel brewing system with six copper-clad fermenters, once used as serving vessels, from a Capital City Brewing Company restaurant in Baltimore, Maryland. (Capital City Brewing is a small chain of brewpubs, mostly in Washington, D.C., and Arlington, Virginia.) The Brau Brothers brewery also has a half-dozen stainless-steel fermenters, a small bottling line, and a cold storage room — all within a 5,000-square-foot building. The bottling line was purchased from the Ithaca Brewing Company (Ithaca, New York), and the labeler was once used at the Dark Horse Brewery (Marshall, Michigan). With their dad's help, they constructed a fair amount of the brewery's essential equipment — keg washer, bottling line, and pasteurizer. The keg washer is a modified Hobart commercial dishwasher. The brewery's pasteurizer was once a forty-foot deli sandwich conveyer line used in Kansas City that Dustin located on eBay. To transport it, the conveyer had to be cut in half. When it arrived in Lucan a transmission system was built to move beer-filled bottles through a modified tunnel for complete pasteurization. Trevor contributed by writing the software for the robotic components.

DON'T MISS THIS

The seasonal releases, festival beers, and a few beers marketed in the Lucan area make a visit to the brewery's tasting room very worthwhile, especially for a chance to taste Old 56. It's a light lager that the Braus make mostly for the locals and appearances at beer festivals. However, if you go to Lucan or a festival that the Brau brothers attend you may get to see Old 56 herself. Old 56 is the name of a fire truck that the city of Lucan purchased new in 1956. In 2009, the Brau brothers bought it from the city with the intent of making it a mascot for the brewery. Despite being over fifty years old the fire engine had only 3,900 miles when the Braus acquired it. They added a few extra emergency features any brewery needs — including a beer-chilling system and tap handles — on the outside of the truck to create a unique, eye-catching tapster on wheels.

BRAU BROTHERS BREWS

Cream Stout 🍺🍺🍺   *Your Ranking_____*
Malty nose. Deep black color with a thin, soft, brown head. Medium bodied. Lots of chocolate and caramel maltiness with a light coffee background and finish. A nice stout with an emphasis on maltiness over dryness. The recipe includes East Kent Goldings and Fuggles hops, with chocolate malt and roasted barley.

Forgotten Flem 🍺🍺   *Your Ranking_____*
A beer made as a tribute to the many southern Minnesota farmers who came from the Flemish region of Belgium. A sweet fruity and yeasty nose. Amber-copper color and a thick, light-tan head. Fruity start, yeast tones in the middle and light sour background. Finishes crisp and dry. Bottle conditioned, so expect it to have a full head and maybe even with a slight haze.

Moo Joos 🍺🍺🍺🍺   *Your Ranking_____*
An oatmeal milk stout with lots of smooth body and creamy chocolate maltiness. Firm malty nose with hints of roasted chocolate malt. Deep, dark black color with a medium soft and creamy head. Full bodied and soft mouth feel. Smooth chocolate maltiness stands out in the flavor profile. Finishes with a light spicy licorice-maltiness and some warmth. Made with additions of lactose in the brew kettle, alongside toasted and flaked oats. Brau Brothers make a special cask-conditioned version of this beer that is infused with cocoa and coconut.

Pale Ale 🍺🍺🍺   *Your Ranking_____*
A light but firm, hoppy nose. Clear bright golden color with a soft, off-white head. Medium bodied and crisp. Great citrus hoppiness in the main flavor. The bitterness continues into the finish. Made with Centennial and Cascade hops. This was the first commercial beer made by Dustin Brau. The initial batch actually ended up more like an imperial IPA, to which Dustin states, "When you screw something up, everybody wants to taste it!"

Pilz (Bohemian Pilsner) 🍺🍺🍺 *Your Ranking_____*

A traditional Bohemian pilsner with distinctive malt flavor and the spicy herbal bitterness from Czech Saaz hops. Begins with a light but firm spicy nose. A bright golden color and bubbly texture that has softness. Overall, light to medium bodied and very effervescent. The maltiness comes through in the body with assertive bitterness from the hops that carry through into the finish. Made with Bohemian Pilsner yeast and lagered for four weeks.

Ring Neck Braun Ale 🍺🍺🍺🍺 *Your Ranking_____*

A brown ale with a malty and roasted nose. Deep brown color and a thin, bubbly, tan head. Medium bodied and round. Lots of toasted oats in the flavor that create a nutty background. Finishes with smooth maltiness. This beer was the first seasonal brew of Brau Brothers. This is a bold nut brown ale made from six different malts, including toasted oats. At nearly 7 percent ABV it is a wonderful fall sipping beer. As you might expect, it is also very popular during hunting season in the Dakotas — of course, Minnesotans like it too.

Rubus 🍺🍺🍺🍺 *Your Ranking_____*

This is a blackberry imperial porter that appears somewhat randomly from Brau Brothers. It is sold in 750mL bottles and can be found at select draft accounts. It is a special favorite on the taps of the Brauhaus in Lucan. This is a bold and flavorful beer. Begins with a warm and inviting nose of roasted maltiness and hints of fruity blackberries. Deep black color with a thin, soft, and bubbly head. Full-bodied and round mouth feel. There is a roasted chocolate maltiness to the beginning with lots of berry flavor in the background. The sweet blackberry tones, amidst the roasted chocolate maltiness, linger in the finish. Rubus is the name for the family of plants that includes blackberries. For those who enjoy flavorful and strong beers as dessert or after a meal, put this one on the list of exceptional beers.

Scotch Ale 🍺🍺🍺🍺 *Your Ranking_____*

This beer was originally just brewed for beer shows and festivals but its following soon called on the Brau Brothers to make it year-round. An inviting, light roasted nose. Rich, hazy copper to bronze color with a bubbly, tan head. Medium to full bodied. Malty sweetness is upfront, but a distinctive smoked background is quick to find itself on the palate. Made with seven different malts and hopped with Styrian Goldings, then fermented with a Scottish yeast. Allow this beer to warm slightly and you'll really notice the smooth, complementary peat-smoked malt. An exceptional beer.

Sheephead 🍺🍺🍺 *Your Ranking_____*

An imperial IPA. Lots of resiny and piney notes in the nose. A light floral nose. Hazy reddish-bronze color with a thick, bubbly, tan head. Medium bodied and round. Sharp resiny hop bitterness through taste and finish. Great lingering hoppiness. Made with Sterling, Willamette, Centennial, and Cascade hops. The name is a reference to the Braus' favorite family card game and a beer that's perfect to celebrate winning and forget losing.

Strawberry Wheat 🍺🍺   *Your Ranking_____*

This is an unfiltered American wheat beer made with 50 percent wheat malt and Styrian Goldings hops. A light malty start with hints of strawberry. Despite being unfiltered, this beer is remarkably clear with a light yellow-golden color and thick, soft, off-white head. Light bodied and bubbly. It has a slight grainy beginning with the sweet strawberry flavor in the background and finish. The aftertaste is also somewhat dry.

Whirly Bird 🍺🍺🍺🍺   *Your Ranking_____*

A smooth, clean oatmeal stout. Firm, malty nose. Deep black color and a soft, tan head. Medium bodied and soft. A nice balance of maltiness up front that has a light bitter background with a clean finish. Its name recalls a bird that got stuck in the building's exhaust fan. The bird continued to whirl about even though life had flown away.

OTHER BRAU BROTHERS BREWS YOU MAY WANT TO TRY

Bancreagie   *Your Ranking_____*

A stronger and smokier version of Brau Brothers' popular Scotch Ale. Made with Scottish Maris Otter and a blend of peat smoked malts. Fermented with an Edinburgh yeast strain. Bancreagie is a reference to the granite aquifer underneath Lucan from which the Brau Brothers get their brewing water. Bancreagie translates from Scottish-Gaelic as a way to describe "white rock." This beer was inspired by the abandoned quarry just outside Lucan.

Frame Straightener   *Your Ranking_____*

A Belgian pale ale. A light yeasty nose. Clear, light copper color and a thin, tan head. The name refers to the building's former use by a manufacturer of auto frame straighteners. That product was once Lucan's number-one export.

Hundred Yard Dash   *Your Ranking_____*

This is an imperial (double) IPA made with hops that grow only about a hundred yards from the Brau Brothers' brew kettle. The Brau Brothers have about six acres of hops growing in the field surrounding their brewery. The varieties that go into this wet -hopped ale include Centennial, Cascade, Mt. Hood, Sterling, and Nugget. It's a fall seasonal that is likely to change from year to year based on the local yield.

Old 56   *Your Ranking_____*

A special, all-malt, light lager made mostly for the local area and beer festivals. Crisp and clean. Its recipe includes Sterling and Willamette hops. Gets its name from the fire truck that the city of Lucan purchased new in 1956, which is now a fixture of the brewery.

**Special Release Beers Brewed
with Local Homebrewers**   *Your Ranking_____*

About once a year Dustin Brau works with homebrewers in Sioux Falls, South Dakota, to make a batch of beer. The recipe is based on the winning entry from their local competition.

MENU

Brau Brothers Brewing Company does not serve food. However, just a few blocks away (north on Main Street) brewery visitors should check out the Brauhaus for a lunch or dinner and experience Brau Brothers beers on tap. Ken and Barb Rechzigel purchased the Brauhaus from Dustin and Mary Brau in 2008. The Rechzigels grew up in Lucan and have remained good friends with the Brau family. The food menu at the Brauhaus stresses homemade items, ranging from pizza to entrées like chicken kiev, ribs, and walleye dinners, along with weekend specials. On Friday and Saturday evenings it's not uncommon for the Brauhaus to serve more people than the entire population of Lucan!

OTHER THINGS TO SEE OR DO IN THE AREA

Perhaps one of the most fitting stops along the way to Lucan is a visit to Granite Falls. The two are only about thirty miles apart. Granite Falls is a town where raising a pint has special meaning. Andrew Volstead was its mayor (1900–1901) and went on to represent the state in the U.S. House of Representatives (1903–23). As chair of the House Judiciary Committee, he wrote the National Prohibition Act of 1919 (a.k.a. the Volstead Act), which reinforced the Eighteenth Amendment. His home in Granite Falls, the Volstead House (163 Ninth Avenue), is a National Historic Landmark and is open by appointment or by chance. It is a wood frame house with a two-story stairwell tower that has a few informational panels about Volstead and the role of farm cooperatives in the early twentieth century. Volstead is buried in the Granite Falls. No matter how you feel about Volstead, Granite Falls is a place to toast both the Eighteenth Amendment and the Twenty-first Amendment that repealed Prohibition.

The community of Redwood Falls is another excellent stop along the way to Lucan. Redwood Falls and Granite Falls are connected by the Minnesota River valley. Redwood Falls, which gives "The Scenic City" its name, runs through Alexander Ramsey Park, Minnesota's largest municipal park at over 217 acres. The park has great picnic areas, and its Ramsey Creek is a well-known trout stream.

About a half-mile west of Redwood Falls is the Redwood County Museum (913 West Bridge Street), which was once the county poor farm and now houses historical artifacts and displays. One of highlights is a foot-and-a-half-long meteorite. There is also a display about Richard W. Sears, the founder of Sears & Roebuck Company, who in 1886 was a depot agent for the Minneapolis and St. Louis Railroad in North Redwood. In June, Redwood hosts the Minnesota Inventors Congress, the nation's oldest such convention.

To the west of Lucan is the town of Marshall. In July Marshall hosts the Festival of Kites, and in August the Lyon County fair is in town.

For outdoor experiences there are several State Wildlife Management Areas near Lucan. The closest, about four miles west, is the Westline State Wildlife Management Area. Other such areas within a short drive include Gales (southwest), Waterbury (south), Mammenga and Willow Lake (southeast), and Daub's Lake (east).

Brau Brothers would make for a great three- to four-day tour that could include visiting the August Schell brewery in New Ulm. When planning a trip to

Brau Brothers always call ahead. Be sure to check the brewery's website for a number of events including BrauFest in June and HopFest in the fall.

BREWERY RATING

	Your Rating	Shepard's Rating	General Description
Location		🍺🍺🍺	For most Minnesotans, getting to Lucan (population 220) does require an investment in time, but the trip is part of the experience that makes a visit to Brau Brothers unique.
Ease of Finding Location		🍺🍺🍺	Once in Lucan it's not difficult to find. The brewery is in the middle of town, just off Main Street. Watch for the water town as a landmark that lets you know you're near the brewery.
Brewery Atmosphere		🍺🍺🍺🍺	This is a working brewery. The stories behind some of the equipment offer special meaning to "hand crafted" beer.
Dining Experience		n/a	Not applicable. However, you might check out the nearby Brauhaus Restaurant, which serves Brau Brothers brews. After all, the Brauhaus is where this brewery began.
The Pints		🍺🍺🍺🍺	When visiting the brewery you are likely to find several beers that are made just for the area, like Old 56. Brau Brothers offers great beer, but it's an example of the journey being part of the experience.

DIRECTIONS

Lucan, Minnesota — no matter how much you like the beer — is best summed up as a destination type of trip. Lucan is about 150 miles southwest of the Twin Cities and some 100 miles northeast of Sioux Falls, South Dakota. Redwood Falls, Granite Falls, and Marshall are larger communities with lodging options. Brau Brothers Brewing is not difficult to find once you arrive in Lucan. It's on Main Street (County Road 10) in a red building adjoining a hops field. If you miss Brau Brothers, you've probably missed Lucan altogether.

Mankato Brewery
Mankato

Visit Date	Signed

ABOUT THE BREWERY

The Mankato Brewery took a few years of planning before finally heating up its brew kettle for the first time in fall of 2011. The brewery is located in North Mankato, near Hiniker Pond and the intersections of U.S. Highways 14 and 169. Local businessman Tim Tupy founded the Mankato Brewery in 2010. Tupy and his wife, Tami, are owners of the LIV Aveda Lifestyle Salon and Spa in Mankato. Before that, Tim Tupy worked in telecommunications with Midwest Wireless, which eventually became part of Verizon. Tupy grew up in the area on an organic farm, which fostered his strong interest in using local ingredients in making his beer. He's especially interested in making beer with locally grown hops. Tupy is the chief executive officer for the company and handles all sales and marketing. In May 2011 Tony Feuchtenberger was hired as brewery president. Feuchtenberger grew up in St. James, Minnesota, about forty-five minutes southwest of Mankato. Feuchtenberger has a degree in education from Ridgewater Community College in Willmar, Minnesota. Both Tupy and Feuchtenberger were homebrewers before starting Mankato Brewery. In the summer of 2011 they hired Mike Miziorko as brewmaster. Before taking the job at Mankato Brewery, Miziorko had worked for the Summit Brewing Company in St. Paul. Miziorko is a 2005 graduate of the American Brewers Guild Program that is based in Salisbury, Vermont. He did his apprenticeship at the Rock Bottom Brewery in downtown Minneapolis. Miziorko brings a unique dimension to his brewing of traditional German and European beers because he speaks both German and Dutch, in part a reflection of his bachelor's degree in German studies from the University of Wisconsin.

The Mankato Brewery consists of a 15-barrel brewing system with a 2,500-barrel annual capacity. The 24,000-square-foot building had been built for Locher Brothers Inc., a Miller beer distributor that moved its operations to Green Isle, Minnesota. From the outside the building has the appearance and character of a common industrial processing and warehouse facility. Before moving in the building required some renovation, but a big selling point to the Mankato Brewery was its 24-foot-high ceiling and 4,000 square feet of cold storage space. Mankato's initial equipment, mostly new, was purchased from Newlands System in 2011. It consists of a brew kettle, three 30-barrel fermenters, one bright tank, keg sanitizer and filler, and a Meheen bottle filler. The brewhouse occupies most of the two-story steel building, but not all of it. Tupy plans to lease some of the remaining space in the building to other businesses.

The Greater Mankato area offers strong possibilities for a local brewery to prosper and flourish. The cities of North Mankato and Mankato are located at the confluence of the Minnesota and Blue Earth rivers, and together make up Minnesota's fourth largest metro area. It's also the home of Minnesota State University–Mankato with its own thriving student population of around 17,000. Overall, there are lots of prospects for entertainment, shopping, eating, annual events, and historical attractions. Beyond the August Schell Brewing Company in nearby New Ulm, greater Mankato has been without a local production brewery for more than a half-century.

Mankato Brewery's core beers include a Golden Ale, a Brown Ale, and an IPA. They are available on draft in area taverns and restaurants and in growlers from the brewery. Mankato Brewery considers its home market to be the nine counties that surround Greater Mankato. As demand for its beer grows, expect the brewery to offer special seasonal and barrel-aged beers.

HISTORY

Mankato has been home to more than a dozen breweries since the 1850s. Among those that stand out is the William and Jacob Bierbauer Brewery, which began in 1856 near North Front and Rock streets. Ownership of that brewery changed hands several times within the Bierbauer family before Prohibition. After 1933 and the repeal of Prohibition Minneapolis businessman Gerald Martin reopened it as the Mankato Brewing Company. The brewery became known for Kato Beer with Gold, White, and Black brands. In 1951 Mankato Brewing Company was purchased by the Cold Spring Brewery, which continued to run it until 1954. Then a group of local Mankato investors bought it back and tried to expand it brands. By 1967 the brewery could not compete with larger Minnesota breweries and was forced to close.

Mankato had a brief flirtation with a brewpub in the early 2000s. The Bandana Brewpub operated from 2003 until 2006. The restaurant and bar, without an operating brewhouse, stayed open until 2008. Its owner, Bob Ahlstom, cited a drop in business and changes in state laws reflecting an intolerance for smoking in public places as reasons for closing.

The owner of today's Mankato Brewery, Tim Tupy, grew up in New Prague,

Minnesota. In the planning phase of his brewery, Tupy became interested in his family ancestors and started wondering if past family members had connections with breweries. What he discovered was that his great-great-great-grandfather Albert Minar started a brewery in New Prague in 1886 with his son Albert Jr. Tupy believes that Albert Sr. actually emigrated from Czechoslovakia and when he arrived in America he listed his occupation as brewer. Albert Jr. eventually left New Prague to train and work at the Christopher Stahlmann Brewing Company in St. Paul. Tupy says family records indicate that Albert Sr. sold his interest in the New Prague brewery to his daughter and son-in-law in the early 1890s and moved to Browerville, Minnesota, where he opened a brewery on eighty acres of land. Minar Brewing Company in Browerville operated from 1892 until 1918. At least for a short time during Prohibition, before closing for good, Minar made soft drinks. Given that heritage, special sodas or even a root beer is something to watch for in the future from Tim Tupy.

DON'T MISS THIS

The use of local ingredients and the small-batch, one-time brews.

MANKATO BREWS

Brown Ale   *Your Ranking*_____

An anticipated early role out beer for the Mankato Brewery. Deep amber color with malty and light nutty tones.

Golden Ale   *Your Ranking*_____

A light-bodied ale with bright golden color. Well balanced and clean.

OTHER MANKATO BREWS YOU MAY WANT TO TRY

India Pale Ale   *Your Ranking*_____

The Mankato Brewery hopes to eventually tap in to the local hop producers to help make this IPA.

Kölsch   *Your Ranking*_____

A beer that is expected to be part of Mankato's offering in the future. While he was at the Summit Brewing Company brewmaster Mike Miziorko created a special version of the Kölsch style that appeared in their Unchained Series of special release beers.

MENU

None. Mankato Brewing Company does not serve food.

OTHER THINGS TO SEE OR DO IN THE AREA

Mankato was originally named "Mahkato" by its early inhabitants, the Dakota. That translates to greenish-blue earth. Today, there are many memorials and buildings in the Greater Mankato area that commemorate the region's history and the diverse ancestry of those who have settled the region. Two such tributes include the Dakota Warrior (101 East Main) and Reconciliation Park (100 North Riverfront Drive). Both sites have large sculptures and call attention to the need for reconciliation and healing among non-Dakota and Dakota people.

For those who enjoy art and sculptures, the CityArt Walking Sculpture Tour features twenty sculptures throughout Mankato and North Mankato. At the Mankato Farmers' Market, which runs May through October (1400 Madison Avenue), you can find not only fresh fruits and vegetables but also flowers, household amenities, and crafts. The Summer Solstice is one of Mankato's major summer events. It features local and regional musicians, artists, and craft and food vendors. The main festivities are held at the Land of Memories Park. Riverfront Park is another site of many festivals and events throughout the year. One to put on your list is the Arts by the River in June. Riverfront Drive on the Mankato side of the Minnesota River between Plum and Vine streets showcases some of the oldest architecture in town dating back to the late nineteenth century.

If you enjoy seeing historic homes, the Hubbard House (606 South Broad Street) was built by R. D. and Mary Esther Hubbard in 1871. The Blue Earth County Historical Society operates the house and offers regular tours. The County Historical Society also coordinates Mankato's Historic Old Town Pub Crawl, which stops at several places for a portal, perhaps even a pint glass, into the city's past.

Also in Mankato is the Sinclair Lewis Summer Home (315 South Broad Street) where in the summer of 1919 Lewis wrote much of his novel *Main Street*. Lewis also enjoyed buggy rides out to the bluffs to enjoy views of the Minnesota River valley. A great view today is from the trails at Bluff and Riverview Parks on the North Mankato side of the river.

West of Mankato on State Highway 68 and U.S. Highway 169 is Minneopa State Park. Minneopa in the Dakota language means "water falling twice," which is a reference to the park's beautiful waterfalls of Minneopa Creek. This region has some of the tallest waterfalls in southern Minnesota. A more secluded 42-foot fall is Minnemishinona Falls, located three miles west of North Mankato along Nicollet County Road 41 (Jodson Bottom Road).

The surrounding area of Mankato offer an abundance of hiking and biking opportunities. The Sakatah Singing Hills State Trail stretches nearly forty miles from Mankato to Fairbault. The Red Jacket Bike Trail follows an abandoned rail line south along the Minnesota River from Mankato. And the Minnesota River Trail connects Sakatah and Red Jacket trails through the heart of Mankato.

The city also plays host to the Minnesota Vikings training camp from late July to mid-August. Practices are held on the Minnesota State University campus and portions are open to the public, although tickets are required for scrimmages. Also in the local sport scene, the Mankato MoonDogs of the Northwoods Baseball League play at Franklin Rogers Park (601 Reed Street) on the east side of town.

Mankato is also about thirty miles east of New Ulm and the August Schell Brewing Company.

BREWERY RATING

	Your Rating	Shepard's Rating	General Description
Location		🍺🍺🍺🍺	The trip to the Mankato Brewery makes for a wonderful long weekend, unless you live in the area so the drive might not be that long or special to the locals. Mankato and North Mankato combined for a population of over 50,000. It's hard to believe that this is the only brewery in town. The location just north of downtown Mankato is a plus for for taking in the other activities and attractions of Greater Mankato.
Ease of Finding Location		🍺🍺🍺	Easy to find off U.S. Highway 14.
Brewery Atmosphere		🍺🍺🍺	A straight forward, no frills working brewery, in a warehouse building whose previous tenant had been a beer distributor.
Dining Experience		n/a	Not applicable.
The Pints		🍺🍺🍺	Still a brewery/work in progress. The initial commitment and investment positions the beer and brewery on a good path for success.

DIRECTIONS

When approaching Mankato from the east on U.S. Highway 14, take the Minnesota Route 60 and U.S. Highway 169 South exit into North Mankato. (For a scenic drive, Highway 169 actually connects Mankato with the Twin Cities.) Proceed on Highway 169—which roughly follows the west bank of the Minnesota River—about 1 mile and turn right (west) onto Webster Avenue. Take the third right (north) onto Center Street and the Mankato Brewery will be on the left (west) side of the road.

Mantorville Brewing Company
Mantorville

ABOUT THE BREWERY

Mantorville Brewing is one of the smallest working breweries in Minnesota. It's also part of a community with a storied brewery past that dates back to the late 1850s. But the most recent brewing chapter in Mantorville began in 1996. The present Mantorville brewery is located on the east side of town along Fifth Street. The town of Mantorville was founded in 1854, and even today it has an old look about it with many distinctive century-old limestone buildings. However, the Mantorville brewery is in a building without much of a past. It was once a two-bay car wash that, "soaking wet," isn't much larger than 1,500 square feet. The brewery emerged from the creative hands and beer passions of a half-dozen local homebrewers who pulled together a system in part converted from used dairy equipment, like the old creamery kettle that's now a brew kettle. Small does indeed describe the brewery's on-site operations, with an annual production that hovers around 150 barrels.

If you want a tour, it is essential to call ahead. The brewing schedule in Mantorville is not regular because the owner, Tod Fyten, has to travel from the Twin Cities on brew days. From Mantorville he mainly supplies fresh draft beer and growlers. You can find it on tap at the historic Hubbell House hotel only a few blocks from the brewery, or if you are lucky enough to be there when brewing is happening you can purchase a growler. However, Fyten also has his brewery licensed to Duluth, Minnesota, where large scale production and bottling is done with help from the Lake Superior Brewing Company. Mantorville Brewing's bottled products include Stagecoach Amber (its flagship beer),

Smoked Porter, and Stagecoach Golden. Tod Fyten also owns two other breweries, St. Croix Brewing and Theodore Fyten Brewing.

HISTORY

John Hirschi founded the first brewery in Mantorville in 1858, known as the Dodge County Brewery. A year later it was purchased by Charles Ginsburg and Henry Naegli, who expanded operations along the east end of Main Street, into the bluff that overlooks the Zumbro River and not far from the location of today's Mantorville brewery. It was regarded as an elaborate brewery for its time, especially for a small town like Mantorville, known more for its limestone quarry and stagecoach stop. Ginsburg's brewery was one of the first in Minnesota to have a hall for events, entertainment, and dancing. The inner workings of the brewery included an elaborate system of cellars and caves, and it was an early adopter of steam power. In 1878 Ginsburg died, supposedly by suicide. His widow took over for a short time, but his partner Henry Naegli assumed ownership. By 1899 Naegli had sold the brewery to Ferdinand Schnagl. It remained in the Schnagl family until 1917. During Prohibition it functioned as a creamery and maker of soft drinks and afterward reopened as Otto's Brewery under the ownership of Otto Schumann. Financial difficulties ultimately forced another change of ownership within a few years. A former brewmaster took over the brewery, but in 1939 it finally closed.

Brewing did not return to Mantorville until 1996 when a group of six homebrewers decided to scale up their hobby to a commercial business. They developed several recipes, with their primary beer being Stagecoach Amber Ale, which they made for the Stagecoach Saloon in the nearby Hubbell House. In 1999 the group of homebrewers hired Tod Fyten as a consultant to help them expand. By 2002 Fyten had assumed full ownership of Mantorville Brewing.

Fyten's original plan was to maintain draft beer production in Mantorville and contract bottling to a larger brewery. He initially hoped the August Schell Brewing Company would help out, but when Schell acquired the Grain Belt label and increased its own production Fyten focused on other options. In 2007 he teamed up with the Sand Creek Brewing of Black River Falls, Wisconsin, and in 2010 he moved his bottling to Lake Superior Brewing Company in Duluth. That strategy distinguishes his brewery from other contract beer companies because Mantorville Brewing is licensed as a brewery in both Mantorville and Duluth.

Fyten also owns St. Croix Brewing Company, which produces St. Croix Cream Ale, Creamy Brown Ale, Cream Stout, Serrano Pepper Ale, and Maple Ale. And, he owns Theodore Fyten Brewing which makes Fytenburg Grand Cru, Grand Cru Blanc and Grand Cru Reserve. Both St. Croix Brewing and Theodore Fyten Brewing have offices in the shadow of St. Paul's once great Joseph Schmidt brewery.

DON'T MISS THIS

When visiting Mantorville give yourself a little extra time for a stop at Hubbell House (502 North Main Street) where you can enjoy a meal and a beer from Mantorville Brewing inside the Stagecoach Bar. Look around this wonderful old hotel that dates back to 1854. If you look closely you might see a framed photo of the Dodge County Brewery taken around 1874.

MANTORVILLE BREWS

Stagecoach Amber   🍺🍺🍺   *Your Ranking_____*

Mantorville's flagship ale. A light malty nose. Hazy reddish-amber color with a marbled tan head. Medium bodied. Firm, caramel malty flavor and clean finish.

Stagecoach Golden   🍺🍺🍺   *Your Ranking_____*

A Kölsch-style beer. No nose. Light straw color with a thin, bubbly, white head. Light bodied and very bubbly. Smooth malty flavor with a firm, crisp, bitterness for the finish. Made with noble hops and Canadian honey malt.

Stagecoach Smoked Porter   🍺🍺🍺🍺   *Your Ranking_____*

Made with Belgian chocolate malt and peat-smoked malt. A firm, roasted nose. Deep black color and a thick, brown head. Medium to full bodied. The chocolate malty flavors are robust with the peat-smoked malt evident in the background and finish of the beer.

OTHER MANTORVILLE BREWS YOU MAY WANT TO TRY

Stagecoach Double Barrel Smoked Porter   *Your Ranking_____*

A special version of the Stagecoach Smoked Porter aged in bourbon barrels. The initial version was made to celebrate the brewery's fifteenth anniversary in 2011.

MENU

None. Mantorville is a working brewery and does not serve food. However, at Hubbell House you can find a great meal and a pint of Mantorville beer. Its dinner menu features steaks, seafood, and chicken entrées.

OTHER THINGS TO SEE OR DO IN THE AREA

Restoration House (540 North Main Street) is a must stop for the brewery history enthusiast. Built in 1856, the structure once served as a county office building and held the county's only jail cell, still in the basement. Behind Restoration House is a log cabin that was once the home of the cooper for the early Mantorville breweries. Inside is a display of old brewery tools that will add to the experience of a tour of the modern Mantorville brewery.

Mantorville offers a lot for visitors. Nearly half of the businesses are antique, art, and gift shops. For Marigold Days in September, craft vendors and antique dealers fill the local riverside park. A few weeks later is the Zumbro Bend Rendezvous, a living history festival with costumed reenactors and demonstrations of what life in a fur trading post and community encampment was like in the seventeenth and eighteenth centuries. There is strong community interest in historical reenactments. In June the nearby community of Wasioja holds its annual Civil War Days, and in August Mantorville hosts the Wasioja Civil War Days Shivaree. The Mantorville Theatre Company puts on summer melodramas and year-round performances at the Mantorville Opera House (5 Fifth Street Northeast). In October Mantorville throws its annual Fall Festival, one highlight of which is a narrated tour of haunted sites in town. The Opera House itself is said to be haunted by unexplainable footsteps and previous theater performers.

BREWERY RATING

	Your Rating	Shepard's Rating	General Description
Location		🍺🍺🍺	Mantorville is a small community west of Rochester. It makes a fun day trip for enjoying the shops and antique stores of Mantorville and Kasson.
Ease of Finding Location		🍺🍺🍺	Not difficult, just requires some planning. I-90 and I-35 are not far from Mantorville.
Brewery Atmosphere		🍺🍺🍺	It's best to call ahead for tours of this small brewery. Larger production and bottling are done in Duluth at the Lake Superior Brewing Company.
Dining Experience	n/a		Not applicable.
The Pints		🍺🍺🍺	Okay experience, enhanced by the journey to the area.

DIRECTIONS

Mantorville is about twenty miles west of Rochester. From Rochester, go west on U.S. 14 to Kasson, then north on Minnesota 57 for about three miles to Mantorville. From the west, exit Interstate 35 at Owatonna and travel east on U.S. 14 to Kasson, then north on Minnesota 57 to Mantorville. Minnesota 57 northbound becomes U.S. 52, which leads to St. Paul (about seventy miles).

Olvalde Farm and Brewing Company
Rollingstone

Visit Date	Signed

ABOUT THE BREWERY

Olvalde Farm and Brewing Company evokes the romantic image of the Flemish farmhouse breweries. Located in rural southwestern Minnesota on a former dairy farm, this small brewery is tucked away in a farm shed and most anyone passing by would never know it exists. What's more, it's only known for one beer that is sold in 750mL bottles!

Owner and brewmaster Joe Pond, an avid homebrewer, allowed his hobby to grow into several professional brewery positions and before long his fascination with beer history and culture introduced him to the European farmhouse brewing traditions. His in-laws welcomed him to their rural Rollingstone farm where he constructed a small farm shed for the 15-barrel brewing system that he purchased in 2009 from a brewery in Columbus, Ohio. Pond also patiently scanned sale ads in newspapers and used his connections with farmers to find former dairy equipment, such as bulk milk tanks that he could modify into two fermenters and a conditioning tank. When it came time to assemble his brewery, he was able to get some help from local metal workers in nearby Winona.

The name "Olvalde" is a reference to the Norse mythology from the thirteenth century. Olvalde was also known as "the emperor of ale," and he made beer for Thrym, who was the god of cold, frost, and winter. When Olvalde died his wealth was said to have been divided by his three sons by measuring it out in their mouths.

Olvalde began with only one beer, the Auroch's Horn, a brew made with honey, wheat, and barley. Pond's brewing philosophy is based on simplicity and a love of history that encourages him to consider older beer styles that are based on locally grown ingredients. Pond hopes to eventually add four rotating seasonals along with several barrel-aged beers.

HISTORY

Brewery owner and brewmaster Joe Pond established the Olvalde Farm and Brewing Company in March 2011. Pond considers his arrival into farm-house brewing as a combination of interest, opportunity, and good luck.

Pond grew up in Lakeville, Minnesota. After graduating from the University of Minnesota in St. Paul with a degree in chemical engineering, Pond worked a few different jobs until in 2002 when he landed a position in Chicago at Goose Island Brewing's Fulton Street bottling plant. At Goose Island his engineering background initially got him involved in issues like solving problems on the packing line and dealing with the brewery's waste water. Eventually he moved into a cellarman position, which also included working in the brewery's lab and even brewing. In 2005 Joe Pond and his wife Dinel decided to move to the Twin Cities where he went to work for the Summit Brewing Company in St. Paul. He remained there for about a year before taking some time off to help with his young and growing family.

The farm that Olvalde is located on belongs to Dinel's mother and father, Carlus and Carolyn Dingfelder. It had been in the family since the 1930s, and at the time of their retirement in 2000 it was a working dairy farm. Joe Pond plans to eventually grow his own hops and barley on the land surrounding the brewery. He even has the goal of building a small malt-house for roasting his own barley.

DON'T MISS THIS

The brewery itself! Located on a farm on Rollingstone's eastern edge, the bre-whouse is located in what appears from the outside to be an ordinary farm shed on the Dingfelder property (the in-laws of brewer Joe Pond).

OLVALDE BREW

The Auroch's Horn   🍺🍺🍺🍺   *Your Ranking_____*
As of 2011, the only beer made by Olvalde. Made with barley, wheat, and honey. A light honey-like nose. Amber-golden color with a thin, bubbly, off-white head. Full bodied. Smooth honey sweetness dominates and lingers into the finish. The honey in this beer comes from Cannon Falls, Minnesota. Sold in 750mL bottles that are hand corked. The beer gets its name from the Auroch, an extinct wild bull, from which European barbarians would take the horn for drinking vessels.

MENU

None. Olvalde Farm and Brewing Company does not serve food. However, if you are looking for a local place to enjoy a meal and share a bottle of Auroch's Horn try Ginny's Supper Club (western edge of Rollingstone on Highway 248).

OTHER THINGS TO SEE OR DO IN THE AREA

Rollingstone is a small town of about 700 people, located about ten miles west of Winona. The Rollingstone Township was organized in 1858 on a plateau between two branches of the Rollingstone River, from which it takes its name. Its Dakota name is Eyan-omen-man-met-pah, which translates to "the stream where the stone rolls." Many of the early settlers to the area had ties to Luxembourg, a small country located between Germany, France, and Belgium. Coincidentally, Luxembourg is known for its own beer heritage.

Nearby Winona is a larger population center and the Winona County History Center (160 Johnson Street) is a good place to learn about the area. It houses a "County Time-Line" exhibit that includes descriptive information about the area's unique geologic formations and other exhibits about early settlement of the area. Summer is a great time to visit a number of festivals in Winona, such as Steamboat Days and the Great River Shakespeare Festival.

Olvalde is one of three breweries in this area, which can make for a great weekend of exploring the Mississippi River and the Great River Road. Nearby Winona is home to Backwater Brewing and to the west about forty-five miles lies the Mantorville Brewing Company.

BREWERY RATING

	Your Rating	Shepard's Rating	General Description
Location		🍺🍺🍺	This is one of the harder to find breweries in Minnesota. Located west of Winona near Rollingstone on a farmstead. No brewery signage makes it even more challenging. But the romance of a true farmhouse brewery makes it a special place among beer enthusiasts.
Ease of Finding Location		🍺🍺	Its location and lack of evidence that the farm has a working brewery make it difficult to find. That's somewhat by design, however, given that brewery owner and brewmaster Joe Pond is only there on brew days. Call ahead before making plans to visit.
Brewery Atmosphere		🍺🍺🍺	A small working brewing that's being put together with used dairy and brewery equipment. The homebrewer will appreciate Pond's ingenuity and creativity for fashioning together this brew system.
Dining Experience		n/a	Not applicable.
The Pints		🍺🍺🍺	Small batch beers and only a few of them.

DIRECTIONS

Rollingstone is located about ten miles west of Winona on Highway 248. The brewery is located on a farm without any signage near the intersection of Highway 248 and County Road 25, roughly on the eastern edge of Rollingstone. If you go, you are asked to call ahead.

City Brewing Company
La Crosse, Wisconsin

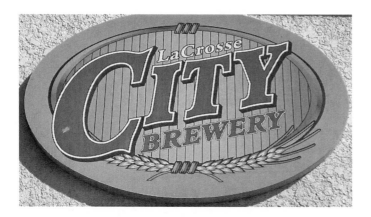

ABOUT THE BREWERY

City Brewery was the name John Gund gave his brewery when it opened in La Crosse in 1864, but the name changed a few years later when Gund sold his interests in the brewery to his partner, Gottlieb Heileman. The brewery still carried the name Heileman when it reached peak production in the early 1980s and became the nation's fourth largest beer maker.

The brewery changed owners several times in the 1990s — Stroh's, Pabst, and even for a short time the City of La Crosse, when debt payments guaranteed by the city were not made by the holding company. In 2000 a group of former G. Heileman executives was able to restructure the company — restoring the City name in the process — and achieve success with a handful of local beer labels alongside a tremendous growth in contract beer making. These former G. Heileman employees revived recipes and processes found in the archives of the 1970s, which included the practice of kraeusening, which had given rise to Heileman's dominant position in the beer market. Kraeusening is a secondary aging process that naturally carbonates beer. It was used in beers such as G. Heileman's Old Style and Special Export.

In 2006 City Brewing Company was purchased by Sabina Bosshard, her husband George Parke, and her three brothers. Sabina had actually been part of the group that purchased the brewery six years earlier. The current facility has capacity for nearly seven million barrels annually. City Brewing Company's contract portfolio contains nearly forty different products.

When visiting La Crosse you will want to make sure to take note of the world's largest six-pack, just north of the City brewery's visitor center. It's actually six lagering tanks, large enough to hold over 7.3 million cans of beer, painted to resemble four-story-tall cans of La Crosse Lager. Yet another major landmark is just across the street from the six-pack—a ten-foot statue of King Gambrinus.

BEERS

The local labels of City Brewing are no longer owned by the brewery, but they are made there. City Light 🍺 is a light-bodied lager with light yellow color and thin flavor. City Lager 🍺🍺 has more color and body than City Light and received a silver medal from the 2000 World Beer Cup competition in the American-style premium lager category. La Crosse Light 🍺🍺 is light to medium bodied and very clean. La Crosse Lager 🍺🍺🍺 is clear golden with a crisp, light hoppiness.

The bulk of City Brewing's beer making is contract brews. Products such as Smirnoff Ice, Mike's Hard Lemonade, Minnesota's Brew Northern Lager, Nighthawk Premium Malt Liquor, Rolling Rock, and even Sam Adams have been made at this brewery.

MENU

None. City Brewing Company does not serve food.

Dempsey's Brewery, Restaurant, and Pub
Watertown, South Dakota

Visit Date	*Signed*

ABOUT THE BREWERY

Dempsey's Brewery, Restaurant, and Pub, located in downtown Watertown, occupies a building that was originally constructed in 1903. For many years it served the community as a food warehouse.

Owner Bill Dempsey grew up as an Army kid, which meant he saw many parts of Europe, including Ireland, Scotland, and Germany. In particular, learning to eat and drink in Germany left him with a special taste for beer. Later, after twenty-five years with the Deli Express Company, he decided to go out on his own and chose Watertown as a place to build his pub with international flair. Inside you'll immediately note the flags of the seven Celtic nations as well as other military flags, various weaponry, and framed pieces of Scottish tartan. On one entire wall there is a forty-foot mural of Dempsey's Castle in Ireland.

Much of the actual brewery equipment came from the Moorhead, Minnesota, brewery called Trapper and Trader, which closed in 1999. The 10-barrel system that includes fermenters, a mash tun, brew kettle, and hot liquor tank occupies its own room behind the bar; serving vessels are located downstairs. Bill Dempsey did much of the remodeling work on the building, including assembling the brewery, a process that took about six months. Dempsey's opened on February 1, 2000.

Dempsey himself is fully involved in the business, playing the roles of bartender, bookkeeper, waiter, busboy, and brewer. You may even find him dressed in a kilt and playing the bagpipes—he's founder and Pipe Major of the Glacial Lakes Marching Band and sometimes plays for patrons.

241

BEERS

Expect a half-dozen Dempsey beers at any visit. The beers reflect the overall Irish and Scottish theme of the brewpub. Perhaps the most appropriate beer name is Battle Axe Blonde 🍺🍺, a light-bodied, clear, golden ale with crisp flavor and light fruity finish. You'll actually find a few battle axes and swords hanging on the walls of the brewpub. The Banshie Pale Ale 🍺🍺 is a hoppy beer that references the female spirit who warns of impending death in Irish folklore. Valkyrie Red 🍺🍺🍺🍺, Dempsey's best seller, is a German-style Oktoberfest that gets its name from Richard Wagner's composition *Ride of the Valkyries*. A beer that shouldn't be overlooked is the Black Bear Stout 🍺🍺🍺🍺, whose name comes from the Scottish bagpipe tune "The Black Bear," which British units play to pipe home the troops. Other beers that make occasional appearances include Honey Brown Wench, a brown ale; Longship Lager, a clear amber lager; and Frostbite Lager, a seasonal favorite.

MENU

Dempsey's varied menu has such signature dishes as Wienerschnitzel and Spätzle, and Irish Boxy. Other selections worthy of consideration include fish and chips, burgers, sandwiches, pastas, and several versions of stir-fry. Among main entrée choices are steak, chicken, pork, fish, shrimp, and ribs. Dempsey's offers a Sunday brunch and a buffet at least one night a week.

Granite City Food and Brewery

Sioux Falls, South Dakota

Granite City
FOOD & BREWERY*

Visit Date	Signed

ABOUT THE BREWERY

Granite City Food and Brewery of Sioux Falls was the second restaurant for the company. It opened in December 2000 on the south side of Sioux Falls, about a half-mile east of Interstate 29 (exit 78, South Louise Avenue). While its atmosphere and décor is very similar to all other Granite Cities, this one also has a beautiful small courtyard with a fountain surrounded by tables. Nearby are a variety of shopping options, including the Empire Mall, several hotels, and a multiplex cinema. No trip to Sioux Falls is complete without a walk through Falls Park, a downtown area along the Sioux River that gives this city its name.

Granite City Food and Brewery operates more than two dozen restaurants in the Midwest, with plans for expansion in the northeast and south. The chain of Granite City restaurants began in St. Cloud, Minnesota. Granite City president Steve Wagenheim spent much of the 1980s and 1990s as chief operating officer and president of Champps Americana, a sports restaurant-bar chair. In 1999 he cofounded Granite City with Bill Burdick, who handled brewing operations for Granite City until he retired in 2006. Burdick owned the popular brewpub Sherlock's Home from 1989 to 2001 in Minnetonka and had been active in the brewing, restaurant, and hospitality industry for many years.

The Sioux Falls Granite City was originally built with a full working brewhouse. However, when the company opened its Fargo location as its third restaurant in the chain, it began using a trademarked process called Fermentus Interruptus, a system developed by Burdick. The process involves a central

243

wort-making facility in Ellsworth, Iowa, that prepares and ships wort to each restaurant, where yeast is added and fermentation begins.

BEERS

Granite City offers four to five standard beers and special seasonals at all of its locations. Among Granite City's Minnesota, North Dakota, and South Dakota stores this one often generates the most beer sales. There is a large number of local homebrewers in Sioux Falls, so occasionally this Granite City will feature a special seasonal brew to entice a visit from them. The Northern Light Lager 🍺🍺 is an American light lager with a bubbly golden color. Wag's Wheat 🍺🍺, the lightest of the Granite City beers, is a slightly cloudy American wheat that has vivid yellow color and a thick white head. The Duke of Wellington 🍺🍺🍺 is a medium- to full-bodied, copper-colored India pale ale that has a solid malty character with a hoppy nose and finish. Brother Benedict's Bock 🍺🍺 is a German-style lager with medium body, deep brown color, and a caramel malty flavor. On a darker note, the Broad Axe Stout 🍺🍺🍺🍺 is medium to full bodied with creamy texture and lots of rich roasted chocolate and caramel flavors. Granite City also does beer blending with its Two Pull, created by mixing the Northern Light and Brother Benedict's Bock. The Admiral Two Pull features the Northern Light and Duke of Wellington IPA.

MENU

The Granite City menu is broad and modestly priced. The company's internal slogan is "give the customer a twenty-five-dollar experience for thirteen dollars." While its menu looks similar across its various stores, the rotating weekly specials add some variety with such choices as Sriracha Tilapia, Cajun Pasta, Sticky Fingers (honey-glazed chicken strips), and the Quarry Burger. The Quarry Burger itself has special meaning after a visit to the actual falls of Sioux Falls.

Granite City features many made-from-scratch menu items, and if you try more than one Granite City you'll find quite a few similarities. Among the most popular items no matter which Granite City restaurant you are in is the open-faced meatloaf. Just as tasty is the London broil.

Granite City has always offered extensive salad selections, ranging from a basic dinner salad to grilled Asian chicken. Expect about ten different sandwiches and a half-dozen burger choices. One of the signatures is the Bleu Peppercorn burger, a half-pound of Angus beef seasoned with black peppercorns and topped with creamy bleu cheese. There are also steaks, seafood, pastas, soups, and a kids' menu. Several of the house beers are integrated into menu items, such as the Ale and Cheddar Soup. Granite City also is well known for serving a Sunday brunch.

Pearl Street Brewery
La Crosse, Wisconsin

Visit Date   Signed

ABOUT THE BREWERY

Pearl Street opened in 1999, when Wisconsin native Joe Katchever returned from making beer in Colorado to open his own brewery in the basement of a La Crosse bar called the Bodega. The Bodega, which is still a local beer aficionado's hangout, is located at intersection of 4th and Pearl Streets, and that cross-street provided the inspiration to the brewery's name. In 2007 Katchever and his father-partner expanded their bottling operations and moved the brewery to its present location in the former La Crosse Footwear building.

Katchever's years in Colorado were spent working at various breweries, including the well-known Tommyknocker Brewery and Pub of Idaho Springs. In 1998 he purchased some equipment from the closed down Squaw Mountain Brewery in Evergreen, Colorado. He and his father packed all they could in a trailer and transported the brewery components to La Crosse. After more than a year of assembling and building, son and father opened Pearl Street Brewery directly under Bodega's bar. On opening day in December 1999, the Bodega, which means public gathering place, was the place to be. Even the mayor of La Crosse turned up for a beer.

Pearl Street's current location in the historic warehouse where La Crosse footwear products were once made is huge — nearly six times larger than Bodega's basement. The brewery now consists of a 30-barrel brew kettle and bottling line. Prior to 2007, Pearl Street was mainly draft-only accounts in the La Crosse area. The expansion has allowed for substantial growth and distribution throughout western Wisconsin and into such cities as Madison and Milwaukee, with little or no bottle distribution into Minnesota. Pearl Street makes several different styles throughout the year, but its four main brews include a pale ale, Hefeweizen, stout, and brown ale. When visiting the brewery on Fridays the Happy Hour Stage in the tasting room area provides a venue for live music to go with the beer. In 2010 Pearl Street was given the People's Choice Award at the eighth annual Between the Bluffs Beer, Wine, and Cheese Festival.

BEERS

Pearl Street Pale Ale 🍺🍺🍺 is a medium- to full-bodied American-style pale ale. It's made with four separate additions of British hops, including "dry-hopping" during fermentation. Pearl Street Pale Ale has some spicy flavors and floral aroma and finishes about 6 percent ABV. It was a silver medal winner at the 2003 World Beer Championships. DTB Brown Ale 🍺🍺🍺 is made with seven specialty malts that are milled and mashed together at the brewery. It has some roasted nutty flavors among a solid malty backbone and finishes at 5.5 percent ABV. DTB won a gold medal at the World Beer Championships in 2003. The brewery has a dark, full-bodied organic stout it calls That's What I'm Talkn' 'bout Rolled Oat Stout 🍺🍺🍺🍺. It showcases oats that Joe Katchever purchases in fifty-pound bags from the People's Co-op of La Crosse. Chocolate and black malt give this beer color and a distinctive, smooth character. It finishes at 6 percent ABV. On the lighter side, El Hefe 🍺🍺🍺🍺 is an unfiltered Bavarian-style Hefeweizen with rich flavors of clove and banana. Weinstephan yeast gives El Hefe its crisp, fruity tones. It ends up around 4.8 percent ABV. The brewery's Lucky Logger Lager 🍺🍺🍺 is amber colored with a smooth, caramel, malty sweetness and a light hoppy finish at 5.5 percent ABV. For seasonal and special release brews, Pearl Street offered the late spring mai-bock called Evil Doppleganger 🍺🍺🍺🍺. At 7.5 percent ABV this beer has a firm bitter background from German Perle and French Strisselspalt hops. The Dankenstein 🍺🍺🍺 is a double (imperial) India pale ale that brewmaster Joe Katchever makes with four additions of hops in the brew kettle. Katchever describes it as throwing everything into the pot, stirring, and ending up with a Frankenstein beer. Watch for the Dankenstein in the brewery's taproom and on select tap accounts. The Oktoberfest season brings out the entire community for the annual multiday celebration. Pearl Street Brewery has its own fall seasonal called Oktoberfest Harvest Ale. In past years it has featured fresh hops picked from the vines on the brewery's front porch.

MENU

For the most part, Pearl Street Brewery is a working brewery. There is a tasting room that is open daily and on Saturday. Occasionally food is served for special promotions.

Potosi Brewing Company
Potosi, Wisconsin

POTOSI BREWING COMPANY

EST. 1852

Visit Date	*Signed*

ABOUT THE BREWERY

On a map you'll notice that Potosi, Wisconsin, is indeed more than a short trip beyond the Minnesota border. But any beer enthusiast and brewery history buff will want to include this as a destination.

In 2008 brewing returned to the Mississippi River town of Potosi with the opening of a restaurant and brewery in the same location that was famous for such labels as Good Old Potosi, Holiday Bock, and Cave Ale. The buildings containing today's Potosi Brewing Company were once home to Wisconsin's fifth largest beer maker, the Potosi Brewing Company, which closed in 1972. Over the next thirty years the building sat vacant, deteriorating and eroding until a massive public restoration effort brought beer back to town.

The current Potosi Brewing Company is more accurately described as a beer museum with a brewpub. In addition to its series of house-made beers, the old brewhouse contains the National Brewery Museum with more than seventy exhibits featuring thousands of pieces of memorabilia and historical artifacts from breweries all across the United States.

The original Potosi brewery was constructed in 1852 and went silent in 1972, a victim of competition from larger, more modern operations. Over the next twenty years the old stone and brick buildings saw little to no upkeep, so by the 1990s the place was just considered an eyesore. In 1995 local artist Gary David bought the brewery's bottling building, directly across the street from the brewhouse. After working to restore it, David decided to also acquire the brewery building. His family and friends joined in and soon the community got involved in the vision of restoring the old brewery to a modern brew-pub. As the idea grew, so did the concept of a private nonprofit entity to create something beyond a restaurant. Community organizers saw great potential for the brewery. In 2000 a group of citizens and brewery history buffs formed the Potosi Brewery Foundation. By 2004 they had made a surprisingly successful pitch to the American Breweriana Association (ABA) to be the home of its National Brewery Museum, beating out competition from such major cities as Milwaukee (the home of Miller) and St. Louis (home of Budweiser). Potosi Brewing Company is considered the only nonprofit brewery in the country.

In July 2008 the $7.5 million Potosi brewery complex opened: National Brewery Museum, restaurant, and brewpub. In addition, given Potosi's location along the 3,000-mile network of scenic highways along the Mississippi River, the complex has also become a welcome stop and interpretative center for the Great River Road. What's more, it is also home to a transportation museum that shows how the movement of goods and material evolved from horse-drawn wagons to steamboats and trucks.

A visit to the National Brewery Museum should be more than a one-time event. Nearly all exhibits are from private collections, many on loan from ABA members across the U.S. In addition to beer bottles, brewery glasses, and bar coasters, the museum has advertising signs, mirrors, rare steins, and old photographs to accompany much of the breweriana. There are exhibits of brewery equipment and even an opportunity to walk inside one of the brewery's old lagering caves.

In May 2009 the controlling Potosi Brewery Foundation hired as its brewmaster Steve Buszka, a former brewer for the well-known Bell's Brewery of Kalamazoo, Michigan. On any trip to this small Grant County town (population 711), you'll find at least four standard beers and a couple of special seasonal offerings at the brewpub. Given the personality of the place, you need to start with Good Old Potosi, made to taste similar to one locals may remember, and it's the brewpub's best seller. In the fall the brewpub hosts an annual brewfest. In 2010 Potosi started bottling many of its most popular beers with the help of the Stevens Point Brewery in Stevens Point, Wisconsin. Buszka likes to remain hands-on even though Stevens Point is nearly two hundred miles north of Potosi. He commonly travels there on brew and bottling days to oversee the making and packaging of his beer.

BEERS

Good Old Potosi 🍺🍺🍺 is a light-bodied golden ale with a mild, malty profile and very clean overall taste. The Holiday Bock 🍺🍺🍺 is another familiar name to those who remember Potosi beer. Steve Buszka's version is a traditional German lager made with Munich malt and Perle hops that pours with beautiful golden-bronze color, medium body, and firm caramel flavor. The Malt Cave Ale 🍺🍺🍺🍺 has great amber color and a bolder malt character accompanied by a mild, hoppy finish. The Cave Ale purist will want to step inside the actual brewery caves that were dug deep into the adjacent hillside in the nineteenth century.

The Snake Hollow IPA 🍺🍺🍺🍺 allows Steve Buszka to show off a bit of his brewery roots from his days at Bell's. With a hazy orange-copper color, the Cascade and Centennial hops provide a firm, bitter body with an assertive citrus nose. Buszka uses nearly a pound of hops in every barrel, which easily make it the hoppiest of the Potosi brews.

Among the seasonal brews that merit a sampling on a summer day trip to Potosi are the Belgian Wit 🍺🍺🍺🍺 with its hints of coriander and orange and a traditional Czech-style pilsner 🍺🍺🍺🍺 that features Pilsen malt and Saaz hops, a clean-tasting lager with a beautiful golden hue.

MENU

The menu of the Potosi Brewing Company has an assortment of soups, sandwiches, burgers, and hearty entrées like steaks, fish, and pasta. It is hard to go wrong with a Good Old Potosi burger and a Snake Hollow IPA. The menu changes periodically, and new entrées often reflect foods of the Great River Road, such as jambalaya from Louisiana or St. Louis–style ribs.

Inside seating for the restaurant is about a hundred, with an additional forty tables outside in the beer garden. In an interesting way, the restaurant's décor and the historic setting present a challenge. The surroundings are so comfortable that people don't just eat and leave, so turning over the tables for the sake of service can be a challenging issue. The centerpiece of the restaurant is a curved bar and arched backbar that was handcrafted (over the course of nearly two thousand hours) by Gary David, his personal donation to the project.

Sand Creek Brewing Company

Black River Falls, Wisconsin

SAND CREEK BREWING COMPANY
BLACK RIVER FALLS, WI
WWW.SANDCREEKBREWING.COM

Visit Date	*Signed*

ABOUT THE BREWERY

This Wisconsin-based brewery has one of the most extensive beer lists of any craft brewery in the Midwest. Sand Creek Brewing Company of Black River Falls is located about two hours southeast of the Twin Cities on Interstate 94. It merits inclusion in the Minnesota brewery guide not only because it distributes a handful of its own brands in Minnesota, but also because it contract brews for a few emerging Minnesota beer companies and licensed breweries, including Fulton Brewery of Minneapolis. It also bottles for Dave's BrewFarm, another Wisconsin brewery that distributes its products in the Twin Cities. Sand Creek makes more than thirty beers plus a dozen of its own brews that are marketed under the Sand Creek and Pioneer Brewing labels.

Sand Creek Brewing occupies a brewery building that goes back to 1856. Ulrich Oderbolz started making beer next to the Black River on the southern edge of downtown Black River Falls. The Oderbolz family suffered heartbreak as sons of brewery founder Ulrich died in tragic accidents. In the late 1880s, eighteen-year-old Charlie fell into a boiling vat of beer. He was able to pull himself out but lived for only a few more hours. Ulrich died in 1900 and his oldest son, Frank, took over the brewery. In the spring of 1911, Frank was boating on the Black River above the falls when the motor on his boat quit and the boat headed for the dam. Others in the boat grabbed hold of the dam and pulled themselves to safety. Frank, who either couldn't get out of the boat or didn't want to lose the boat, stayed aboard and went over the dam. His body was found several days later in the rocks downstream. Other family members op-

250

erated the brewery until they sold it to the Badger Brewing Company in 1913. Badger brewed beer until Prohibition and didn't reopen afterward.

The original Oderbolz brewery building was made of wood. In 1901 it was torn down and the present brick building was erected on the original basement and foundation. Between Prohibition and the 1990s it had various uses. Most locals remember the building as the Trask turkey-processing plant. The brick house across the street from the brewery was once the home of the Oderbolz family.

Brewing returned to the three-story brick structure in 1996 when brothers Dave and Jim Hellman purchased and renovated it. In 1997 they produced their first kegs of Pioneer Lager and Pioneer Pale Ale. In 1998 the Hellman brothers purchased the Wisconsin Brewing Company brands and moved production of that Wauwatosa, Wisconsin, brewery to Black River Falls. In 2004 the Hellmans decided to focus more on beer distribution, so they began looking for a buyer. They didn't have to look very far; their brewmaster, Todd Krueger, was interested. He teamed up with fellow Wisconsin brewery owners Cory Schroeder and Jim Wiesender, who had started Sand Creek Brewing near Downing, Wisconsin, in 1999. Schroeder and Wiesender were operating a 7-barrel brewery in a small garage belonging to Schroeder's family on a hundred-year-old dairy farm. Schroeder and Wiesender fabricated the brewery with recycled dairy equipment and aggressive Internet purchases, but were looking to expand. Krueger, Wiesender, and Schroeder formed a partnership and became the primary owners in a joint brewing operation of Sand Creek and Pioneer breweries. Today the brewery is run by Krueger and Wiesender. Schroeder still has a small part-ownership, along with a couple of other brewery employees.

The brewery's own labels are Sand Creek and Pioneer, but Sand Creek is the dominant in-house brand. The brewery makes beer for several contract accounts in Minnesota, Wisconsin, Iowa, Missouri, and Illinois.

BEERS

With so many beers in its portfolio Sand Creek offers a great brewery tour with ample tasting opportunities. There are too many beers to mention them all but several favorites should be pointed out. Among the core Sand Creek brews, the Golden Ale 🍺🍺🍺 is a light-colored and bubbly American ale with a slightly sweet, malty flavor and a clean finish. The Sand Creek English Style Special Ale 🍺🍺🍺🍺 is reddish-brown with toasted or toffee tones. Hoppy beer fans will enjoy the bitterness of Wild Ride IPA 🍺🍺🍺, which offers nearly sixty IBUs. On the maltier side, Sand Creek makes a very nice Scottish Ale 🍺🍺🍺🍺 that features nine different types of malt and a combination of French and English yeasts, creating a clove-like background with a somewhat high alcohol content of nearly 8.5 percent ABV. Badger Porter 🍺🍺🍺 gets its flavor from Belgian and American dark roasted malts. Badger Porter was originally produced by Wisconsin Brewing before Sand Creek purchased the label. Its bigger brother, Sand Creek Imperial Porter 🍺🍺🍺🍺, offers darker color along with lots of rich malty flavor and warmth. The imperial porter is a limited release that isn't always available. Another darker beer worth watching for is Oscar's Chocolate Oatmeal Stout 🍺🍺🍺🍺. It won a gold medal at the 2000 World Beer Cup. One Planet Ale 🍺🍺🍺 is a tribute to locally grown ingredients. Black River Falls is in a cranberry-growing area, and in the fall the brewery makes Cranberry Ale with local cranberry juice. Ulrich's Authentic Doppel-bock, another seasonal brew, is warm and rich in chocolate malt.

Sand Creek offers a few beers marketed with the Pioneer label, including Black River Red 🍺🍺🍺, a Märzen-style Oktoberfest lager with ruby-red color and solid malty flavor. This beer won a gold at the 2000 World Beer Cup. The Pioneer Lager 🍺🍺🍺🍺 is a flagship for the Pioneer brands. It's a true Bavarian-style lager with an amber color and sweet malty flavor.

MENU

None. Sand Creek Brewing Company does not serve food.

Toppling Goliath Brewing Company
Decorah, Iowa

Visit Date	Signed

ABOUT THE BREWERY

Toppling Goliath is a reference to the craft brewers taking on the big beer giants. Considering that the Toppling Goliath Brewing Company began with just a 12-gallon brewing system, that image seems to work well as a description!

Owner Clark Lewey and his wife Barb opened the Toppling Goliath Brewing Company in 2009 in a building on the northwest edge of downtown Decorah. Their production brewery, a 10-barrel system, was established in May 2010 on Decorah's eastside. Toppling Goliath beers are found in several Decorah taverns. Access to the production brewery is limited, but if you want to taste several Toppling Goliath brews the original location is the place to go. It really serves as a glorified brewery taproom in a small brick and metal building with a burgundy roof that locals claim was Decorah's first fast food burger joint. Most will remember its more recent use as a flower shop. Inside, there are a handful of tables but Toppling Goliath really lives up to the image of the little guy taking on the behemoth. The bar itself is pretty small, with only a half-dozen stools or maybe ten seats if you don't mind rubbing elbows with close friends or getting to know the locals.

Brewmaster Mike Saboe has been making beer at Toppling Goliath since May 2010. Saboe grew up in nearby West Union and attended the University of Iowa with plans to enter the pharmacy field. While taking all those science classes he developed an interest in homebrewing that was further encouraged by his friends and family who enjoyed his beer. When he graduated in 2009 he decided to give brewing his full attention and took a job at Hub City Brewing in Stanley, Iowa. After a year Saboe landed the brewer position at Toppling Goliath.

Visitors to Toppling Goliath will want to go directly to the taproom because the main brewery doesn't allow walk-ins without an appointment. Also, it's a good idea to check the taproom's hours because it doesn't normally open until late afternoon.

BEERS

The Toppling Goliath taproom will offer three or four of the brewery's beers for most visits. Dorothy's New World Lager 🍺🍺 is a light golden California common beer with mild citrus tones. It's considered the brewery's flagship beer and is named after Lewey's grandmother, Dorothy. Hop heads have several choices, including Tsunami Pale Ale 🍺🍺🍺, which has a firm bitter backbone. Lewey was on a trip to the Oregon coast when the crashing waves of the Pacific provided the inspiration for this beer. The Golden Nugget IPA 🍺🍺🍺 is the number one seller in the taproom. It's made with five different varieties of hops. The recipe was written for a local hop lover who donated locally grown Nugget hops to make the beer. The PseudoSue 🍺🍺🍺, named after the largest T-Rex fossil ever discovered, is a milder pale ale with some nice grapefruit and citrus tones and a slightly lighter body than the brewery's other hoppy offerings. Other beers to watch for throughout the year include the Kettle Clogger, a west coast IPA, and the Hop Smack, a citrusy double IPA. The Rush Hollow Maple Ale was Toppling Goliath's first seasonal. It is a golden-colored ale that is made with maple syrup from the Rush Family Farm in Iowa's Allamakee County. If you're looking for something with deeper color the Dark Shadow Stout is smooth and creamy and the Watershed Wheat is a tribute to Clark Lewery's love of the outdoors with a portions of the proceeds from the beer given to watershed projects in northeast Iowa.

MENU

The emphasis at Toppling Goliath taproom is on the beer. You can order from a list of light appetizers like chips, salsa, and dips or if you are hungry there is a collection of local takeout and delivery menus.

Worth Brewing Company
Northwood, Iowa

ABOUT THE BREWERY

The term "small brewery" doesn't quite describe Worth Brewing. "We've been called a nano-brewery," laughs owner Peter Ausenhus. Worth Brewing in Northwood, Iowa, just four miles south of the Minnesota state line, claims to be one of smallest licensed breweries in the country. This nano-brewery makes beer in 10-gallon batches with an annual capacity of around seventy-five barrels. Ausenhus thinks only one or two other commercial systems in the country are this small, and he equates the equipment he uses for his entire brewery with what some microbreweries use to experiment with recipes before they ramp up to full production. His Sabco system is actually somewhat common among large-scale homebrewers, but is still small for any commercial brewery or brewpub. However, the size actually works in Ausenhus's favor by allowing him to always keep something new on tap.

The brewery opened on St. Patrick's Day of 2007 in the former Worth County State Bank building, constructed in 1886. The bank moved out in 1907, and the building sat vacant until the local utility company took it over and occupied it until 2006.

In remodeling, Ausenhus worked hard to restore the building's century-old character. A false ceiling and altered walls were removed, exposing original plaster walls, woodwork, and moldings that add to today's charm. Visitors who look closely will see that the utility company's stained-glass sign has been restored and backlit with great care. Such details reflect a commitment not only to this building but to the Northwood Central Avenue Historic District, which comprises nearly fifty structures. One of the most striking features is the very small bar that seems appropriate for such a small brewery. It's a former bank teller cage from the nineteenth century. When the bank moved out, the teller cage traveled around town — a veterinarian's office, stables, a Chevrolet garage. It spent several years in the local home and garage of Gary and Nancy Hengesteg before they donated it to the Worth County Historical Society. Since the historical society didn't have space to display it or store it, the bar is now on loan to Worth Brewing. Ausenhus needed a forklift to move it into place just before the new storefront windows were installed for the brewery's opening in 2007.

Peter Ausenhus's own history is worth noting. He worked at Summit Brewing in St. Paul from 1995 to 1996 before working for Northern Brewer in the St. Paul retail store. He and his wife, Margaret Bishop, moved to Northwood in 1999. Prior to that he was an avid homebrewer and certified beer judge.

Worth Brewing has five year-round beers plus several specialty and seasonal brews worth watching for.

BEERS

The Brown Ale 🍺🍺🍺🍺 is Worth's best seller. It's a medium-bodied, American-style brown made with two-row barley and English chocolate malt, along with Palisade and German Tettnang hops. The Pale Ale 🍺🍺🍺 is the brewery's flagship beer. It has a firm bitterness from magnum and whole-leaf centennial hops. When available, batches in the fall and early winter may feature some of Ausenhus's home-grown Cascade hops in the recipe. The Field Trip IPA 🍺🍺🍺 was introduced in 2009 for the Ragbrai (Register's Annual Great Bicycle Ride Across Iowa). This hoppy brew features Centennial and Cascade hops and it proved to be the favorite of a team by the name of "One More." The Dillon Clock Stopper 🍺🍺🍺 is a pre-Prohibition style of beer made with malted barley and 15 percent flaked maize. The beer gets its name from L. T. Dillon, a longtime jeweler who made the iconic Northwood street clock that still keeps track of time for the community. A little lighter version of the Brown Ale is Worth's English Mild 🍺🍺 made with floor-malted barley, flaked oats, Glacier hops, and an English yeast strain. The Oatmeal Stout 🍺🍺🍺🍺 has a hardcore following among locals. Made with English pale malt and roasted barley, this is a velvety smooth stout with great flavor, mouth feel, and color. Ausenhus likes to keep at least one specialty brew on tap each month. A few to watch for include the Helles Bock in spring, Farmhouse Brown in summer, a smoked Kellerbier in fall, and a Russian imperial stout in winter.

MENU

Worth Brewing has a limited menu consisting mostly of appetizers. Selections include a Greek hummus plate with a hearty olive-based Mediterranean dip and pita bread and a Mexican plate with homemade taquito dip, chicken, cream cheese, cilantro, and tortilla chips. The Ploughman's Lunch consists of several cheeses, salami, and tomato brochette with ciabatta bun. But nothing goes better with a Worth Brown Ale than the Bavarian plate of bratwurst, kraut, and homemade red cabbage.

Minnesota's Contract Breweries

BANK BEER COMPANY (HENDRICKS)

BARD'S TALE BEER COMPANY (MINNEAPOLIS)

BLUE DIAMOND BREWING COMPANY (ST. PAUL)

BRAINERD LAKES BREWERY (BRAINERD)

FINNEGANS INC. (MINNEAPOLIS)

HAUENSTEIN BEER (SLEEPY EYE)

LAKEMAID BEER COMPANY (MINNEAPOLIS)

PIG'S EYE BREWING COMPANY (WOODBURY)

All of Minnesota's contract breweries maintain corporate offices in Minnesota but do not have standalone beer-making facilities of their own. They contract with another brewery to make their beer, and they stress their own identity and assume responsibility for marketing the beer as their own. For many contract breweries, the company owner and brewmaster have close working relationships with the contract beer maker and often travel to the brewery on days their product is being brewed and packaged.

Some of these breweries have plans for production facilities and someday may house their own working brewery. Meanwhile, hiring someone else to make the beer allows them to establish their brands and generate revenue without the costs of finding a large building to house a brewery, purchasing equipment, paying for labor, and, in some instances, transporting and distributing beer.

They operate under various kinds of licenses — brewery, alternating proprietorship, beer marketing company, and distributorship. Despite some stereotyping of contract brewing, this guidebook doesn't make any gross generalizations about quality — rather, you should judge for yourself.

Bank Beer Company
Hendricks

ABOUT THE COMPANY

The Bank Beer Company makes beer for the wild side — that is, profits from its beer go to help wildlife conservation efforts in Minnesota and surrounding states. Minnesota native Jason Markkula, a homebrewer and outdoorsman with a big passion for social entrepreneurship, started the company in 2009. Markkula's idea for merging his love of hunting and beer with a public-good component began after leaving his job of ten years in the power tool industry to return to college. After graduating from the University of St. Thomas with a degree in entrepreneurship, he created Beer for Wildlife (beerforwildlife .com), which provides the overall philanthropic philosophy of the Bank Beer Company.

Profits from the sale of its two flagship brews, Rooster Lager (targeted to pheasant hunters) and Walleye Chop (for fishing enthusiasts), are directed through Beer for Wildlife to Pheasants Forever's Build a Wildlife Area program. The money helps to purchase land that is then turned over to state governments for wildlife habitat preservation and public recreational use. The dollars from Bank Beer sales are added to donations from Pheasants Forever, then matched with grants from the Minnesota Department of Natural Resources and the U.S. Fish and Wildlife Service, thereby tripling Markkula's efforts at selling beer.

Bank Beer's first product, Rooster Lager, is commonly found on store shelves during hunting season, roughly from October through April. Walleye Chop is offered during the fishing season, or May through September. In the

259

fall, the brewery does a sampler pack that includes both beers, along with any special seasonal brews that Markkula develops for limited distribution.

HISTORY

Jason Markkula grew up in the Twin Cities and continues to live there. His tie to Hendricks came through his love of hunting and frequent trips to the area, and his involvement in Pheasants Forever. He was a driving force in developing a Pheasants Forever chapter there, and for many years has volunteered his time to the organization's Build a Wildlife Area campaign through fund raising and participating in habitat restoration projects.

In 2006, Markkula jumped at an opportunity to buy a historic three-story bank building in downtown Hendricks. Within three years he had turned the abandoned structure into a hunting lodge for himself and friends that he refers to as the Bank Inn. Constructed in the early 1900s, the building was one of three local banks. Following the 1930s and the Great Depression it became home to a local cafe, but by the 1970s it was vacant and falling into disrepair. Markkula's personal commitment to the project and the local community led to naming his beer business the Bank Beer Company. The bank building is incorporated into the company's logo.

Markkula dreams that someday, if people continue to like his beer, his bank building might even contain a working brewery. For now, small quantities of beer are stored there for distribution across southwest Minnesota and eastern South Dakota. He has plans for a tasting and sampling room and a gift shop.

Since the first batch of Rooster Lager was made in 2009, Bank Beer Company has relied on the Cold Spring Brewing Company to make its products. Distribution of Rooster Lager and Walleye Chop has quickly spread in states where pheasant hunting and walleye fishing are popular—Minnesota, North and South Dakota, Iowa, Nebraska, and Wisconsin. Markkula often travels to Cold Spring on brewing days to personally take part in making his beer.

BANK BEER COMPANY BREWS

Rooster Lager 🍺🍺🍺🍺 *Your Ranking*_____
An amber lager similar to a Märzen/Oktoberfest. In addition to the base malts of special roast and caramel, it is fermented with a German yeast strain. The beer has a light malty aroma. Its color is a clear deep bronze with a soft, tan head. Smooth caramel maltiness dominates the body. Finishes clean.

Walleye Chop 🍺🍺🍺 *Your Ranking*_____
Also an amber lager, but lighter in color with a sharper bitterness to the flavor and finish with additions of Cascade hops. Begins with a light malty nose. Clear amber-copper color and a soft, marbled tan head. Medium bodied and soft. Nice malty start with hoppy tones in the background. The bitterness is most evident in the finish. Overall, sharp and clean with an emphasis, but not dominance, of hop character.

OTHER BANK BEERS YOU MAY WANT TO TRY

1876 Rye Ale *Your Ranking_____*

A dark amber ale. Firm dryness alongside light chocolate and caramel sweetness. The spicy flavor from the malted rye really comes through and compliments the roastedness from the chocolate malt. Named after the year that Jesse James attempted to rob the First National Bank of Northfield, Minnesota. The local residents were successful in fighting off eight bank robbers, including Jesse and Frank James, in a shootout on the street. Two of the bank robbers were killed in the gunfight and several others were tracked down during the largest manhunt in U.S. history at the time. But the James brothers managed to escape to Missouri. Proceeds from this beer go to the Northfield Historical Society. A limited release that is bottled with the help of Brau Bothers Brewing of Lucan. When first introduced in 2011 this beer became an immediate best seller for the Bank Beer Company.

Black Lager *Your Ranking_____*

Made in small batches for draft accounts and for the assorted sampler pack. Watch for this as a dark seasonal brew, possibly for winter. In 2011 Jason Markkula, in collaboration with Brau Brothers Brewing of Lucan, developed a recipe based on the German Schwarzbier style. His plan was to make a beer that would raise funds to support the work of the National Wild Turkey Federation.

Bard's Tale Beer Company
Minneapolis

Visit Date   Signed

ABOUT THE COMPANY

When Craig Belser and Kevin Seplowitz were told they could no longer drink beer they decided to change the rules of the game. Belser and Seplowitz were homebrewers who discovered they had celiac disease, a digestive disorder involving intolerance of gluten. Gluten is found in many cereal grains—including wheat, rye, and barley—commonly used in making beer. The beer-loving pair couldn't envision their lives without beer and they knew others who felt the same, so they made it their mission to bring beer to fellow celiacs. The disease affects roughly 1 in 133 people in the United States. There is no medication, and many who have it deal with it by watching their diet and avoiding gluten.

Belser and Seplowitz discovered each other via e-mail while researching gluten-free beer on the Internet. After learning that sorghum could be substituted for cereal grains in beer, Belser experimented with recipes in his garage. Sorghum-based beer is not a new invention, and a handful of gluten-free beers are on the market. But this beer claims to be the first gluten-free beer and the only one with malted sorghum, which provides more mouth feel and malt-like qualities to the beer. Bard's Tale Beer Company was established in 2005 with headquarters in Plymouth (northwest of Minneapolis). Bard's Tale is brewed by Matt Brewing Company of Utica, New York, and is distributed in over forty states and parts of Canada.

HISTORY

Belser is from Lee's Summit, Missouri, and Seplowitz from Norwalk, Connecticut, but chief executive officer Brian Kovalchuk calls Minneapolis home, and when he took the job in 2007 he set up the company headquarters in the Twin Cities.

Kovalchuk grew up in the Twin Cities and has maintained a home in Minneapolis throughout his career and various positions across the country. He's a graduate of the University of Minnesota's Carlson School of Management with an MBA, and he has served on the board of directors of the Metropolitan Minneapolis YMCA.

From 2001 to 2006 Kovalchuk commuted from Minneapolis as president and CEO for Pabst Brewing in San Antonio, Texas. Focusing on rebuilding the Pabst brands, he led the management team that oversaw restructuring of Pabst and the resurgence of Pabst Blue Ribbon. Before that, he had commuted between Minneapolis and the East Coast while working for New Jersey–based Benetton Sportsystem.

By 2007 he was looking for a change and wanted to cut back on cross-country commutes. His goal was to find work in the Twin Cities and stay at home, closer to his then teenage daughter. When he met Belser and Seplowitz, he saw great potential for their product and signed on, with the condition that the company would be based in Minneapolis.

Initially called Bard's Dragon's Gold, the first batches were made with the help of the Flying Bison Brewing Company of Buffalo, New York. Large-scale production of Bard's was subsequently started at the Gordon Biersch Breweries, a brewery and brewpub chain based in San Jose, California. By October 2008, the name was changed to just Bard's Tale and brewing was shifted to the Matt Brewing Company of Utica, New York. Matt Brewing is also known as the maker of Saranac Beers. As the Bard's Tale brand grows, some production may shift back to Gordon Biersch.

Company founders Craig Belser and Kevin Sepowitz turned to medieval times in selecting the name of their beer. In Gaelic and British culture a bard refers to a professional poet, such as William Shakespeare, Robert Burns, or William Wordsworth. Some even consider Minnesota native and songwriter Bob Dylan to fit that definition. The name may also remind some of the fantasy role-playing computer game created in the mid-1980s called *The Bard's Tale* or the board game *Dungeons & Dragons*, but there's no connection.

BARD'S BREW

Bard's Gold 🍺🍺🍺🍺 *Your Ranking*_____
An American-style lager made with malted sorghum, Hallertauer Hersbrucker and Tettnang hops, and a strain of German lager yeast. Begins with a light, sweet, fruity aroma. Clear copper color with a medium bubbly, off-white head. Medium bodied and bubbly. Smooth, sweet caramel flavor with a light fruity background. A light, sweet finish. For a beer without traditional brewer's malts, this beer has remarkable body and caramel malt-like flavor. One has to appreciate this beer for being gluten free.

Blue Diamond Brewing Company

St. Paul

Visit Date	*Signed*

ABOUT THE COMPANY

Blue Diamond was once part of the Minnesota Brewing Company's family of beers. The label — then called Diamond Blue — was purchased by Frank Yarusso in 2002, when the assets of Minnesota Brewing were liquidated, along with Brewer's Cave beers, another former label of Minnesota Brewing. Brewer's Cave is a tribute to Christopher Stahlmann, a Bavarian immigrant who ran a brewery in the caves along the Mississippi River in order to take advantage of their natural springs. Stahlmann's brewery eventually became the Jacob Schmidt Brewing Company and later the Minnesota Brewing Company.

When Yarusso resurrected Brewer's Cave Beer and Blue Diamond in 2002 he teamed up with Siegfried Plagens, who knew both Jacob Schmidt and Minnesota Brewing very well. Plagen had been brewmaster for both. Yarusso and Plagens worked together to recreate the recipes. Yarusso's Blue Diamond Brewing Company consists of the premium beer brands Blue Diamond Lager and Blue Diamond Light as well as the Brewer's Cave series, which includes Caramel Lager and Black Barley Ale. He also makes a few other specialty beers under contract, such as Riverside Resort Light for Don Laughlin's Riverside Resort Hotel and Casino in Nevada.

HISTORY

Blue Diamond owner Frank Yarusso is a graduate of Johnson High School in St. Paul. Upon graduation and a stint in the Marines, he returned to the Twin

Cities and purchased the Scotch Mist nightclub in Minneapolis. By the late 1970s he had joined his uncle as part owner of the Yarusso Brothers Restaurant on St. Paul's east side. In the 1980s, Yarusso decided he wanted to open a restaurant in Arizona, but plans fell through and instead he took a job distributing Minnesota Brewing Company products in the southwestern states.

From its Arizona home base in the 1990s, Yarusso worked the distribution and export side of the beer business, even working on agreements to send beer to China. Eventually, due to family concerns, he moved back to St. Paul. Taking the advice of former Minnesota Brewing CEO Dick McMahon, he began looking into owning his own beer labels, to protect distribution rights and take charge of running things. In 2002 he purchased the Diamond Blue and Brewer's Cave labels through the bank after Minnesota Brewing was forced to close—changing the name of his flagship brew slightly, to Blue Diamond. He formed the Blue Diamond Brewing Company and began contracting its production with the Cold Spring Brewing Company of Cold Spring, Minnesota. Blue Diamond Brewer's Cave beers are sold throughout Minnesota.

BLUE DIAMOND AND BREWER'S CAVE BREWS

Blue Diamond Lager 🍺🍺🍺   *Your Ranking_____*
The company's flagship brew. Light grainy nose. Golden to amber color with thin, soft, white head. A sharp, clean, crisp pilsner. This is what it is, and those who enjoy the American lager style will find this above average.

Brewer's Cave Caramel Lager 🍺🍺   *Your Ranking_____*
A light malty nose. Amber to bronze color and a tan bubbly head. Medium bodied and round. Solid caramel maltiness with a light smoky finish with a light sourness.

OTHER BLUE DIAMOND AND BREWER'S CAVE BREWS YOU MAY WANT TO TRY

Blue Diamond Light   *Your Ranking_____*
Light bodied and straw to golden color. Made with pale malts and Yakima hops.

Brewer's Cave Amber Wheat Ale   *Your Ranking_____*
Made with barley, wheat, and Vienna malts, with Cluster and Tettnang hops. Amber color with slight fruity hint of apple and toffee bitterness.

Brewer's Cave Roasted Black Barley Ale   *Your Ranking_____*
Made with barley, caramel Carapils, roasted barley, and black barley malt, with Cascade and Brewers Gold hops. A deep nutty flavor. Amber to bronze color.

Riverside Resort—Light Beer   *Your Ranking_____*
This beer is made exclusively for Don Laughlin's Riverside Resort Hotel and Casino in Laughlin, Nevada. Laughlin grew up on a farm near Owatonna, Minnesota. As a boy he got involved in setting up slot machines for local pubs.

When his high school insisted he choose school or the business, he left school. Laughlin moved to Nevada in 1966 and opened up a ten-room motel in what would become a city bearing his name. He and Yarusso met in 2000 and shortly after entered into an agreement to produce Riverside Resort beer in Minnesota to be shipped to Nevada.

Brainerd Lakes Brewery
Brainerd

Visit Date   Signed

ABOUT THE COMPANY

Even though the Brainerd Lakes Brewery didn't actually have beer for sale until 2010 it was already winning awards. The owners worked with the Adventure Creative Group of Brainerd to design labels and packaging for their "yet to be" brewery, and, in 2009, a year before they officially offered beer, the labels won an Addy award for creativity.

Brainerd Lakes Brewery was established in 2008 by local residents Jesse Grant and Dan Stanifer. For the next two years they worked on perfecting recipes and developing a business plan that initially relies on contract brewing by Lake Superior Brewing. As a sign that they intend to grow and eventually own a fully operating brewery in Brainerd, they leased a historic building for their company offices in the former Northern Pacific Center. In 2010 they moved into the century-old engine house, known as Building #7. They plan to grow their company slowly and establish their beer locally before investing in brewery equipment. However, their company offices have a gift shop and growlers of three or four of their beers for sale. Their goal is to have their own full brewery by 2015.

Brainerd Lakes Brewery released its first two beers in 2010. Despite their award winning labels, which were based on each beer's style, Grant and Stanifer launched their brewery with beer names and labels that identify with what the region is known for, including fishing themes such as One-Eye Pike and First Pull IPA. Other brews that make up the Brainerd Lakes portfolio include a brown ale, a Kölsch, a rhubarb crisp, a cranberry wheat, and a hazelnut brown.

HISTORY

Dan Stanifer and Jesse Grant met in 2004 as construction contractors and got to know each other over beers. Both grew up in Brainerd. Jesse went to high school there, and Dan moved to Michigan for a while before moving back in 1998. Early on, Dan was the one with the intense homebrewing hobby. Jesse likes to joke that when he first learned that Dan liked to brew he invited him to a party and asked he if would bring some of his beer. The first year Dan brought one keg. The following year he showed up with two kegs, and within four years he was bringing many more. They got to know each other over more beers and various construction jobs, and one morning at 4 a.m. Jesse sent Dan an e-mail stating, "Okay, I've got a really dumb idea. What do you think about opening a brewery?" Dan's response was immediate, to the effect of "So now I've got to teach you how to make beer."

Three years later Brainerd Lakes Brewery had an office in Building #7 of the Northern Pacific Center, which once served as the firehouse for a sprawling railroad complex that dates back to the nineteenth century. The two-story brick structure sits just a few hundred feet from the railyard's former power plant where the giant smokestacks still stand and take their place among the most visible landmarks in the Brainerd skyline.

Stanifer and Grant aren't the first to run a brewery in Brainerd. However, it has been some time since commercial beer making was part of the community. A man named John Hoffman is credited with running the first brewery in Brainerd in the early to middle 1870s. Not much is known about Hoffman's brewery. By 1881 another brewery had emerged, this one run by Peter Ort, a local saloonkeeper who started making beer to supply his tavern. Ort's early version of a brewpub led to the formation of the Brainerd Brewing Company by 1887. It had several owners before it closed in 1915.

BRAINERD LAKES BREWS

First Pull IPA 🍺🍺🍺   *Your Ranking*_____
An IPA made with Chinook and Amarillo hops. Light citrus-hoppy nose. Golden-copper color with a medium to thick tan head. Medium bodied and bubbly. Firm spicy and piney hoppiness with a lingering bitter finish. Its name is a reference to hoping the boat motor starts on the first pull.

One-Eyed Pike 🍺🍺   *Your Ranking*_____
A filtered wheat beer. Light yeasty nose with a hint of sourness. Slightly hazy, with a yellow to straw color. Light to medium bodied with an overall smooth texture. Light yeasty flavor with a hint of graininess in the background and a touch of sourness in the finish.

Tilted T-Ale 🍺🍺🍺🍺   *Your Ranking*_____
This dark brown ale was developed by the Brainerd Lakes Brewery as a special brew for the independent film *Tilt*, much of which was shot in the Brainerd area in 2010. Light roasted chocolate malt within the nose. Dark, almost black with bronze highlights and a thick, soft, brown head. Full bodied, bubbly, and smooth. Lots of chocolate and caramel maltiness. A hint of licorice-like spici-

ness with warmth and dryness in the finish. This beer was a limited release brew in 2011.

OTHER BRAINERD LAKES BREWS YOU MAY WANT TO TRY

Brown-Eyed Mutt   *Your Ranking*_____

An American brown ale with lots of chocolate malt flavor. Fermented with London ale yeast.

Grandma Sarge   *Your Ranking*_____

This Kölsch pays tribute to Dan Stanifer's grandmother, whom he remembers fondly for her pet poodle named Sarge. Her real name was Vera, but all her children knew her as Grandma Sarge. When Stanifer and Grant decided to make beer, Grandma Sarge brought to their attention a beer recipe that belonged to her father, who brewed beer in their home during Prohibition. Stanifer and Grant tweaked the original wheat-based beer into a Kölsch.

Rhubarb Crisp   *Your Ranking*_____

A light-bodied red lager. Rhubarb gives it a reddish tint. Stanifer developed the recipe as a modified Kölsch. He says that rhubarb is pretty prolific in the area. A lot of his friends liked it so it's considered a seasonal beer for Brainerd Lakes.

30 Below IPA   *Your Ranking*_____

Not your everyday IPA. This beer is made with Kölsch yeast and Amarillo hops.

Finnegans Inc.
Minneapolis

Visit Date	Signed

ABOUT THE COMPANY

This beer puts meaning to the phrase "Drink like you care!" Finnegans Irish Amber is a beer with a philanthropic cause. Profits from every pint of Finnegans goes to fighting poverty. Finnegans has grown from the hands and heart of Jacquie Berglund, a local woman who set out to make a difference, one pint at a time. Berglund established Finnegans to make money for social causes. It's an idea very similar to that of actor Paul Newman, who created a line of salad dressings and other products whose profits go to charities. Berglund's merchandise is Finnegans Irish Amber, a contract beer made by Summit Brewing Company that is sold throughout the Twin Cities and much of Minnesota. As of 2010, an agreement with Super Targets took this deep reddish ale to several Upper Midwest states and beyond.

The concept is pure social entrepreneurism where the profits fund local not-for-profit groups that address issues like poverty. Berglund says she's always wanted to help communities help themselves. About two-thirds of the sales of Finnegans are in the Twin Cities, and so, Berglund says, about two-thirds of the profit goes back into the Twin Cities area. She says that she was brought up in challenging economic conditions and understands the importance of donations and charity. She describes the impact of Finnegans's proceeds as reaching small, nonprofit organizations that offer innovative and sustainable approaches to dealing with the working poor. She eventually wants to be more than a beer company, and hopes that the efforts created by Finnegans Irish Amber inspire other philanthropic endeavors.

HISTORY

Jacquie Berglund grew up near the Twin Cities in White Bear Lake and Mah-tomedi. After attending Augsburg College, in 1990 she moved to Paris where she earned a master's degree in international relations. She went on to put the degree to work in assistance and sustainable development programs in north-ern regions of Russia. In 1997 she moved back to Minnesota and eventually landed a marketing job with the CARA Pub Group — owners of several popular Minnesota restaurants, one of which is the downtown Minneapolis Irish pub called the Local. In 2000 Berglund approached owner Kieran Folliard with the idea of a beer to fund local philanthropic causes. Berglund says her social en-trepreneurism captured Folliard's imagination too, and together they set out to devote the profits of a single product, a beer, to creating social impact.

All of this wasn't exactly easy. Berglund had to figure out with attorneys how to create a for-profit beer company (Finnegans) and also a not-for-profit entity to handle proceeds (Finnegans Community Fund). The beer company contracts with the Summit Brewing Company to make the beer and pay the ex-penses associated with brewing and management before profits are donated to the fund. Between 2000 and 2010, these two symbiotic entities worked to give more than $150,000 to projects and services that build social capital in the communities with the hope of addressing issues associated with poverty. Berglund tracks sales to ensure that dollars are given back to communities where the beer generated the profit. A board of directors governs the decisions of where profits will go. Berglund is president and founder of both entities.

Early on Berglund worked with James Page Brewing Company brewmaster James Hoeft and brewery president Dave Anderson to develop recipe ideas. She wanted to focus on the quaffable qualities of an Irish ale because, from her experi-ence at the Local, she was aware that as drinkers grow in their sophistication and ap-preciation of beer they look for more flavor, color, and body. Therefore, Berglund says, Finnegans was designed to have broad appeal, a brew that lighter beer drinkers would eventually gravitate to. As for the name "Finnegans," she and Folliard drew inspira-tion from the James Joyce novel *Finnegans Wake*, which, she says, just seemed like a great name for a beer. The perceptive beer enthusiast may note a dash of spuds in the recipe; the original version of the beer was called CARA's Irish Potato Ale.

A fun place to grab a meal and a Finnegan's Irish Amber is at the Local (931 Nicollet Mall), where the idea for this brew began. Another fun place to find a pint of Finnegan's is at Brit's Pub (1110 Nicollet Mall), where you can also com-pete in lawn bowling on the pub's roof.

FINNEGANS BREWS

Irish Amber 🍺🍺🍺   *Your Ranking_____*
Deep clear copper color with a light malty nose and firm malty body. Smooth soft texture. A great session beer and very versatile meal brew. A solid malty flavor. Made with a light amount of potato.

OTHER FINNEGAN BREWS YOU MAY WANT TO TRY

In the future, watch for a special, limited edition of Finnegans. Founder Jacquie Berglund also hopes to add other product to her portfolio.

Hauenstein Beer
Sleepy Eye

Visit Date	Signed

ABOUT THE COMPANY

Hauenstein Beer is owned by Al and Rae Ann Arneson, who also own Arneson Distributing, a company that helps get a number of Minnesota beers on store shelves, including Grain Belt, Cold Spring, Brau Brothers, and Lift Bridge.

Al and Rae Ann Arneson purchased a Grain Belt distributorship, based in Sleepy Eye and known as Barthel Beverage, in 1972. As their territory and brands grew, the Arnesons, with the help of the August Schell brewery, added root beer and Buddy's sodas to their list of products in the mid-1980s. The name 1919 Root Beer is a reference to the first year of Prohibition, and its recipe is based on the type of soda that August Schell would have made then. Hauenstein is a local favorite sold in liquor stores around New Ulm. Earlier versions appeared in eight-pack containers.

HISTORY

The history of Hauenstein beer goes back to 1864 when John Hauenstein and Andreas Betz started their brewery not far from where August Schell was making beer. By the early 1870s Hauenstein was the sole owner. The original brewery structures were heavily damaged by a tornado in 1881. But Hauenstein rebuilt and over the years expanded the brewery and its production. Hauenstein and Schell at the time were similar in size, both approaching nearly 20,000 barrels a year.

Hauenstein reopened after Prohibition in 1933 and continued to grow until the 1960s, but brewery structures in New Ulm's South Park area (1601 Jefferson Street), which is now occupied, in part, as a private residence.

In 1970 the Hauenstein labels were acquired by Grain Belt and production was moved to St. Paul. A few years later, in 1974, G. Heileman acquired Hauenstein when it purchased Grain Belt. In 1996 Al and Rae Ann Arneson bought the Hauenstein label from Heileman Brewing with the intent to initially make it under contact with Minnesota Brewing Company. However, after Minnesota Brewing closed it became a beer made under contract by August Schell.

HAUENSTEIN BREWS

Hauenstein 🍺🍺 *Your Ranking_____*

An American lager. Grainy nose. Clear light golden color. Very bubbly. Thin, soft, white head. Mild malty flavor with a crisp finish. Lightly hopped.

Lakemaid Beer Company
Minneapolis

_____   _____
Visit Date   Signed

ABOUT THE COMPANY

It seems like a rather simple premise — beer for those who also enjoy fishing. The marketing behind this brew focuses on the drinking preferences of male anglers and their tendency after a long day of fishing to embelish their conversations about the big one that got away. The beer is a light- to medium-bodied American lager that is brewed by the August Schell Brewing Company. However, the beer company is owned by the Minneapolis advertising firm of Pocket Hercules.

Lakemaid Beer is also sold on the notion that scantily clad mermaids just might actually exist in the freshwaters of Minnesota. The packaging features twelve mermaids in various colored bikinis, and each one has the tail section of a different game fish. The bottle labels, collector items for some, include Miss Muskie, Miss Salmon, Miss Sturgeon, Miss Walleye, and Miss Sunfish, just to name a few. Company partner Jack Supple says many of the women who grace the labels are local Minnesota girls, and he adds there's a waiting list to become a Lakemaid mermaid. Supple even laughs that the company tries to match the mermaid with the personality of the model, explaining that to be Miss Sunfish you need to have a "perky" disposition.

Lakemaid Beer's fame might have just as much to do with its popular bottle. Under each cap there's a fish tale, ranging from a 49-pound muskie or a 12-pound walleye to how your minnow died and even the dreaded hooked boot. Supple says the caps are merely game pieces and beer drinking fishing enthusiasts figure out various games to play with them. Some bars have even been known to host fishing tournaments based on the random nature of what you turn up, or what "gets landed at the bar," as the bottles are opened. When the company attempted to introduce its beer in cans in 2009, the passion for the bottle caps and the games they inspired created such a backlash the company decided to stay with bottles.

Lakemaid Beer is mainly available in Minnesota's lake country. It's offered from early May, around the opening of fishing season, through October. It's also available in portions of Wisconsin, Michigan, Iowa, North Dakota, South Dakota, and Nebraska where beer drinkers seem to share a common problem—fishing. It's sold in 6- and 12-packs of bottles and on limited draft accounts. Given the light-hearted advertising associated with Lakemaid Beer one might not take it as a serious beer. However, next time you walk into a northern liquor store, notice the amount of shelf and cooler space dedicated to this popular brew and you can't help but conclude it has found a market niche. Furthermore, a portion of the sales is dedicated to the International Game Fish Association for freshwater game fish research, conservation, and habitat restoration projects.

HISTORY

The Lakemaid Beer Company is owned by Pocket Hercules, a branding, advertising, and public relations firm based in Minneapolis that was begun in 2005 by Jack Supple, Jason Smith, and Tom Camp. The beer was launched in 2008 as a collaboration among Pocket Hercules, Rapala (fishing equipment), and the August Schell Brewing Company of New Ulm. The August Schell brewery, through direct involvement of company president Ted Marti, devised the recipe for the beer, which continues to be made there.

Pocket Hercules is somewhat of a hybrid company, with projects ranging from public relations to product development. It also owns Tiny Footprint Coffee, an effort with Roastery 7, a Twin Cities specialty coffee roaster. Part of the proceeds from its sales go to reforestation in the Mindo Cloudforest in Ecuador, which helps offset carbon credits and make it a carbon negative product.

Part of the inspiration for Lakemaid Beer comes from Jack Supple's long-time working relationship with Rapala. Over the years that association has led to numerous conversations about the existence of freshwater mermaids. Somewhere in those discussions, laughs Supple, the mermaid of Rainy Lake, a stone sculpture on the Minnesota–Ontario border, was mentioned as proof of their existence. The statue was carved in 1932 by Minneapolis architect Gordon Schlichting near the Silver Island Narrows of Rainy Lake.

The creativity of Lakemaid Beer Company's parent company, Pocket Hercules, is also on display in Minnesota's northern lake country in the style of the old Burma-Shave signs once common in the 1920s. The signs, actually large billboards, are deployed in sets of five. One of the most humorous debuted in 2011 with signs one through five reading: At The Cabin, Near The Beaches, We Share The Fridge, With Jumbo Leeches, Lakemaid Beer.

LAKEMAID BREWS

Lakemaid Beer 🍺🍺🍺   *Your Rating_____*

A light, sweet, malty nose with hints of graininess and earthiness. Clear yellow-copper and very effervescent. A medium, soft, white head. Light to medium bodied, soft and bubbly texture. A firm malty flavor with a light hoppy background. This American lager has more flavor and body than most fishing and boating beer with a very clean finish.

OTHER LAKEMAID BREWS YOU MAY WANT TO TRY

Lakemaid Winter Edition   *Your Rating*_____

Offered in winter 2010. Same beer, but just an unsuccessful advertising campaign depicting mermaids wearing fur bikinis and fur hats.

Pig's Eye Brewing Company
Woodbury

Visit Date   Signed

ABOUT THE COMPANY

So what's in a name? Pig's Eye is somewhat like the maiden name for St. Paul! In its early days before Minnesota was a territory — and when what we know as St. Paul was little more than a trading post — Pierre Parrant, a fur trapper, established an encampment along the Mississippi River and eventually settled in Fountain Cave just below what became downtown St. Paul. The cave provided artesian water for his still. As fur trading declined Parrant became even more of a bootlegger. His distinguishing feature was his blind eye, with its sinister white ring around the pupil. That physical abnormality along with his personal attributes lent him the name Pig's Eye. Parrant was so popular that letters in the 1830s merely had to mention "Pig's Eye" in the address and they got to their recipient. Father Lucien Galtier, a Catholic priest, named his small log chapel nearby for St. Paul and applied the name to the settlement as well.

Over 150 years later, when Minnesota Brewing Company made plans to reopen the old Schmidt brewery on the west side of St. Paul on the banks of the Mississippi River, it held a contest to name the brewery and its inaugural beer brand. The name most often suggested was Pig's Eye, but the company's advertising agency disregarded popular opinion and opted for the second choice, Landmark. After the company's Landmark labels were not received by the public as well as hoped, Pig's Eye Pilsner and Pig's Eye Lean Light were introduced in June 1992 and enjoyed immediate acceptance.

Pig's Eye Brewing is licensed as a brewery, but its beers are made by City Brewing in La Crosse, Wisconsin. Its main offices are in Woodbury. Pig's Eye

Brewing has about a half-dozen beers in its portfolio. It includes the main Pig Eye's Pilsner, along with Pig's Eye Lean Light and Pig's Eye Ice. The brewery's brands are distributed in more than a dozen states.

HISTORY

Pig's Eye Brewing was established in 2002. Its owners have a wealth of midwestern brewing experience. Jeff Crawford and Phil Gagné had been driving forces at Minnesota Brewing in St. Paul. When tough beer times forced that brewery to close, Crawford and Gagné purchased the Pig's Eye labels. At their peak, as part of the Minnesota Brewing Company, Pig Eye's brands were available in forty-nine states.

Crawford grew up in Forest Lake. His background includes experience in sales and operations with Pabst Brewing Company, G. Heileman Brewing Company (now City Brewing Company of La Crosse, Wisconsin), and Coors Brewing Company (now MillerCoors). At Minnesota Brewing he was the vice president of sales.

Phill Gagné grew up in North St. Paul. He held positions with G. Heileman and August Schell Brewing. At Minnesota Brewing, Gagné was assistant brewmaster alongside Siegfried Plagens from 1992 until 2000 and later brewmaster from 2000 to 2002.

The Minnesota Brewing Company developed the Pig's Eye brand in 1992. Minnesota Brewing was located in the former Schmidt brewery just a few miles west of downtown St. Paul. The Jacob Schmidt Brewing Company was originally the Christopher Stahlmann Brewery, which began operations in 1855. As the Schmidt Brewing Company it was eventually purchased by G. Heileman, which continued to operate it until 1990 when the brewery was forced to close. A group of investors led by Bruce Hendry purchased it and formed Minnesota Brewing in 1991. Minnesota Brewing also brought back the Grain Belt brands that it purchased along with the brewery.

With the success of Pig's Eye and Grain Belt other beers were added to Minnesota Brewing's beer list, including Red Amber Ale, Ice, Dark, and NA. In 1996, however, the brewery chose to emphasize other proprietary brands, including contract brews such as Pete's Wicked Ale. By the late 1990s Pig's Eye distribution had fallen to just five states (of which Minnesota remained one). In 2002, when Minnesota Brewing closed, the Pig's Eye family of beers were sold to former company employees Crawford and Gagné.

PIG'S EYE BREWS

Pig's Eye Lean Light 🍺🍺🍺🍺   *Your Ranking*_____

A gold medal winner in the American-style low carbohydrate light lager category at the 2005 Great American Beer Festival and a bronze medal in 2003. A solid example of the light beer style. No nose. Light, clear straw color with a thin, soft, white head. Light body with a smooth texture. Crisp, light hoppiness with a fast, clean finish.

Pig's Eye Pilsner 🍺🍺🍺   *Your Ranking*_____

The flagship brew of Pig's Eye Brewing, introduced in 1992. Winner of a bronze medal in the international-style pilsner category at the 2007 Great American

Beer Festival and a silver medal in 2004. Begins with light, crisp, hoppy, grainy nose. Clear light golden and bubbly with a soft, white head. Light bodied. Crisp, light, but firm hoppy background and clean finish. The beer features Cluster, Cascade, and Fuggle hops.

Pit Bull High Gravity Ice Malt Liquor 🍺🍺   *Your Ranking_____*
Light grainy nose. Clear golden color and a medium soft off-white head. Full bodied with a light warmth from the alcohol. Sweet malty flavor and finish. Finishes at 10.2 percent ABV. Packaged in 16-ounce and 24-ounce cans and 40-ounce bottles. A bronze medal winner in the strong ale or lager category in the 2006 Great American Beer Festival.

OTHER PIG'S EYE BREWS YOU MAY WANT TO TRY

Milwaukee Select and Milwaukee Select Light   *Your Ranking_____*
An American-style lager.

Pig's Eye Ice   *Your Ranking_____*
This beer was first made in 1994 and reintroduced in 2007. It won a silver medal in 1994 Great American Beer Festival. Light straw color with a thin, off-white head. Smooth texture but well balanced. Finishes at 5.9 percent ABV.

Sturgis Beer   *Your Ranking_____*
A special pale, light golden lager made for the Sturgis, South Dakota, motor-cycle rally. Sold in commemorative 12-ounce cans.

BREWERIES TO WATCH

MINNEAPOLIS–ST. PAUL AIRPORT BREWS

BEER TASTINGS AND FESTIVALS

BOOKS FOR THE BEER TRAVELER

WEBSITES FOR THE BEER TRAVELER

DIRECTORY OF MINNESOTA BREWERIES AND BREWPUBS

DIRECTORY OF JUST OVER THE BORDER BREWERIES
AND BREWPUBS

MINNESOTA'S BREWING PAST

BEER STYLES

TERMS COMMONLY HEARD ON BREWERY TOURS

INDEX

Breweries to Watch

As of fall 2011 there are several new Minnesota brewers in the early stages of development. These breweries "yet to be" range from just beginning to acquiring a building and constructing the brewhouse. These are a few breweries and brewmasters to watch for in the future.

612 BREW

612 Brew gets its name from the area code for Minneapolis. The brewery is the concept of homebrewing friends Robert Kasak, Emily and Joe Yost, Ryan Libby, and Adit Kalara. The group of five has been homebrewing together for several years, and much of their brewing has taken place in Kasak's Uptown Minneapolis garage. By 2011 they had built their own nano-brewery, a 1-barrel system, that is used for recipe development and test batches. The anticipated beers of 612 include a Porter made with Chinook and Cascade hops, an IPA that finishes at 70 IBUs, and a summer German lager made with grated ginger called Mary Ann that's a big hit with fans of *Gilligan's Island*. The brewery's flagship beer is a pale ale called Six Ale. The pale ale and IPA are expected to be the initial releases of this brewery once it up and producing. For updates go to http://612brew.com.

BIG WOOD BREWING COMPANY

Big Wood Brewing grew out of the decline in the economy and specifically hard times for the hardwood flooring industry. Steve Merila, the president Lon Musolf Distributing, a hardwood flooring company in Vadnais Heights, did what he said he needed to do to help his customers find some "positive mojo." Merila's idea was to start a brewery and offer beer to cheer up his clientele during the downturned economy. Merila's Big Wood Brewery started as a 10-gallon Sabco Brew-Magic system in the back of his 30,000-square-foot flooring business. Merila actually takes customers into the brewery through a side door in his office, almost giving one the impression of a hidden speakeasy. While he has his federal brewer's permit, Merila isn't actually selling beer. Instead he gives most of what he makes to his customers and occasionally takes small kegs to events. He doesn't plan to keep the brewery in his flooring company office long term. His dream is to build a 30-barrel brewhouse in White Bear Lake. Merila took much of 2011 to work on the financing plan with partners Matt Lunstrom of Burnsville and Jason Medvec of White Bear Lake. Initial brews of Big

Wood Brewery include Morning Wood, a coffee stout made with Minnesota's own Caribou Coffee; an American pale ale called Forest Ale, with a piney and resiny bitterness; the Big Wood Imperial IPA; and a smooth roasted nut brown ale. For updates go to http://bigwoodbrewery.com.

CANAL PARK BREWING COMPANY

Once completed, Canal Park Brewing should provide some great views of Lake Superior. Developer and local hotel entrepreneur Rocky Kavajecz is creating this three-story brewpub on the site where the Duluth Spring Company was formerly located. Duluth Spring once made equipment for heavy trucks and Zamboni ice resurfacers. Kavajecz razed the building and began site preparation in spring 2011. Kavajecz also owns the Canal Park Lodge and Canal Park Inn, in addition to several other hotels in northern Wisconsin, including the Hotel Chequamegon in Ashland. His Canal Park Brewing Company is only four hundred feet from the shore of Lake Superior. The initial design includes a two and a half story brewery tower where the main components of the brewhouse will be. On the lake side, deck seating will take advantage of the view. Canal Park Brewing is set up for both ales and lagers. For updates go to www.thecpbc.com.

CLYDE PARK BAKERY, RESTAURANT, AND BREWERY

The Clyde Park Bakery, Restaurant, and Brewery opened in 2010 on Duluth's near south side in a 36,000-square-foot, three-story-high factory building constructed in 1889 for Clyde Iron Works. The restaurant, bakery, and events center components were first to start up. The remaining part of the business plan that is yet to be implemented calls for a brewhouse. Clyde Park operations manager Steve Eto has described the ultimate brewery vision as something similar to the Rock Bottom brewpub experience. Eto was actually the general manger of the Rock Bottom brewpub in downtown Minneapolis when it opened in 1993. There's certainly a lot of space to work with in this former factory that once produced cranes and derricks, some of which were used to construct the Panama Canal. Even still today, a 60-foot hoist that factory workers used to move heavy equipment around remains in the building. It's not just a focal point but a conversation piece. In 2011 Clyde contracted with Lake Superior Brewing of Duluth to make a house brown ale simply called "Clyde." The beer has rich malty flavor and a reddish-bronze color. Expansion plans for a brewhouse at Clyde have been put on hold while the restaurant and events center establishes itself. In the meantime, the contract brews from Lake Superior make this a great place to visit. For updates go to www.clydeparkduluth.com.

EXCELSIOR BREWING COMPANY

This brewing partnership began with Little League. John Klick, Jon Lewin, and Patrick Foss met while watching their kids play baseball. Their discussions in the stands led them to form their own team, one that just may bring Excelsior its first commercial brewery. Their planning started in 2010 and eventually led them to jointly purchasing a Sabco Brew-Magic, a professional-level pilot brewing system they have used to try out recipes and determine core beers for their yet-to-be brewery. Through much of 2011 they worked with the community of Excelsior to make changes to local ordinances that would be necessary to allow a brewery and onsite growler sales. The group's goal is to make about 3,000 barrels of beer a year, but they have experienced significant challenges in finding a building large enough for a brewery. All three partners plan to keep their day jobs and hire a brewmaster to run the brewery. Lewin works for a local real-estate company, Foss owns a human resources consulting firm, and Klick is a partner in a promotional products company. For updates go to www.excelsiorbrew.com.

FITGER'S PRODUCTION BREWERY

This well-established Duluth brewpub has designs on setting up its own production brewery. Fitger's has been making beer since 1997 in the former Fitger's Brewing Company building (600 East Superior Street), which was original constructed in the 1880s. Fitger's beers are in demand and space is limited in its current 10-barrel brewhouse, which houses more than fifty fermenters and storage tanks across two floors of the old brewery building. You will find Fitger's beers not only in the brewpub but also in its companion bar, the Red Star Lounge, which is just across the hallway in the old brewery complex. There's always an assortment of Fitger's brews at Burrito Union (1332 East 4th Street), which the owners of Fitger's opened in 2007. Then in 2011 they followed that with Tycoon's Zenith Alehouse (132 East Superior Street) in Duluth's old City Hall building. Their plans to expand their brewing capacity have focused on their 2010 purchase of the Carlson Bookstore Building (206 East Superior Street), just a few blocks from their current brewpub. Fitger's owners Tim Nelson and Rod Raymond have plans that include a cafe, bakery, events center, sound studio, and a new production brewery. For updates go to http://brewhouse.net.

READS LANDING BREWING COMPANY

Reads Landing hasn't had a brewery in more than a century, since the Burkhardt Brewery closed its doors in 1909. Reads Landing is located along the Mississippi River between Red Wing and Winona. Former contractor Bob Nihart took a building that had been in his family since the 1930s and renovated it to include a bar and restaurant. The building was once home to the Anchor Inn during 1950s and early 1960s. His great aunt ran the restaurant and lived upstairs. It later was used as a family cabin. Nihart's dream is to add a working brewhouse by 2012. The building is one of just a few structures besides private residences in Reads Landing. It stands less than a hundred feet from the Mississippi and its large windows look out on the water. Nihart is planning an ale brewery, with expectations that he'll have at least four beers on all the time. His homebrewing experience has allowed him to create a very nice pale ale worth trying on any visit.

SURLY BREWING

Surly Brewing has seen nothing but tremendous growth since it made its first beers in 2006. Production figures in 2010 reached nearly 12,000 barrels, up almost 30 percent from the year before. Twin Cities demand for Surly has grown so fast that the Brooklyn Center brewery has struggled to keep up and had to pull back on the out-of-state distribution of its products. Company founder and president Omar Ansari sees even more potential for growth and has plans for a new $20 million facility that he says will make his Surly a "destination brewery." His idea is to build a two-story, 60,000-square-foot building with a rooftop deck, beer garden, 250-seat restaurant with a thirty-foot bar, and an events center. The expansion would increase his brewery's overall annual capacity to 100,000 barrels. In 2011 Ansari went to work on getting Minnesota state laws changed, which would allow breweries of a certain size to sell pints of their beer at their brewery. In anticipation of the construction jobs, permanent jobs, and tax revenues the project would create, mayors of both Minneapolis and St. Paul have been trying to entice Ansari to build in their city. After success in the Minnesota legislature, Ansari's focus turned to raising the finances necessary to make his expansion dream a reality.

TIN WHISKERS

The brainchild of three University of Minnesota School of Engineering graduates. The name Tin Whiskers is actually an obscure engineering term used to describe a crystalline metallurgical phenomenon where spontaneous growth of tiny hair-like filaments form on a metallic surface. When it happens, it can cause a short that causes a device to fail. The engineering minds behind the brewery are George Kellerman, Jeff Moriarty, and Jacob Johnson. All three are Minnesota natives and work at Spectrum Design Solutions, a Minneapolis engineering firm. Their goal is an ale production brewery in Roseville. Kellerman likes to point to the bold assertive beers of Surly Brewing as a source of inspiration for getting them through the phase of business planning and financing in 2011.

Minneapolis–St. Paul Airport Brews

Beer is one of the best incentives to arrive early at the airport or to make the most of time between connecting flights. And, compared with other large terminals, the Minneapolis–St. Paul Airport (MSP) is above average in the opportunities for travelers who enjoy good local beer. Finding a good beer in such settings can be a challenge, given that those passing through may be under time constraints. That is, unless a flight has been delayed, and then all the more reason to sit and enjoy a quality brew.

Over the past decade, airports seem to have expanded dramatically the types of shops, restaurants, and amenities they offer the flyer. These businesses are inside secured areas of most airports and are commonly managed by a concessionaire, who may lease a popular local business name and its concepts. Concessionaires with ties to breweries and brewpubs have been cropping up in many major airports across the country, from large international hubs to regional terminals. While you won't likely see any brew kettles or lagering tanks within the airport terminals themselves, such venues still can make traveling for the beer enthusiast pleasurable.

More than a dozen places in MSP sell beer. Among those, a handful make an extraordinary commitment to Minnesota craft beer. A few of the well-known favorites to look for at MSP include Summit, Schell, and Surly. If you find those Minnesota tap handles you will not be disappointed.

AXEL'S BONFIRE

Axel's Bonfire is built on the popular Axel's restaurants in the Twin Cities area. The company was founded by Linda Young and Charlie Burrows in 1996. Both had long associations in restaurant and food service, including Champps Americana, where they met. The name honors Young's father, Axel.

Axel's Bonfire offers a full bar with several great beer choices. What distinguishes this restaurant from others is a commitment to offering a house beer called Bonfire Lager, currently made under contract by the August Schell Brewing Company of New Ulm. It's a medium-bodied beer with a deep bronze color and bubbly white head. Bonfire Lager has a firm, solid caramel maltiness to its flavor and finish. Over the years, Axel's Bonfire has relied on other breweries to make its house beer, most of which have been medium-bodied reds, ambers, or deep golden beers. Other taps at Axel's commonly feature other Minnesota favorites like Summit Extra Pale Ale. Axel's southwestern-inspired menu features wood-fire cooking of ribs, chicken, seafood, and steaks.

IKE'S

Ike's two locations at MSP are spinoffs of a popular downtown Minneapolis bar and restaurant (50 South Sixth Street) and its retro theme in the spirit of post-WWII with blue plate specials and Eisenhower-era shakes and malts. One of its signature staples is the Original Ike's Burger.

Ike's on Summit (Concourse F, Gate 7) provides a wide selection of Minnesota-made Summit beers. This is a good location to find year-round favorites like Summit's Extra Pale Ale, Great Northern porter, and the Pilsner. You may also find a few of the brewery's seasonals and the occasional limited release Unchained Summit brews. Tasting flights of as many as six Summit brews are available, along with a diverse food menu and made-to-order breakfast omelets.

Ike's Food and Cocktails (Main Mall) offers travelers a sit-down dining experience in an atmosphere that feels more like a supper club or classic steakhouse with its large booths and wooden accents. The beer list at Ike's Food and Cocktails includes several Summit beers; however, it's not as extensive as the Ike's on Summit location. Ike's in the main mall is also likely to have beers from Surly as well as more than a dozen domestic and import bottled selections. In addition to a standard food menu, Ike's Food and Cocktails features a carving station as well as steaks and ribs and complimentary cookies or cinnamon rolls for all tables.

O'GARA'S RESTAURANT

This is the airport location of St. Paul's well-known O'Gara's Bar and Grill. James Freeman O'Gara opened the doors of the original O'Gara's tavern (164 Snelling Avenue) in 1941. Initially the pub catered to local residents who manufactured supplies and munitions for the WWII effort. What today is the restaurant's Green Room was once the barber shop of Carl Schulz, the father of Charles, creator of the cartoon strip Peanuts.

In 1996 O'Gara's started making beer with the help of the local father-and-son team of Larry and Brian Benkstein. Larry had worked for the St. Paul Malt House, which processed grain for the Stroh's brewery when it operated in St. Paul. Larry pretty much ran the brewery side of O'Gara's in St. Paul until 2007, when the St. Paul tavern stopped making its own beer.

At MSP, O'Gara's offers Summit and Grain Belt Premium on tap, among a handful of big brewery beers. O'Gara's also has a variety of bottled imports. The menu choices include burgers, fish and chips, and sandwiches.

ROCK BOTTOM RESTAURANT AND BREWERY

Rock Bottom is part of a national chain of brewpubs, including a downtown Minneapolis location (800 LaSalle Plaza), owned by a company that operates more than a hundred businesses under several brands, such as Old Chicago, the Chophouse, and Sing Sing Dueling Piano Bars. The company's namesake brewpub has about thirty locations, making it one of the largest brewpub chains in the country.

At MSP, Rock Bottom's décor, food menu, and beer selections will look familiar to travelers who have visited one of the brewpubs before. As one might expect, it's just a bit scaled down from the larger freestanding locations.

The beer here is made at Rock Bottom's Westminster, Colorado, brewpub. You can expect a core array of brews from lighter wheats to full-bodied stouts. The Rock Bottom Wheat is a crisp and flavorful Belgian Wit beer with a rich golden hue and citrus notes. The Singletrack Copper Ale is a beer more recognizable to those who frequent Rock Bottoms in Colorado. It's smooth and malty and it captured a bronze medal in the 2004 World Beer Cup. For those who enjoy a darker beer, the Bighorn Nut Brown is full-bodied with a firm maltiness alongside tones of raisin and cocoa with the bitterness of Willamette hops. Erik the Red is a Vienna-style lager whose name reflects Minnesota's fascination with all things Viking. The Rock Bottom in downtown Minneapolis makes an ale version of this beer that offers more caramel maltiness. Itasca Extra Pale Ale is copper color with bitterness from four different varieties of hops. The MSP rendition has a bit more citrus to the aroma, with hints of assertive piney bitterness to its body. At the MSP Rock Bottom you'll find a food menu that offers burgers, large salads, and sandwiches.

THE LODGE

To some, the Lodge may appear to be just another bar with a north woods theme. But the Lodge deserves acknowledgment from thirsty beer travelers for its level of rustic Midwest authenticity in what's on tap. Craft beer enthusiasts will be familiar with the name Leinenkugel's, and the Lodge always has a couple of Leinies on tap or in bottles. Leinenkugel Brewing Company of Chippewa Falls, Wisconsin, about eighty miles east of the Twin Cities, has been a fixture of the region for over 150 years. At the Lodge, look for the brilliant reddish-amber lager called Leinenkugel's Red or the light bubbly Honeyweiss. Also check out the bottled selections for the silky smooth black lager called Leinenkugel's Creamy Dark—perfect for waiting for a late-night flight.

The Lodge is what MSP considers a "quick service" consessionaire. That means that while you can find a selection of beer and bar drinks, the menu is pretty light and could best be described as "grab and run" (or "grab and fly"). Certainly nothing wrong with quick service, given that many who walk past the Lodge have an itinerary. After all, there's always time for a Leinies.

SURDYK'S FLIGHTS

Surdyk's came to MSP in 2010 as a wine market and bar, a new concept in airport concessions. Travelers can stop in for a local beer like Summit and Lift Bridge or a glass of wine. It's a great place for a hot or cold sandwich or even specialty cheeses that make excellent beer or wine companions (but remember—you cannot take open alcoholic beverages onto the plane).

Surdyk's began as a grocery store in Minneapolis in 1934. Owner Joseph Surdyk purchased one of the first liquor licenses available in Minneapolis after the repeal of Prohibition, figuring that selling liquor, in addition to groceries, would bolster the family income. Today, Surdyk's lays claim to "The Midwest's Largest Liquor Store." Jim Surdyk, grandson of Joseph, currently operates the Minneapolis store at 303 East Hennepin Avenue—just a few blocks from the store's original location. Over the years, three generations of Surdyks have run the business.

OTHER AIRPORT BEER VENUES WORTHY OF A LAYOVER

Akron–Canton Airport (CAK)—Great Lakes Brewing Company (Post-Screening area)

Atlanta Hartsfield–Jackson International Airport (ATL)—SweetWater Brewery and Draft House & Grill (Concourse B, near Gates 10–11)

Baltimore Washington International Airport (BWI)—DuClaw Brewing Company (Main Terminal)

Boston Logan International Airport (BOS)—Harpoon Brewing (Terminal A, near Gates 18–22)

Chicago O'Hare Airport (ORD)—Goose Island Beer Company (Terminal 1, Concourse C, near Gates 8–10)

Cincinnati Northern Kentucky International Airport (CVG)—Bluegrass Brewing Company (Concourse C, Gate 79); and Samuel Adams Brewpub (Terminal 3, Gate 18; and Concourse A, Gate 18)

Cleveland Hopkins International Airport (CLE)—Gordon Biersch Brewing Company (Concourse D); and Great Lakes Brewing (Concourse C)

Denver International Airport (DEN)—New Belgium Brewing (Concourse B, Regional Jet Terminal); and Rock Bottom Restaurant and Brewery (Concourse C)

Detroit Metro Airport (DTW)—Heineken Lounge (McNamara-Main Terminal, near Gate A73)

Indianapolis International Airport (IND)—Granite City Food and Brewery (Concourse A)

Los Angeles International Airport (LAX)—Gordon Biersch Brewing Company (Terminals 1 and 8); and Karl Strauss Brewing (Terminal 7)

Madison / Dane County Regional Airport (MSN)—Great Dane Pub and Brewing Company (near Gate 8)

Miami International Airport (MIA)—Samuel Adams Brewpub (North, Terminal D)

Milwaukee, General Mitchell International Airport (MKE)—Miller Brewhouse (Main Terminal)

New York, Kennedy (JFK)—Samuel Adams Brewpub (Delta Terminal and International Terminal 4)

Philadelphia International Airport (PHL)—Jet Rock Bar and Grill with about 4 dozen taps (Concourses B, D, and F)

Portland International (PDX)—Laurelwood Brewing Company (Concourses A and E)

Reno–Tahoe International Airport (RNO)—Brew Brothers (Terminal Lobby)

Salt Lake City International (SLC)—Squatters Beer and Wasatch Brewing (Terminal 2, Concourse C)

San Francisco International Airport (SFO)—Gordon Biersch Brewing Company (Terminal 3, Boarding Area F)

Seattle–Tacoma International (SEA)—Seattle Taproom (Concourse B)

St. Louis International Airport (STL)—Schlafly Tap Room (Concourse B)

Washington, DC, Dulles International Airport (IAD)—Old Dominion Brewing Co. (Concourse B, Gate 19)

Washington, DC, Reagan National Airport (DCA)—Gordon Biersch Brewing Company (Terminal C, Gate 37)

Beer Tastings and Festivals

Attending a beer festival or a beer tasting is an excellent way to discover some of Minnesota's best beers. Such events occur all around the state. It's always a good idea to check a few websites or even call the local chamber of commerce for more information and to confirm date, time, location, driving directions, cost, and phone numbers. Dates, sponsors, and other details can change.

Many Minnesota breweries and brewpubs will hold their own special events that feature tastings and brewmaster dinners. Some even are organized around charitable causes. There are also quite a number of regional and national events that could be of interest depending upon where you live and how much you like to travel.

Festivals can be especially rewarding for those who like to try many different beers from many different breweries. Tickets to such events, however, can be challenging to obtain. The most popular festivals can sell out in a few hours. Some even use a mail-in lottery for awarding the right to purchase tickets.

Beer dinners and special tastings tied to a brewpub can be equally gratifying, but for different reasons. Such dinners will often pair the talents of the brewmaster with the restaurant's chef. They may range from a few straightforward offerings to a multiple course meal. Also, such tastings aren't just organized by breweries or brewpubs. There are a growing number of fine restaurants that recognize the power of pairing beer with their best cuisine. Some of those restaurants sponsor unique beer dinners for which they invite a local brewmaster to appear alongside their chef. While the event list that follows is by no means all-inclusive, it does offer some ideas that can add to weekend or vacation plans and your search for the perfect pint.

Brooklyn Center
Surly Darkness Day   October

Caledonia
Caledonia Bluff Country Brewfest   June

Cloquet
Big River Brewfest   September

Elk River
Taste of Elk River   May

Lucan
    Braufest   June
    Brau Brothers' Hop Fest   October

Lutsen
    Hopped Up Caribou Beer Festival   July

Minneapolis
    City Pages Beer Festival   June
    Minnesota Monthly Food & Wine Experience   March
    Autumn Brew Review   September
    Minneapolis Beer Fest   September
    Oktoberfest (Mississippi River Front Festival)   September

Minnetonka
    Hooray for IPA   July

New Ulm
    Bockfest   February
    Bavarian Blast   July
    Schells Anniversary Party   July
    Oktoberfest   September–October

St. Cloud
    Craft Beer Expo   January

St. Paul
    Upper Mississippi Mashout   January
    St. Paul Winter Carnival   January
    Winterfest   February
    Firkin Fest   March
    Summer Beer Festival   June
    Highland Fest (Beer Dabbler)   July
    Muddy Pig Annual Belgian Beer Fest   September

Stillwater
    Winter Wine Down   February
    Annual Brewers Bazaar   May

OUT-OF-STATE EVENTS IN THE REGION AND BEYOND

Amana, Iowa
    Festival of Iowa Beers   September

Black River Falls, Wisconsin
    Great Tastes Festival   May

Chetek, Wisconsin
    Chetek Brews and Rib Fest   July

Chicago, Illinois
Chicagoland Brewpub-Microbrewery Shootout   January
Day of the Living Ales   March
Chicago Beer Society's Annual Spring Beer Tasting and Dinner   May
Summer Beer Festival by Illinois Craft Brewers Guild   July
Chicago Beer Society's Annual Fall Beer Tasting and Dinner   November

Chilton, Wisconsin
Wisconsin Microbrewers Beer Fest   May

Chippewa Falls, Wisconsin
Northwest Beer Festival   May

Denver, Colorado
Great American Beer Festival   September

Des Moines, Iowa
Des Moines Craft Brew Festival   May

Eagle River, Wisconsin
Great Northern Beer Festival   June

Eau Claire, Wisconsin
Clearwater Beer Festival   September

Fargo, North Dakota
Fargo Beer Festival   October

La Crosse, Wisconsin
Between the Bluffs — Beer, Wine, and Cheese Festival   April
Oktoberfest   late September

Lake Mills, Wisconsin
Tyranena Oktoberfest Bike Ride   October

Madison, Wisconsin
Great Taste of the Midwest   August

Middleton, Wisconsin
Bockfest (Capital Brewery)   February

Milwaukee, Wisconsin
Food and Froth   February
Blessing of the Bock   March
Germanfest   July
Oktoberfest   September

Minocqua, Wisconsin
Ice Cold Beer Fest   January
Brewfest   July

Mount Horeb, Wisconsin
Thirsty Troll Brewfest   September

Potosi, Wisconsin
Potosi Brewfest   August

Racine, Wisconsin
Great Lakes Brew Fest   September

Superior, Wisconsin
Gitchee Gumee Brewfest   April

Wisconsin Dells, Wisconsin
Wisconsin Dells on Tap   October

Books for the
Beer Traveler

Apps, Jerry. *Breweries of Wisconsin*. Madison: University of Wisconsin Press, 1992 (revised 2005).

Asbury, Herbert. *Gem of the Prairie: An Informal History of the Chicago Underworld*. Garden City, NY: Garden City Publishing, 1942.

Association of Brewers, comp. *Evaluating Beer*. Boulder, CO: Brewers Publications, 1993.

Beaumont, Stephen. *The Great Canadian Beer Guide*. Toronto: McArthur, 2002.

———. *Premium Beer Drinker's Guide: The World's Strongest, Boldest and Most Unusual Beers*. Buffalo, NY: Firefly Books, 2000.

———. *Stephen Beaumont's Brewpub Cookbook: 100 Great Recipes from 30 Great North American Brewpubs*. Boulder, CO: Brewers Publications, 1998.

———. *A Taste for Beer*. Pownal, VT: Storey Publishing, 1995.

Bice, John. *Tap into the Great Lakes: A Guide to the Brewpubs and Microbreweries of Michigan, Indiana, Illinois,Ohio, and Wisconsin*. Holt, MI: Thunder Bay Press. 1999.

Boteler, Alison. *Gourmet's Guide to Cooking with Beer*. Beverly, MA: Quarry Books, 2009.

Buxton, Ian., ed. *Beer Hunter, Whisky Chaser: New Writing on Beer and Whisky in Honour of Michael Jackson*. Poland: Classic Expressions, 2009.

Ditky, Alan S., ed. *The Beverage Testing Institute's Buying Guide to Spirits*. New York: Sterling Publishing, 1999.

Dornan, Marc, ed. *The Beverage Testing Institute's Buying Guide to Beer*. New York: Sterling Publishing, 1999.

Eckhardt, Fred. *Essentials of Beer Style: A Catalog of Classic Beer Styles for Brewers and Beer Enthusiasts*. Portland, OR: Fred Eckhardt Communications, 1989.

Flanagan, John T. *Theodore Hamm in Minnesota: His Family and Brewery*. St. Paul, MN: Pogo Press, 1989.

Glover, Brian. *The Complete Guide to Beer*. New York: Anness Publishing, 2000. Original titled *The World Encyclopedia of Beer*.

Hales, Steven D. *Beer & Philosophy*. Malden, MA: Blackwell Publishing, 2007.

Harris, Moira. *Louise's Legacy: Hamm Family Stories*. St. Paul, MN: Pogo Press, 1998.

————. *The Paws of Refreshment: A History of Hamm's Beer Advertising.* St. Paul, MN: Pogo Press, 2000.

Hieronymus, Stan, and Daria Labinsky. *The Beer Lover's Guide to the USA: Brewpubs, Taverns, and Good Beer Bars.* New York: St. Martin's Griffin, 2000.

Hoverson, Doug. *Land of Amber Waters: The History of Brewing in Minnesota.* Minneapolis: University of Minnesota Press, 2007.

Jackson, Michael. *Michael Jackson's Beer Companion: The World's Great Beer Styles, Gastronomy, and Traditions.* 2d ed. Philadelphia: Running Press, 2000.

————. *Michael Jackson's Pocket Beer Book.* UK: Mitchell Beazley, 2000.

————. *The New World Guide to Beer.* Philadelphia: Running Press, 1997.

————. *The Simon and Schuster Pocket Guide to Beer.* New York: Fireside, 1996.

————. *Ultimate Beer.* New York: DK Publishing, 1998.

Lindberg, Richard. *To Serve and Collect: Chicago Politics and Police Corruption from the Lager Beer Riot to the Summerdale Scandal, 1855–1960.* Carbondale: Southern Illinois University Press, 1998.

Macintosh, Julie. *Dethroning the King: The Hostile Takeover of Anheuser-Busch, an American Icon.* Hoboken, NJ: John Wiley & Sons, 2011.

Mercer, Todd Bryant. *Bike and Brew America: Midwest Region.* Boulder, CO: Brewers Publications, 2001.

Mosher, Randy. *The Brewer's Companion.* Seattle: Alephenalia Publications, 1995.

————. *Tasting Beer.* North Adams, MA: Storey Publishing, 2009.

Nachel, Marty. *Beer across America: A Regional Guide to Brewpubs and Microbreweries.* Pownal, VT: Storey Publishing, 1995.

Nachel, Marty, and Steve Ettlinger. *Beer for Dummies.* New York: IDG Books, 1996.

Ogg, Bryan J. *Peoria Spirits.* Peoria, IL: Peoria Historical Society, 1996.

Oliver, Garrett. *The Brewmaster's Table.* New York: HarperCollins, 2003.

————. *The Oxford Companion to Beer.* New York: Oxford University Press, 2012.

Okrent, Daniel. *Last Call: The Rise and Fall of Prohibition.* New York: Scribner, 2010.

One Hundred Years of Brewing: A Complete History of the Progress Made in the Art, Science and Industry of Brewing during the Nineteenth Century. Chicago: H. S. Rich, 1903. Compiled by *Western Brewer* trade journal and reprinted by Arno Press in 1974.

Papazian, Charlie. *Microbrewed Adventures.* New York: HarperCollins, 2005.

————. *The New Complete Joy of Home Brewing.* New York: Avon Books, 1991.

Perozzi, Christina, and Hallie Beaune. *The Naked Pint: An Unadulterated Guide to Craft Beer.* New York: Perigee, 2009.

Protz, Roger. *The Taste of Beer.* New York: Sterling Publishing, 2000.

————. *The Ultimate Encyclopedia of Beer.* London: Carlton Books, 1998.

————. *The World Beer Guide.* London: Carlton Books, 2000.

Rabin, Dan, comp., and Carl Forget, ed. *Dictionary of Beer and Brewing.* Boulder, CO: Brewers Publications, 1998.

Rhodes, Christine P., ed. *The Encyclopedia of Beer*. New York: Henry Holt, 1997.

Robertson, James D. *The Beer-Taster's Log: A World Guide to More Than 6000 Beers*. Pownal, VT: Storey Publishing, 1996.

Saunders, Lucy. *Best of American Beer and Food: Pairing and Cooking with Craft Beer*. Boulder, CO: Brewers Publications, 2007.

Shepard, Robin. *The Best Breweries and Brewpubs of Illinois: Searching for the Perfect Pint*. Madison: University of Wisconsin Press, 2003.

———. *Wisconsin's Best Breweries and Brewpubs: Searching for the Perfect Pint*. Madison: University of Wisconsin Press, 2001.

Skilnik, Bob. *Beer and Food: An American History*. Chattanooga, TN: Jefferson Press, 2007.

———. *The History of Beer and Brewing in Chicago, 1833–1978*. St. Paul, MN: Pogo Press, 1999.

———. *The History of Beer and Brewing in Chicago: Volume II*. Haverford, PA: Infinity Publishing, 2001.

Smith, Gregg. *The Beer Enthusiast's Guide: Tasting and Judging Brews from around the World*. Pownal, VT: Storey Publishing, 1994.

———. *A Beer History: A Day at a Time through the Year*. Pittsburgh, PA: Whitmore Publishing, 2005.

———. *Beer in America: The Early Years, 1587–1840*. Boulder, CO: Siris Books, 1998.

Sneath, Allen Winn. *Brewed in Canada: The Untold Story of Canada's 350-Year-Old Brewing Industry*. Toronto: Dundurn Group, 2001.

Snyder, Stephen. *The Brewmaster's Bible*. New York: HarperPerennial, 1997.

Standage, Tom. *A History of the World in Six Glasses*. New York: Walker & Company, 2005.

Van Wieren, Dale P. *American Breweries II*. West Point, PA: Eastern Coast Breweriana Association, 1995.

Wells, Ken. *Travels with Barley: A Journey through Beer Culture in America*. New York: Free Press / Simon and Schuster, 2004

Wood, Heather, comp. *The Beer Directory: An International Guide*. Pownal, VT: Storey Publishing, 1995.

Yaeger, Brian. *Red, White, and Brew: An American Beer Odyssey*. New York: St. Martin's, 2008.

Yenne, Bill. *Great American Beers*. St. Paul, MN: MBI Publishing, 2004.

Websites for the Beer Traveler

BEER RATING AND GENERAL BEER INFORMATION

American Brewery History Page: www.beerhistory.com
American Homebrewers Association: www.beertown.org
Associated Beer Distributors of Illinois: www.abdi.org
B is for Beer: www.BisforBeer.com
BeerAdvocate: www.beeradvocate.com
Beer Books: www.beerbooks.com
Beer Church: www.beerchurch.com
Beer Expedition: www.beerexpedition.com
The Beer Information Source—Virtual Library of Beer and Brewing:
    www.beerinfo.com
Beer Judge Certification Program: www.mv.com/ipusers/slack/bjcp
Beer Lovers World: www.beer-lover.com
Beerme database of beers and breweries: www.beerme.com
Beertown: Home of the Association of Brewers: www.aob.org
Beer Travelers: www.beertravelers.com
Beer Trips and Travel: www.beertrips.com
Beer World Database: www.dailyglobe.com/beer
Beverage Testing Institute (BTI): www.tastings.com
The Brewery: Total Homebrewing Information: www.brewery.org
BrewPubZone: www.brewpubzone.com
BrewsTraveler Guides: www.brewstraveler.com
Chicago Beer History Website: www.chicagolandbeerhistory.com
Chicago Beer Society: www.chibeer.org
Indiana State Fair Brewer's Cup Competition: http://hbd.org/indiana
Iowa Brewpub and Brewery Information: www.beerstuff.com/ibg
Marcobrau Beer Pages (Chicago and Illinois): www.marcobrau.com
Michael Jackson's The Beer Hunter—World Guide to Beer:
    www.beerhunter.com
Michigan Beer Guide: www.michiganbeerguide.com/beerguide.asp
Michigan Brewers Guide: www.michiganbeerguide.com/beerguide.asp
Minnesota Beer Wholesalers Association: www.mnbwa.com
Minnesota Home Brewers Association: www.mnbrewers.com
Museum of Beer and Brewing: www.brewingmuseum.org
Pubcrawler: www.pubcrawler.com
RateBeer: www.ratebeer.com

The Real Beer Page: www.realbeer.com
Siebel Institute of Technology: www.siebelinstitute.com
Stephen Beaumont's World of Beer: http://worldofbeer.com

BREWERS' GUILDS

American Brewers Guild: www.abgbrew.com
Illinois Craft Brewers Guild: www.illinoisbeer.com
Indiana, Brewer's Guild of: www.theoysterbar.com/guild.htm
Iowa Brewers Guild: www.beerstuff.com/ibg/
Michigan Brewers Guild: www.michiganbrewersguild.org
Minnesota Craft Brewers Guild: www.mncraftbrew.org
Wisconsin Brewers Guild: www.wibrewersguild.org

BEER NEWSPAPERS AND MAGAZINES

Ale Street News: www.alestreetnews.com
All About Beer: www.allaboutbeer.com
American Brewer: www.ambrew.com
Beer Connoisseur Magazine: www.beerconnoisseur.com
Brewing Techniques: www.brewingtechniques.com
Brew Magazine: www.brewmag.com
Brew Your Own: http://byo.com
Celebrator Beer News: www.celebrator.com
Draft: www.draftmag.com
Great Lakes Brewing News: www.greatlakes.brewingnews.com

MINNESOTA HOMEBREW CLUB WEBSITES

Boreal Brewers (Bemidji): borealbrewers.org
Brewers in Chaos (St. Paul): 651-603-8541
Cloudy Town Brewers (St. Cloud / Sauk Rapids):
    www.cloudytownbrewers.org
Cross River Alliance of Zymurgists (Eden Prairie): mgbehrendt@mn.rr.com
Jack of All Brews (Waconia): www.jackofallbrews.org
Minnesota Home Brewers Association (Edina): www.mnbrewers.com
Minnesota Timberworts (Rochester): Renkly.Gregory@mayo.edu
Run River Wort Hogs (Anoka): rrworthogs@yahoo.com
Saint Paul Homebrewers Club (St. Paul): www.sphbc.org
Three Rivers United Brewers (Hastings): mike_hopman@yahoo.com
Up North Brewing Club (Champlin): www.upnorthbrewing.com

Directory of Minnesota Breweries and Brewpubs

BRAINERD
Brainerd Lakes Brewery
1511 Northern Pacific Road,
Building #7
Brainerd, MN 56401
GPS Coordinates: N 46°21.386'
W 94°10.951'
Established: 2008
Production (approximate barrels/
year): brewed by Lake Superior
Brewing (Duluth)
Website:
www.brainerdlakesbrewery.com
E-mail: see website
Facebook: yes
Telephone: 218-330-8550 or
218-820-9775
Gift Shop: yes (see website)
Mug Club: no
Growlers: yes
Tours: yes
Tasting: yes
Distribution: northern Minnesota
Makes Own Line of Soft Drinks: no
Bar Toys: none
Bar Stools: none
Beer Garden/Outside Seating: no
Tourism: Brainerd Lakes Chamber of
Commerce, 800-450-2838
(www.explorebrainerdlakes.com)

BROOKLYN CENTER
Surly Brewing Company
4811 Dusharme Drive
Brooklyn Center, MN 55429
GPS Coordinates: N 45°02.566'
W 93°19.462'

Established: 2006
Production (approximate barrels/
year): 12,000 bbl (2010)
Website: www.surlybrewing.com
E-mail: beer@surlybrewing.com
Facebook: yes
Telephone: 763-535-3330
Gift Shop: yes
Mug Club: no
Growlers: no
Tours: yes (call and see website)
Tasting: yes
Distribution: Minnesota and
Wisconsin
Makes Own Line of Soft Drinks: no
Bar Toys: none
Bar Stools: none
Beer Garden/Outside Seating: no
Tourism: Brooklyn Center Commu-
nity Chamber of Commerce /
North Hennepin Area Chamber
of Commerce, 763-424-6744
(www.nhachamber.com);
City of Brooklyn Center
(http://ci.brooklyn-center.mn.us)

COLD SPRING
Cold Spring Brewing Company
219 Red River Avenue, North
Cold Spring, MN 56320
GPS Coordinates: N 45°27.532'
W 94°25.737'
Established: 1998 (current owner-
ship); 1874 (dates back to the
Michael Sargl Brewery)
Production (approximate barrels/
year): 45,355 bbl (2010)

Website:
www.coldspringbrewery.com
E-mail: see website
Facebook: no
Telephone: 320-685-8686
Gift Shop: yes
Mug Club: no
Growlers: no
Tours: yes
Tasting: yes
Distribution: national distribution of
several brands
Makes Own Line of Soft Drinks: yes;
also health drinks and mineral
water
Bar Toys: none
Bar Stools: none
Beer Garden/Outside Seating: no
Tourism: Cold Spring Chamber of
Commerce, 320-685-4186; City
of Cold Spring, 320-685-3653
(www.coldspring.govoffice.com);
St. Cloud Area Convention and
Visitors Bureau, 800-264-2940
(www.granitecountry.com)

DULUTH
Carmody Irish Pub and Brewing
308 East Superior Street
Duluth, MN 55802
GPS Coordinates: N 46°47.406'
W 92°05.639'
Established: 2009 (brewpub); 2005
(pub)
Production (approximate barrels/
year): 150 bbl (2010)
Website: www.carmodyirishpub.com
E-mail: carmodyirishpub@yahoo.com
Facebook: yes
Telephone: 218-740-4747
Gift Shop: yes
Mug Club: no
Growlers: yes
Tours: yes
Tasting: yes
Distribution: through brewpub only
Makes Own Line of Soft Drinks: no
Bar Toys: none
Bar Stools: 12
Beer Garden/Outside Seating: no

Tourism: Duluth Convention and
Visitors Bureau, 800-4Duluth
[438-5884]
(www.visitduluth.com)

Dubh Linn Irish Brewpub
109 West Superior Street
Duluth, MN 55802
GPS Coordinates: N 46°47.136'
W 92°05.974'
Established: 2011 (brewpub); 2006
(pub)
Production (approximate barrels/
year): no estimate available
Website: www.dubhlinnpub.com
E-mail: dubhlinnduluth@yahoo.com
Facebook: yes
Telephone: 218-727-1559
Gift Shop: yes
Mug Club: no
Growlers: no
Tours: yes
Tasting: yes
Distribution: through brewpub only
Makes Own Line of Soft Drinks: no
Bar Toys: 2 shuffle boards, 4 pool
tables, 3 electronic dart boards
Bar Stools: 15-plus
Beer Garden/Outside Seating: no
Tourism: Duluth Convention and
Visitors Bureau, 800-4Duluth
[438-5884]
(www.visitduluth.com)

Dubrue
211 East 2nd Street
Duluth, MN 55805
GPS Coordinates: N 46°47.441'
W 92°05.885'
Established: 2011
Production (approximate barrels/
year): no estimate available
Website: www.dubrue.com
E-mail: bob@dubrue.com
Facebook: yes
Telephone: 218-341-0988
Gift Shop: yes
Mug Club: no
Growlers: yes
Tours: yes

Tasting: yes
Distribution: Duluth area and north-
east Minnesota
Makes Own Line of Soft Drinks: no
Bar Toys: none
Bar Stools: 2 and a small tasting area
Beer Garden/Outside Seating: no
Tourism: Duluth Convention and
Visitors Bureau, 800-4Duluth
[438-5884]
(www.visitduluth.com)

Fitger's Brewhouse
600 East Superior Street
Duluth, MN 55802
GPS Coordinates: N 46°47.515'
W 92°05.510'
Established: 1997 (brewpub); 1995
(restaurant)
Production (approximate barrels/
year): 2,500 bbl (2010)
Website: www.brewhouse.net
E-mail: brew@brewhouse.net
Facebook: yes
Telephone: 218-279-2739
Gift Shop: yes
Mug Club: no
Growlers: yes
Tours: yes
Tasting: yes
Distribution: draft beers in Duluth
Makes Own Line of Soft Drinks: yes
Bar Toys: none
Bar Stools: 8
Beer Garden/Outside Seating: yes
Tourism: Duluth Convention and
Visitors Bureau, 800-4Duluth
[438-5884]
(www.visitduluth.com)

Lake Superior Brewing Company
2711 West Superior Street
Duluth, MN 55806
GPS Coordinates: N 46°45.662'
W 92°07.974'
Established: 1994
Production (approximate barrels/
year): 2000 bbl (2010)
Website:
www.lakesuperiorbrewing.com

E-mail:
info@lakesuperiorbrewing.com
Telephone: 218-723-4000
Gift Shop: yes
Mug Club: no
Growlers: yes
Tours: yes
Tasting: yes
Distribution: northern Minnesota and
northern Wisconsin
Makes Own Line of Soft Drinks: yes
(High Bridge Root Beer)
Bar Toys: none
Bar Stools: 3
Beer Garden/Outside Seating: no
Tourism: Duluth Convention and
Visitors Bureau, 800-4Duluth
[438-5884]
(www.visitduluth.com)

EAGAN
Granite City Food and Brewery
3330 Pilot Knob Road
Eagan, MN 55121
GPS Coordinates: N 44°50.198'
W 93°09.996'
Established: 2005 (store #10)
Production (approximate barrels/
year): 770 bbl (2010)
Website: www.gcfb.net
E-mail: egan@gcfb.net
Facebook: yes
Telephone: 651-452-4600
Gift Shop: yes
Mug Club: yes
Growlers: yes
Tours: yes
Tasting: yes
Distribution: bottled products in
Minnesota, Iowa, North Dakota,
and South Dakota
Makes Own Line of Soft Drinks: no
Bar Toys: none
Bar Stools: 15
Beer Garden/Outside Seating: yes
Tourism: Eagan Convention and
Visitors Bureau, 866-324-2620
or 651-675-5546
(www.eaganmn.com)

ELY
BoatHouse Brewpub and
Restaurant
47 East Sheridan Street
Ely, MN 55731
GPS Coordinates: N 47°54.199′
    W 91°51.944′
Established: 2008 (brewpub); 2007
    (restaurant)
Production (approximate barrels/
    year): 100 bbl (2010)
Website:
    www.boathousebrewpub.com
E-mail: boathouse@frontiernet.net
Facebook: yes
Telephone: 218-365-4301
Gift Shop: yes
Mug Club: no
Growlers: yes
Tours: yes
Tasting: yes
Distribution: through brewpub only
Makes Own Line of Soft Drinks: no
Bar Toys: pool table, dartboard
Bar Stools: ~12
Beer Garden/Outside Seating: no
Tourism: Ely Chamber of Commerce,
    800-777-7281 or 218-365-6123
    (www.ely.org)

HENDRICKS
Bank Beer Company
Hendricks, MN 56136
GPS Coordinates: N 44°30.354′
    W 96°25.550′
Established: 2009
Production (approximate barrels/
    year): brewed by the Cold
    Spring Brewing Company
Website: http://beerforwildlife.com
E-mail:
    jmarkkula@beerforwildlife.com
Facebook: yes
Telephone: not provided
Gift Shop: yes (see website)
Mug Club: no
Growlers: no
Tours: no
Tasting: no
Makes Own Line of Soft Drinks: no

Distribution: Minnesota and parts of
    North Dakota, South Dakota,
    Iowa, and western Wisconsin
Bar Toys: none
Bar Stools: none
Beer Garden/Outside Seating: no
Tourism: City of Hendricks,
    507-275-3192
    (www.hendricksmn.com)

LUCAN
Brau Brothers Brewing Company
201 First Street
Lucan, MN 56255
GPS Coordinates: N 44°24.653′
    W 95°24.474′
Established: 2006 (Brau Brothers
    Brewing Company); 2000 (Brau-
    haus brewpub); 1998 (Brauhaus
    restaurant)
Production (approximate barrels/
    year): 2,100 bbl (2010)
Website:
    www.braubrothersbrewing.com
E-mail: dustin@braubeer.com
Facebook: yes
Telephone: 507-747-BEER [2337]
Gift Shop: yes
Mug Club: no
Growlers: yes
Tours: yes
Tasting: yes
Distribution: Minnesota and parts of
    North Dakota, South Dakota,
    Iowa, Michigan, and Wisconsin
Makes Own Line of Soft Drinks: no
Bar Toys: none
Bar Stools: none
Beer Garden/Outside Seating: no
Tourism: Redwood Falls Area Cham-
    ber and Tourism, 800-657-7070
    or 507-637-2828
    (www.redwoodfalls.org)

MANKATO
Mankato Brewery
1119 Center Street
North Mankato, MN 56003
GPS Coordinates: N 44°10.952′
    W 94°00.835′

Established: 2011
Production (approximate barrels/
   year): no estimate available
Website: www.mankatobrewery.com
E-mail: info@mankatobrewery.com
Facebook: yes
Telephone: 507-386-2337
Gift Shop: yes
Mug Club: no
Growlers: yes
Tours: yes
Tasting: yes
Distribution: Mankato, its surround-
   ing counties, and select ac-
   counts in the Twin Cities
Makes Own Line of Soft Drinks: no
Bar Toys: none
Bar Stools: limited seating in the
   tasting area
Beer Garden/Outside Seating: no
Tourism: Greater Mankato Con-
   vention and Visitors Bureau,
   507-385-6660
   (www.greatermankato.com) and
   (www.visitgreatermankato.com)

MANTORVILLE
Mantorville Brewing Company
101 East Fifth Street
Mantorville, MN 55955
GPS Coordinates: N 44°04.002′
   W 92°45.222′
Established: 2002 (complete own-
   ership by Tod Fyten); 1996 (as
   current Mantorville Brewery)
Production (approximate barrels/
   year): 100 bbl (2010) of keg and
   growler production at this loca-
   tion; bottled products are made
   through arrangement with the
   Lake Superior Brewing Com-
   pany (Duluth)
Website: http://mantorvillebeer.com
E-mail: info@mantorvillebeer.com
Facebook: yes
Telephone: 651-387-0708
Gift Shop: yes
Mug Club: no
Growlers: yes
Tours: yes (call ahead)

Tasting: yes (call ahead)
Distribution: Minnesota
Produces Own Line of Soft Drinks:
   yes (Teddy's Root Beer)
Bar Toys: none
Bar Stools: ~2
Beer Garden/Outside Seating: no
Tourism: Mantorville Chamber of
   Commerce, 800-313-8687
   (www.mantorvilletourism.com/
   Mantorville_Tourism/Home.html)

MAPLE GROVE
Granite City Food and Brewery
11909 Main Street North
Maple Grove, MN 55369
GPS Coordinates: N 45°05.448′
   W 93°25.938′
Established: 2004 (store #10)
Production (approximate barrels/
   year): 971 bbl (2010)
Website: www.gcfb.net
E-mail: maplegrove@gcfb.net
Facebook: yes
Telephone: 763-416-0010
Gift Shop: yes
Mug Club: no
Growlers: yes
Tours: yes
Tasting: yes
Distribution: bottled products in
   Minnesota, Iowa, North Dakota,
   and South Dakota
Makes Own Line of Soft Drinks: no
Bar Toys: none
Bar Stools: 15
Beer Garden/Outside Seating: yes
Tourism: Maple Grove Chamber
   of Commerce / North Hennepin
   Area Chamber of Commerce,
   763-424-6744
   (www.nhachamber.com); City
   of Maple Grove, 763-494-6000
   (www.ci.maple-grove.mn.us)

MINNEAPOLIS
Bard's Tale Beer Company
P.O. Box 24835
Minneapolis, MN 55424

Also maintains a business office in
　　Plymouth, Minnesota
Established: 2005
Production (approximate barrels/
　　year): brewed by Matt Brewing
　　of Utica, New York
Website: www.bardsbeer.com
E-mail: info@bardsbeer.com
Facebook: yes
Telephone: 877-440-2337
Gift Shop: no
Mug Club: no
Growlers: no
Tours: no
Tasting: no
Distribution: 43 states
Makes Own Line of Soft Drinks: no
Bar Toys: none
Bar Stools: none
Beer Garden/Outside Seating: no

Boom Island Brewing Company
2207 2nd Street, North
Minneapolis, MN 55411
GPS Coordinates: N 45°00.097'
　　W 93°16.818'
Established: 2011
Production (approximate barrels/
　　year): no estimate available
Website:
　　www.boomislandbrewing.com
E-mail:
　　kevin@boomislandbrewing.com
Facebook: yes
Telephone: 612-227-9635
Gift Shop: yes
Mug Club: no
Growlers: yes
Tours: yes
Tasting: yes
Distribution: Twin Cities area
Makes Own Line of Soft Drinks: no
Bar Toys: none
Bar Stools: none
Beer Garden/Outside Seating: no
Tourism: Greater Minneapolis
　　Convention and Visitors Associ-
　　ation, 888-676-6757
　　(www.minneapolis.org)

Finnegans Inc.
619 South 10th Street, Suite 100
Minneapolis, MN 55404
GPS Coordinates: N 44°58.196'
　　W 93°15.957'
Established: 2000
Production (approximate barrels/
　　year): brewed by Summit Brew-
　　ing Company
Website: www.finnegans.org
E-mail: info@finnegans.org
Facebook: yes
Telephone: 763-315-6442
Gift Shop: no
Mug Club: no
Growlers: no
Tours: no
Tasting: no
Distribution: Minnesota and several
　　Upper Midwest states
Makes Own Line of Soft Drinks: no
Bar Toys: none
Bar Stools: none
Beer Garden/Outside Seating: no

Fulton Brewery
414 6th Avenue, North
Minneapolis, MN 55401
GPS Coordinates: N 44°59.088'
　　W 93°16.742'
Established: 2011 (Fulton Brewery
　　began operations in Minneapo-
　　lis); 2009 (Fulton Beer)
Production (approximate barrels/
　　year): 1,100 bbl (2010); bottled
　　products made by Sand Creek
　　Brewing Company
Website: http://fultonbeer.com
E-mail: info@fultonbeer.com
Facebook: yes
Telephone: 612-568-8416
Gift Shop: yes
Mug Club: no
Growlers: yes
Tours: yes
Tasting: yes
Distribution: Twin Cities
Bar Toys: none
Bar Stools: several seats in the tast-
　　ing area of brewery

Beer Garden/Outside Seating: no
Tourism: Greater Minneapolis
Convention and Visitors Association, 888-676-6757
(www.minneapolis.org)

Harriet Brewing
3036 Minnehaha Avenue
Minneapolis, MN 55406
GPS Coordinates: N 44°56.832′
W 93°14.012′
Established: 2011
Production (approximate barrels/
year): 600 bbl (2011)
Website: www.harrietbrewing.com
E-mail: info@harrietbrewing.com
Facebook: yes
Telephone: 612-225-2184
Gift Shop: yes
Mug Club: no
Growlers: yes
Tours: yes (call ahead)
Tasting: yes
Distribution: Twin Cities
Makes Own Line of Soft Drinks: no
Bar Toys: none
Bar Stools: none
Beer Garden/Outside Seating: no
Tourism: Minneapolis Chamber
of Commerce, 612-370-9100
(www.minneapolischamber.org);
Longfellow Neighborhood,
(www.ci.minneapolis.mn.us/
neighborhoods/longfellow
_profile_home.asp)

Herkimer Pub and Brewery
2922 Lyndale Avenue, South
Minneapolis, MN 55408
GPS Coordinates: N 44°56.961′
W 93°17.301′
Established: 1999
Production (approximate barrels/
year): 790 bbl (2010)
Website: http://theherkimer.com
E-mail: info@theherkimer.com
Facebook: yes
Telephone: 612-821-0101
Gift Shop: yes

Mug Club: no
Growlers: no
Tours: yes
Tasting: yes
Distribution: through brewpub only
Makes Own Line of Soft Drinks: yes
(Triplecaff, energy drink)
Bar Toys: shuffleboard
Bar Stools: 35
Beer Garden/Outside Seating: yes
Tourism: Greater Minneapolis
Convention and Visitors Associ-
ation, 888-676-6757
(www.minneapolis.org)

Lakemaid Beer Company
(parent company, Pocket Hercules)
510 First Avenue North, Suite 210
Minneapolis, MN 55403
GPS Coordinates: N 44°58.809′
W 93°16.455′
Established: 2008
Production (approximate barrels/
year): brewed by the August
Schell Brewing Company in
New Ulm
Website: www.lakemaidbeer.com
E-mail:
brewmaster@lakemaidbeer.com
Facebook: yes
Telephone: 612-435-8313
Gift Shop: yes (see website)
Mug Club: no
Growlers: no
Tours: no
Tasting: no
Distribution: Lakes areas of Minne-
sota, Iowa, Michigan, Nebraska,
North Dakota, South Dakota,
and Wisconsin.
Makes Own Line of Soft Drinks: no
Bar Toys: none
Bar Stools: none
Beer Garden/Outside Seating: no
Tourism: Greater Minneapolis Con-
vention and Visitors Association,
888-676-6757
(www.minneapolis.org)

Minneapolis Town Hall Brewery
1430 Washington Avenue South
Minneapolis, MN 54454
GPS Coordinates: N 44°58.395'
    W 93°14.863'
Established: 1997
Production (approximate barrels/
    year): 1,200 bbl (2011)
Website: www.townhallbrewery.com
E-mail: info@townhallbrewery.com
Facebook: yes
Telephone: 612-339-8696
Gift Shop: yes
Mug Club: no
Growlers: yes
Tours: yes
Tasting: yes
Distribution: through brewpub and
    select draft accounts
Makes Own Line of Soft Drinks: yes
    (root beer)
Bar Toys: pool table, dartboards
Bar Stools: 20
Beer Garden/Outside Seating: yes
Tourism: Greater Minneapolis
    Convention and Visitors Associ-
    ation, 888-676-6757
    (www.minneapolis.org)

**Rock Bottom Restaurant and
Brewery**
800 LaSalle Plaza
Minneapolis, MN 55402
GPS Coordinates: N 44°58.579'
    W 93°16.589'
Established: 1993 (store #3); 1991
    (Rock Bottom's first brewpub)
Production (approximate barrels/
    year): 1,330 bbl (2010)
Website: www.rockbottom.com
E-mail:
    minneapolis@rockbottom.com
Facebook: yes
Telephone: 612-332-2739
Gift Shop: yes
Mug Club: yes
Growlers: yes
Tours: yes
Tasting: yes
Distribution: through brewpub only

Makes Own Line of Soft Drinks: yes
    (sarsaparilla)
Bar Toys: 5 pool tables, dartboard,
    video games, Internet access
Bar Stools: 20
Beer Garden/Outside Seating: yes
Tourism: Greater Minneapolis
    Convention and Visitors Associ-
    ation, 888-676-6757
    (www.minneapolis.org)

MINNETONKA
Lucid Brewing Company
6020 Culligan Way
Minnetonka, MN 55345
GPS Coordinates: N 44°53.703'
    W 93°26.961'
Established: 2011
Production (approximate barrels/
    year): no estimate available
Website: www.lucidbrewing.com
E-mail: info@lucidbrewing.com
Facebook: yes
Telephone: 612-810-9324
Gift Shop: yes
Mug Club: no
Growlers: yes
Tours: yes (call ahead)
Tasting: yes (call ahead)
Distribution: southwest Twin Cities
Makes Own Line of Soft Drinks: no
Bar Toys: none
Bar Stools: none
Beer Garden/Outside Seating: no
Tourism: City of Minnetonka,
    952-939-8200
    (www.eminnetonka.com)

NEW BRIGHTON
Barley John's Brew Pub
781 Old Highway 8 Southwest
New Brighton, MN 55112
GPS Coordinates: N 45°02.165'
    W 93°11.904'
Established: 2000
Production (approximate barrels/
    year): 750 bbl (2010)
Website: www.barleyjohns.com
E-mail: info@barleyjohns.com
Facebook: yes

Telephone: 651-636-4670
Gift Shop: yes
Mug Club: yes (Barley Beer Society)
Growlers: yes
Tours: yes
Tasting: yes
Distribution: through brewpub only
Makes Own Line of Soft Drinks: no
Bar Toys: none
Bar Stools: 5
Beer Garden/Outside Seating: yes
Tourism: New Brighton Mounds
Chamber of Commerce,
651-631-1906
(www.ci.new-brighton.mn.us)

NEW ULM
August Schell Brewing Company
P.O. Box 128
1860 Schell Road
New Ulm, MN 56073
GPS Coordinates: N 44°17.413′
W 94°26.910′
Established: 1860
Production (approximate barrels/
year): 116,000 bbl (2010)
Website: www.schellsbrewery.com
E-mail: schells@schellsbrewery.com
Facebook: yes
Telephone: 507-354-5528 or
800-770-5020
Gift Shop: yes
Mug Club: no
Growlers: no
Tours: yes
Tasting: yes
Distribution: the Midwest
Makes Own Line of Soft Drinks: yes
(1919 Root Beer and Buddy's
Sodas)
Bar Toys: none
Bar Stools: none, but German Beer-
hall tasting room
Beer Garden/Outside Seating: no
Tourism: New Ulm Area Chamber
of Commerce/Visitors Informa-
tion Center, 888-463-9856 or
507-233-4300
(www.newulm.com)

ROLLINGSTONE
**Olvalde Farm and Brewing
Company**
16557 County Road 25
Rollingstone, MN 55969
GPS Coordinates: N 44°05.642′
W 91°48.566′
Established: 2011
Production (approximate barrels/
year): 500 barrels (2011)
Website: www.olvalde.com
E-mail: info@olvalde.com
Telephone: 507-205-4969
Gift Shop: yes (see website)
Mug Club: no
Growlers: no
Tours: very limited (call ahead)
Tasting: very limited (call ahead)
Distribution: 750mL bottles in
Twin Cities and southwestern
Minnesota
Makes Own Line of Soft Drinks: no
Bar Toys: none
Bar Stools: none
Beer Garden/Outside Seating: no
Tourism: Winona Area Chamber of
Commerce, 507-452-2272
(www.winonachamber.com)

ROSEVILLE
Granite City Food and Brewery
851 Rosedale Center
Roseville, MN 55113
GPS Coordinates: N 45°00.773′
W 93°10.157′
Established: 2006 (store #17)
Production (approximate barrels/
year): 870 bbl (2010)
Website: www.gcfb.net
E-mail: roseville@gcfb.net
Facebook: yes
Telephone: 651-209-3500
Gift Shop: yes
Mug Club: yes
Growlers: yes
Tours: yes
Tasting: yes
Distribution: bottled products in Min-
nesota, Iowa, North Dakota, and
South Dakota

Makes Own Line of Soft Drinks: no
Bar Toys: none
Bar Stools: 15
Beer Garden/Outside Seating: yes
Tourism: Roseville Visitors Association, 651-633-3002
(www.visitroseville.com)

Pour Decisions Brewing Company
1744 Terrace Drive
Roseville, MN 55113
GPS Coordinates: N 45°01.460′
W 93°10.445′
Established: 2011
Production (approximate barrels/year): 800 bbl (2011)
Website:
http://pourdecisionsbrewery.com
E-mail:
info@pourdecisionsbrewery.com
Facebook: yes
Telephone: 651-56POUR1
[567-6871]
Gift Shop: yes
Mug Club: yes (frequent growler club)
Growlers: yes
Tours: yes
Tasting: yes
Distribution: Twin Cities area
Makes Own Line of Soft Drinks: yes
Bar Toys: none
Bar Stools: ~15, with additional seating in tasting room
Beer Garden/Outside Seating: no
Tourism: Roseville Visitors Association, 651-633-3002
(www.visitroseville.com)

ST. CLOUD
Granite City Food and Brewery
3945 2nd Street South
St. Cloud, MN 56301
GPS Coordinates: N 45°33.017′
W 94°12.385′
Established: 1999 (store #1)
Production (approximate barrels/year): 777 bbl (2010)
Website: www.gcfb.net
E-mail: st.cloud@gcfb.net

Telephone: 320-203-9000
Gift Shop: yes
Mug Club: yes
Growlers: yes
Tours: yes
Tasting: yes
Distribution: bottled products in Minnesota, Iowa, North Dakota, and South Dakota
Makes Own Line of Soft Drinks: no
Bar Toys: none
Bar Stools: 30
Beer Garden/Outside Seating: yes
Tourism: St. Cloud Area Convention and Visitors Bureau, 320-251-4170
(www.granitecountry.com)

McCann's Food and Brew
3308 3rd Street North
St. Cloud, MN 56303
GPS Coordinates: N 45°33.501′
W 94°11.940′
Established: 2007 (McCann's); 1996 (as OHara's)
Production (approximate barrels/year): 150 bbl (2010)
Website:
http://mccannsfoodandbrewpub.com
E-mail: yes (see website)
Facebook: yes
Telephone: 320-217-5800
Gift Shop: yes
Mug Club: yes
Growlers: yes
Tours: yes
Tasting: yes
Distribution: through brewpub only
Makes Own Line of Soft Drinks: no
Bar toys: pool tables, dartboards, shuffleboard
Bar stools: 3 bars, each with 10 to 15 barstools
Beer garden/outside seating: no
Tourism: St. Cloud Area Convention and Visitors Bureau, 320-251-4170
(www.granitecountry.com)

ST. LOUIS PARK
Granite City Food and Brewery
5500 Excelsior Boulevard
St. Louis Park, MN 55416
GPS Coordinates: N 44°55.903'
    W 93°20.938'
Established: 2006 (store #15)
Production (approximate barrels/
    year): 785 bbl (2010)
Website: www.gcfb.net
E-mail: st.louispark@gcfb.net
Facebook: yes
Telephone: 952-746-9900
Gift Shop: yes
Mug Club: yes
Growlers: yes
Tours: yes
Tasting: yes
Distribution: bottled products in Min-
    nesota, Iowa, North Dakota, and
    South Dakota
Makes Own Line of Soft Drinks: no
Bar Toys: none
Bar Stools: 30
Beer Garden/Outside Seating: yes
Tourism: City of St. Louis Park,
    952-924-2500 (www.stlouis-
    park.org); TwinWest Chamber of
    Commerce, 763-450-2220
    (www.twinwest.com)

Steel Toe Brewing Company
4848 35th Street, West
St. Louis Park, MN 55416
GPS Coordinates: N 44°56.478'
    W 93°20.469'
Established: 2011
Production (approximate barrels/
    year): no estimate available
Website: www.steeltoebrewing.com
E-mail: brewer@steeltoebrewing.com
Facebook: yes
Telephone: 952-955-9965
Gift Shop: yes
Mug Club: yes (frequent growler
    club)
Growlers: yes
Tours: yes
Tasting: yes
Distribution: Twin Cities area

Makes Own Line of Soft Drinks: no
Bar Toys: none
Bar Stools: limited seating in tasting
    room
Beer Garden/Outside Seating: no
Tourism: City of St. Louis Park,
    952-924-2500 (www.stlouis-
    park.org); TwinWest Chamber of
    Commerce, 763-450-2220
    (www.twinwest.com)

ST. PAUL
Blue Diamond Brewing Company
25 North Dale Street, #112
St. Paul, MN 55102
GPS Coordinates: N 44°56.523'
    W 93°07.570'
Established: 2002 (labels pur-
    chased from Minnesota Brewing
    Company)
Production (approximate barrels/
    year): brewed by Cold Spring
    Brewing Company
Website:
    www.bluediamondbrewingco
    .com
E-mail: info@bluediamondbrewingco
    .com
Facebook: yes
Telephone: 651-216-7550 or
    651-221-0899
Gift Shop: yes (see website)
Mug Club: no
Growlers: no
Tours: no
Tasting: no
Distribution: Minnesota
Makes Own Lines of Soft Drinks: no
Bar Toys: none
Bar Stools: none
Beer Garden/Outside Seating: no
Tourism: St. Paul Convention and
    Visitors Bureau, 651-265-4900
    or 800-627-6101
    (www.visitsaintpaul.com);
    St. Paul Chamber of Commerce,
    651-223-5000
    (www.saintpaulchamber.com);
    general event information (www
    .downtownstpaul.com)

Flat Earth Brewing Company
2035 Benson Avenue
St. Paul, MN 55116
GPS Coordinates: N 44°54.496'
    W 93°09.267'
Established: 2007
Production (approximate barrels/
    year): 774 bbl (2010)
Website: www.flatearthbrewing.com
E-mail:
    brewer@flatearthbrewing.com
Facebook: yes
Telephone: 651-698-1945
Gift Shop: yes
Mug Club: no
Growlers: yes
Tours: yes (see website)
Tasting: yes (see website)
Distribution: central Minnesota
Makes Own Line of Soft Drinks:
    occasionally
Bar Toys: none
Bar Stools: none
Beer Garden/Outside Seating: no
Tourism: St. Paul Convention and
    Visitors Bureau, 651-265-4900
    or 800-627-6101
    (www.visitsaintpaul.com);
    St. Paul Chamber of Commerce,
    651-223-5000
    (www.saintpaulchamber.com);
    general event information
    (www.downtownstpaul.com)

Great Waters Brewing Company
426 St. Peter Street
St. Paul, MN 55102
GPS Coordinates: N 44°56.804'
    W 93°05.827'
Established: 1997
Production (approximate barrels/
    year): 650 bbl (2010)
Website: www.greatwatersbc.com
E-mail: yes (see website)
Facebook: yes
Telephone: 651-224-2739
Gift Shop: yes
Mug Club: yes (Masters of Beer Ap-
    preciation, MBA)
Growlers: yes

Tours: yes
Tasting: yes
Distribution: through brewpub only
Makes Own Line of Soft Drinks: yes
    (root beer)
Bar Toys: none
Bar Stools: 10
Beer Garden/Outside Seating: yes
Tourism: St. Paul Convention and
    Visitors Bureau, 651-265-4900
    or 800-627-6101
    (www.visitsaintpaul.com);
    St. Paul Chamber of Commerce,
    651-223-5000
    (www.saintpaulchamber.com);
    general event information
    (www.downtownstpaul.com)

St. Croix Brewing Company
P.O. Box 16545
St. Paul, MN 55116
Offices currently co-located with
    Theodore Fyten Brewing
    Company
363 Webster Street
St. Paul, MN 55102
GPS Coordinates: N 44°55.803'
    W 93°07.480'
Established: 2003 (ownership by Tod
    Fyten); 1995 (by Karl Bremer)
Production (approximate barrels/
    year): 20 bbl (2010) of keg and
    growler production at Mantor-
    ville Brewing Company; bottled
    products are made through ar-
    rangement with the Lake Supe-
    rior Brewing Company
Website: http://stcroixbeer.com
E-mail: tod@stcroixbeer.com
Facebook: no
Telephone: 651-387-0708
Gift Shop: yes (see website)
Mug Club: no
Growlers: yes
Tours: not regular (call ahead)
Tasting: not regular (call ahead)
Distribution: Minnesota
Makes Own Line of Soft Drinks: yes
    (Teddy's Root Beer)
Bar Toys: none

Bar Stools: none
Beer Garden/Outside Seating: no
Tourism: St. Paul Convention and
  Visitors Bureau, 651-265-4900
  or 800-627-6101
  (www.visitsaintpaul.com);
  St. Paul Chamber of Commerce,
  651-223-5000
  (www.saintpaulchamber.com);
  general event information
  (www.downtownstpaul.com)

Summit Brewing Company
910 Montreal Circle
St. Paul, MN 55102
GPS Coordinates: N 44°54.798'
  W 93°08.424'
Established: 1986
Production (approximate barrels/
  year): 100,000 bbl (2010)
Website: www.summitbrewing.com
E-mail: info@summitbrewing.com
Facebook: yes
Telephone: 651-265-7800
Gift Shop: yes
Mug Club: no
Growlers: no
Tours: yes (call ahead and see
  website)
Tasting: yes
Distribution: Minnesota and
  regionally
Makes Own Line of Soft Drinks: no
Bar Toys: none
Bar Stools: 12, with large tasting
  room
Beer Garden/Outside Seating: yes
Tourism: St. Paul Convention and
  Visitors Bureau, 651-265-4900
  or 800-627-6101
  (www.visitsaintpaul.com);
  St. Paul Chamber of Commerce,
  651-223-5000
  (www.saintpaulchamber.com);
  general event information
  (www.downtownstpaul.com)

Theodore Fyten Brewing Company
363 Webster Street
St. Paul, MN 55102

GPS Coordinates: N 44°55.803'
  W 93°07.480'
Established: 1999
Production (approximate barrels/
  year): 30 bbl (2010) of keg and
  growler production at Mantor-
  ville Brewing Company; bottled
  products are made through ar-
  rangement with the Lake Supe-
  rior Brewing Company
Website: http://fytenburgbeer.com
E-mail: info@fytenburgbeer.com
Facebook: no
Telephone: 651-387-0708
Gift Shop: yes (see website)
Mug Club: no
Growlers: yes
Tours: not regular (call ahead)
Tasting: not regular (call ahead)
Distribution: Minnesota
Makes Own Line of Soft Drinks: yes
  (Teddy's Root Beer)
Bar Toys: none
Bar Stools: none
Beer Garden/Outside Seating: no
Tourism: St. Paul Convention and
  Visitors Bureau, 651-265-4900
  or 800-627-6101
  (www.visitsaintpaul.com);
  St. Paul Chamber of Commerce,
  651-223-5000
  (www.saintpaulchamber.com);
  general event information
  (www.downtownstpaul.com)

Vine Park Brewing Company
1254 West 7th Street
St. Paul, MN 55102
GPS Coordinates: N 44°55.344'
  W 93°08.085'
Established: 2004 (by Andy Grage
  and Dan Justesen); 1995 (by
  David Thompson)
Production (approximate barrels/
  year): 100 bbl (2010)
Website: www.vinepark.com
E-mail: andy@vinepark.com
Facebook: yes
Telephone: 651-228-1355
Gift Shop: yes

Mug Club: no
Growlers: yes
Tours: yes
Tasting: no
Distribution: growlers only through
Vine Park
Makes Own Line of Soft Drinks: yes
(root beer and cream soda)
Bar Toys: none
Bar Stools: none
Beer Garden/Outside Seating: no
Tourism: St. Paul Convention and
Visitors Bureau, 651-265-4900
or 800-627-6101
(www.visitsaintpaul.com);
St. Paul Chamber of Commerce,
651-223-5000
(www.saintpaulchamber.com);
general event information
(www.downtownstpaul.com)

SLEEPY EYE
Hauenstein Beer
120 7th Avenue Northeast
Sleepy Eye, MN 56085
GPS Coordinates: N 44°17.932'
W 94°42.805'
Established: 1996 (label acquired by
Al and Rae Ann Arneson); 1864
(dates back to the John Hauen-
stein Brewery of New Ulm)
Production (approximate barrels/
year): brewed by August Schell
Brewing Company
Websites: www.hauensteinbeer.com,
arnesondistributing.com
E-mail: schells@schellsbrewery.com
Facebook: yes
Telephone: 507-794-7472
Gift Shop: no
Mug Club: no
Growlers: no
Tours: no
Tasting: no
Distribution: central Minnesota
Makes Own Line of Soft Drinks: yes
(Buddy's Sodas and 1919 Root
Beer with August Schell Brewing
of New Ulm)
Bar Toys: none

Bar Stools: none
Beer Garden/Outside Seating: no
Tourism: New Ulm Area Chamber
of Commerce/Visitors Information Center, 888-463-9856 or
507-233-4300
(www.newulm.com)

STILLWATER
Lift Bridge Brewery
1900 Tower Drive
Stillwater, MN 55082
GPS Coordinates: N 45°02.336'
W 92°49.905'
Established: 2011 (Lift Bridge Brew-
ery); 2008 (Lift Bridge Beer
Company)
Production (approximate barrels/
year): 2,000 bbl (2010); bottled
products made by Cold Spring
Brewing Company
Website: www.liftbridgebrewery.com
E-mail: see website or
Sales@LiftBridgeBrewery.com
Facebook: yes
Telephone: 888-430-2337
Gift Shop: yes
Mug Club: no
Growlers: yes
Tours: yes
Tasting: yes
Distribution: Minnesota and western
Wisconsin
Makes Own Line of Soft Drinks: no
Bar Toys: none
Bar Stools: 3
Beer Garden/Outside Seating: no
Tourism: Greater Stillwater Chamber
of Commerce, 651-439-4001
(www.ilovestillwater.com)

Stillwater Brewing Company
402 Main Street, North
Stillwater, MN 55082
GPS Coordinates: N 45°03.563'
W 92°48.435'
Established: 2011
Production (approximate barrels/
year): no estimate available

Website:
www.stillwaterbrewingco.com
E-mail:
info@stillwaterbrewingco.com
Facebook: yes
Telephone: 651-472-5552
Gift Shop: yes
Mug Club: yes (frequent growler
club)
Growlers: yes
Tours: yes
Tasting: yes
Distribution: Stillwater area
Makes Own Line of Soft Drinks: no
Bar Toys: none
Bar Stools: none
Beer Garden/Outside Seating: no
Tourism: Greater Stillwater Chamber
of Commerce, 651-439-4001
(www.ilovestillwater.com)

TWO HARBORS
Castle Danger Brewery
3067 East Castle Danger Road
Two Harbors, MN 55616
GPS Coordinates: N 47°06.759'
W 91°32.419'
Established: 2011
Production (approximate barrels/
year): no estimate available
Website:
www.castledangerbrewery.com
E-mail:
castledangerbrewery@frontier
.com
Facebook: yes
Telephone: 218-834-5800
Gift Shop: yes
Mug Club: no
Growlers: yes
Tours: yes (call ahead)
Tasting: yes (call ahead)
Distribution: Two Harbors to Duluth
Makes Own Line of Soft Drinks: yes
Bar Toys: none
Bar Stools: none
Beer Garden/Outside Seating: no
Tourism: Two Harbors Area Chamber
of Commerce, 218-834-6200
(www.twoharborschamber.com)

WALKER
Leech Lake Brewing Company
P.O. Box 1364
195 Walker Industries Boulevard
Walker, MN 56484
GPS Coordinates: N 47°06.168'
W 94°36.788'
Established: 2010
Production: (approximate barrels/
year): 900 bbl (2011)
Website:
http://leechlakebrewing.com
E-mail:
brewmaster@leechlakebrewing
.com
Facebook: yes
Telephone: 218-507-4746
Gift Shop: yes
Mug Club: no
Growlers: yes
Tours: yes
Tasting: yes
Distribution: Leech Lake area and
parts of northern Minnesota
Makes Own Line of Soft Drinks: no
Bar Toys: none
Bar Stools: none; tasting room
Beer Garden/Outside Seating: no
Tourism: Leech Lake Tourism
Bureau, 800-735-3297
(www.leechlake.org)

WINONA
Backwater Brewing Company
1429 West Service Drive (Westgate
Shopping Center)
Winona, MN 55987
GPS Coordinates: N 44°02.881'
W 91°40.546'
Established: 1995
Production (approximate barrels/
year): 125 bbl (2010)
Website:
www.westgatewellingtons.com/
Wellingtons/BrewPub.html
E-mail: see website or
cc-gardy@hotmail.com
Facebook: yes
Telephone: 507-452-2103
Gift Shop: no

Mug Club: no
Growlers: no
Tours: not regular (call ahead)
Tasting: yes
Distribution: through brewpub only
Makes Own Line of Soft Drinks: yes
(root beer)
Bar Toys: attached bowling alley
Bar Stools: ~20
Beer Garden/Outside Seating: yes
Tourism: Winona Area Chamber of
Commerce, 507-452-2272
(www.winonachamber.com)

WOODBURY
Pig's Eye Brewing Company
World Headquarters (not a brewery)
10107 Bridgewater Parkway
Woodbury, MN 55129
GPS Coordinates: N 44°55.357'
W 92°54.067'
Established: 2002 (by Phil Gagné
and Jeff Crawford); 1992 (origi-
nally developed by Minnesota
Brewing Company)

Production (approximate barrels/
year): brewed by City Brewery in
La Crosse, Wisconsin
Website: www.pigseyebeer.com
E-mail:
pierreparrant@pigseyebeer.com
Facebook: yes
Telephone: 651-734-1661
Gift Shop: yes (see website)
Mug Club: no
Growlers: yes
Tours: yes
Tasting: yes
Distribution: Minnesota and 15-plus
other states
Makes Own Line of Soft Drinks: no
Bar Toys: none
Bar Stools: none
Beer Garden/Outside Seating: no
Tourism: Woodbury Chamber of
Commerce, 651-578-0722
(www.woodburychamber.org)

Directory of Just Over the Border Breweries and Brewpubs

ASHLAND, WISCONSIN
South Shore Brewery
808 West Main Street
Ashland, WI 54806
GPS Coordinates: N 46°35.243'
W 90°53.542'
Established: 1995
Production (approximate barrels/year): 1,200 bbl (2010)
Website:
www.southshorebrewery.com
Facebook: yes
E-mail:
southshorebrewery@charter internet.com
Telephone: 715-682-4200 or 715-682-9199
Gift Shop: yes
Mug Club: no
Growlers: yes
Tours: yes
Tasting: yes
Distribution: Wisconsin and Minnesota
Makes Own Line of Soft Drinks: no
Bar Toys: game room with dart boards and pool table
Bar Stools: about 10 in Deep Water Grille and about 30 in The Alley
Beer Garden/Outside Seating: no
Tourism: Ashland Chamber of Commerce, 715-682-2500 (www.visitashland.com)

BLACK RIVER FALLS, WISCONSIN
Sand Creek Brewing Company
320 Pierce Street
Black River Falls, WI 54615
GPS Coordinates: N 44°17.563'
W 90°51.116'
Established: 2004 (Sand Creek purchased Pioneer Brewing Company and the two operate in the Black River Falls location); 1999 (Sand Creek Brewing Company, Downing); 1995 (Pioneer Brewing Company, Black River Falls)
Production (approximate barrels/year): 7,200 bbl (2010)
Website:
www.sandcreekbrewing.com
E-mail: see website
Facebook: yes
Telephone: 715-284-7553
Gift Shop: yes
Mug Club: no
Growlers: yes
Tours: yes
Tasting: yes
Distribution: regionally depending upon the brands
Makes Own Line of Soft Drinks: no
Bar Toys: none
Bar Stools: ~6
Beer Garden/Outside Seating: no
Tourism: Black River Area Chamber of Commerce, 800-404-4008 (http://blackrivercountry.net)

DECORAH, IOWA
Toppling Goliath Brewing Company
310 College Drive (taproom location)
Decorah, IA 52101
GPS Coordinates: N 43°18.497'
W 91°47.830'
Established: 2010 (production brew-
ery); 2009 (small brewery and
taproom)
Production (approximate barrels/
year): 225 bbl (2010)
Website: www.tgbrews.com
E-mail: barb@tgbrews.com;
chelsea@tgbrews.com
Facebook: yes
Telephone: 563-387-6700
Gift Shop: yes
Mug Club: yes (frequent growler
club)
Growlers: yes
Tours: yes (call ahead for tours of
production brewery)
Tasting: yes
Distribution: Decorah and northeast
Iowa
Makes Own Line of Soft Drinks: no
Bar Toys: none
Bar Stools: ~8–10
Beer Garden/Outside Seating: yes
Tourism: Decorah Area Chamber of
Commerce, (563) 382-3990 or
800-463-4692
(www.decoraharea.com);
Winneshiek County Convention
& Visitors Bureau, 800-463-4692
(www.visitiowa.org/winneshiek
.html)

FARGO, NORTH DAKOTA
Granite City Food and Brewery
1636 42nd Street
Fargo, ND 58103
GPS Coordinates: N 46°51.353'
W 96°51.032'
Established: 2001 (store #3)
Production (approximate barrels/
year): 786 bbl (2010)
Website: www.gcfb.net
E-mail: fargo@gcfb.net
Facebook: yes
Telephone: 701-293-3000
Gift Shop: yes
Mug Club: yes
Growlers: yes
Tours: yes
Tasting: yes
Distribution: bottled products in
North Dakota, South Dakota,
Iowa, and Minnesota
Makes Own Line of Soft Drinks: no
Bar Toys: none
Bar Stools: ~ 30
Beer Garden/Outside Seating: yes
Tourism: Fargo-Moorhead Con-
vention and Visitors Bureau,
800-235-7654 or 701-282-3653
(www.fargomoorhead.org)

LA CROSSE, WISCONSIN
City Brewing Company
925 South 3rd Street
La Crosse, WI 54601
GPS Coordinates: N 43°48.184'
W 91°15.207'
Established: 2006 (current owner-
ship); 1864 (original John Gund's
City Brewery)
Production (approximate barrels/
year): no estimate available
Website: www.citybrewery.com
E-mail: inquiries@citybrewery.com
Facebook: yes
Telephone: 608-785-4200
Gift Shop: yes
Mug Club: no
Growlers: no
Tours: yes
Tasting: yes
Distribution: several contract brands
with international distribution
Makes Own Line of Soft Drinks: no
Bar Toys: none
Bar Stools: none
Beer Garden/Outside Seating: no
Tourism: La Crosse Area Con-
vention and Visitors Bureau,
800-658-9424 or 608-782-2366
(www.explorelacrosse.com)

Pearl Street Brewery
1401 Saint Andrew Street
La Crosse, WI 54603
GPS Coordinates: N 43°50.053′
   W 91°14.193′
Established: 2007 (current location);
   1999 (original location at 4th and
   Pearl)
Production (approximate barrels/
   year): 1,083 bbl (2010)
Website:
   www.pearlstreetbrewery.com
E-mail: info@pearlstreetbrewery.com
Facebook: yes
Telephone: 608-784-4832
Gift Shop: yes
Mug Club: no
Growlers: yes
Tours: yes
Tasting: yes
Distribution: La Crosse and southern
   Wisconsin
Makes Own Line of Soft Drinks: no
Bar Toys: Ping-Pong and foosball
   tables
Bar Stools: 10
Beer Garden/Outside Seating: yes
Tourism: La Crosse Area Con-
   vention and Visitors Bureau,
   800-658-9424 or 608-782-2366
   (www.explorelacrosse.com)

MENOMONIE, WISCONSIN
Das Bierhaus
120 6th Avenue, West
Menomonie, WI 54751
GPS Coordinates: N 44°52.632′
   W 91°55.838′
Established: 2006
Production (approximate barrels/
   year): 200 bbl (2010)
Website: www.dasbierhaus-wi.com
E-mail: bavarianbrewery@gmail.com
Facebook: yes
Telephone: 715-231-3230
Gift Shop: yes
Mug Club: yes
Growlers: yes
Tours: yes
Tasting: yes

Distribution: through brewpub only
Makes Own Line of Soft Drinks: yes
   (root beer)
Bar Toys: none
Bar Stools: ~15
Beer Garden/Outside Seating: no
Tourism: Greater Menomonie
   Area Chamber of Commerce,
   715-235-9087
   (www.menomoniechamber.org)

Lucette Brewing Company
910 Hudson Road
Menomonie, WI 54751
GPS Coordinates: N 44°52.520′
   W 91°56.410′
Established: 2010
Production (approximate barrels/
   year): 3,000 bbl (2011)
Website: www.lucettebrewing.com
E-mail: info@lucettebrewing.com
Facebook: yes
Telephone: 715-233-2055
Gift Shop: yes (see website)
Mug Club: no
Growlers: no
Tours: yes
Tasting: yes
Distribution: western Wisconsin and
   Twin Cities area
Makes Own Line of Soft Drinks: no
Bar Toys: none
Bar Stools: none
Beer Garden/Outside Seating: no
Tourism: Greater Menomonie
   Area Chamber of Commerce,
   715-235-9087
   (www.menomoniechamber.org)

NEW RICHMOND, WISCONSIN
Brady's Brewhouse
230 South Knowles Avenue
New Richmond, WI 54017
GPS Coordinates: N 45°07.235′
   W 92°32.250′
Established: 2011 (brewpub); 2010
   (restaurant)
Production (approximate barrels/
   year): no estimate available

Website:
www.bradysbrewhouse.com
E-mail: info@bradysbrewhouse.com
Facebook: yes
Telephone: 715-246-9960
Gift Shop: yes
Mug Club: yes (loyalty club)
Growlers: yes
Tours: yes
Tasting: yes
Distribution: through brewpub only
Makes Owl Line of Soft Drinks: yes
(root beer)
Bar Toys: dart boards, video games,
hockey table
Bar Stools: ~20
Beer Garden/Outside Seating: no
Tourism: New Richmond Area
Chamber and Visitors Bureau,
715-246-2900 or 800-654-6380
(www.newrichmondchamber
.com)

NORTHWOOD, IOWA
Worth Brewing Company
826 Central Avenue
Northwood, IA 50459
GPS Coordinates: N 43°26.638'
W 93°13.204'
Established: 2007
Production (approximate barrels/
year): 73 bbl (2010)
Website: www.worthbrewing.com
E-mail: brewer@worthbrewing.com
Facebook: yes
Telephone: 641-324-9899
Gift Shop: yes
Mug Club: yes
Growlers: yes
Tours: yes
Tasting: yes
Distribution: through brewpub only
Makes Own Line of Soft Drinks: no
Bar Toys: none
Bar Stools: ~2–4
Beer Garden/Outside Seating: no
Tourism: Northwood Area Chamber
of Commerce, 641-324-1075
(www.northwoodchamber.org)

POTOSI, WISCONSIN
Potosi Brewing Company
209 South Main Street
Potosi, WI 53820
GPS Coordinates: N 42°40.491'
W 90°43.573'
Established: 2008 (brewpub); 1852
(original brewery)
Production (approximate barrels/
year): 1,600 bbl (2010)
Website: www.potosibrewery.com
E-mail: info@potosibrewery.com
Facebook: yes
Telephone: 608-763-4002
Gift Shop: yes
Mug Club: yes
Growlers: yes
Tours: yes
Tasting: yes
Distribution: Wisconsin
Makes Own Line of Soft Drinks: yes
(Princess Potosa Root Beer)
Bar Toys: none
Bar Stools: ~12
Beer Garden/Outside Seating: yes
Tourism: Potosi/Tennyson Chamber
of Commerce, 608-763-2261
(www.potosiwisconsin.com)

RIVER FALLS, WISCONSIN
Rush River Brewing Company
990 Antler Court
River Falls, WI 54022
GPS Coordinates: N 44°53.465'
W 92°38.304'
Established: 2007 (current location);
2004 (began in Maiden Rock,
Wisconsin)
Production (approximate barrels/
year): 4,000 bbl (2010)
Website: www.rushriverbeer.com
E-mail: info@rushriverbeer.com
Facebook: yes
Telephone: 715-426-2054
Gift Shop: yes
Mug Club: no
Growlers: yes
Tours: yes (call ahead and see
website)

Tasting: yes
Distribution: Twin Cities and parts of
    southern Wisconsin
Makes Own Line of Soft Drinks: no
Bar Toys: none
Bar Stools: none
Beer Garden/Outside Seating: no
Tourism: River Falls Area Chamber
    of Commerce and Tourism
    Bureau, 715-425-2533
    (www.rfchamber.com/
    TourismHome.htm)

SIOUX FALLS, SOUTH DAKOTA
Granite City Food and Brewery
2620 South Louise Avenue
Sioux Falls, SD 57104
GPS Coordinates: N 43°31.277′
    W 96°46.298′
Established: 2000 (store #2)
Production (approximate barrels/
    year): 868 bbl (2010)
Website: www.gcfb.net
E-mail: siouxfalls@gcfb.net
Facebook: yes
Telephone: 605-362-0000
Gift Shop: yes
Mug Club: yes
Growlers: yes
Tours: yes
Tasting: yes
Distribution: bottled products in
    South Dakota, North Dakota,
    Iowa, and Minnesota
Makes Own Line of Soft Drinks: no
Bar Toys: none
Bar Stools: ~25
Beer Garden/Outside Seating: yes
Tourism: Sioux Falls Convention and
    Visitors Bureau, 800-333-2072
    or 605-336-1620
    (www.siouxfallscvb.com)

SUPERIOR, WISCONSIN
Thirsty Pagan Brewing
1623 Broadway
Superior, WI 54880
GPS Coordinates: N 46°43.597′
    W 92°06.156′

Established: 2006 (as Thirsty Pagan);
    1999 (as Twin Ports Brewing
    Company)
Production (approximate barrels/
    year): 450 bbl (2010)
Website:
    www.thirstypaganbrewing.com
E-mail:
    steve@thirstypaganbrewing.com
Facebook: yes
Telephone: 715-394-2500
Gift Shop: yes
Mug Club: no
Growlers: yes
Tours: yes
Tasting: yes
Distribution: through brewpub only
Makes Own Line of Soft Drinks: no
Bar Toys: none
Bar Stools: ~10
Beer Garden/Outside Seating: yes,
    but small
Tourism: Superior-Douglas County
    Chamber of Commerce,
    800-942-5313 or 715-394-7716
    (www.visitsuperior.com)

WATERTOWN, SOUTH DAKOTA
Dempsey's Brewery, Restaurant, and Pub
127 North Broadway
Watertown, SD 57201
GPS Coordinates: N 44°54.160′
    W 97°06.828′
Established: 2000
Production (approximate barrels/
    year): 325 bbl (2010)
Website:
    www.dempseysbrewpub.com
E-mail: dempseys@iw.net
Facebook: yes
Telephone: 605-882-9760
Gift Shop: yes
Mug Club: yes
Growlers: yes
Tours: yes
Tasting: yes
Distribution: through brewpub only

Makes Own Line of Soft Drinks: yes
(Prohibition style root beer)
Bar Toys: darts, video games
Bar Stools: ~12
Beer Garden/Outside Seating: yes
Tourism: Watertown Convention and
Visitors Bureau, 800-658-4505
or 606-753-0282
(www.watertownsd.com)

WILSON, WISCONSIN
Dave's BrewFarm
2470 Wilson Street
Wilson, WI 54027
GPS Coordinates: N 44°58.411'
W 92°10.551'
Established: 2009
Production (approximate barrels/
year): 600 bbl (2010)
Website: www.brewfarm.com;
http://davesbrewfarm.blogspot
.com

E-mail: davesbrewfarm@gmail.com
Facebook: yes
Telephone: 612-432-8130
Gift Shop: yes
Mug Club: no
Growlers: yes
Tours: yes
Tasting: yes
Distribution: Twin Cities and western
Wisconsin
Makes Own Line of Soft Drinks: no
Bar Toys: none
Bar Stools: ~5
Beer Garden/Outside Seating: noth-
ing formal, just a few picnic
tables on the back patio
Tourism: Dunn County, Wisconsin
(http://dunncountywi.govoffice2
.com)

Minnesota's Brewing Past

AN ABBREVIATED HISTORY OF THE STATE'S
BEER-MAKING HERITAGE

Commercial brewing in Minnesota began at about the same time the Minnesota Territory was formed. Anthony Yoerg, a Bavarian immigrant, is credited with establishing Minnesota's first brewery sometime around 1849. Yoerg chose an area just south of what is now downtown St. Paul on the east bank of the Mississippi River (near today's Irvin Park). He later moved his brewery across the river to a location (229 Ohio) that allowed him to expand and excavate caves into the bluff for lagering his beer.

By the time Minnesota became a state in 1858, more than three dozen breweries had emerged. Minnesota's natural resources helped foster its early brewing industry: productive soils for growing barley, abundant forests for making barrels, and certainly not the least was abundant water for the beer itself as well as ice for storage and lagering.

Another important component was a growing population of German and Irish immigrants who brought knowledge of making beer and a love for enjoying it. At the time of statehood Minnesota's population was approximately 150,000. By 1870 it had grown to about 440,000, and 20 percent claimed German heritage and another 20 percent claimed Irish descent. By 1880 the population was nearly 780,000 and the number of breweries had grown to more than 120. It was during these years that a number of Minnesota's beer barons emerged. Brewers such as Jacob Schmidt, Theodore Hamm, August Schell, Jacob Bernhardt, and August Fitger came to prominence and created iconic images that linger today in cities like St. Paul, New Ulm, and Duluth.

After Prohibition the Minnesota brewing industry followed national trends. Initially many small-town breweries tried to come back during the 1930s, but by the end of World War II the age of brewery mechanization fueled mergers and consolidation. Few breweries except for the largest could compete with aggressive industry trends. Many of the once mighty breweries—including Hamm's, Grain Belt, Montgomery, Hauenstein, Mankato, and Fitger's—closed or sold off their most popular brands in the late 1960s and 1970s.

Today's small breweries and brewpubs reflect a renaissance of craft brewing that began in the 1980s with changes in federal law. This ushered in a host of small brewpubs and revived interest in small, local, artisan-craft beer. Bert Grant's Yakima Brewing and Malting Company of Yakima, Washington, is credited with beginning the brewpub movement in 1982.

It was a few more years before Minnesota would follow states like Washington. James Page Brewing Company of Minneapolis was created in 1986 and is often cited as the the state's first microbrewery of the modern area. However, that same year Mark Stutrud opened Summit Brewing Company in St. Paul. It took a few more years for Minnesota brewpubs to arrive. In 1989 Taps Waterfront Brewpub opened in Minneapolis as the state's first brewpub. That same year Bill Burdick opened Sherlock's Home in Minnetonka. Burdick deserves much recognition for getting directly involved in changing the state's laws pertaining to brewpubs that have allowed the industry to grow. Unfortunately, of these early trail blazers in Minnesota's most recent brewing chapter, only Summit continues today.

Despite some tough times for small brewers in the 1990s, a new generation with distinctive brews and approaches to making them has emerged. Beyond Summit Brewing a handful of notables include Flat Earth (St. Paul), Surly (Brooklyn Center/Minneapolis), Barley John's Brew Pub (New Brighton), Minneapolis Town Hall Brewery (Minneapolis), and Fitger's Brewhouse (Duluth). These are just a few that seem to be establishing their own place in Minnesota brewing history.

It is indeed a great time to be enjoying Minnesota beer.

MINNESOTA BREWERIES WE HAVE KNOWN AND LOVED (SINCE 1933)

Since Prohibition ended in 1933, Minnesota has seen nearly fifty breweries and brewpubs come and go. The following listing is a partial reference for those interested in tracing brewpubs and breweries in the years since the repeal of Prohibition. Minnesota had many breweries before Prohibition. By some estimates another 200-plus breweries existed in Minnesota between 1849 and 1918. There are many fine historians who have provided excellent resources describing them in more detail. Some of their work was used to expand the information below. For those interested in more comprehensive historical listings of past Minnesota breweries see Dale Van Wieren's *American Breweries II*, Doug Hoverson's *Land of Amber Waters: The History of Brewing in Minnesota*; and *One Hundred Years of Brewing*, a supplement to the *Western Brewer* originally published in 1903.

Minnesota Brewpub Entities, 1989–2010
 All American Grill & Brewhouse—Waverly, 2007–9
 Bandana Brewery—Mankato, 2003–6
 BrauHaus—Lucan, 2004–6 (restaurant continues)
 The Brew Station—Shakopee, 1999–2002
 Clubhaus Brewpub—Rochester, 1994–99
 District Warehouse Brewing Co.—Minneapolis, 1996–99
 Green Mill—Albert Lea, 2003–4
 Green Mill—St. Paul, 1995–2006
 Harwell's Steakhouse and Brewery—Shakopee, 2002–3
 Hops—Eden Prairie, 2001–5
 Hops—Maple Grove, 1999–2005
 O'Gara's—St. Paul, 1996–2007

O'Hara's Brew Pub—St. Cloud, 1996–2007
Shannon Kelly's Brewpub—St. Paul, 1995–97
Sherlock's Home—Minnetonka, 1989–2002
Taps Waterfront Brewpub & Comedy Gallery / Main Street Brewery—
Minneapolis, 1989–91
Trader & Trapper—Moorhead, 1998–99
Union Station/First City Brewery and Grill—Bemidji, 1997–2006
Vittorio's—Stillwater, 1997–2001
Watertower Brewing—Eden Prairie, 1997–2003

Minnesota Brewery Entities, 1933–2010
Alexandria Brewery / Brewing Company—Alexandria, 1935–43
Ambleside Brewing Company—Minneapolis, 1997–98
Duluth Brewing & Malting Company—Duluth, 1933–66
  Prior brewery names/owners and approximate dates: Duluth Brewing
  & Malting Company (1896–1920).
Engesser Brewing Company—St. Peter, 1933–42
  Matthew Engesser (1856–80); Matthew Engesser and Sons (1880–88);
  Engesser Brewing Company (1888–1920).
Ernst Fleckenstein Brewing Company—Faribault, 1933–64
  Some evidence suggests this brewery may have existed as early as
  1857. Ernst Fleckenstein (1872–1901); Ernst Fleckenstein Brewing Co.
  (1901–20).
Falls Breweries/Brewing—Fergus Falls, 1935–51
  J. K. O'Brien (1882–83); Aberle & Ahrentz (1883–84); Andreas Aberle
  (1884–93); Charles J. Bender (1893–96); Andreas Aberle (1896–1900);
  Anton Meyer (1901); Andreas Aberle & John Bauer (1901–3); John
  Bauer (1903–7); Theodore Hubner (1907–8); Fergus Falls Brewing
  (1908–20); Premier Brewing Company (1933–35).
Fitger Brewing Company—Duluth, 1933–72
  Sidney Luce (1857–65); Nicholas Decker (1865–77); Michael Fink &
  Company, Lake Superior Brewing Company (1877–85); A. Fitger &
  Company (1885–1903); Fitger Brewing Company (1903–20).
Fred Beyrer—Chaska, 1934–55
  Records suggest the first brewery was started at this location in 1866
  by Henry Young and Charles May. Fred Beyrer (1906–20).
Glacial Lakes Brewing Company—New York Mills, 1997–2001
Gluek Brewing Company—Minneapolis, 1933–64
  Gottlieb Gluek & John Rank, Mississippi Brewery (1857–62); Gottlieb
  Gluek (1862–80); G. Gluek & Sons (1880–93); Gluek Brewing Com-
  pany (1894–1920).
Goodhue County Brewing Company—Red Wing, 1948–51
  William Heising, City Brewery (1861–73); Christina Heising (1873–77);
  Remmler's Estate / Adolph Remmler's Brewery (1877–1920); Remmler
  Brewing Company (1934–48).
Grain Belt Breweries (Minneapolis Brewing Company)—Minneapolis,
1967–75 (1933–67)
  John Orth Brewing Company (1850–90); Minneapolis Brewing and
  Malting Company (1890–93); Minneapolis Brewing Company (1893–
  1920).

Hamm's Brewing Company—St. Paul, 1933–1975
Andrew Keller, Pittsburg Brewery/Excelsior (1860–64); Theodore
Hamm (1864–96); Theodore Hamm Brewing Company (1896–1920).
James Page Brewing Company—Minneapolis, 1986–2005
John Hauenstein Company—New Ulm, 1933–69
John Hauenstein and Andreas Betz (1864–69); John Hauenstein &
John Toberer (1869–71); John Hauenstein (1871–1900); John Hauen-
stein Brewing Company (1900–1920).
Kiewel Brewing Company—Little Falls, 1933–61
Leo P. Brick (1880–84); Little Falls Brewing Company (1884–88); Marin
& Medoed (1888–91); Peter Medoed (1881–92); R. J. Koch (1892–
93); Jacob Kiewel (1893–99); Jacob Kiewel Brewing Company (1899–
1920).
Mankato Brewery—Jordan, 1946–54
Nicolin & Gehring (1866–67); Gehring & Paier (1867–85); Schutz & Kai-
ser (1885–1903); Schutz & Hilgers City Brewery (1902–18); Schutz &
Hilgers Jordan Brewery (1934–46).
Mankato Brewing Company—Mankato, 1933–67 (owned by Cold
Spring Brewing Company, 1951–54).
William and Jacob Bierbauer (1856–62); William Bierbauer (1863–94);
William Bierbauer Estate (1894–1903); Louisa Bierbauer (1903–5); Wil-
liam Bierbauer Brewing Company (1905–20).
Mantorville Brewing Company—Mantorville, 1937–39
Some evidence suggests that this brewery may have existed as
early as 1858 as the John Hirchi Brewery. Charles Ginsberg, Dodge
County Brewery (1874–79); Henry Naegli (1877–79); Anna Gins-
berg (1879–84); Henry Naegli (1884–93); Henry Naegli Jr. (1893–99);
Ferdinand Schnagl (1899–1906); Ferdinand Schnagl Estate (1906–7);
Anna Schnagl (1907–10); Anna Schnagl Estate (1911); John George
Schnagl (1911–17); Otto's (Schumann) Brewery, Inc. (1934–37).
Midwest Brewing Company—Red Wing, 1935–37
Some records suggest that this brewery may have also operated
under the name John Melander from 1874 to 1882. Phillip Hoffman
(1857–68); Christina Hoffman (1868–1871); Christina Christ (1871–
1872); Jacob Christ, Red Wing Brewery (1872–90); Christina Christ
(1890–93); Red Wing Brewing Company (1893–1904); Zimmerman &
Featherston (1904–9); Red Wing Brewing Company (1909–20); Red
Wing Brewing Company (1934–35).
Minnesota Brewing Company—St. Paul, 1991–2002
Christopher Stahlmann, Cave Brewery (1854–82); Christopher Stahl-
mann Brewing Company (1882–98); St. Paul Brewing Company
(1898–1900); Jacob Schmidt Brewing Company (1900–1920); Jacob
Schmidt Brewing Company (1933–54); Pfeiffer Brewing Company /
Jacob Schmidt Brewing Company (1954–62); Associated Brewing /
Pfeiffer, Schmidt (1962–72); G. Heileman Brewing Company
(1972–90).
Montgomery Brewing Company—Montgomery, 1933–43
John and Matthais Chalupsky (1882–91); Murphy, Sheehy & Merz
(1891–93); Handsuch & Pexa (1893–98); Joseph Handsuch (1898–

1905); Joseph Handsuch & Edward Richter, City Brewery (1905–13); Montgomery Brewing Company (1913–19).

Peoples Brewing Company—Duluth, 1933–57
The Peoples Brewing Company (1907–20).

Peter Bub Brewery—Winona, 1935–69
Some records indicate that other names may have been involved with this brewery in the 1860s and 1870s, including Weisbrod, Garlock, Rath, and Burmeister. Jacob Weisbrod (1856–70); Peter Bub / Sugar Loaf Brewery (1870–1911); Sugar Loaf Brewery / Peter Bub Estate (1911–20); Peter Bub Estate (1933–35).

St. Cloud Brewing Company—St. Cloud, 1933–39
This brewery may have been operated by Fritz Herberger as early as 1857. John Brick (1876–82); Brick and Legler (1882–84); Preiss and Wimmer (1884–1900); Preiss and Wimmer Brewing Company (1900–12); Preiss Brewing Company (1912–20).

Yoerg Brewing Company—St. Paul, 1933–52
Anthony Yoerg (1849–96); Yoerg Brewing Company (1896–1920).

Beer Styles

Beer styles fit rather loosely into two general classifications known as ales and lagers. These two distinctions correspond to the type of yeast used. Ales are made at relatively warm temperatures, roughly 60 to 70 degrees Fahrenheit, and require less time to ferment. They are made with strains of yeast that are active in the warmer upper portions of the fermentation vessel. Ales tend to have fruity flavors, more assertive tastes and aromas, and especially bitter tones. They are considered the older, more traditional beers. Lagers are created by colder fermentation and aging temperatures that slow down the activity of the yeast, and in turn can reduce the production of fruity esters that in some cases create a mellower or cleaner beer. Lagers are made with strains of yeast that are active in colder temperatures, usually at the bottom of the fermentation vessel. They became more popular once mechanical refrigeration became possible. Keep in mind that ales and lagers share many characteristics, so, unless the brewer specifies which beers are which, it can be difficult if not impossible for even the best beer connoisseur to tell the difference.

Within the general classifications of ales and lagers there are subgroups referred to as styles. The brewing industry recognizes approximately one hundred different styles of beer, and some of the styles have substyles. For example, a stout is an ale and can include such substyles as American stout, dry (Irish) stout, oatmeal stout, or even Russian imperial stout.

For the most part, the beer styles recognized today evolved over centuries through trial and error in brewing processes. Brewers may have been making beer in less than ideal situations, trying different grains, varying the amount of hops or spices, or looking for less costly ingredients. While some styles may initially have been created by accident, many years of consistent brewing helped establish particular beers as accepted styles. In recent years the number of defined styles for competitively judged beer events have further defined, perhaps even refined, the list of beer styles.

The following list of styles is not meant to be all-inclusive; rather, it is offered as a guide to some of the most common beer styles you'll run across as you travel Minnesota. There are a number of good beer websites that provide a comprehensive listing. See, for example, the Brewers Association (www.brewers association.org), the Beer Judge Certification Program (www.bjcp.org), and the World Beer Cup (www.worldbeercup.org).

As you travel and experience the differences in beer flavors it is good to keep in mind that many craft brewers often do not want to be held to strict style definitions. Because they brew smaller batches, they like to experiment.

That may mean they begin with a general style and expand its characteristics, combining their creativity and their insights into what local beer drinkers want. It doesn't make the beer wrong or bad, but it might not be fair to give the beer a bad mark for a style it really did not intend to be.

In the following section I have provided examples of many of the most common styles. Where possible, and where there is a Minnesota beer I found to be a strong representation of that style, you'll find the name of the beer followed by the Minnesota brewpub or brewery that produces it. I have also included a few examples made outside Minnesota, with the brewer's name and location in parentheses.

ALES

Ales are characterized by fermentation at warmer temperatures. They are made with what are commonly referred to as a top-fermenting yeast; that is, the yeast is active in the upper portions of the fermentation vessel. Ales generally require shorter aging processes. Compared with lagers, they are often distinguished by a greater variety of colors and more robust flavors, including fruity tones.

Alt

Alt (the German word for "old") usually has a malty nose, a color that is orange or copper to brown, medium body, and assertive bitterness with a light fruity background. Some alts will have a dry finish due to the large amounts of hops. While considered traditional German ale, some well-known northern German alts are closer to a lager because they are fermented with ale yeast at lower lager-style temperatures.

Examples: Alt, Herkimer Pub and Brewery; BWCA Alt, Fitger's Brewhouse; Schmaltz's Alt, August Schell Brewing Company.

Amber or Red Ale
American Amber or Red

Amber or red ale can have either a mild to strong hop aroma or some malty caramel nose. The light copper to light brown color and tan head most commonly distinguish them. Reds are very similar, often with a more vivid red hue (hence the name) and clearer color. Body is medium to full; carbonation is moderate. They usually are well balanced between maltiness and hoppiness, yet ample hops provide a crispness if not slight emphasis to bitterness.

Examples: High Bank Amber Ale, McCann's Food and Brew; Horizon Red Ale, Summit Brewing Company; Stump Jumper, Vine Park Brewing Company.

Irish Red

Irish ale has a malty or toffee nose, dark bronze color, and often a reddish hue. It is medium to full bodied. Malty sweet flavors dominate, with low hoppiness.

Examples: Finnegans Irish Ale, Finnegans; O'Byrne's Irish Red, Great Waters Brewing Company.

Barley Wine
American style

Often made with American hops, the American-style barley wine is hoppier in both nose and taste than the English style. Barley wine has the strongest, most robust and assertive character of the ales. The nose is often fruity. The color is dark, sometimes with a bronze hue. It has full-bodied and viscous texture, and intense malt body with fruity overtones. High alcohol content and thick texture provide a very smooth taste experience. Finish can be very warm. To truly appreciate a barley wine, drink it from a snifter or tulip glass.

Examples: Old Redbeard, Fitger's Brewhouse; Old Foghorn (Anchor Brewing, San Francisco, California).

English style

The English-style barley wine features British hops and gives more attention to the malty character. Barley wine has the strongest, most robust and assertive character of the ales. The nose is often fruity. The color is dark, sometimes with a bronze hue. It has full-bodied and viscous texture, and intense malt body with fruity overtones. There is some hoppiness, but the balance is more to the malty flavors. It has high alcohol content. A thick texture provides a very smooth taste experience. Finish can be very warm. To truly appreciate a barley wine, drink it from a snifter or tulip glass.

Examples: Old Man Winter Warmer, Lake Superior Brewing Company; Winter Warlock, Flat Earth Brewing Company; Old Nick (Young & Company, England).

Belgian Ale
Abbey

Abbey refers more to the tradition of monastery brewing and is not a defined style. They are not always brewed in an abbey but they may be licensed by one.

Examples: Abbaye de Leffe (Leffe Blonde, Belgium, imported by Wetten Importers).

Dubbel

Dubbel originated at monasteries in the Middle Ages. It has a rich malty nose; sometimes clove or spiciness is evident. Color is dark golden to dark amber with a thick, long-lasting head. Body is medium to full and often warm. Flavor has rich maltiness with a fruity background. The finish is usually warm from the alcohol content.

Examples: Emma's Yuletide Ale, Great Waters Brewing Company; La Trappe Dubbel (Trappistenbier Brauwerij "De Schapskooi," Koningshoeven, Holland, imported by All Saint's Brands, Minneapolis); Ommergang (Brewery Ommergang, Cooperstown, New York).

Flanders Oud Bruin (Brown) or Oud Red Ale

These are considered sour beers with strong fruity qualities. They are light to medium bodied. The Flanders brown may offer light roasted maltiness in flavor and aroma with a acidic sourness. The Flanders red may have less aroma but a sharp sour flavor and fruity finish. Hops generally play only a minor part in the task associated with this style.

Example: Rode Haring (Flanders Red), Flat Earth Brewing Company.

Grand Cru

Not a definitive style, rather used as a vague designation for a Belgian beer considered to be of high quality, and high in alcohol and pale in color. Often a seasonal beer, and originally a celebratory beer for weddings and important events.

Examples: Collaboration (Cherry) Grand Cue, Minneapolis Town Hall Brewery and Fitger's Brewhouse; Fytenburg Grand Cru, Theodore Fyten Brewing Company; Rodenbach Grand Cru (Brouwerij Rodenbach, Belgium).

Saison

Saison originated in the French-speaking part of Belgium. Often a seasonal beer (e.g., summer), it was traditionally brewed at the end of winter. Characteristics include fruity nose with some light hoppiness, a pale orange body with a thick head, light to medium body, bitter hoppiness with a strong fruity background.

Examples: CynicAle, Surly Brewing Company; Farm Girl Saison, Lift Bridge Brewery; Forgotten Flem, Brau Brothers Brewing Company; Hennepin (Brewery Ommergang, Cooperstown, New York); Monette-Saison (Brasserie Dupont, Belgium, imported by Banbery & Dewulf).

Strong

Belgian ales are sometimes distinguished by color into further categories as either pale or dark. Belgian strong ales are commonly brewed with Belgian candi sugar and are well attenuated. Most are low in bitterness and big on the fruity sweetness and intense maltiness. Herbs and spices are sometimes used to offer some light flavors. The high alcoholic characteristics can be deceiving.

Examples: El Diablo, Fitger's Brewhouse; Duvel (Brouwerij Duvel Moortgat, Belgium).

Trappist

By Belgian law, Trappist ales must be brewed at a Trappist monastery, and by European law they can come from only the six abbeys of the Trappist order that still brew. The term "abbey" or "Trappist style" is applied to beers that closely follow this style but do not originate at a Trappist monastery. Golden to deep amber color, they are often fruity and bittersweet. Characteristically these Belgians are brewed with candi sugar in the kettle and are bottle-conditioned.

Example: Red Label (Chimay, Belgium, imported by Belukus Marketing).

Tripel

Tripel is complex from beginning to end. The nose is a competition between malty and fruity aromas. The color is pale golden to deep gold with a light, bubbly, white head. It is medium bodied, crisp, and often very effervescent. A malty sweetness is balanced with both hops and fruity overtones. The finish is dry. Overall, strong fruity bursts, yet warm and smooth.

Example: Bermuda Triangle, Flat Earth Brewing Company.

Witbier or White Beer

Witbier has a sweet, citrus nose, often with hints of orange, herbs, or spice. Color is pale yellow or straw color and generally cloudy, with a light, soft, white head. It has light to medium body. Malty, it even has a hint of musty qualities, all accented with coriander, citrus, and spice.

Examples: Belgian Wit, Minneapolis Town Hall Brewery; Breakwater Wit, Fitger's Brewhouse; Little White Lie, BoatHouse Brewpub and Restaurant; Scandia Ale, Summit Brewing Company.

Bière de Garde
This French beer has a malty to fruity nose. Color is clear and sparkling gold, copper, or even reddish. It has a light to medium body, with moderate to high carbonation, and a medium to full malty flavor. Light hints of caramel and toffee are common. Traditionally served in a corked bottle, it is meant to be aged in a cellar as wines are. Its name means "beer for keeping."

Examples: Ovni, Flat Earth Brewing Company; Rendezvous (Lakefront Brewery, Milwaukee, Wisconsin); Bière de Garde (Brasserie Castelain, Bénifontaine, France, imported by Vanberg & Dewulf).

Brown Ale
American
This brown was adapted by American brewers who wanted stronger hop flavors. The nose has a hoppy aroma. The color is dark amber to dark brown with a thick, tan head. It is medium bodied and sometimes dry. The hop bitterness dominates, despite assertive maltiness. There are often some toasty qualities in the background. With its high hop qualities, the finish is usually dry.

Examples: Bender, Surly Brewing Company; Brooklyn Brown Ale (Brooklyn Brewery, Brooklyn, New York).

Mild
It has a slight, mild, malty nose. The color can be medium dark brown, deep copper, or mahogany. Light to medium body; low carbonation; low or no hop flavor and finish. It is malty but usually well balanced.

Examples: Dark Mild, Barley John's Brew Pub; Mild, Surly Brewing Company.

Northern English
Also called nut brown ale, it is known for its dryer, nuttier maltiness. With little or no hop aroma, it is more likely to have a malty or even roasted nose. Color is dark golden to light brown. Light to medium bodied, it has a soft sweetness with strong nutty character that dominates a caramel malt body. A dry finish.

Examples: Big Mike D's Nut Brown, Stillwater Brewing Company; Chestnut Hill, Lift Bridge Brewery; Nut Brown Ale (South Shore Brewery, Ashland, Wisconsin); Newcastle Brown Ale (Scottish & Newcastle Breweries, Newcastle-upon-Tyne, England); Nut Brown Ale (Samuel Smith's Old Brewery, Yorkshire, England).

Southern English
Nose is malty, sometimes with a light fruitiness. Color is dark brown and almost opaque. Medium bodied, it has a gentle sweetness with a malty dominance. There should be some hoppiness in the background, but nutty roasted tones are not appropriate.

Examples: Brown Trout, Great Waters Brewing Company; Brown Ale (Capital Brewery, Middleton, Wisconsin).

Cask Ale
Cask-conditioned beers are served from their cask (or keg) under their own carbonation. Several styles (most commonly ales) are offered in this manner. Cask-conditioned ale is served the traditional British way, on draught from a

hand pump rather than through lines that are pushed by pressurized tanks of carbon dioxide. They may seem "flat" or at least much less effervescent. Cask-conditioned ales are also commonly served at cellar temperatures of 50 to 55 degrees Fahrenheit, which is considerably warmer than most American beer drinkers are used to. Cask-conditioned ales are sometimes referred to as "live" beers because they are naturally self-carbonated during a secondary fermentation process that occurs in the cask.

Examples: Great Waters Brewing Company is an excellent place to try various beers on cask.

Cream Ale

Cream ale is a hybrid of an American pale lager fermented as an ale. May sometimes be referred to as a "sparkling ale." Corn or rice may be used as adjuncts. It has a light hoppy aroma and a pale straw to light golden color. It is light bodied with a smooth texture and well carbonated. A sweet graininess within a light malt character and even light hoppy background. This sweetness leaves almost a floury, or grainy, impression. However, generally well balanced and overall a clean flavor profile.

Example: Cream Ale, Barley John's Brew Pub; Cream Ale, Castle Danger Brewery.

Extra Special Bitter (ESB)

A light amber to copper color with medium to medium-high bitterness. Expect some hoppines in the aroma and flavor, however the maltiness comes through in a defining sweetness. The ESB is a medium-bodied beer with mild carbonation. It is also commonly found on cask in brewpubs. An ESB is very close in style to what some brewers distinguish as the "Special Bitter" or "Best Bitter," which is golden to copper colored and somewhat less assertive in both hop and malty qualities. The ESB has emerged to mean something like best premium or even the word "large" on a package. The ESB has become recognized as its own style and in England it is very closely tied to Fuller's Brewery. In America it is more widely applied to bitter beers with a strong malty backbone and recipes that commonly have both American and English ingredients.

Examples: Broken Paddle ESB, Minneapolis Town Hall Brewery; Summit ESB, Summit Brewing Company; Witchtree ESB, Fitger's Brewhouse.

Golden or Blonde Ale

A soft, light malty flavor and a fruity or light hoppy nose. The blonde color is clear pale straw to deep golden. Most often blonde is light and thin, but it can range to medium bodied and soft. The fruitiness or hoppiness is in the background and usually well balanced with the maltiness.

Examples: Entry Point Golden Ale, BoatHouse Brewpub and Restaurant; Golden Prairie Blond Ale, Great Waters Brewing Company; Lighthouse Golden Ale, Fitger's Brewhouse.

India Pale Ale (IPA)
American IPA

An adaptation of the British IPA, it is lighter in color than most British versions, and the hoppy aroma may be more assertive. Somewhat bolder and cleaner, it is made with American malt and hops to create a crisper profile. Most often it has a strong, aromatic, hoppy nose, deep golden color, medium body, and assertive hoppiness. Finish is often dry and long lasting.

Examples: El Niño Double Hopped IPA, Fitger's Brewhouse; Furious, Surly Brewing Company; Sweet Child of Vine, Fulton Brewery.

Black IPA

Sometimes referred to as a black pale ale or a Cascadian dark ale. Very dark color and strong hoppy character. A moderate degree of caramel maltiness and a roasted but not burnt flavor. An American twist on the IPA and often made with U.S. grown hops.

Examples: ERB, Minneapolis Town Hall Brewery; IBA (India Black Ale), Dubrue.

British IPA

The British IPA has a strong, floral, hoppy nose and a color that ranges from gold to deep copper. Some versions may appear hazy or slightly cloudy, but generally it's a clear beer. It is smooth and medium bodied and has a very strong hop flavor with assertive bitter taste. A warm, strong, bitter finish is also common.

Examples: 47° North, Leech Lake Brewing Company; Sam Smith's India Ale (Samuel Smith's Old Brewery, Yorkshire, England).

Imperial IPA

The imperial IPA is also called a double IPA. They are commonly gold to reddish amber in color, with medium to full-bodied mouth feel. The imperial IPA has a strong hop profile that features resiny and citrus tones. Some robust malty sweetness in the background adds complexity to the flavor profile. Because they can be quite strong, the finish will have some alcoholic warmth.

Examples: Abrasive Ale, Surly Brewing Company; Sheephead, Brau Brothers Brewing Company.

Kölsch (also Koelsch)

The Kölsch name can be applied only to beers from Köln (Cologne), Germany, brewed to strict legal standards, including 10 to 20 percent wheat. It is considered a blonde alt beer. It has a light hoppy nose and a clear pale to light golden color. It is light to medium bodied and soft. It has a light fruity body and a crisp hoppy background. Some have a dry finish.

Examples: Kayak Kölsch, Lake Superior Brewing Company; Stagecoach Golden, Mantorville Brewing Company.

Lambic
Framboise

A lambic made with raspberry; framboise often has a cloudy reddish color. It has a strong fruity body and may be sour. It is light to medium bodied and highly carbonated. Typically it has very light or no hop flavor. The fruit will dominate.

Examples: Raspberry Tart (New Glarus Brewing Company, New Glarus, Wisconsin); St. Louis Framboise (Brouwerij Van Honsebrouck, Belgium).

Gueuze

Gueuze is traditionally made by blending young and old lambic, producing a smoother beer. Most often it has a fruity nose, but it can be sour, earthy, or even woody. Color is gold to amber and slightly cloudy. It can be intensely sour and acetic, but it is better balanced than the unblended lambic.
Example: Gueuze Cuvée Renée (Brouwerij Lindemans, Belgium).

Kriek

Kriek is a lambic made with cherries. Traditionally the cherries are not crushed but the skins are lightly broken and added to the beer in the cellar. Some young lambic is also added. It has a fruity nose and pink color. It is light to medium bodied and highly carbonated. Kriek can be intensely sour and acetic, but it is better balanced than the unblended lambic.
Example: Kriek (Brouwerij Lindemans, Belgium).

Unblended

The straight lambic-style ale most often has a fruity nose, but it can be sour, earthy, or even woody. Color is yellow to golden and cloudy. Light to medium bodied, it has strong, sour, acidic flavor. Traditionally the lambic style is open fermented with naturally occurring yeast.
Examples: Very few straight lambics are bottled.

Pale Ale

American Pale Ale

An adaptation of the original British style, American pale ale is generally considered crisper and more hoppy than the English pale ale. They tend to emphasize American ingredients, most notably American varieties hops and types of malts. Despite the reference to "pale" in the name, most are a clear, rich golden to amber color. They often have moderate to high hop flavor, light to medium body, and high carbonation.
Examples: Starfire Pale Ale, Fitger's Brewhouse; Angry Planet, Flat Earth Brewing Company; Pale Ale, Summit Brewing Company; Pale Ale (Sierra Nevada Brewing, Chico, California).

Belgian Pale Ale

This pale ale has firm hoppy bitterness with pronounced tones of yeasty-spiciness. Light to modest amounts of hoppiness will be found in the nose. Light golden to deep amber colored and light to medium bodied. There is a complex blend of hoppiness, fruity esters, and spicy notes. Low maltiness is common. Some dryness to the finish may be evident.
Example: Belgian-Style Pale Ale, Flat Earth Brewing Company;

English Pale Ale

More balanced with a firm underlying maltiness and not the assertive hoppy bitterness of its American cousin. Often golden to copper colored with an earthy and herbal hop character. Medium hop bitterness in the flavor and aroma. This is a medium-bodied beer that is low to medium in malty flavor with some light fruity esters within the flavors and aromas.
Examples: Curley Tail, Flat Earth Brewing Company; Pilot Pub Ale, Boat-House Brewpub and Restaurant.

Porter
American Porter
Sometimes referred to as the Robust Porter. American versions of porter are often drier and hoppier. It has a roasted malt or coffee nose and a dark brown to black color. It is medium to full bodied. It differs from the English porter with more assertive malty flavor that can include strong coffee tones and roasted dryness. Hoppiness is evident to even dominant.

Examples: Driven Snow, Leech Lake Brewing Company; Great Northern Porter, Summit Brewing Company; Anchor Porter (Anchor Brewing, San Francisco, California).

Baltic Porter
The aroma will include rich malty sweetness with hints of toffee and nuttiness. Deep dark brown color, sometimes with brilliant ruby-bronze tints. This porter has a complex flavor profile with layers of sweetness in chocolate and caramel malts with hints of roasted coffee, nuttiness, molasses, or even fruity currants. The finish may offer tones of licorice. The style originates from the Baltic Sea region and was influenced by English porters and the Russian imperial stouts.

Example: Odin, Minneapolis Town Hall Brewery.

English or British Porter
Sometimes referred to as a brown Porter. This style of porter originated in England as a blend of beers and was a precursor to stout. It has a malty nose with a mild roastedness. Hoppiness should be low to moderate. Color is brown to dark brown. Medium bodied. The flavor is maltier with some roasted tones, but generally it is sweeter, even with hints of chocolate malt, than the American porter style.

Examples: Flag Porter (Darwin, England); Sam Smith's Taddy Porter (Samuel Smith's Old Brewery, Yorkshire, England).

Imperial Porter
Often considered an American invention, this strong porter is full bodied, very dark brown to black in color with strong caramel and coca-like sweetness. Some fruitiness is common, but not overpowering. Some bitterness from both the black malt and hops, but any bitterness should complement the malty flavor and body of this style.

Example: Rubus, Brau Brothers Brewing Company

Robust Porter
Black in color and assertive roasted maltiness with hints of cocoa and caramel sweetness. Often has a sharp bitterness of black malt, as opposed to burnt flavors or intense resiny-hoppy bitterness. Medium to full bodied mouth feel.

Example: Edmund Fitzgerald Porter (Great Lakes Brewing Company, Cleveland, Ohio)

Scottish style
Scottish ales tend to emphasize malt qualities and give less attention to hoppiness. In part, this reflects the use of brown malts and a brewing process that features longer boiling periods. The common varieties of Scottish ales are light, heavy, and export. Historically these distinctions carried labels of the shilling

currency, which reflected the price charged per barrel of beer in the nineteenth century. For example, 60 shilling was used for light Scottish ales, 70 shilling for heavy, 80 shilling for export, and above 90 shilling for Scotch ale and Wee Heavy. Almost all are malty, sweet, and full bodied. They often range from dark amber to brown or even bronze color with thick, creamy heads. A strong malty nose is common. The taste is dominated by maltiness. Some may have a faint smokiness. Heavier versions may even have a warmth, especially in the finish.

Examples: Loch Leech Monster, Leech Lake Brewing Company; Kilt Lifter Ale (Pike Brewing, Seattle, Washington).

Scotch Ale and Wee Heavy

The maltiness can be strong but not overwhelming in these beers. They begin with an assertive aromatic malty nose. There is some roastedness that may even be in competition with the malt aroma. A peaty or smoky character is common. The color is dark amber to brown. It can be full bodied and thick. There is intense maltiness and even some hints of caramelization. The Wee Heavy is fermented at temperatures cooler than that used for most ales, leading to a clean but still strong malty flavor. Wee Heavy is the name for Scotch ale in pubs in Scotland.

Examples: Hope and King Scotch Ale, Minneapolis Town Hall Brewery; Scotch Ale, Brau Brothers Brewing Company; McEwan's Scotch Ale (McEwan and Younger, Fountain Brewery, Scotland, imported by Scottish & Newcastle).

Specialty Ales

Fruit flavored

An important characteristic of quality fruit beer is balance. The fruit should complement the style and not overwhelm other characteristics. Color and texture of the fruit beer will vary depending upon style. Nose, taste, and finish should provide a distinctive opportunity for the fruit but not a venue to overpower the beer.

Examples: Apricot Wheat, Fitger's Brewhouse; Rubus, Brau Brothers Brewing Company; Flat Earth Brewing Company is well known for making a series of infused porters.

Rauchbier

Rauchbier is smoke flavored, and its smoky aroma ranges from faint to very assertive. Usually clear and dark, the color can be black, brown, or dark copper. It has medium body and smooth texture. While the smoke flavor may vary among brewers, it should remain in balance with the smooth maltiness of the body.

Example: Northern Waters Smoked Helles, Fitger's Brewhouse.

Roggenbier

A German rye beer made with large portions of rye. It has pronounced sourness with some spicy qualities from the malt. These beers are often bottle conditioned and unfiltered.

Example: Roggenbier (150th Anniversary Series), August Schell Brewing Company.

Stout
American Stout
Inspired by Irish and English styles, the American stout features more hoppy aromas and bitter flavors. It has a light, mild hoppy or even roasted nose. Color is dark to black. Medium bodied, it has some malty flavors but a dry bitter dominance, and less fruity esters than an English or Irish stout.

Examples: Obsidian Stout (Deschutes Brewing, Bend, Oregon); Stout (Sierra Nevada Brewing, Chico, California).

Dry (Irish) Stout
Irish stout is deep black in color and it looks thick. The head is off-white to tan, very thick, and long lasting. It has a coffee or roasted nose, medium body, and creamy texture. A sharpness or sourness comes through in the beginning, but the strong hoppy body provides a dry or even tart finish. Overall, the Irish stout is smooth and creamy, but dry and tart.

Example: Guinness (St. James Gate Brewery, Dublin, Ireland).

Oatmeal Stout
Oatmeal stout has a mild, roasted nose. It is black with a thick, creamy head. It is full bodied and smooth, sometimes oily or resin-like. There is medium malty sweetness and mild hoppiness with a slight malty dominance. A nutty finish is not uncommon.

Examples: Big Boat Oatmeal Stout, Fitger's Brewhouse; Black H_2O Oatmeal Stout, Minneapolis Town Hall Brewery; Boadicea, Summit Brewing Company; Sir Duluth, Lake Superior Brewing Company; Sam Smith's Oatmeal Stout (Samuel Smith's Old Brewery, Yorkshire, England).

Russian Imperial Stout
This style of stout was brewed to stand up to sea voyages from Britain to the Baltic and is said to have been popular with the Russian Imperial Court. It actually belongs in a category of strong ales. It has an intense roasted nose with fruity esters in the background. It is very full bodied and creamy. Usually low carbonation will add to a thick texture. The taste is a complex blend of heavy roasted maltiness and fruity tones. The high alcohol levels provide a rich, smooth, yet lingering dryness. Imperial stouts are usually found in winter months.

Examples: Darkness, Surly Brewing Company; Russian Roulette, Minneapolis Town Hall Brewery.

Sweet (English) Stout
This stout, also known as a milk stout, has a mild, roasted nose. Some may have fruity or even light hoppy aromas. Color is very dark amber to black. A full body and creaminess may accentuate the malty dominance in the flavor. While this stout still isn't truly sweet, the malts dominate and the roastedness may stand out above any mild hoppy flavor.

Examples: Broad Axe Stout, Granite City Food and Brewery; Sam Adams Cream Stout (Boston Beer Company, Jamaica Plain, Massachusetts).

Strong Ale

Often referred to as old ales, strong ales most commonly have deep amber colors but can be deep bronze to black. They have full bodied and assertive, sweet, malty flavors, sometimes with a light fruity background or accent.

Example: Winter Ale, Summit Brewing Company.

Wheat Beer (Weisse)
American Wheat and Honey Wheat

The American wheat style is known for its hoppy aroma. The color is straw to golden, and clarity depends upon whether it has been filtered. The head is typically white and bubbly and long lasting. Light to medium bodied, the taste has a light graininess. Fruitiness and hoppiness dominate.

Example: Honey Weisse (Leinenkugel Brewing, Chippewa Falls, Wisconsin).

Bavarian Hefeweizen, Weizen, and Weissebier

The traditional wheat-based ale originating in southern Germany. Made with at least 50 percent wheat. "Hefe" is the German word for yeast, indicating the beer is bottle conditioned. Expect a Hefeweizen to be cloudy. Unlike the American wheat style, the German or Bavarian Weizen is marked by a strong vanilla and clove-like, even banana nose. The color is pale straw to dark reddish golden. It is light to medium bodied and creamy. A soft grainy flavor consists of spicy clove and fruity esters. A strong banana taste is common. The finish is crisp and bubbly. Although it is found year round, the German wheat beer is ideally suited for summer drinking.

Examples: Lester River Hefeweizen, Fitger's Brewhouse; Weihenstephaner Hefe Weissbier (Bayerische Staatsbrauerej Weihenstephan, Germany).

Berliner Weisse/Weissbier

This northern Germany style is Berlin's classic white beer. Wheat malt content is typically under 50 percent. A fruity nose may appear sour. Color is pale straw to light golden. Light bodied and highly carbonated, it has very distinctive sour fruitiness that dominates.

Example: Weisse (Berliner Kindl Braueri, Germany).

Dunkelweizen

This dark version of the Weizen has low hoppiness, so the spicy aromas are evident in its nose. Color ranges from amber to light brown. It is light to medium bodied but usually highly carbonated, so it's often considered a very refreshing beer. The Dunkel style is known for its complex malt and fruity tones. Wheat content in the recipe is 25 percent or less.

Examples: Dunkel Weisse, Herkimer Pub and Brewery; Paulaner Hefe Weizen Dunkel (Brauerei Paulaner, Germany).

Krystal Weizen

This traditional wheat beer originated in southern Germany. It can have a light assertive fruitiness and, like the Bavarian Weizen, its qualities also include a spiciness, such as cloves. Krystal refers to the filtering of the Bavarian Weizen.

Examples: Kristall Weizen, Minneapolis Town Hall Brewery; Weissbier Kristallklar (Hofbrau Kaltenhausen Edelweiss, Austria).

Weizenbock
The Weizenbock offers the fruity and yeasty tones of the Dunkelweizen, with the rich maltiness and strength of the bock. Expect a strong fruity nose. The color is light amber to dark brown and cloudy. Medium to full bodied, it has strong earthy flavors marked by fruitiness and maltiness, but the fruitiness dominates. Some clove spiciness is common. There may be smoky overtones.

Example: Aventinus (Private Weissbierbrauerei G. Schneider and Sohn, Germany); Weihenstephaner Vitus (Bayerische Staatsbrauerej Weihenstephan, Germany).

Wheat Wine
A bold and strong wheat-based beer made with 50 percent or more wheat malt. A light fruity nose. Medium to full bodied. A deep amber color. Residual sweetness with fruity esters and low hoppiness. Some bready or honey-like flavor is common.

Example: Wheat Wine, Fitger's Brewhouse.

Winter Warmer
A relatively modern version of the strong ale style. Malty nose and flavor and dark bronze to black color. Often offers an alcoholic warmth that lends charac-ter. Commonly a winter seasonal.

Example: Winter Ale, Vine Park Brewing Company.

LAGERS

Lagers are characterized by fermentation at colder temperatures. They are made with what is commonly referred to as a bottom-fermenting yeast, mean-ing that the yeast is active in the lower portions of the fermentation vessel. Their color is lighter than most ales, most often a shade of golden or bronze, except for the bock and schwarzbier styles, which are much darker. Lagers are a younger style of beers, most having been refined since the mid-nineteenth century and especially in the twentieth century, when mechanical refrigeration came to the brewing industry.

American Lager
Classic American Pilsner
Also called the pre-Prohibition pilsner, this style was brought to the U.S. by immigrant German brewers. It was made not only before but also after Pro-hibition; however, its popularity was strongest in the years before. The style emerged as American brewers worked with ingredients they could get locally. Corn and later rice became components to the recipe, and also U.S. grown hops. It's known for its low to medium grainy or earthy nose. Yellow to golden color. Light to medium-bodied mouth feel. A grainy or earthy maltiness stands out.

Examples: Hauenstein, Arneson Distributing and August Schell Brewing Company; Capital Super Club (Capital Brewery, Middleton, Wisconsin).

Dark American Lager
Dark lager has little or no aroma, or a very faint, light roasted nose. The color is a clear and deep copper to dark brown with a long-lasting bubbly head. Light to medium bodied and smooth, it is crisp with subtle sweetness and roasted tones. The darker caramel malts may provide some dominance to a crisp hoppy background. Finish, if at all, can be slightly sweet.
Example: Schell Dark, August Schell Brewing Company.

Light American Lager
American light lager has a very light or no nose. If an aroma is present it may be a faint fruity or very light flowery hoppiness. The color is pale straw to pale gold. It has light body and thin texture. The flavor is generally clean and crisp. There may be some sweetness, but more often a dryness is evident from the high carbonation. "Light" requires that it have fewer calories than the same style without the light label. In America, Miller Lite has become synonymous with the American light lager style. Miller Lite is known for its "Tastes great, less filling" slogan and its emphasis on fewer calories. In Canada and Australia, the term "light" usually indicates lower amounts of alcohol.
Example: Blue Diamond Light, Blue Diamond Brewing Company; Pig's Eye Lean Light, Pig's Eye Brewing Company; Miller Lite (Miller Brewing, Milwaukee, Wisconsin).

Premium American Pilsner
American Premium has a very light or no nose. If an aroma is present it may be a faint fruity or very light flowery hoppiness. Color is pale straw to pale gold. It is light bodied and thin textured. The flavor is generally fast and crisp. It may have some sweetness, but more often a dryness is evident from the high carbonation. "Premium" brands generally use fewer adjuncts and provide a stronger flavor and body than standard American lagers. The premium label is often applied in the mass marketing of certain lagers to create an up-scale image and to identify the brewery's best lager.
Examples: Handy's Lager, Herkimer Pub and Brewery; Miller Genuine Draft (Miller Brewing, Milwaukee, Wisconsin).

Standard American Pilsner
Little or no aroma. Light bodied, crisp, dry, and highly carbonated. Pale straw to yellow-golden color. Some grainy maltiness will dominate, but hoppy finish gives a very clean and thirst quenching impression. Overall, low hoppy bitterness and high carbonation. Corn, rice, or sugar adjuncts are often used.
Examples: Lakemaid Beer, Lakemaid Beer Company (Pocket Hercules); Pig's Eye, Pig's Eye Brewing Company; Miller High Life (Miller Brewing, Milwaukee, Wisconsin).

Bock
Bock (Bavarian) Traditional
The traditional-style bock originated in and gets its name from the city of Einbeck in northern Germany. Bock also means goat in German, which is used on many labels and in many variations of the name. The bock has a firm malty nose and brilliant deep amber to bronze color. It can be medium to full bodied. It offers a rich, complex maltiness with strong caramel flavors. Some roasted-

ness is in the background but it is kept quiet and only as an accent. The hoppiness is low to moderate. Its finish can be raisiny.

Examples: Bock, August Schell Brewing Company; Split Rock Bock, Lake Superior Brewing Company; Hacker-Pschorr Dunkeler Bock (Hacker-Pschorr Brauerei, Germany).

Doppelbock

A very strong malty nose and virtually no hoppiness. Color is deep, clear gold to dark brown. Full bodied, it has rich maltiness and a strong roasted complement without a burnt flavor. It is smooth and warm to the finish. Fruity esters can be common but not overwhelming. Hop bitterness is evident but not excessive.

Examples: Doppel Bock, August Schell Brewing Company; Intoxicator Doppelbock, Rock Bottom Restaurant and Brewery; Spaten Optimator (Spaten-Franziskaner Brau, Germany).

Doppelbock, Blonde

Similar to the doppelbock, however the term "blonde" refers to a light color, often rich golden to copper. The doppelbock's flavor should feature malty sweetness, especially fresh and lightly toasted caramel malt character.

Example: Blonde Doppelbock (Capital Brewery, Middleton, Wisconsin)

Eisbock

A specialty from Kulmbach, Germany, Eisbock is made by freezing a bock or Doppelbock and removing the ice to concentrate the flavor and alcohol content. It has a malty nose and golden to dark brown color. Full bodied, it has strong malty dominance and no hop flavor. A warming sensation comes from the high alcohol content.

Examples: Eisbock (New Glarus Brewing Company, New Glarus, Wisconsin); Bayrisch G'frorns Eisbock (Kulmbacher Reichelbrau, Germany).

Helles Bock/Maibock

Helles Bock has a moderate to strong malty nose. As the German word "Helles" indicates, this bock is light or pale in color—clear, deep golden to amber, with a thick, soft, long-lasting white head. Medium bodied, it has a rich malty flavor that provides an assertive and sweet perception without being syrupy. Maibocks are considered a spring (May) seasonal.

Examples: Maifest, August Schell Brewing Company; Maibock, Summit Brewing Company; Ayinger Maibock (Privatbrauerei Aying, Germany).

European Lager
Bohemian (Czech) Pilsner

The style originated in Plzen (Pilsen), which is situated in the western half of the Czech Republic. The Bohemian pilsner is therefore sometimes called a Czech pilsner, another reference to its geographic origin. The style dates back to the 1840s. Its defining characteristics include its clarity and a color that ranges from light golden to amber, topped with dense and soft white head. It is known for a moderate bitterness, yet you should still have some balance with its malty underpinnings to the aroma and flavor. You may even find light toasted or biscuit-like character. The Bohemian pilsner, and especially Pilsner Urquell, is often considered the standard by which all pilsners are measured.

Examples: Pilsner, Summit Brewing; Park Point Pilsner, Fitger's Brewhouse; Pilsner Urquell (Pilsner Urquell, Czech Republic, imported by Guinness Import Company).

Dortmunder Export

The color is clear and light golden with a bubbly white head. With light to medium body and hoppiness, there should be good balance between the hops and malt. The strongest trait is in its balance. It is clean tasting and not fruity. Dortmunder Export is not as malty as a Munich Helles or as hoppy as a Bohemian pilsner. This style originates from the German city of Dortmund. The term "export" was originally applied as a notation of strength and was important in German tax law.

Example: Dortmunder Local Export, Minneapolis Town Hall Brewery; Dortmunder Union Original (Dortmunder Union Brauerei, Germany).

German Pilsner

Northern German pilsner is considered to be very similar to the Bohemian pilsner style but it is drier in bitterness and finish. It has a flowery nose and a straw to gold color with a soft, white head. Light to medium bodied, it has crisp and dry hoppiness, clean taste, no fruitiness, and long-lasting dry finish. Recipes feature German noble hop varieties.

Example: Bitburger Premium Pilsner (Privatbrauerei Th. Simon, Germany).

Munich Dunkel

Malt nose has hints of chocolate and toffee. The color is amber to dark brown with a reddish hue. Medium to full bodied and firm. The rich Munich malt dominates this beer. Both roasted tones and hoppiness are restrained and only lightly in the background. It usually has a crisp, light, hoppy finish. When compared with an American dark lager, the Munich Dunkel tends to be fuller bodied with sweet tones from the German malts.

Examples: High Point Dunkel, Herkimer Pub and Brewery; Ayinger Altbairisch Dunkel (Brauerei Aying, Germany)

Munich Helles

The nose is malty, with just a hint of hoppiness. Color is clear and yellow-golden with a soft, white head. Medium to full bodied, it has a clean malt dominance, despite a strong hop complement that gives a balanced impression. This is a Bavarian version of light lager, distinctively malty.

Examples: Hell, Surly Brewing Company; Munich Helles, Vine Park Brewing Company; Spaten Premium Lager (Spaten-Franziskaner Brau, Germany).

Oktoberfest/Märzen

Oktoberfest has a malty nose with light roastedness in the background. Color is dark gold to bronze. Medium bodied and creamy, it has a complex maltiness that may have light roasted tones. Its malty character is smooth and rich. There is a clean, crisp hoppiness in the background. Finish is clear, fast, and lightly bitter. Traditionally brewed in the spring, Oktoberfest is stored in caves or cellars during the summer until the autumn celebrations.

Examples: Oktoberfest, August Schell Brewing; Oktoberfest, Lake Superior Brewing Company; Spaten Oktoberfest (Spaten-Franziskaner Brau, Germany).

Schwarzbier
This German black lager has a malty nose with hints of roasted character. It is very dark, with a reddish or bronze hue. Light to medium bodied, it has a complex malt and hop balance that allows the chocolate malts to come out somewhat dry. The finish is lightly bitter and fast.

Examples: Black Bavarian (Sprecher Brewing Company, Glendale, Wisconsin); Schwarzbier (Das Bierhaus, Menomonie, Wisconsin).

Vienna
The nose is malty, the color is reddish amber to light brown. Light to medium bodied, Vienna has a soft and malty body with a light hoppiness in the finish. It is made with Vienna malt, and roasted malt characteristics impart a light nutty or toasty aroma and taste.

Examples: FireBrick, August Schell Brewing; Red (Leinenkugel Brewing Company, Chippewa Falls, Wisconsin); Negra Modelo Dark Lager (Cerveceria Modelo, Mexico).

Specialty Lagers
Kellerbier or Zwickelbier
Commonly associated with an unfiltered and cellared lager; however, many brewery competitions indicate it can be a lager or an ale. They are not pasteurized. Expect them to be hazy to cloudy, with some yeasty aroma and flavors but not in overpowering amounts. Commonly well balanced between the malt and hops. "Keller" in German means cellar. The term Zwickelbier comes from the sampling cock, called a "zwickel" in German, that is used to take samples from the cask during fermentation. While similar to the Kellerbier, traditionally Zwickelbier may have been lighter, less hoppy, and more effervescent and was served as soon as fermentation ended.

Example: Sky Pilot, Herkimer Pub and Brewery.

Malt Liquor
Neither malt nor liquor dominates. Sometimes it is made with cheaper sugars. Usually it is a high alcohol version of an American lager

Example: Pit Bull High Gravity Ice Malt Liquor, Pig's Eye Brewing Company; Mickey's Malt Liquor (Miller Brewing, Milwaukee, Wisconsin).

HYBRID, MIXED, SPECIALTY BEERS

Barrel- and Wood-Aged Beer
Can be any lager, ale, or hybrid beer that has been aged for a period of time in a wooden barrel or in contact with wood. The intent by the brewer is to impart the character of the wood and/or the flavor of what was previously in the barrel (e.g., bourbon, whiskey, wine, etc.). Depending upon the kind of barrel and its previous use, the resulting beer will have a complex blend of flavors.

Examples: Czar Jack (Bourbon Barrel) Russian Imperial Stout, Minneapolis Town Hall Brewery; Dark Knight, Barley John's Brew Pub.

California Common Beer
Widely referred to as Steam Beer. The modern interpretation of the style has been defined by the Anchor Brewing Company of San Francisco, which actually trademarked the name Anchor Steam Beer in 1981. Because of that, other breweries often shy away from using "steam beer" in their name. The style emerged as an attempt to make a lager-type of beer without strict refrigeration controls. The beer is fermented at temperatures that are on the warm end for lagers and the cool end for ales. The nose is a complex combination of hoppy, fruity, and citric aromas. It has medium body and medium to high carbonation. Substantial bitterness stands out, with a dry finish.

Examples: Element 115, Flat Earth Brewing; Duluth Steam, Fitger's Brewhouse; Anchor Steam (Anchor Brewing, San Francisco, California).

Gluten-Free Beer
Can be any lager, ale, or hybrid beer made from fermentable grains that do not contain gluten. Beers that fit this distinction do not contain malts from barley, wheat, oats, or rye. Gluten-free beers will follow the characteristics of whatever style the brewer is making.

Examples: Bard's Gold, Bard's Tale Beer Company; Lakefront New Grist (Milwaukee, Wisconsin)

Ice Beer
Ice beers have been frozen during fermentation. This freezing can rob the beer of some characteristics and increase others. For example, water freezes before alcohol, and when the ice crystals are separated from the beer the concentration can thereby increase. Ice beer is considered an American adaptation of the Eisbock style, but specific federal regulations apply to its production and marketing.

Examples: Pig's Eye Ice, Pig's Eye Brewing Company; Mickey's Ice (Miller Brewing, Milwaukee, Wisconsin).

Session Beer
Often used to describe any lager, ale, or hybrid that is lower in strength and well balanced in flavor. Generally these beers do not exceed 5 percent ABV. They are often referred to as "very drinkable" beers because they allow the drinker to have more than one in a session without feeling full or overwhelmed by the alcohol.

Examples: The Pubstitute, Pour Decisions Brewing Company; West Bank Pub Ale, Minneapolis Town Hall Brewery.

MEADS

Meads are made with honey, water, and yeast. They can offer many characteristics of beer, such as sweetness, dryness, and effervescence. They are often recognized for long fermentation times and sweet, honey-like flavors.

Braggot or Bracket
Braggot meads are made with both honey and malt. The amount of honey must be greater than half of the fermentables, otherwise it is more likely a honey-enhanced beer.

Melomel
Melomel is made with fruit. Both nose and color are enhanced by the type of fruit used. More specifically, a Cyser is a mead made with apples, and a Pyment is a mead made with grapes.

Metheglin
A mead made with herbs and species. While the honey aromas are evident, their assertiveness depends upon what spices are used.

Traditional Mead
The honey is evident in both the nose and the taste. The color ranges from gold to amber and usually clear, and most have only light bubbly heads or no head at all. Meads are full bodied and smooth, almost wine-like in their texture. They will finish smooth and warm.

Terms Commonly Heard on Brewery Tours

ABV (alcohol by volume)—A measure of the alcohol content expressed as a percentage of the volume of alcohol per volume of beer.

ABW (alcohol by weight)—A measure of the alcohol content expressed as a percentage of the weight of alcohol per volume of beer. The ABW figure is approximately 20 percent lower than the ABV.

adjunct—Any ingredient that is added to the mash besides the traditional four ingredients of water, hops, yeast, and malt. Such additives are commonly unmalted grains or cheaper fermentable sugars. Oats, corn, wheat, rice, and glucose are common examples.

aeration—The specific act of exposing or inducing air during the brewing process.

aftertaste—The linger taste, sometimes combined with aroma, after the beer has been swallowed.

alcoholic (as part of the flavor profile)—The warming taste from higher levels of ethanol.

ale—A beer brewed from top-fermenting yeast.

alpha acids—The bittering compounds found in hops that are extracted when hops are boiled with wort.

aroma (also called bouquet or nose)—The fragrance or odor that emanates from the beer.

aromatic hops—Hops that lend strong aroma to the beer. Sometimes also called finishing hops.

astringent (as part of the flavor profile)—A harsh, medicinal tannic taste that can create a puckering sensation when extreme.

balance—The proportion of malt flavor to hoppy bitterness in a beer.

balling—A measure of the density of sugars in wort.

beer engine—A hand pump that draws the beer out of a cask. Often features a curved spout that allows the glass to be filled from the bottom up.

bierstube—A beer hall or large pub/tavern that specializes in beer.

bittering hops—Hops that impart bitterness in the flavor profile of the beer's taste.

bomber—A large bottle of beer, commonly 22 to 25 ounces (650–750 ml).

bottle-conditioned—When secondary fermentation and maturation occur after the beer is placed in the bottle.

brew kettle—The vessel in which wort is boiled.

CAMRA (Campaign for Real Ale)—An independent, voluntary organization based in Europe that advocates for real or cask-conditioned ales, real pubs, and consumer rights.

carboy—A large glass container or bottle with a narrow neck that is commonly used in homebrewing as a fermentation vessel. Usually five to ten gallons in size.

cask—A large vessel used for storage and secondary fermentation. Traditionally it would have been a wooden barrel; in modern times it more commonly refers to a stainless-steel half-barrel keg (approximately 15.5 gallons).

cask conditioned—When secondary fermentation and maturation occur in the keg or barrel. Beer is often served directly from that vessel.

cellarman—The person responsible for taking care of the beer while it remains in storage.

chill haze—Cloudiness from protein-tannins that precipitate in beer at low temperature.

conditioning—The period of maturation intended to impart natural carbonation, develop flavor, and settle or clarify the fermenting beer.

contract beer—Beer made by one brewery and then marketed by another company.

decoction mashing—A traditional German technique for brewing lager beers that is aimed at maximizing the conversion of starch.

diacetyl—A volatile compound produced by yeast in the fermentation cycle. While it is a desired character in some ales, in certain instances it is unwanted. Extreme amounts can create a butter or butterscotch flavor similar to partially popped and buttered popcorn.

DMS (dimethyl sulfide)—A sulfur compound most commonly associated with lagers. At high levels in beer it can be associated with vegetal flavors, such as cooked corn or cabbage.

draft/draught beer—Beer drawn from kegs or cask, usually through a tap.

dry hopping—The addition of hops to the fermenting or aging beer. Intended to increase the aroma and/or the hop flavor of the beer.

effervescence—A bubbly or fizzing appearance.

esters—Flavor compounds that are formed by the interaction of alcohol from certain yeasts with organic acids. They can be desirable or undesirable depending upon the beer style. Commonly associated with fruity-type flavors, such as banana or pear. Too much results in solvent-like tastes.

extract/malt extract—Malt in the form of concentrated syrup or powder and reactivated with water during the preparation of wort.

final/terminal specific gravity—The measurement of the beer's density after fermentation is complete.

firkin—A cask or keg with a quarter-barrel capacity. More commonly associated with the English unit of volume (in English units a firkin is approximately nine gallons).

flavoring hops—The hops added to boiling wort for bitter taste, as opposed to finishing and aromatic hops.

Gambrinus (King Gambrinus)—The legendary king of Flanders in the Middle Ages, considered the first patron of beer lovers (although not a patron saint). He was not a brewer but a popular ruler with a joyous and infectious way of life. He is said to have had a large appetite for and enjoyment of beer. His likeness is found in many breweries, such as a large mural in the lobby of Fitger's Inn and Hotel in Duluth and a ten-foot statue outside City Brewery (former G. Heileman) in La Crosse, Wisconsin.

grist—The mixture of milled grains that creates the wort.

growler—A large jar, jug, or special container (usually one-half gallon) for take-home beer from a brewpub or brewery.

heavy beer—A beer with high density or high gravity (original wort gravity of 1.050 or higher). Such beers usually look thick and have full-bodied mouth feel from immense amounts of ingredients that go into making them. They can have high alcohol content, but this term is more appropriately used to describe high specific gravity.

hogshead—A 54-gallon cask of beer (for wine the measure is 63 gallons). The hogshead was first standardized by Parliament in 1423.

hop back—A type of strainer, or sealed chamber, that is used to separate the spent hops from the wort after boiling. It helps retain hop aroma compounds that would normally be driven off when the hops contact the hot wort.

hot liquor tank—A container with reheated water to be used in the brewing process, commonly water that is infused directly into mashing or sparging.

hydrometer—A instrument for measuring specific gravity of liquids as compared to that of water.

IBUs (international bittering units)—The system of measuring and expressing bitterness in beer.

infusion mashing—A process in which the mash is not boiled but is sprayed, soaked, and/or steeped with hot water. The wort, followed by hot water, is sparged or filtered over the spent grains. In single infusion mashing water is added all at once and the mash is held at a steady temperature. In step infusion mashing some of the water is held back and heated to a carefully maintained temperature.

jockey box—Most commonly a picnic cooler with externally mounted tap handles. It has tubes or piping coils for each tap and is filled with ice to rapidly cool beer as an open tap pulls it through the system. Often used at beer festivals.

krausening—A method of conditioning the fermenting beer that adds a small amount of young fermenting wort to a fully fermented batch. The intent is to initiate secondary fermentation and natural carbonation.

lactic acid—A chemical compound that imparts a flavor similar to sour milk. For most beer styles it is an undesirable trait of bacteria contamination in fermentation and aging resulting in a sour, yogurt-like taste. In some beer styles like the Belgian lambic, however, small amounts are desirable.

lactobacillus—A bacteria that is used like yeast to ferment wort sugars into lactic acid. This commonly adds a fruity, sour flavor to the beer. Undesirable for most beer styles, but a sought-after characteristic in some styles, such as lambics.

lager—Beer made with bottom-fermenting yeast.

lagering—The storage and aging of beer at low temperature, usually below 50 degrees Fahrenheit.

lauter tun—The vessel where the mash settles and the wort is strained or sparged from spent grains.

malt—Grain that has been malted.

malt extract—Malt in the form of concentrated syrup or powder and re-activated with water during the preparation of wort.

malting—The process of converting barley into malt. It involves encouraging grains to germinate by soaking them in water and then halting germination by drying or roasting the grains.

mash—The mixture of grist that is soaked and cooked in water to release the fermentable sugars.

mash tun—The container where mash is mixed and turned into wort.

mouth feel—The beer's body or texture. A description of how it feels in the mouth.

original gravity—The specific gravity of the wort prior to fermentation.

oxidation—Exposure to oxygen. May cause stale or wet cardboard flavors.

pasteurization—The application of intense heat to beer after it has been bottled, canned, or kegged to stop fermentation and/or to kill bacteria in an effort to stabilize the product.

phenols—These volatile compounds contribute to flavor and aroma. In certain styles, such as wheat beers, they are welcome, with spicy clove-like and fruity banana esters. In excessive concentrations they can create solvent or medicinal qualities.

pitching—The addition of yeast into the wort once it has cooled.

plato—An expression of specific gravity as measured by a saccharometer.

pony keg—A quarter-barrel measure (7.75 gallons).

primary fermentation—The initial stage of fermentation at which most of the fermentable sugars in the wort are converted to alcohol and carbon dioxide gas by the yeast. Depending upon the beer style, this usually lasts from two to seven days.

priming—The addition of sugars into fermented beer at bottling in order to initiate a small amount of additional fermentation in a sealed bottle to carbonate the beer. In homebrewing a common priming sugar is corn sugar or syrup.

racking—The process of transferring fermented beer into packaging, such as bottles, cans, and kegs.

real ale—Unpasteurized, cask-conditioned beer that completes fermentation and maturation in the keg or barrel.

Reinheitsgebot—The German Purity Law of 1516 that permitted only three ingredients in beer: barley, hops, and water.

rouser—A brewer's paddle.

rousing—To stir. Often used when serving wheat beers directly from the bottle. Homebrewers may also use this to describe rocking the fermentation vessel to re-suspend the yeast.

saccharification—The process of converting malt starch to fermentable sugars.

secondary fermentation—The second stage of fermentation that occurs in closed vessels. Depending upon the beer style, it may last from a few weeks to several months.

session beer—A beer, usually relatively low in alcohol strength, that allows one to drink several at one sitting without becoming inebriated or too full.

small beer—A term originating in England to describe a weak beer.

smoked malt—Malt that has been dried (kilned) by open fire. Such malt commonly imparts a smoky or deeply roasted flavor to the beer.

sparging—During mashing spent grains are used as a filter for the mash as it is transferred from the lauter tun. The spent grains are also sprayed with hot water to extract the remaining fermentable sugars.

specific gravity—The density of a liquid compared to that of water.

spent grains—The grain husks remaining after the wort is made.

SRM (standard reference method)—An analytical method the American Society of Brewing Chemists uses to describe the color of beer.

stillion—An X-shaped cradle that holds wooden casks.

stubbie—A short glass bottle that is shorter and flatter than standard bottles. Stubbies typically hold 11.2 ounces.

tannin—A nontechnical term for phenols. Tannins cause dry and puckered mouth feel.

texture—How the beer feels in the mouth.

three-tier system—Following Prohibition some states mandated that beer distribution go through three entities—brewer, wholesaler, and retailer.

tied house—A system by which a pub, inn, or saloon is "tied" to a single brewery and sells only its products.

torrefication—A process of quick heating grain (wheat and/or barley), causing it to expand like popcorn, thereby making it easier to mash.

turbidity—Cloudiness in beer.

two-stage fermentation—Primary and secondary fermentation carried out in two containers. A common process in homebrewing.

ullage—The space at the top of the bottle, cask, or barrel between the beer and the top of the container.

underback—The container that receives the wort as it flows from the mash tun.

weeping barrel—A brewer's term for a leaking barrel or cask.

wild yeast—Commonly used to describe airborne yeast that is not deliberately used, cultured, or under the control of the brewer.

wort—The sugar solution created by the boiling of malt and hops before it is fermented into beer.

yard of ale—A three-foot-long drinking glass, usually with a wooden stand, that holds about a quart of beer.

yeast bite—A sour, rotten, off-flavor or aroma of yeast in beer. One potential cause is overpitching yeast.

zymology—The science of fermentation.

Index

ACE Engineering, 63
Adventure Creative Group, 267
Aerial Lift Bridge (Duluth), 179, 185–86
Ahlstom, Bob, 227
Aiple, Frank, 107
airport beer, Minneapolis–St. Paul, 287–91
Akron, Ohio, 290
Albany, New York, 112
Alcohol and Tobacco Tax and Trade Bureau (TTB), 139
ales, xiv, 329–40
Alexander Ramsey Park, 224
Alley (pub), 188–89. *See also* South Shore Brewery
Allied Beverage Tanks, 148
Amana, Iowa, 293
Ambleside Brewing Company, 138
American Breweriana Association (ABA), 248
American Brewers Guild, 79, 226
American Fur Company, 116, 132
American Homebrewers Association (AHA), xx, 185
Ames, Iowa, 10
Amsoil Arena, 165, 169
Anchor Inn, 285
Anderson, David, xi, 138–40. *See also* Dave's BrewFarm
Anderson, Nick, 143–44. *See also* Rush River Brewing Company
Andi's Closet, 182
Angry Minnow Brewpub, 130
Anheuser-Busch Brewing Company, 158, 248
Anneke, Percy, 173. *See also* Fitger's Brewhouse

Ansari, Becca, 118. *See also* Surly Brewing Company
Ansari, Omar, 118–20, 286. *See also* Surly Brewing Company
Ansbach, Germany, 113
antiquing, 27, 52, 75, 76, 84, 104, 109, 110, 113, 162, 217, 233, 234
Antwerp, Belgium, 31, 141
Aplington, Iowa, 103
appearance, xviii
appetizers, with beer, xxii
Arbor Lakes, 49
Archdiocese and Cathedral of St. Paul, 107
Arctic Craft Brewery, 136
Arizona, 265
Arlington, Virginia, 220
Arneson, Al and Rae Ann, 272–73. *See also* Hauenstein Beer
Arneson Distribution, 272
aroma/bouquet/nose, xiv–xv
Arrowhead region, 147, 160
Arts by the River, 229
Ashland, Wisconsin, 174, 188–89, 284. *See also* South Shore Brewery
Atlanta, Georgia, 290
Augsburg College, 271
August Schell Brewing Company, x, xi, xii, 160, 205–13, 224, 227, 229, 232, 272, 274, 275, 287
Ausenhus, Peter, 255–56. *See also* Worth Brewing Company
Autumn Brew Review, xi, 293
Axel's Bonfire, 287

Backwater Brewing Company, x, 214–18, 237

Badger Brewing Company, 251
bagpipes, 98, 241, 242
Bakken Museum, 104
Baltimore, Maryland, 220, 290
Bamberg, Germany, 121
Bandana Brewery, 227
Bank Beer Company, 259–61, 304
Bank Inn, 260
Bard's Tale Beer Company, 262–63,
    246, 305
Barker's Island, 179, 185
barley, growing, 219–20
Barley John's Brew Pub, x, 23–28, 93,
    308–9
Barley's (Dominican Republic), 118
Barley Wine, 35, 37, 88, 104, 178, 184,
    191
Barthel Beverage, 272
baseball, 5, 7, 13, 14, 18, 36, 83, 104,
    229, 284
Bavarian Blast, 293
Bayfront Festival Park, 177
Beaver Bay, 158
bed and breakfast, 60, 125, 157, 212,
    216–17
beer and food, xxii–xxvi
BeerAdvocate, 119
beer barons, 323
Beer Dabbler, 293
Beer for Wildlife, 259
beer garden, x, 286
Beerhalter, John, 173. *See also* Fitger's
    Brewhouse
Beer Judge Certification Program
    (BJCP), 92
beer styles, xiv, xx, 328–46
Bélanger, Bo, 174, 188–89. *See also*
    South Shore Brewery
Belgium, 29, 92, 93, 125, 131, 141, 191,
    221, 237
Belgrade, Montana, 103
Bell Museum, 89
Bell's Brewery, 30, 215, 248
Belsele, Belgium, 31
Belser, Craig, 262, 263. *See also* Bard's
    Tale Beer Company
Benkstein, Brian, 288
Benkstein, Larry, 288
Benzberg Brewery, 206

Berglund, Jacquie, 270, 271. *See also*
    Finnegans Inc.
Berkeley, California, 172
Bernhardt, Jacob, 206. *See also* August
    Schell Brewing Company
Betty's Pies, 160
Between the Bluffs Beer, Wine and
    Cheese Festival, 246, 294
Beverage International, 3
Beverage Testing Institute (BTI), xx,
    183
Biermann, Eric, 78, 79, 80. *See also*
    Lucid Brewing Company
Big River Brewfest, 292
Big Wood Brewing, 283–84
biking trails/paths, 13, 18, 32, 38, 48,
    52, 60, 65, 104, 116, 132, 159,
    186, 198, 212, 229, 256
Bishop, Margaret, 256. *See also* Worth
    Brewing Company
Black River Falls, Wisconsin, 139, 232,
    250–52, 293. *See also* Sand Creek
    Brewing Company
Blair, Bob, 167, 168. *See also* Dubrue
Blessing of the Bock, 294
Blomquist, Eric, 115–16. *See also* Sum-
    mit Brewing Company
Bloomington, Indiana, 183
Blue Diamond Brewing Company, 4,
    264–66
Blue Earth County Historical Society,
    229
Blue Earth River, 227
Bluegrass Brewing Company, 290
Bluff Park, 229
BoatHouse Brewpub and Restaurant,
    xi, 147–51
Bock Brats, 212
Bockfest (Middleton, Wisconsin), 294
Bockfest (New Ulm), 293
Boddingtons, 168
Bodega, 245
Boelens, Kris, 31
Bois Forte Heritage Center and Cultural
    Museum, 151
Boo, Rick, 153. *See also* Carmody Irish
    Pub and Brewing
Boom Island Brewing Company, 29–33,
    306

Boom Island Park, 30
bootlegging, 277
Bossard, Sabina, 239. *See also* City
Brewing Company
Boston, Massachusetts, 183, 290
bottling line, xi, 8, 44, 74, 112, 119, 183,
186, 196, 219, 220, 245, 247
Boulder, Colorado, 11
Boulder Beer Company, 11
Boundary Waters Canoe Area Wilder-
ness (BWCAW), 147, 148, 149,
150, 151, 160, 174
Bowerville, 228
Boy River, 198
Brady's Brewhouse, 134–35
Brainerd, 148, 267–69. *See also* Brain-
erd Lakes Brewery
Brainerd Brewing Company (1887–15),
268
Brainerd Lakes Brewery, 182, 267–69,
301
Brau, Brady, 219, 220. *See also* Brau
Brothers Brewing Company
Brau, Dale, 219. *See also* Brau Brothers
Brewing Company
Brau, Dustin, 219, 220, 221, 223, 224.
See also Brau Brothers Brewing
Company
Brau, Mary, 219, 220, 224. *See also*
Brau Brothers Brewing Company
Brau, Trevor, 219, 220, 221. *See also*
Brau Brothers Brewing Company
Brau Brothers Brewing Company, xi, xii,
219–26, 260, 272; Braufest, 225,
293; Hop Fest, 293
Brauerei Zum Hirsch, 112
Braufest, 225, 293
Brauhaus, 219, 220, 224, 225. *See also*
Brau Brothers Brewing Company
Bremer, Karl, 126. *See also* St. Croix
Brewing Company
Brew Brothers, 290
Brewers Bazaar, 76, 109, 293
Brewer's Cave, 264–66. *See also* Blue
Diamond Brewing Company
Brewery Boelens, 31
Brewery Ommegang, 183
Brewfest (Minocqua, Wisconsin), 294
brewing process, xxviii–xxix

Brew-Magic, 283, 284
brewmaster dinners, 292
brew-on-premise, 129, 130, 131
brewpub, definition, xxvii
Bridge of Hope, 18
Briese Malting, 126
Bright Spot Tavern and Liquors, 84
Brit's Pub, 271
Brödd, Jesse, 63. *See also* Harriet
Brewing
Brooklyn Center, xi, xii, 118–23, 285–
86, 292. *See also* Surly Brewing
Company
Brouwerij der Trappisten van Westmalle,
31, 93
Brown, Earle, 122
Brown University, 10
Bruce Hitman Heron Rookery, 7
Bruzek, Mark, 147–51. *See also* Boat-
House Brewpub and Restaurant
Bryan, Maurice, 3. *See also* Cold Spring
Brewing Company
Bryant-Lake Bowl, 71
Buffalo, New York, 263
Build a Wildlife Area, 259, 260
Burdick, Bill, 9–12, 45–46, 96, 200, 243.
See also Granite City Food and
Brewery
Burns, Robert, 263
Burnsville, 283
Burrito Union, 173
Burrows, Charlie, 287
Burwell, Charles, 80
Burwell Art Fair, 80
Busch, Gottlieb, 173. *See also* Fitger's
Brewhouse
Buszka, Steve, 248. *See also* Potosi
Brewing Company

Caledonia Bluff Country Brewfest, 292
California, 91, 119, 158, 159, 172, 206,
254, 263, 290
Cameron, Nick, 167, 168. *See also*
Dubrue
Camp, Tom, 275. *See also* Lakemaid
Beer Company
Camp Depression, 159
Canada, 148, 149, 151, 159, 179, 262,
275

Canal Park (Duluth), 155, 156, 165, 169, 176, 179, 180, 185, 186, 284
Canal Park Brewing Company, 284
Canal Park Inn, 284
Canal Park Lodge, 284
Cannon Falls, 236
Canton, Ohio, 290
Capital City Brewing Company (Washington, DC), 220
Caribou Coffee, 284
Carlson, Jake, 148, 149. See also BoatHouse Brewpub and Restaurant
Carlson, Joel, 148, 149, 150. See also BoatHouse Brewpub and Restaurant
Carlson Bookstore Building, 173, 285
Carlson School of Management (University of Minnesota), 41, 263
Carmody, Agnes, 153. See also Carmody Irish Pub and Brewing
Carmody Irish Pub and Brewing, xi, 152–56, 165, 168, 169, 179, 186, 302
casinos, 169, 198, 264
Cass Lake, 198
Castle Danger Brewery, xi, xii, 157–61
Castle Haven Cabins, 158, 161. See also Castle Danger Brewery
Cathedral Hill neighborhood, 60, 127
Cathedral of St. Paul, 127
Cave Brewery, 278
caves, 60, 76, 109, 217, 232, 248, 264, 323
Cedar Lake Trail, 44, 104
Chain of Lakes, 62, 65
Champps Americana, 9–10, 45, 200, 243. See also Granite City Food and Brewery
Chang, Dan, 143, 144. See also Rush River Brewing Company
cheese, with beer, xxii
Chequamegeon Bay, 188
Cherokee Park, 116
Chetek Brews and Rib Fest, 293
Chicago, Illinois, 148, 168, 172, 191, 211, 215, 236, 290, 294
Chicago Beer Society, 293, 294
Chicagoland Brewpub-Microbrewery Shootout, 294
Chilton, Wisconsin, 126, 294

China, 265
Chippewa Falls, Wisconsin, 195, 289
Chippewa National Forest, 195
Choo Choo Bar and Grill, 190
Christiansen, Jon, 141, 142. See also Lucette Brewing Company
Christopher Stahlmann Brewing Company, 228, 264, 278
Cigar City Brewing, 79
Cincinnati, Ohio, 206, 290
City Brewery (La Crosse, Wisconsin), 217, 239–40, 277–78
City Pages, 24; Beer Festival, 293
Civilian Conservation Corps, 151
Civil War Days, 233
Clark, Wendel, 15. See also McCann's Food and Brew
Clear Lake, Wisconsin, 136
Clearwater Beer Festival, 294
Cleveland, Ohio, 290
Cleveland Institute of Music, 30
Cloquet, 292
Clubhaus Brewpub, 215
Clyde Park Bakery, Restaurant, and Brewery, 182, 185, 284
Coborn's Leech Lake Cruises, 198
Coborun, Dan, 3. See also Cold Spring Brewing Company
Coborun, Mabel, 3. See also Cold Spring Brewing Company
coffee shops and roasters, 32, 36, 65, 88, 87, 160, 182, 275, 284
Cold Spring, 3–8. See also Cold Spring Brewing Company
Cold Spring Brewery, 3–8, 16, 74, 186, 227, 260, 265, 272, 276
Collins, Clint, 163. See also Dubh Linn Irish Brewpub
Cologne, Germany, 183
Colorado, 68, 102, 136, 139, 183, 196, 245, 289, 290, 294
Colorado Springs, Colorado, 136
Columbus, Ohio, 235
Complete Joy of Home Brewing, 196
Concord, California, 79
Concord Singers of New Ulm, 211
Connecticut, 263
contract brewing company, definition, xxvii
Cooperstown, New York, 183

Coors Brewing Company, 3, 11, 278
Cottonwood River, 206, 212, 213
Council for the Arts, 211
County Cork (Ireland), 162
Covington Inn Bed and Breakfast, 60
Craft Beer Expo, 293
Craft Brewers Conference, 119
Craft Brew Festival (Des Moines), 294
cranberries, 149, 251, 252, 267
Crawford, Jeff, 278. See also Pig's Eye
Brewing Company
Creighton University, 55
Cronk, Trevor, 73, 74. See also Lift
Bridge Brewery
Crooked Pint Ale House, 84
Crosby Farm Regional Park, 116
Crosby Lake Business Park, 117
Cruaser, Hellen, 24

Dakota Warrior, 228–29
Dark Horse Brewery, 220
Das Bierhaus (Menomonie, Wisconsin),
136–37
Daub's Lake State Wildlife Management
Area, 224
Dave's BrewFarm, xi, 138–40, 250
David, Gary, 247, 249. See also Potosi
Brewing Company
Day, Frank, 96
Decker, Nicholas, 172. See also Fitger's
Brewhouse
Decorah, Iowa, 253–54. See also
Toppling Goliath Brewing
Company
Deep Water Grille, 188–89. See also
South Shore Brewery
Deer Brand Beer, 206, 208, 209,
210–11. See also August Schell
Brewing Company
De Koninck Brewery, 141
Delafield, Wisconsin, 141
Dempsey, Bill, 241
Dempsey's Brewery, Restaurant, and
Pub, 241–42
Dempsey's Castle, 241
Denver, Colorado, 96, 139, 196, 290,
294
Des Moines, Iowa, 11, 294
desserts, with beer, xxiii
Detroit, Michigan, 290

Deutsche Strasse Bed and Breakfast,
212
Dewitt-Seitz Marketplace, 155
Diamond Blue, 264, 265. See also Blue
Diamond Brewing Company
Diley, Jim, 41–42, 43. See also Fulton
Brewery
Dillon, L. T., 256
Dingfelder, Carlus, 236
Dingfelder, Carolyn, 236
District Warehouse Brewing Company,
68
Dixon, Pamela, 138. See also Dave's
BrewFarm
Dodder River, 163
Dodge County Brewery, 233
Doemens Academy, 141
Dorothy Molter Museum, 150–51
Dromeshauser, Bob, 182, 183, 185.
See also Lake Superior Brewing
Company
Dubh Linn Irish Brewpub, xi, 162–66,
179, 186, 302
Dublin, Ireland, 164
Dubrue, xi, 155, 165, 167–70, 186
DuClaw Brewing Company, 290
Duff, Tim, 148. See also BoatHouse
Brewpub and Restaurant
Du Lhut, Daniel Greysolon, 184
Duluth, 124, 151–56, 160, 162–88,
231–34, 284–85, 302–3. See also
specific brewery
Duluth Art Institute, 165, 179
Duluth Brewing. See Dubrue
Duluth Brewing and Malting Company,
183
Duluth Children's Museum, 165
Duluth City Hall, 285
Duluth Clinic, 167, 170
Duluth Entertainment and Convention
Center, 165, 169
Duluth Playhouse, 165
Duluth Spring Company, 284
Duluth–Superior Harbor, 186
Duluth Superior Symphony Orchestra,
30, 165, 169
Dunn Bros, 36
Durkhardt Brewery, 285
DuVernois, Bob, 54–55. See also Great
Waters Brewing Company

Dwyer, Alyssa, 78, 79. *See also* Lucid
    Brewing Company
Dylan, Bob, 154, 174, 179, 263
Dylan Fest, 174, 179
Dzubar, Paul, 84. *See also* Minneapolis
    Town Hall Brewery

Eagan, 46, 48–49. *See also* Granite City
    Food and Brewery
Eagan Community Center, 48
Eagle Lake, 50
Eagle River, Wisconsin, 294
Eagles Nest Lake, 149
Eastern Arizona College, 182
Eau Claire, Wisconsin, 294
Eden Prairie, 126
Edinburgh, Scotland, 10
Eelpout, 148, 149, 150, 198
Eighteenth Amendment, U.S. Constitu-
    tion, 224
Elk River, 292
Ellsworth, Iowa, 10, 46, 200, 244.
    See also Granite City Food and
    Brewery
Elm Creek Park, 50
Ely, xi, 147–51. *See also* BoatHouse
    Brewpub and Restaurant
Ely-Winton History Museum, 151
Empire Mall, 243
Enger Park, 186
England, Kristen, 91, 92, 93. *See also*
    Pour Decisions Brewing
    Company
England, Orsolya, 92. *See also* Pour
    Decisions Brewing Company
English, Dr. Nancy, 154
entrees, with beer, xxiii
Eto, Steve, 284
Eugene H. Hagel Arboretum, 122
Evergreen, Colorado, 245
Excelsior, 80, 104, 284–85. *See also*
    Excelsior Brewing Company
Excelsior Brewing Company, 284–85
Experimental Theatre Company, 83

Falls Park, 243
Famous Dave's, 38, 39
Fargo, North Dakota, 45, 148, 200–201,
    243, 294. *See also* Granite City
    Food and Brewery

farmers' markets, 49, 65, 80, 135, 164,
    229
farmhouse breweries, 235, 236
Fermentus Interruptus, 10–11, 46, 200,
    243
Festival of Iowa Beers, 293
Festival of Kites, 224
festivals, beer, 292–95
Feuchtenberger, Tony, 226. *See also*
    Mankato Brewery
finish/aftertaste, xix
Fink, Michael, 172. *See also* Fitger's
    Brewhouse
Finnegans Community Fund, 271
Finnegans Inc., 270–71
Firestone Walker Brewing, 74
First National Bank of Northfield, Min-
    nesota, 260
Fish Lake, 50
fishing, 149, 198, 274, 275
Fitger, Arthur, 171. *See also* Fitger's
    Brewhouse
Fitger Brewing Company (before 1972),
    173, 285
Fitger's Brewhouse Brewery and Grille,
    x, xi, xii, 84, 173, 182, 134–35,
    155–56, 165, 167, 168, 169, 183,
    186, 190, 285
Fitger's Brewery Complex, 171, 173,
    174, 182
Fitger's Hotel, 171
Fitger's Production Brewery (planned),
    285
Fitger's Spark Plug, 173
Fitzgerald, F. Scott, 60
Fitzgerald Theatre, 59
Flandrau Fest, 212
Flandrau State Park, 212
Flat Earth Brewing Company, xi, 34–39,
    65, 73, 74, 79, 117, 128, 132
Florida, 107, 290
Flying Bison Brewing Company, 263
Folliard, Kieran, 271
Fond du Luth Casino, 169
food and beer, pairing, xxii–xxvi
Food and Froth, 294
football, 83, 154
Forest Lake, 35, 278
Fort Collins, Colorado, 183
Fort Snelling, 38, 48, 65, 116, 132

Foss, Patrick, 284. *See also* Excelsior Brewing Company
Fountain Cave, 277
Four Firkins, 105
France, 237
Franken, Al, 104
Frankenstein system, 40, 168
Frederick Weisman Art Museum, 89
Freeport, 7, 14
French beer, 184
Friedman, Thomas, 104
Fulton Brewery, 32, 40–44, 65, 90, 250, 306–7
Fyten, George Jr., 125
Fyten, John, 125
Fyten, Tod, 124, 125, 126, 127, 217, 231, 232. *See also* Mantorville Brewing Company; St. Croix Brewing Company; Theodore Fyten Brewing Company

G. Heileman Brewing Company, 5, 210, 239, 273, 278
Gagné, Phil, 278. *See also* Pig's Eye Brewing Company
Gales State Wildlife Management Area, 224
Galtier, Father Lucien, 277
Gambrinus, 240
gangsters, 55
garage brewers: Bard's Tale, 262; Dubrue, 167, 168, 170; Fulton, 40, 41; Harriet, 63, 66; Sand Creek, 251; 612 Brew, 283; Surly, 119, 122
Gardner, Chris, 214. *See also* Backwater Brewing Company
Gardner, Geoff, 215. *See also* Backwater Brewing Company
Gardner, Paul, 215. *See also* Backwater Brewing Company
General Mills, 41
Georgia, 290
Germanfest (Milwaukee), 294
German immigration, 323
German Park, 211
Germany, 79, 92, 103, 111, 112, 113, 114, 119, 121, 126, 131, 136–37, 141, 148, 172, 176, 183, 191, 205, 206, 207, 210, 211, 219, 237, 241

Gibbs Farm Museum of Pioneer and Dakota Life, 27
Ginny's Supper Club, 236
Ginsberg, Charles and Anna, 232
Gitchee Gumee Brewfest, 179, 295
Glacial Lakes Marching Band, 241
glassware, xiv–xv, xvi–xvii
Gleason, Ed, 153. *See also* Carmody Irish Pub and Brewing
Gleason, Liz, 153. *See also* Carmody Irish Pub and Brewing
Glensheen Mansion, 179
Glockenspiel, 132, 211
Gluek Brewing Company, 3, 4, 83. *See also* Cold Spring Brewing Company
gluten-free beer, 191, 262, 263
Glynn, Brad, 73, 74, 75, 76. *See also* Lift Bridge Brewery
Glynn, Gwen, 75. *See also* Lift Bridge Brewery
Golden Valley, 41
Gooseberry Falls State Park, 159, 160, 161, 179, 186
Goose Island Beer Company, 236, 290
Gordon Biersch Brewing Company, 263, 290, 291
Gräfelfing, Germany, 103
Grage, Andy, 129, 130, 131, 132. *See also* Vine Park Brewing Company
Grain Belt, 30, 205, 207, 210, 272, 273, 278, 288. *See also* August Schell Brewing Company
Grand Avenue (St. Paul), 60
Grand Marais, 160
Grand Portage, 159
Grande, Peter, 41–42. *See also* Fulton Brewery
Grandma's Marathon, 185, 186
Grandma's Saloon and Grill, 185
Granite City Food and Brewery, 45–53; corporate offices, 52; Eagan, 48–49; Fargo, North Dakota, 200–201; Indianapolis, Indiana, 290; Maple Grove, 49–50; Roseville, 50–52, 93, 209–10; Sioux Falls, South Dakota, 243–44; St. Cloud, 9–14, 18, 96; St. Louis Park, 52–53, 104

Granite Falls, 224, 225
Grant, Jesse, 267, 268. *See also* Brainerd Lakes Brewery
Grant County (Wisconsin), 248
Great American Beer Festival, 139, 294; medal winning beers, 24, 69, 85, 86, 87, 88, 99, 113, 114, 115, 120, 178, 208, 209, 278, 279
Great Dane Pub and Brewing Company, 290
Great Depression, 260
Great Lakes, xi, 89, 155, 157, 158, 159, 160, 161, 164, 165, 169, 171, 172, 179, 180, 183, 184, 185, 186, 188, 189, 284, 290, 295
Great Lakes Aquarium, 155, 165, 169, 179, 185
Great Lakes Brew Fest, 295
Great Lakes Brewing Company, 290
Great Northern Beer Festival, 294
Great River Bluffs State Park, 216
Great River Road, 216, 218, 237, 248
Great Taste of the Midwest (Madison, Wisconsin), 294
Great Tastes Festival (Black River Falls, Wisconsin), 293
Great Waters Brewing Company, x, 39, 54–61, 117, 132, 148, 183
Green Bay Packers, 71
Green Isle, 227
Green Mill Restaurants, 84
Green Room, 288
Grumpy's Bar, 93
Guinness, 152, 162, 163–64
Gund, John, 239. *See also* City Brewing Company
Guthrie Theatre, 84

Hackensack, 142
Haggarty, John, 84. *See also* Minneapolis Town Hall Brewery
Hall, Matt, 74. *See also* Lift Bridge Brewery
Hamm, William, 54, 55
Hamm's Bear, 56
Happy Gnome, 41, 76
Harpoon Brewing Company, 183, 290
Harriet Alexander Nature Center, 51, 93
Harriet Brewing, xii, 62–66, 90, 307

Harriet Island, 60
Harriet Lake, 62, 63
Hauenstein Beer, 272–73
Haug, Todd, 118, 119. *See also* Surly Brewing Company
Haun, B. J., 91, 92. *See also* Pour Decisions Brewing Company
haunted sites, 233
Hawaii, 168, 183
Hay City Stage, 83
Hayward, Wisconsin, 130
Heartland State Trail, 198
Heimertingen, Germany, 112
Heineken Lounge, 290
Heinzelmännchen, 211
Hellman, Dave, 251. *See also* Sand Creek Brewing Company
Hellman, Jim, 251. *See also* Sand Creek Brewing Company
Henderson, Nevada, 141
Henderson, Pete, 215
Hendricks, 259–61. *See also* Bank Beer Company
Hendry, Bruce, 278
Hengesteg, Gary and Nancy, 256
Hennepin Center for the Arts, 100
Hennepin Island Park, 43
Hennepin Theatre Trust, 100
Hennepin Trail Corridor, 50
Henry H. Sibley House, 38, 116, 132
Herimertingen, Germany, 114
Heriot-Watt University, 10, 96
Heritagefest, 211
Herkimer Pub and Brewery, 65, 67–72
Hermann the German, 211
Hermanutz, Eugene, 4. *See also* Cold Spring Brewing Company
Hiawatha, light rail service, 44, 65, 66, 90, 101
Hieronymus, Stan, 92
Highland Fest, 293
Highland National Golf Course, 116
Highway 61, 154, 157, 159–60, 161, 179, 186
hiking trails/areas, 13, 38, 48, 50, 60, 80, 104, 116, 132, 147, 150, 159, 160, 179, 186, 198, 229
Hill, James J., 60
Hilltop Park, 186
Hirchi, John, 232

Hoag, Don, 182. *See also* Lake Superior
    Brewing Company
Hobo Band, 206
Hoeft, James, 271
Hofbrauhaus (Munich, Germany), 119
Hoffman, Brian, 41–42. *See also* Fulton
    Brewery
Holdingford, 7, 14
Holland, 125
homebrewers/homebrewing, xiii, xx, 11,
    15, 16, 23, 24, 30, 31, 35, 40, 41,
    63, 66, 68, 73, 74, 78, 79, 91, 92,
    102, 105, 110, 112, 118, 119, 120,
    126, 129, 130, 131, 133, 139, 148,
    149, 153, 157, 172, 182, 185, 191,
    214, 215, 220, 223, 226, 231, 232,
    235, 237, 244, 253, 255, 256, 259,
    262, 267, 268, 283, 285
Hoops, Dave, 84, 171–72, 175, 176,
    177. *See also* Fitger's Brewhouse
Hoops, Mike, 82, 84, 171, 177, 183.
    See also Minneapolis Town Hall
    Brewery
HopFest, 225
Hopped Up Caribou Beer Festival, 293
Hoppy Brewing Company (Sacramento,
    California), 79
Hops Restaurant and Brewery, 54
Hotel Chequamegon, 284
Houlton, Wisconsin, 76
Hoverson, Doug, 324
Hubbard House, 229
Hubbell House, 231, 232, 233
Hub City Brewing, 253–54
Hubert H. Humphrey Metrodome, 82,
    89, 100
Hungary, 92
Hunter, George, 157–58, 159. *See also*
    Castle Danger Brewery
Hurnerbräu Brewery, 113

IBM, 195, 196
Ice Cold Beer Fest, 294
Idaho Springs, Colorado, 245
Iguadona Lake, 198
Ike's, 288
Illinois Craft Brewers Guild, 294
Illinois, 95, 148, 168, 172, 191, 211,
    215, 236, 251, 290, 294
Indiana, 95, 183, 290

Indianapolis, Indiana, 290
International Eelpout Festival, 198
International Game Fish Association, 275
International Wolf Center, 151
Iowa, 95, 102, 103, 200, 220, 244, 251,
    253–54, 255–57, 260, 275, 293,
    294. *See also* Toppling Goliath
    Brewing Company; Worth Brewing
    Company
Ireland, 162, 241
Irish folklore, 162, 242
Irish immigration, 323
Iron Range, 141, 147, 158, 159, 184
Irvine Park neighborhood, 130, 323
Isaac Staples Sawmill, 106, 107, 110
Island Glass Company, 24
Italy, 138
Itasca State Park, 96, 198
Ithaca, New York, 220
Ithaca Brewing Company, 220
Izumo Brewing, 63

Jackson, Michael, 10
Jacob Bierebauer Brewery, 227
Jacob Leinenkugel Brewing Company,
    125, 289
Jacob Schmidt Brewing Company, 112,
    125, 128, 130, 232, 264, 277, 278
James, Jesse, 260
Jameson Whiskey, 162
James Page Brewing Company, 24,
    125, 271
Jamrozy, Chad, 68. *See also* Herkimer
    Pub and Brewery
Jay Cooke State Park, 186
Jean Baptiste Fairbault House, 38, 116,
    132
Jet Rock Bar and Grill, 290
John Hauenstein Brewing Company,
    205
John Hoffman Brewery, 268
John Lind House, 211
Johnny's Bar, 112
Johnson, Jacob, 286. *See also* Tin
    Whiskers
Joseph James Brewing, 141
Joseph Schlitz Brewing Company, 173
Joyce, James, 271
Judd, John, 182, 183. *See also* Lake
    Superior Brewing Company

Jungle Theatre, 71
Justesen, Dan, 129, 130, 131, 132.
    See also Vine Park Brewing
    Company

Kailua Kona, Hawaii, 183
Kalamazoo, Michigan, 30, 215, 248
Kalara, Adit, 283. *See also* 612 Brew
Kansas City, Missouri, 11, 46, 142, 220
Kasak, Robert, 283. *See also* 612 Brew
Katchever, Joe, 245. *See also* Pearl
    Street Brewery
Kato Beer, 227
Kauai, Hawaii, 74
Kavajecz, Rocky, 284. *See also* Canal
    Park Brewing Company
Kayak Festival, 160
keg washer, 143, 220
Keillor, Garrison, 7, 14, 59
Keisling House, 211
Kellerman, George, 286. *See also* Tin
    Whiskers
Kentucky, 125
Keoki Brewing Company, 74
KeyKeg, 107
Kimmick, Norbert, 107
King Boreas, 58, 59
King Gambrinus, 171, 240
Kirriemuir, Scotland, 96
Kleinschmidt, Dale, xi, 181, 182.
    See also Lake Superior Brewing
    Company
Klick, John, 284. *See also* Excelsior
    Brewing Company
Knauss, Steve, 190. *See also* Thirsty
    Pagan Brewing
Knauss, Susan, 190. *See also* Thirsty
    Pagan Brewing
Knife Lake, 151
Knife River, 160
Knipps, Gerhard, 107, 126
Kona Brewing Company, 168, 183
Kovalchuk, Brian, 263. *See also* Bard's
    Tale Beer Company
kraeusening, 239
Kramer and Seberger brewery, 10
Krueger, Todd, 251. *See also* Sand
    Creek Brewing Company
Kuszuba, Frank, 175. *See also* Fitger's
    Brewhouse

La Crosse, Wisconsin, 210, 217, 218,
    239–40, 245–46, 277–78, 294.
    See also City Brewing Company;
    Pearl Street Brewery
Lady in the Moon, 190
lagering caves, 248
lagers, xiv, 340–46
Lake Calhoun, 65
lake country, 275
Lake County Historical Society, 160
Lake Erie, 172
Lake George, 10
Lake Harriet, 65–66, 71. *See also* Har-
    riet Brewing
Lake Huron, 172, 175
Lake Johanna, 7
Lakeland, 126
Lakemaid Beer Company, 274–76.
    See also August Schell Brewing
    Company
Lake Mills, Wisconsin, 294
Lake Minnetonka, 80
Lake Ontario, 172
Lake Pepin, 143
Lake Superior, 155, 156, 157, 158, 159,
    160, 161, 171, 172, 175, 179, 180,
    184, 186, 188, 191, 284
Lake Superior Brewing Company (1882–
    85), 173. *See also* Fitger's Brew-
    house
Lake Superior Brewing Company, xi, xii,
    125, 155, 160, 168, 179, 181–87,
    231, 232, 234, 267, 284
Lake Superior Maritime Museum, 155,
    165, 169
Lake Superior Ojibwe Gallery, 165
Lake Superior Railroad Museum, 155,
    165
Lake Vermillion, 148
Lakeville, 236
Lake View Coffee House, 182
Lake Wobegon, 7, 14
Landmark Beer, 277
Landmark Center, 59
Land of Amber Waters (Hoverson), 324
Land of Memories Park, 229
large brewery, definition, xxvii
LaSalle Plaza, 95, 96, 100, 101, 288
Laughlin, Don, 264, 265–66
Laughlin, Nevada, 264, 265–66

Laughlin's Riverside Resort Hotel and Casino, 264, 265
Laumb, Chris, 15. *See also* McCann's Food and Brew
Laurelwood Brewing Company, 290
Leavenworth, Henry, 65
L'Ecosse, 84
Leech Lake Brewing Company, 195–99
Leech River, 198
Lee's Summit, Missouri, 263
Legacy Award, 207
Lewey, Barb, 253. *See also* Toppling Goliath Brewing Company
Lewey, Clark, 253, 254. *See also* Toppling Goliath Brewing Company
Lewin, Jon, 284. *See also* Excelsior Brewing Company
Lewis, Sinclair, 229
Libby, Ryan, 283. *See also* 612 Brew
Lift Bridge Brewery, 34, 73–77, 272, 289
Lightening Boy Brewery, 103
Lincoln Park (Duluth), 181
Lind, Daniel, 158. *See also* Castle Danger Brewery
Lind, Debbie, 158. *See also* Castle Danger Brewery
Lind, Dwight, 158. *See also* Castle Danger Brewery
Lind, Edgar, 158. *See also* Castle Danger Brewery
Lind, Marcus, 158. *See also* Castle Danger Brewery
Linden Hills, 62
Local (pub), 271
Locher Brothers, Inc., 227
Lodge, the, 289
Logging and Rail Museum, 109
Longfellow, Henry Wadsworth, 39
Longfellow neighborhood, 66
Long Lake, 27
Lon Musolf Distributing, 283. *See also* Big Wood Brewing Company
Loring Park, 71
Los Angeles, California, 158, 290
Louisiana, 206
Louisville, Kentucky, 125
Lovejoy, Harriet, 65

Lucan, xi, xii, 219–26, 260, 293. *See also* Brau Brothers Brewing Company
Luce, Sidney, 173. *See also* Fitger's Brewhouse
Lucette Brewing Company, 78–81, 141–44
Lumberjack Days, 76
Lunstrom, Matt, 283. *See also* Big Wood Brewing Company
Lutsen, 293
Luxembourg, 191, 237
Lyndale neighborhood, 144
Lyn-Lake neighborhood, 71

Macalester College, 119
Macallan's Scotch, 37
Mac and Jack's Brewery, 143
MacFarlane, Clint, 157, 158, 159. *See also* Castle Danger Brewery
MacFarlane, Jamie, 158. *See also* Castle Danger Brewery
Madison, Wisconsin, 245–46, 290, 294
Maiden Rock, Wisconsin, 143
Mall of America, 48, 90, 116
Mammenga State Wildlife Management Area, 224
Mankato, 226–30, 304–5. *See also* Mankato Brewery
Mankato Brewery (Mankato), xi, 226–30, 304–5
Mankato Brewing Company (1933–67), 227
Mankato Farmer's Market, 229
Mankato MoonDogs, 229
Mantorville, 217, 231–34. *See also* Mantorville Brewing Company
Mantorville Brewing Company, x, 124, 182, 217, 231–34, 237
Mantorville Opera House, 234
Mantorville Theatre Company, 233
Maple Grove, 46, 49–50. *See also* Granite City Food and Brewery
Maple Grove Arboretum, 50
Maple Grove Art Center, 50
Marigold Days, 233
Marinette, Wisconsin, 135
Maritime Pacific Brewing Company, 215
Markkula, Jason, 259–60. *See also* Bank Beer Company

Marshall, 220, 224, 225
Marshall, Michigan, 220
Marti, Alfred, 206. *See also* August
Schell Brewing Company
Marti, Emma, 206. *See also* August
Schell Brewing Company
Marti, George, 206. *See also* August
Schell Brewing Company
Marti, Jace, 207. *See also* August Schell
Brewing Company
Marti, Jodi, 207. *See also* August Schell
Brewing Company
Marti, Ted, 207, 210, 275. *See also*
August Schell Brewing Company
Marti, Warren, 206–7, 210. *See also*
August Schell Brewing Company
Martin, Gerald, 227
Martin Farm, 122
Maryland, 220, 290
Massachusetts, 183, 290
Matt Brewing Company, 262, 263
Maxim, Mike, 162, 163. *See also* Dubh
Linn Irish Brewpub
Maxim, Mike, Sr., 162. *See also* Dubh
Linn Irish Brewpub
McAlpine, Nathan, 153, 190–91. *See
also* Thirsty Pagan Brewing
McCann, Nick, 15. *See also* McCann's
Food and Brew
McCann's Food and Brew, 15–19
McClure, Scot, 83. *See also* Minneapo-
lis Town Hall Brewery
McElevey, Charlie, 112
McKenzie, Bob, 11, 12, 96, 97, 98.
See also Rock Bottom Restaurant
and Brewery
McMahon, Dick, 265
Medvec, Jason, 283. *See also* Big
Wood Brewing
Melges Bakery, 211
Memphis, Tennessee, 30
Mendota, 38, 116, 132
Menomonie, Wisconsin, 136–37, 141–
44. *See also* Das Bierhaus; Lucette
Brewing Company
Merila, Steve, 283. *See also* Big Wood
Brewing
mermaids, 274–76
Messier, John, 79. *See also* Lucid Brew-
ing Company

Metropolitan Minneapolis YMCA, 263
Mexicali, Mexico, 196
Miami, Florida, 290
Michigan, 144, 153, 215, 220, 248,
267, 275, 290; Upper Peninsula,
84, 163
Mickey's Dining Car, 59, 61
microbrewery, definition, xxvii
Microbrewery Shootout, 294
Middleton, Wisconsin, 83, 294
Midtown Farmer's Market, 65
Midwest Beer Notes, 125
Mike's Hard Lemonade, 240
Miley, Mike, 153. *See also* Carmody
Irish Pub and Thirsty Pagan
Mill City Museum, 43, 89
Miller Brewhouse, 290
Miller Brewing Company, 210
MillerCoors, 190, 210, 227, 248, 278
Milton, West Virginia, 107
Milwaukee, Wisconsin, 245–46, 248,
290, 294
Minar, Albert, Jr., 228
Minar, Albert, Sr., 228
Minar Brewing Company, 228
Minhas Craft Brewery, 10, 11
Minneapolis, xi, xii, 12, 14, 23–133, 138,
210, 226, 250, 262–63, 264–65,
270–71, 274–76, 286, 287–91, 293,
305–8. *See also specific brewery*
Minneapolis–St. Paul Airport (MSP), 48,
90, 95, 116, 132, 287–91
Minneapolis Beer Fest, 293
Minneapolis Brewing Company, 210
Minneapolis Grain Exchange, 125
Minneapolis North Loop, 43
Minneapolis Queen, 32
Minneapolis Riverfront District, 89
Minneapolis Sculpture Garden, 100
Minneapolis Stockyard and Packing
Company, 27
Minneapolis Theatre District, 43
Minneapolis Town Hall Brewery, xi, xii,
32, 35, 65, 82–90, 171, 177
Minneapolis Warehouse District, 32, 33,
43, 83, 101
Minnehaha Bike Trail, 65
Minnehaha Falls, 65
Minnehaha Park, 38–49, 116
Minnemishinona Falls, 229

Minneopa State Park, 229
Minnesota Amateur Baseball Hall of
   Fame, 13, 18
Minnesota and St. Louis Railroad, 224
Minnesota Bluegrass and Old-Time
   Music Festival, 7
Minnesota Brewing Company, 130, 182,
   264, 265, 273, 277, 278
Minnesota Business Magazine, 207
Minnesota Department of Natural Re-
   sources, 259
Minnesota Department of Revenue, 181
Minnesota Gophers, 83
Minnesota Hall of Fame Museum, 211
Minnesota History Center, 59, 127–28
Minnesota Home Brewers Associa-
   tion, 79
Minnesota Inventors Congress, 224
Minnesota Landscape Arboretum, 80
Minnesota Marine Art Museum, 217
Minnesota Monthly Food and Wine
   Experience, 293
Minnesota Museum of American Art, 59
Minnesota Opera, 29
Minnesota Orchestra, 29
Minnesota Public Radio, 7, 59
Minnesota River, 38, 48, 116, 132, 212,
   213, 224, 227, 229, 230
Minnesota Science Museum, 59
Minnesota State Capitol, 59
Minnesota State Fair, 92, 93
Minnesota State University–Mankato,
   227, 229
Minnesota Timberwolves, 43, 100
Minnesota Transportation Museum, 60
Minnesota Twins, 43, 99
Minnesota Valley National Wildlife
   Refuge, 48, 116
Minnesota Vikings, 71, 89, 229
Minnesota Wild, 59
Minnetonka, 46, 78–81, 96, 200, 243,
   293. *See also* Lucid Brewing
   Company
Minnetonka Civic Center, 80
Minnetonka Farmer's Market, 80
Minnetonka Summer Festival, 80
Minocqua, Wisconsin, 294
Mississippi Brewing Company, 5
Mississippi River, 13, 18, 30, 32, 38, 43,
   48, 60, 82, 89, 100, 111, 116, 122,
127, 132, 143, 198, 206, 210, 215,
   216, 217, 218, 237, 247, 248, 264,
   277, 285, 323
Mississippi River Front Festival, 293
Missoula, Montana, 74
Missouri, 142, 220, 251, 260, 263, 290
Mixed Blood Theatre, 89
Miziorko, Mike, 116, 226–27, 228.
   See also Mankato Brewery
Monroe, Wisconsin, 10
Montana, 74, 102, 103
Moondance Ranch and Adventure Park,
   198
Moore, John, 24, 25, 27. *See also* Bar-
   ley John's Brew Pub
Moore, Nick, 25. *See also* Barley John's
   Brew Pub
Moore, Rosie, 27. *See also* Barley
   John's Brew Pub
Moorhead, 241
MoreBeer, 79
Morgan, Anne, 107, 108. *See also* Still-
   water Brewing Company
Morgan, Betram, 108. *See also* Stillwa-
   ter Brewing Company
Morgan, Zachary, 106, 107, 108, 109.
   See also Stillwater Brewing Com-
   pany
Morgan Creek Vineyards, 212
Moriarty, Jeff, 286. *See also* Tin
   Whiskers
moto-i, 68
Mounds View, 79
Mount Horeb, Wisconsin, 295
Mpls.St.Paul magazine, 130
Mr. Beer Kit, 42
Muddy Pig, 128, 293
Muddy Pig Annual Belgian Beer Fest,
   293
Mullen, Colin, 24. *See also* Barley
   John's Brew Pub
Munich, Germany, 119, 141, 191
Munsinger and Clemens Gardens, 13
Muriel Sahlin Arboretum, 51, 93
Murphy, Elizabeth, 162, 163. *See also*
   Dubh Linn Irish Brewpub
museums, xi, 13, 27, 38, 43, 52, 59, 60,
   80, 89, 100, 104, 109, 150, 151,
   155, 165, 169, 174, 205, 207, 211,
   217, 224, 247, 248

Nab, R. J., 11, 46. *See also* Granite City Food and Brewery
Naegli, Henry, 232
nano-brewery, 255
NASA, 35
NASCAR, 56
National Brewery Museum, xi, 247, 248
National Register of Historic Places, 6, 30, 32, 43, 55, 59, 109, 205, 211
natural areas, 4, 7, 48, 50, 51, 52, 89, 116, 122, 173, 206, 212, 216, 224, 259, 260, 264
NBA, 43, 100
Nebraska, 95, 260, 275
Nederland, Colorado, 11
Nelson, Tim, 172, 173, 285. *See also* Fitger's Brewhouse
Nelson, Willie, 177
Nevada, 141, 264–66, 290
New Belgium Brewing, 183, 290
New Brighton, 23–28, 308–9. *See also* Barley John's Brew Pub
New Holland, Michigan, 144
New Holland Brewing Company, 144
New Jersey, 263
Newlands System, 73, 227
Newman, Bill, 112
New Orleans, Louisiana, 206
New Prague, 227–28
New Richmond, Wisconsin, 134–35. *See also* Brady's Brewhouse
New Ulm, 205–13, 224, 227, 229, 272, 275, 293. *See also* August Schell Brewing Company
New York, 112, 183, 220, 262, 290
NFL, 71, 229
NHL, 59
Nice Ride, 65, 89
Nicollet Island, 32
Nicollet Mall, 100, 101, 271
Nihart, Bob, 285. *See also* Reads Landing Brewing Company
North American Bear Center, 151
North Carolina, 106
North Dakota, 112, 115, 148, 220, 243, 244, 260, 275, 294. *See also* Granite City Food and Brewery
North Dakota State University, 148
North Mankato, 226, 227, 229, 230
North Mississippi Regional Park, 122

North Shore Scenic Railroad, 155, 165, 179
Northern Ale Stars, 182
Northern Brewing Company, 6, 186, 190
Northern Lights Casino, 198
Northern Pacific Center, 267, 268
Northern Waters Smokehaus, 155
Northfield, 260
Northwood, Iowa, xii, 255–57. *See also* Worth Brewing Company
Northwood Central Avenue Historic District, 255–56
Northwoods Baseball League, 14, 229
Norton, John, 55. *See also* Great Waters Brewing Company
Norwalk, Connecticut, 263
Norway, 158
note taking, xix
Nussbaum, Joe, 104

Oasis Brewery, 11
O'Byrne, Sean, 54–55, 58. *See also* Great Waters Brewing Company
Oderbolz, Charlie, 250. *See also* Sand Creek Brewing Company
Oderbolz, Frank, 250. *See also* Sand Creek Brewing Company
Oderbolz, Ulrich, 250. *See also* Sand Creek Brewing Company
Odonata Beer Company, 79
O'Gara, James Freeman, 288
O'Gara's Restaurant, 288
O'Hara, Tim, 16
O'Hara's Restaurant, 16. *See also* McCann's Food and Brew
Ohio, 95, 206, 235, 290
Ojibwe, 13, 151, 165, 197
Oktoberfest, 65, 246; Duluth, 179; La Crosse, Wisconsin, 294; Milwaukee, Wisconsin, 294; Minneapolis, 293; New Ulm, 212, 293
Old Chicago, 288
Old Dominion Brewing Company, 291
Old North Shore Road, 160
Old Town Pub Crawl, 229
Olvalde Farm and Brewing Company, 217, 235–38, 309
O'Neel, Cory, 11, 46. *See also* Granite City Food and Brewery
One Hundred Years of Brewing, 324

Ontario, Canada, 275
orchestras, 29, 30, 165, 169, 217
Oregon, 68, 103, 118, 122, 168, 290
Oregon State University, 168
organic, 35, 226, 246
Orpheum Theatre, 100
Ort, Peter, 268. *See also* Brainerd Brewing Company
Orth's Brewery, 84
Oster, John, 4. *See also* Cold Spring Brewing Company
Otto's Brewery, 232
Otto's Pub and Brewery, 103

Pabst Brewing Company, 210, 239, 263, 278
Padelford, Zach, 158. *See also* Castle Danger Brewery
Palomino Building, 101
Pantages Theatre, 100
Papazian, Charlie, 30, 196
Paris, France, 18, 271
Parke, George, 239. *See also* City Brewing Company
Park Point, 176
Park Rapid, 198
Park Square Theatre, 55
Parrant, Pierre, 277
Paso Robles, California, 74
pasteurizer, 219, 220
Paulaner Brewery, 68
Paul Bunyan, 141, 142
Pavek Museum of Broadcasting, 52, 104
Peace Coffee, 65, 88
Pearl Street Brewery (La Crosse, Wisconsin), 217, 245–46
Pelican Pub and Brewery, 103
Pennsylvania, 103, 130, 290
Peoria, Illinois, 84
Peter Bub Brewery, 215, 217
Peters, Ferdinand, 4. *See also* Cold Spring Brewing Company
Petz, Ryan, 41–42. *See also* Fulton Brewery
Pheasants Forever, 259, 260
Philadelphia, Pennsylvania, 130, 290
Pierson, Jim, 73, 74. *See also* Lift Bridge Brewery
Pig's Eye Brewing Company, 277–78

Pike, Zebulon, 38, 116, 132
Pike Island, 116
Pillsbury Company, 24
Pioneer Brewing Company, 250, 251
Plagens, Siegfried, 182–83, 264, 278
Plymouth, 262
Pocket Hercules, 274, 275. *See also* Lakemaid Beer Company
Polfus, Chris, 134, 135. *See also* Brady's Brewhouse
Pond, Dinel, 236. *See also* Olvalde Farm and Brewing Company
Pond, Joe, 217, 235–36, 237. *See also* Olvalde Farm and Brewing Company
Portland, Oregon, 118, 290
Potosi Brewery Foundation, 248
Potosi Brewfest, 295
Potosi Brewing Company, xi, 247–49, 295
Pour Decision Brewing Company, 91–94
Powderhorn Park, 71
Pratt Institute, 68
Pre-Prohibition, 83, 109, 158, 208, 227, 251, 256
Prohibition, 4, 5, 76, 83, 107, 109, 158, 159, 173, 206, 210, 211, 217, 220, 224, 227, 228, 232, 251, 256, 269, 272, 289, 323, 324
Prohibition Act, 224
Pulaski, Wisconsin, 168
Pyramid Brewing, 172

Quale, Lee, 136. *See also* Das Bierhaus
Quetico Provincial Park, 150

Racine, Wisconsin, 295
Ragbrai (Register's Annual Great Bicycle Ride Across Iowa), 256
Rail House Brewing Company, 135
railroad, 5, 43, 109, 127, 142, 155, 165, 179, 190, 212, 224, 267, 268
Rainy Lake, 275
Ramsey County Courthouse, 59, 117
Ramsey Creek, 224
Rapala, 275
Raymond, Rod, 172, 173, 285. *See also* Fitger's Brewhouse
Reads Landing Brewing Company, 285
Rechzigel, Barb, 224

Rechzigel, Ken, 224
Reconciliation Park, 229
Red Cedar River, 142
Red Hook Brewery, 112
Red Jacket Bike Trail, 229
Red River Trail, 6, 18
Red Star, 173
Red Star Lounge, 285
Red Wing, 143, 217, 218, 285
Redwood County Museum, 224
Redwood Falls, 224, 225
regional brewery, definition, xxvii
Reinheitsgebot (German Purity Law of
    1516), xxviii, 137
Renegade Theater Company, 169
Reno, Nevada, 290
Restoration House, 233
Rhode Island, 79
Richardson, Blake, 68. See also Her-
    kimer Pub and Brewery
Ridgeway Community College, 226
Rifakes, Pete, 83, 84. See also Minne-
    apolis Town Hall Brewery
Riggs, Dudley, 83–84
Rine, Tom, 24
Rinker, Steve, 73, 74. See also Lift
    Bridge Brewery
River Falls, Wisconsin, 143–44. See also
    Rush River Brewing Company
Riverfront Park, 229
Riverside Park, 142
Rivertown Art Festival, 76, 109
Riverview Park, 229
Roastery 7, 275
Rochester, 218, 234
Rock Bottom Restaurant and Brewery,
    11, 12, 32, 65, 90, 95–111, 119,
    226, 284, 288–89, 290
Rogers Park, 229
Rollingstone, 235–38. See also Olvalde
    Farm and Brewing Company
Rollingstone River, 237
root beer, 5, 24, 125, 130, 132, 151,
    182, 206, 207, 215, 228, 272
Rosebrook Park, 93
Rosedale Center, 27, 50–52, 93
Rosetown Playhouse, 51
Roseville, 46, 50–52, 91–94, 92, 286,
    309–10. See also Granite City

Food and Brewery; Pour Decisions
    Brewing Company
Roseville Skating Center, 51
Rush Family Farm, 254
Rush River Brewing Company, 143–44
Russell Creamery, 190
Russ Kendall's Smoke House, 160

Sabco Brew-Magic (brewing system),
    255, 283, 284
Saboe, Mike, 253. See also Toppling
    Goliath Brewing Company
Sacramento, California, 79
Sakatah Singing Hills State Trail, 229
Sakrison, Andy, 148. See also Boat-
    House Brewpub and Restaurant
Salisbury, Vermont, 79, 226
Salt Lake City, Utah, 290
Samuel Adams Brewpub, 290
San Antonio, Texas, 263
Sand Creek Brewing Company (Black
    River Falls, Wisconsin), 41, 139,
    232, 250–52
San Diego, California, 119
San Francisco, California, 34, 172, 290
San Jose, California, 263
Sargl, Michael, 4. See also Cold Spring
    Brewing Company
Sauer, Nancy, 190. See also Thirsty
    Pagan Brewing
Sauer, Rick, 135, 153, 190. See also
    Brady's Brewhouse; Thirsty Pagan
    Brewing
Scanlon, Dewey, 154
Schell, Adolph, 206. See also August
    Schell Brewing Company
Schell, August, 205, 206, 210. See also
    August Schell Brewing Company
Schell, Otto, 206, 207. See also August
    Schell Brewing Company
Schell, Theresa, 205, 206. See also
    August Schell Brewing Company
Schell Bock Fest, 212
Schlafly Tap Room, 290
Schletty, Tim, 141, 142. See also
    Lucette Brewing Company
Schnagl, Ferdinand, 232
Schoneman, August, 103. See also
    Steel Toe Brewing

Schoneman, Hannah, 103. *See also* Steel Toe Brewing
Schoneman, Jason, 102, 103. *See also* Steel Toe Brewing
Schroeder, Cory, 251. *See also* Sand Creek Brewing Company
Schultz, Carl, 288
Schultz, Charles, 288
Schumann, Otto, 232
Schwarz, Dan, 73, 74. *See also* Lift Bridge Brewery
scoring beer, xx
Scotch Mist nightclub, 264–65
Scotland, 241
Sears, Richard W., 224
Seattle, Washington, 83, 112, 143, 215, 290
Seattle Taproom, 290
Seplowitz, Kevin, 262, 263. *See also* Bard's Tale Beer Company
series of beers, 24, 99, 112, 115–16, 139, 172, 175, 176, 201, 206, 207, 208, 211, 238, 264
Seven Corners, 82
Shakespeare, William, 263
Shannon Kelly's Brewpub, 68
Sharks, pool hall, 163
Sherlock's Home, 9–11, 46, 96, 200, 243. *See also* Granite City Food and Brewery
Shingobee Recreational Area, 198
Shoppes at Arbor Lakes, 49
Siebel Institute of Technology and World Brewing Academy, 24, 68, 74, 103, 112, 138, 141, 148, 153, 172, 191, 215
Silver Island Narrows, 275
Sinclair Lewis Summer Home, 229
Sing Sing Piano Bars, 288
Sioux Falls, South Dakota, 45, 46, 68, 200, 220, 223, 225, 243–44. *See also* Granite City Food and Brewery
Sivertson Gallery, 160
612 Brew, 283
Sleepy Eye, 272–73. *See also* Hauenstein Beer
Smith, Gina, 196. *See also* Leech Lake Brewing Company

Smith, Greg, 195. *See also* Leech Lake Brewing Company
Smith, Jason, 275. *See also* Lakemaid Beer Company
soda/soft drinks, brewer makers: August Schell, 206, 272; Mankato, 228, 309; Vine Park, 129, 130, 132
Soudan Underground Mine State Park, 151
South China Brewing Company, 11
South Dakota, 68, 200, 220, 223, 225, 241–42, 243–44, 260, 275, 279. *See also* Dempsey's Brewery, Restaurant, and Pub; Granite City Food and Brewery
South Shore Brewery, 174, 188–89
South Washington Avenue District, 84
Southwest Minnesota State University, 220
Sovereign Grounds, 87
Sowards, Jason, 62–65. *See also* Harriet Brewing
Sowards, Tanya, 63. *See also* Harriet Brewing
Spalt, Germany, 15
Sparky Abrasives, 118, 119, 121
Spectrum Design Solutions, 286
Spirit Mountain, 186
Split Rock Lighthouse, 160, 179, 186
Squatters Beer and Wasatch Brewing Company, 290
Squaw Mountain Brewery, 245
SS *William A. Irvin*, 155, 165, 169, 185
St. Anthony Falls, 32; Heritage Trail, 43
St. Augusta, 18
St. Cloud, 3, 7, 9–14, 15–19, 45, 200, 243, 293. *See also* Granite City Food and Brewery; McCann's Food and Brew
St. Cloud State University, 14, 79
St. Croix Brewing Company, 107, 124–28, 132, 182, 232
St. Croix River, 76, 106, 109, 126–27
St. Francis Hotel, 55
St. James Gate Brewery, 164
St. John's University, 42
St. Louis, Missouri, 248, 290
St. Louis Bay, 184

St. Louis Park, 46, 52–53, 62, 63, 102–5. *See also* Granite City Food and Brewery; Steel Toe Brewing
St. Louis Park and Recreation Center, 52
St. Louis River, 186
St. Mary's University–Winona, 217
St. Paul, 34–39, 54–61, 73, 74, 107, 111–17, 119, 124–28, 129–33, 134, 138, 141, 181, 182, 183, 206, 226, 234, 236, 264–66, 270, 273, 277–78, 287–91, 293. *See also specific brewery*
St. Paul Home Grown Economy Project, 112
St. Paul Homebrewers Club, 91
St. Paul Malt House, 288
St. Paul Summer Beer Festival, xi
St. Paul Winter Carnival, 58, 59, 293
Stair, Robbie, 143, 144. *See also* Rush River Brewing Company
Stanifer, Dan, 267, 268. *See also* Brainerd Lakes Brewery
Stanley, Iowa, 253–54
Stanley, James, 108. *See also* Stillwater Brewing Company
Stanley, Justin, 106, 107, 108, 109. *See also* Stillwater Brewing Company
State College, Pennsylvania, 103
State Theatre, 100
Steamboat Days, 237
Stearns County, 13
Steel Toe Brewing Company, 34, 52, 102–5
Stevens Point Brewery, 74, 139, 248
Stillwater, 34, 73–77, 106–10, 126, 134, 293. *See also* Lift Bridge Brewery; Stillwater Brewing Company
Stillwater Brewing Company, 106–10
Stockyard Days, 27
Stone Arch Bridge, 32, 43, 89
Stroh Brewing Company, 24, 74, 239, 288
Sturgis, South Dakota, 279
Stutrud, Mark, 111, 112, 113, 115. *See also* Summit Brewing Company
styles of beer, 328–46

Subak, Laura, 24, 25, 27. *See also* Barley John's Brew Pub
Sugar Loaf Bluff, 217
Sugar Loaf Brewery, 217
Summit Brewing Company, xi, xii, 39, 111–17, 119, 128, 130, 132, 143, 181, 183, 226, 236, 256, 270, 271, 287, 288, 289
Summit Hill, 127
Superior, Wisconsin, 135, 153, 179, 186, 190–91, 295. *See also* Thirsty Pagan Brewing
Superior Hiking Trail, 160, 177
Superior National Forest, 148
Supple, Jack, 274, 275. *See also* Lakemaid Beer Company
Surdyk, Jim, 289
Surdyk, Joseph, 289
Surdyk's Flights, 289–90
Surly Brewing Company, xii, 50, 52, 118–23, 160, 285–87, 288, 292
Surly Darkness Day, xi, 292
SweetWater Brewery and Draft House & Grill, 290
symphony, 29, 30, 165, 169, 217

Tacoma, Washington, 290
Tahoe, Nevada, 290
Tampa, Florida, 79
Target Center, 43, 100
Target Field, 32, 43, 44, 90, 99–100, 101
taste/flavor, xv, xviii–xix
Taste of Elk River, 292
Taste of Minnesota, 60
taster chart, xxi
Technical University of Munich, 137
Templeton Rye Spirits (distillery), 220
Texas, 263
texture or mouth feel, xviii
theaters, 18, 51, 52, 55, 59, 71, 80, 83, 84, 89, 90, 95, 96, 100, 104, 169, 200, 217, 233, 234
Theodore Fyten Brewing Company, 124–28, 132, 232
Theodore Hamm Brewing Company, 39, 54, 55–56, 190
Theodore Wirth Park, 71
Thirsty Pagan Brewing, 135, 153, 155, 186, 190–91
Thirsty Troll Brewfest, 295

Thomasser, Fred, 112
Thomasser, Tom, 112. *See also* Summit
    Brewing Company
Thompson, David, 130. *See also* Vine
    Park Brewing Company
Thompson, Scott, 130. *See also* Vine
    Park Brewing Company
Three Rivers Park District, 50
Timber Lodge Steakhouse, 52
Tin Whiskers, 286
Tiny Footprint Coffee, 275
Tommyknocker Brewery and Pub, 245
Tonnis, Bryon, 96
Toppling Goliath Brewing Company,
    253–54
Tower, 158, 159
Town Hall Tap, 84. *See also* Minneapolis
    Town Hall Brewery
Trampled by Turtles, 177
Transportation Museum, 248
Trapper and Trader, 241
travel tips, xiii
Troutdale, Oregon, 168
Tupy, Tami, 226. *See also* Mankato
    Brewery
Tupy, Tim, 226, 227, 228. *See also*
    Mankato Brewery
Twenty-first Amendment, U.S. Constitu-
    tion, 224
Twin Cities, 23–133, 136, 138, 143, 217,
    220, 225, 230, 231, 236, 250, 260,
    263, 264–65, 275, 285–86, 287–91.
    See also Minneapolis; St. Paul
Twin Ports Brewing Company, 135, 153,
    190. *See also* Thirsty Pagan
Two Harbors, xi, xii, 157–61, 179, 186.
    See also Castle Danger Brewery
Tycoon's Zenith Alehouse, 173, 285
Tyranena Oktoberfest Bike Ride, 294

University of California–Davis, 172
University of Cincinnati, 62
University of Illinois, 83
University of Iowa, 253
University of Minnesota, 41, 63, 79, 80,
    82, 89, 92, 122, 236, 263, 286; Du-
    luth, 153, 158, 165, 169, 191
University of Missouri, 11
University of Montana, 74
University of St. Thomas, 259

University of Washington, 83
University of Wisconsin, 92; Stout, 130
Upland Brewing Company, 183
Upper Mississippi Mashout, 30, 31, 32,
    65, 131, 293
Upper Mississippi River Wildlife Ref-
    uge, 216
Uptown neighborhood, Minneapolis, 67,
    71, 143, 283
U.S. Beer Open Championships, recog-
    nized beers, 207, 208, 209, 210
U.S. Coast Guard, 185
U.S. Fish and Wildlife Service, 259
Utah, 290
Utica, New York, 262

Vadnais Heights, 283
Vale, Erin, 68. *See also* Herkimer Pub
    and Brewery
Vale, Gustavo de Toledo, 67, 68, 70.
    See also Herkimer Pub and
    Brewery
Van Wie, Mark, 55. *See also* Great
    Waters Brewing Company
Vendome Copper and Brass Works,
    125
Vermont, 226
Veterans Memorial Amphitheatre, 52
Vine Park Brewing Company, x, 39, 117,
    128, 129–33
vineyards, 207, 212
Virginia, 220
Virginia, Minnesota, 148
Volstead, Andrew, 224
Volstead Act, 224

Wabasso, 220
Wachsmann Brerutechnik, 63
Wagenheim, Steve, 9–11, 12, 45–46, 47,
    96, 200, 243. *See also* Granite City
    Food and Brewery
Wagner, Richard, 242
Walker, 195–99. *See also* Leech Lake
    Brewing Company
Walker Art Center, 100
Walker Bay Days, 198
walking trails, 7, 13, 32, 43, 48, 50, 51,
    52, 59, 60, 65, 71, 80, 89, 93, 100,
    104, 113, 116, 160, 165, 169, 179,
    180, 186, 211, 229

Walnut Street Brewery, 96
Waraju Distillery, 211
Warner, John, 35. *See also* Flat Earth Brewing Company
Washington, 68, 112, 143, 215, 290
Washington, D.C., 220, 291
Washington County Courthouse, 109
Washington County Historical Society, 109
Wasioja, 233
Waterbury State Wildlife Management Area, 224
waterfalls, 39, 65, 116, 159, 160, 179, 186, 229
Water Street Brewery, 141
Watertower Brewing, 126
water towers (as landmarks), 73, 77, 94, 105, 171, 180, 225
Watertown, South Dakota, 241–42. *See also* Dempsey's Brewery, Restaurant, and Pub
Weingart, Udo, 15
Wellington's Backwater Brewing Company. *See* Backwater Brewing Company
Welsch, Kevin, 29–32. *See also* Boom Island Brewing Company
Welsch, Qiuxia, 30. *See also* Boom Island Brewing Company
West Acres Shopping Center, 200
Western Michigan University, 30
Westgate Bowl, 215, 218
Westline State Wildlife Management Area, 224
Westminster, Colorado, 289
West Union, Iowa, 253
West Virginia, 107, 108
wet hop, 122, 219
White Bear Lake, 107, 271, 283
Wiesender, Jim, 251. *See also* Sand Creek Brewing Company
Wilber, Robert, 136, 137. *See also* Das Bierhaus
William Kuether Brewing Company, 136
William S. Brewing Company, 112
Williamson, Cathie, 35. *See also* Flat Earth Brewing Company
Williamson, Jeff, 34. *See also* Flat Earth Brewing Company

William Younger Brewing Company, 10
Willow Lake State Wildlife Management Area, 224
Wilmarth, L. C., 188. *See also* South Shore Brewery
Wilson, Mike, 141, 142. *See also* Lucette Brewing Company
Wilson, Wisconsin, 138–40. *See also* Dave's BrewFarm
wind-powered brewery, 138–39
wine, 88, 97, 129, 138, 142, 207, 212, 246, 289, 293, 294
Wine Company (St. Paul), 138
Winona, 214–18, 235, 285. *See also* Backwater Brewing Company
Winona County History Center, 237
Winona State University, 217
Winona Symphony Orchestra, 217
Winter Carnival (St. Paul), 293
Winterfest (St. Paul), 293
Winter Wine Down, 293
Wisconsin, 75, 95, 83, 103, 118, 126, 130, 134–35, 136–37, 138–40, 141–44, 148, 153, 163, 168, 174, 179, 186, 188–89, 190–91, 210, 217–18, 220, 232, 239–40, 245–46, 247–49, 250–52, 260, 275, 277–78, 284, 289, 290, 293, 294. *See also specific brewery*
Wisconsin Brewing Company, 251
Wisconsin Dells on Tap, 295
Wisconsin Microbrewers Beer Fest, 294
Wittenburg, Germany, 125
Wolf Brewery, 76, 107, 109
Wolfe Park, 52, 104
Wolf Tongue Brewery, 11
Woodbury, 277–78. *See also* Pig's Eye Brewing Company
Wordsworth, William, 263
World Beer Championships, recognized beers, 183, 184, 185, 246
World Beer Cup, recognized beers, 113, 114, 240, 251, 252, 238, 289
World War II, 288, 323
Worth Brewing Company, xi, 255–57
Worth County Historical Society, 256
Worth County State Bank, 255
worthouse, 10–11, 46, 200, 244.

See also Granite City Food and
Brewery
Wurttemberg, Germany, 211

Xcel Energy Center, 59, 132

Yarusso, Frank, 264, 265. See also Blue
Diamond Brewing Company

Yarusso Brothers Restaurant, 265
Yost, Emily and Joe, 283. See also 612
Brew
Young, Linda, 287. See also Axel's
Bonfire

Zumbro Bend Rendezvous, 233